£25

TOWN AND COUNTRYSIDE
IN THE
ENGLISH REVOLUTION

TOWN
AND
COUNTRYSIDE
IN THE
ENGLISH
REVOLUTION

edited by R. C. Richardson

MANCHESTER
UNIVERSITY PRESS
Manchester and New York

*distributed exclusively in the USA
and Canada by St. Martin's Press*

Published by Manchester University Press
Oxford Road, Manchester M13 9PL, UK
and Room 400, 175 Fifth Avenue, New York, NY 10010, USA

Distributed exclusively in the USA and Canada
by St. Martin's Press, Inc.,
175 Fifth Avenue, New York, NY 10010, USA

British Library Cataloguing-in-Publication Data
A catalogue record for this book is available from the British Library

Library of Congress Cataloging-in-Publication Data
applied for

ISBN 0 7190 3462 0 *hardback*

Printed in Great Britain
by Biddles Limited, Guildford and King's Lynn

CONTENTS

LIST OF TABLES

NOTES ON CONTRIBUTORS

Barry Coward

Dr Coward is Reader in History at Birkbeck College, University of London, and is the author of *The Stuart Age* (1980), *The Stanleys, Lords Stanley and Earls of Derby, 1385–1672* (1983), *Social Change and Continuity in Early Modern England, 1550–1750* (1988), and *Oliver Cromwell* (1991).

Ann Hughes

Dr Hughes has lectured at the University of Manchester since 1980. She previously worked for The Open University. She is the author of *Politics, Society and Civil War in Warwickshire, 1620–1660* (1987) and *The Causes of the English Civil War* (1991) and the co-editor, with Richard Cust, of *Conflict in Early Stuart England* (1989). She is currently working on religious debate and confrontation in the 1640s and 1650s.

Keith Lindley

Dr Lindley is Senior Lecturer in History at the University of Ulster at Coleraine. In 1987–88 he was Visiting Fellow at Clare Hall, Cambridge. His publications include *Fenland Riots and the English Revolution* (1982), as well as a number of articles and essays, mostly on seventeenth-century England. He is currently completing a book on popular politics and religion in London during the English Revolution.

C. B. Phillips

Dr Phillips has lectured in economic history at the University of Manchester since 1969. He has published articles on the Civil War period, the landed gentry, the iron industry, urban history, and on the use of computers in historical research and in history teaching. His edition of the *Lowther Family Estate Books, 1617–75* appeared in 1979.

R. C. Richardson

Dr Richardson has been Head of the History/Archaeology Department at King Alfred's College, Winchester since 1977. In 1982 and 1988 he was Visiting Professor of History at the University of Southern Maine. His publications include: *Puritanism in Northwest England* (1972), *The Debate on the English Revolution* (1977, 2nd edn., 1988), *The Study of History. A Bibliographical Guide* (1988), *British Economic and Social History. A Bibliographical Guide* (1976, 2nd edn. 1984, with W. H. Chaloner), *The Urban Experience. English, Scottish and Welsh Towns, 1450–1700* (1983, with T. B. James), *Freedom and the English Revolution* (1986), with G. M. Ridden). He also contributed to volume five of the *Agrarian History of England and Wales, 1640–1750* (ed. Joan Thirsk, 1986). He is the General Editor of the Manchester University Press historical bibliography series and co-editor of the journal *Literature and History*. Currently he is completing a book entitled *Images of Oliver Cromwell*.

NOTES ON CONTRIBUTORS

Ian Roy

Dr Roy is Senior Lecturer in History at King's College, University of London, where he has taught for over thirty years. He has written a number of articles and edited texts on the Civil War, and on the cities of Oxford, Worcester and Gloucester in the mid-seventeenth century. He has been Literary Director of the Royal Historical Society and a trustee of the Royal Armouries.

David Harris Sacks

Dr Sacks is currently Associate Professor of History and Humanities at Reed College in Portland, Oregon, having previously taught at Harvard. In Spring 1989 he was a Fellow of the Center for the History of Freedom at Washington University, St Louis and in the following academic year a Fellow of the Folger Shakespeare Library. He is the author of *Trade, Society and Politics in Bristol, 1500–1640* (1985) and *The Widening Gate. Bristol and the Atlantic Economy, 1450–1700* (1991). He has published articles in *Past and Present* and *Social History* and essays in various symposia. He is currently completing a book on English political culture in the sixteenth century.

David Scott

Dr Scott holds a research post at the Institute of Historical Research, University of London, and works with the History of Parliament Trust. Previously he taught at the University of York. His doctoral research was on 'Politics, Dissent and Quakerism in York, 1640–1700' and he has a publication on this subject scheduled to appear in the Borthwick Papers series.

Buchanan Sharp

Dr Sharp is Professor of History at the University of California, Santa Cruz. He is the author of *In Contempt of All Authority. Rural Artisans and Riot in the West of England, 1586–1660* (1980). Currently he is working on a study of English food riots in the period 1347 to 1547.

Joan Thirsk

Dr Thirsk was Senior Research Fellow in Agrarian History at the University of Leicester and then, from 1965 until her retirement, Reader in Economic History at the University of Oxford. She is General Editor of the *Agrarian History of England and Wales* and editor of volumes four and five (covering the period 1500 to 1750), for which she also wrote several chapters. Her other publications include *English Peasant Farming* (1957), *Economic Policy and Projects* (1978), *The Rural Economy of England. Collected Essays* (1986), and *Seventeenth-Century Economic Documents* (1972, co-edited with J. P. Cooper).

PREFACE

Despite the unflagging interest among historians in the English Revolution insufficient attention has so far been given to the actual experience of the upheavals and consequent readjustments within urban and rural contexts. The two fields of urban and agrarian history, indeed, attract different specialists and, characteristically, are taught separately to students. This volume – though diverse in content and approach – seeks to overcome this traditional separation of subject matter and examines the extent to which town and countryside shared the same problems (or not as the case may be) and raises questions about whether the English Revolution was urban led, about winners and losers, and the shifting political balance.

As editor I count myself fortunate in having assembled such a distinguished transatlantic team of contributors. My thanks go to them and to Jane Carpenter at Manchester University Press.

In the interests of clarity spelling in quotations from seventeenth-century prose material has been modernised.

R.C. Richardson

CHAPTER ONE

TOWN
AND
COUNTRYSIDE
IN THE
ENGLISH
REVOLUTION

R. C. Richardson

> the Drum shall speak
> In every Village warre, the Rurall swaine
> Shall leave his tillage, Shepheards leave the plaine.
> ... the Glebe Land
> Shall unmanured and untilled stand.
> The plough shall be neglected, and the corn,
> By th'horse hoofs trampled, fade before full born
> 'Tis fit for sickle. Graziers sell away
> Their beasts, lest kept they prove the souldiers pay

(John Abbot (alias Rivers), *The Fable of Philo* (1645), pp. 13–14.
Quoted in J. Turner, *The Politics of Landscape*, Oxford, 1979, p. 91)

Towns are like electric transformers. They increase tension, accelerate the rhythm of exchange and constantly recharge human life. They were born of the oldest and most revolutionary division of labour: between work in the fields on the one hand and the activities described as urban on the other ... Towns generate expansion and are themselves generated by it. But even when towns do not create growth from scratch, they undoubtedly channel its course to their own advantage. And growth can be perceived in the towns and cities more clearly than anywhere else.

(F. Braudel, *Civilisation and capitalism: fifteenth to eighteenth centuries.
I: The structures of everyday life*, London, 1981, p. 479)

[1]

The English Revolution was enacted in both town and countryside and its effects have variously been played down or underlined. Alan Everitt sees the mid-century upheavals as 'tragic but temporary' and as only one – harvest failure, malnutrition and disease being others – 'of a succession of problems to which society at the time was peculiarly vulnerable'. Charles Carlton, on the other hand, in a recent essay has described the English Civil Wars as 'the bloodiest conflict in relative terms in English history', with death rates exceeding those later experienced in the First World War.[1] In this, as in other aspects of this period, we enter fiercely contested ground. As part of the debate much has been written in the last thirty years or so on the local and regional aspects of this crisis period. Most conspicuously a large number of studies have appeared of individual counties and their communities, with Alan Everitt's pioneering work on Kent (1966) paving the way and opening what has since become a considerable controversy.[2] The interpretations of the gentry's place in seventeenth-century society and politics which R. H. Tawney and H. R. Trevor Roper and others advanced during the 1940s and 1950s have been extended and tested at the local level in studies of Northamptonshire, East Anglia, South West Wales, Yorkshire and Lancashire.[3] The interactions between London and the provinces have been explored in investigations of the Eastern Association by Clive Holmes, in John Morrill's *The Revolt of the Provinces* (1976), in Anthony Fletcher's *Reform in the Provinces. The Government of Stuart England* (1986), and in Andrew Coleby's county study of Hampshire.[4] 'History from Below' – a growth area generally in historical studies – has entered the local field in studies of popular politics and religion in Cambridgeshire, the Fens, and the West Country.[5] A great deal has been published on rural society and the changing patterns of agriculture in the seventeenth century, much of it the work of Joan Thirsk, a contributor to this volume.[6] Individual towns and cities in this period – such as Newcastle, Exeter, Lincoln, Norwich, Chester, Worcester and London – have found their historians, and Roger Howell and others have begun to make a general assessment of the urban experience and urban allegiances during the Revolutionary period.[7] Nonetheless, it is clear that so far less attention has been paid to the urban settings of the English Revolution than to the experience of the countryside and the gentry in this period. And by and large town and countryside have been separately compartmentalised by historians who have developed special interests in either one or the other. This book breaks new ground, therefore, in bringing the urban and the rural between the same covers, and in raising questions about the variety of their experience and the inter-relationships which connected them. This chapter attempts to establish the parameters by surveying the principal points of contact between town and countryside and by asking how such an understanding can help us to make sense of the successive phases of the English Revolution.

England in the early seventeenth century was not highly urbanised. Most towns were small – many of them exceedingly small – and neither physically nor demographically were they dominant. London, with a massive and occupationally diverse population of 400,000 in 1650, was in every sense the great exception – even more so than in earlier centuries since the gap separating the capital from other towns and cities had widened.[8] Norwich, the second city of the kingdom at this time and the largest of the provincial capitals, had only about 20,000 inhabitants. Bristol's residents numbered around 15,000. York and Oxford had populations of 12,000 and 8,000 respectively. Southampton had about 4,000 and Winchester, well past its medieval prime, only about 3,000.

Given the small size of most towns in this period it followed that there was no absolute contrast between the economies, social life, and behavioural patterns of town and countryside, though towns obviously had much higher population densities, a more organised cultural life, and closer and more regular contacts with the wider world. Most towns – even London – still contained essentially rural features such as gardens, orchards, grazing land, and heaths, and the sight and smell of animals of all kinds were familiar. In seventeenth-century Falkirk, the townsfolk brought out their cows when the herdsman blew his horn in the high street.[9] 'Farm' animals were sometimes reared and not just butchered in towns. The medieval walls and gates of a town or city emphasised its separation from the rural hinterland which lay beyond, but the existence of suburbs in practice blurred the distinction between the urban and rural worlds.[10] It was a distinction which drama and poetry, for political and moral reasons, still insisted on, but it was ideology rather than social and economic realities which enforced the polarities of city comedy and the poetry of landscapes and country estates.[11]

The points of contact between town and countryside on the eve of the Civil War, in fact, were numerous and strong, but infinitely varied according to the size and character of the town, the regional economy surrounding it, and the different opportunities and demands of arable and pastoral areas. First and most basically there was a demographic link between them. Most town dwellers had migrated from the countryside. Urban communities at this time, it is clear, did not grow as the result of the natural increase of their indigenous populations; death rates normally exceeded birthrates. On the eve of the Civil War less than 10 percent of the population of Canterbury had been born there.[12] It was a phenomenon replicated elsewhere.

Occupational links also connected town and countryside. For obvious reasons much urban employment was bound up with the various stages of processing what had been produced in the countryside. Bakers, brewers, butchers, and tanners are occupations of this kind which spring immediately to mind, but the different branches of the finishing stages in the cloth industry involved others. Taken together, jobs of this sort provided employment for about a third of the population of Gloucester at this time. Its ruling elite, too, was dominated by the leading figures in such occupations.[13]

The matter of food supply also placed town and countryside in a position of mutual, if not always comfortable and respectful, dependence. Most – though not all – food consumed in towns (and hay for all the horses) had to be drawn in from the surrounding countryside, and the more sizeable the town the larger the providing area needed to be. London's population doubled in the first half of the seventeenth century and its demand for provisions, obviously, grew at the same rate. The food supply of the capital, therefore, involved a complicated, highly organised network which extended to most of England and to parts of Wales, Scotland and Ireland.[14] Middlemen plied their trade to make the system work and made good profits into the bargain. Farmers and market gardeners for their part became economically dependent on their urban customers, though much haggling before transactions were concluded was part of the relationship.[15]

Many towns functioned as local and regional marketing centres and thus had an indispensable role in the economic relationships which connected the urban and rural populations. There were over 800 of these market towns in the seventeenth century, and their large number is itself a revealing comment on the close and intimate connections between town and countryside and on the multiplicity of local economies which existed in this period.[16] Industry connected town and countryside for the obvious reason that much industrial activity was located in rural areas, not in towns. Towns, therefore, acted as collecting, finishing, and distributing centres; Kendal is a good example of such industrial interdependence.[17] In this pre-factory age there were relatively few manufacturing towns. But as well as being focal points for the reception and distribution of raw materials and goods, market towns were also financial and social centres.

The fact that towns were centres of administration and professional services brought them into another set of two-way relationships with the countryside and those who lived there. Assizes and Quarter Sessions were based in towns and their jurisdictions extended outwards. Scriveners, lawyers, and doctors invariably practised within towns. Shopkeepers were an essentially urban phenomenon. So were inns and innkeepers. 'There is no town', wrote the great French historian Fernand Braudel, 'that does not impose upon its hinterland the amenities of its market, the use of its shops, its weights and measures, its moneylenders, its lawyers, even its distractions. It has to dominate an empire, however tiny, in order to exist'.[18]

In varying degrees towns were also religious centres for their localities and regions. The Reformation emphasised the religious role of towns – medieval monasteries had operated chiefly in, sometimes remote, rural areas – and not just in a diocesan sense. Towns and the availability of preaching were increasingly correlated. Puritanism's social foundations, as its modern historians have shown, were principally urban.[19]

Social connections strengthened the bonds between town and countryside still further. Towns occupied a key place in the transmission of news. Kinship networks united the rural and urban worlds. Prosperous merchants or tradesmen often tended to convert some of their wealth into a country estate. And for political as well as social reasons the links between the gentry and the towns could be close and involve mutual self-interest. (Winchester, for example, was tentatively admitting gentry as freemen of the city from the late sixteenth century.) A large proportion of borough MPs were drawn from the country gentry. So when historians talk of 'county communities' in this period, it is clear that that concept must in some respects accommodate the towns.[20]

The relationship between town and countryside on the eve of the Civil War thus had many facets. These did not always work harmoniously. Producers and consumers of food could have fundamentally opposite views on prices. The activities of urban middlemen operating in the countryside could be bitterly resented. So could overbearing gentry intrusions and interference in town life and government. Urban administrators resolutely tried to fend off the endemic problem of the rural poor. But town and countryside had a way of exporting their respective problems to each other. Harvest failure in the countryside – to take the most extreme case – could entail desperate difficulties for the towns. A commercial recession, on the other hand, reverberated back from ports and market towns to rural areas and inescapably led to cutbacks in industrial production in the countryside.

This complex pattern of relationships between town and countryside was affected by the upheavals and readjustments of the English Revolution in various ways. First, the onset of Civil War imposed the problem of allegiance as a complicating factor in the connecting links between urban and rural areas. Generalisations on this subject are notoriously difficult. To describe a locality or town as either Royalist or Parliamentarian is misleading in a number of respects and underestimates the prevailing trend of neutralism.[21] It was rare indeed to find unanimous allegiance to one side in the same place. Competing factions jostled for power; terms like 'Royalist Newcastle' or 'Parliamentarian Bradford' refer chiefly to the dominant elite of the places in question.[22] Moreover, it has to be remembered that both towns and rural areas changed hands in the course of the war and that there was an essential distinction between towns themselves and their (usually imported) garrisons. The real problems came in counties such as Leicestershire which were equally divided, or where there were pockets of rival loyalty in a region largely in the hands of the other side.[23] The sieges of Corfe Castle in Dorset, Basing House in Hampshire, Lathom House in Lancashire, and Brampton Bryan in Herefordshire are dramatic examples of the consequences.[24] But contrasting allegiances in adjacent localities not only led inevitably to political tension but also produced economic difficulties since supply lines and distribution networks were affected. Rival Civil War loyalties strained at times to breaking point the economic interdependence of town and countryside.

Civil War in England, it is true, was less prolonged and devastating than the Thirty Years War in Germany.[25] The armies involved were relatively small, many 'battles' were little more than skirmishes, and some areas of the country saw little or no fighting. There were no serious harvest failures before 1647 so prices generally remained stable. The capacity to pay (increased) taxes evidently remained. Some places positively benefited from the war. Army contracts for swords, shoes and uniforms brought considerable gains to towns like Birmingham and Northampton.[26] And as the price of horses shot up in the 1640s those in the right places with large supplies of them could make a killing.[27]

Nonetheless, in the most fiercely contested areas both town and countryside experienced disruption, loss and destruction. Towns were both more defensible than the countryside and more prone to be targets. The Severn Valley was one of the major cockpits of fighting. Bristol was twice besieged in 1643 and 1645. Tewkesbury and Malmesbury changed hands several times. Cirencester was sacked by Prince Rupert in 1643. These and other towns in the region suffered plundering and fire raids.[28] Winchester's sufferings at the hands of both sides in the Civil War were harrowing. Waller, Ogle and Cromwell all inflicted severe damage between 1642 and 1645. But the major dramatic moments in the Civil War history of Winchester and other towns should not make us overlook the endemic, small-scale harassment by roving bands of soldiers of both sides, always on the look out for loot, provisions, and horses.[29]

As well as the physical damage there was economic dislocation. The corporation of Hull informed Parliament in 1645 that 'by their decay of trade, continual making and re(pair)ing of fortifications, their constant charge in watching and warding the Town, and their insupportable losses at sea (by Pirates or otherwise) ... the town is utterly disabled of itself'. The West Riding textile industry collapsed in view of the problems encountered in production, quality control and marketing.[30] Long distance movement of goods and the operation of credit and payment arrangements were amongst the most serious economic difficulties occasioned by the Civil War. The West Country and Welsh clothiers, for example, struggled in vain to get their goods through the war zones to London. For the countryside in areas near the fighting or crossed by rival armies the hardships involved the loss of livestock, crops, timber, equipment, acts of vandalism, the rounding up of horses, and the mounting difficulties experienced in getting produce to market. Non-payment of rent, increased taxation, mounting debt, and sequestration of estates all had a place among the problems encountered by landowners.[31] Troop movements cut across established lines of communication between towns and their rural hinterlands. And the presence of a garrison not only strained the urban economy in which it was immediately placed – 5,000 troops swelled Winchester's native population of 3,000 in 1643[32] – but also placed serious burdens on the rural hinterland and interrupted the characteristic rhythms of rural life. Petitioners from the Manshead Hundred of Bedfordshire argued passionately in 1644 that they were completely unable to contribute any more to the defence of the garrison at Newport Pagnell. So much had been seized from them already, they pleaded, that 'now being seedtime they have not horses to plough or sow their land'. Petitioners from Cleveland in 1647 made much the same case. 'Some ... have neither oxen left to till the ground nor seed to sow the same withall'. Country folk from Cheshire had a similar lament. 'For money they are so exhausted betwixt free quartering of our own (men) and plundering by the enemy', a Parliamentarian officer reported, that 'their daily taxations and their weekly mises [levies] for these garrisons that they are subject to, that they profess that, being restrained from selling that little cheese which is most of their sustenance, they are not able to contribute any more unless they should sell the very clothes off their backs and their wives' and children's'.[33]

Towns acquired new responsibilities and roles in the 1640s and 1650s which affected their relationships with the surrounding countryside. Towns had strategic significance. Usually against their own will, they were made centres of military operations in the Civil War period and therefore exercised a military dominance over the adjacent countryside. Instances of the privations suffered by countrymen have already been mentioned. When we find repeated examples of military requisitioning of horses, carts, even pickaxes and spades, we begin to appreciate the depths of rural antipathy to soldiers and the plight to which small farmers could be temporarily reduced.

In the 1640s and 1650s towns continued to be the kind of administrative centres that they had always been. The differences were that new administrative structures were imposed and new policies carried out. The County Committees of the 1640s operated from an urban base.[34] So did Cromwell's Major Generals after 1655. New taxation policies – and record levels of taxation – and the new religious programme spread outwards from towns. With the Anglican church and its structures and ceremonies officially abolished, new systems were devised – the Presbyterian experiment is the most obvious example – and towns were the spearhead of their advance. The different aspects of the business of handling the defeated Royalists were dealt with not just in London but in the urban administrative centres of the provinces; assessment, composition fines, the Decimation Tax, all these penalties on Royalist landlords were settled in the towns. New opportunities arose in these circumstances for further urban investment in the countryside, either by buying confiscated land or by providing loans to distressed landlords. The redistribution of land and the settlement of disputes and grievances connected with the Civil War did much to promote the consolidation of the urban-based profession of the law.[35]

There was much rural resistance, it is clear, to many of the policies of the interregnum, and the survival of Anglicanism, despite all attempts to suppress it, is an example. The Clubmen and the Diggers expressed rural alienation and initiatives in the 1640s. From another perspective, the growth of Quakerism, primarily a rural movement in its formative stages, provides further evidence of the countryside's refusal to toe the official line.[36]

It is not the argument of this chapter, however, nor of this book that the English Revolution was a primarily urban phenomenon imposed on a hostile and resentful countryside. The English Revolution by its nature has to be classified as both urban and rural, though it is worth remarking that the apparent political deceleration of the 1650s was accompanied by a shift away from the towns towards the countryside; under the Instrument of

Government the proportion of county members in the House of Commons was increased by 45 percent. Only one town in the while country had the capacity to be so significant in its impact on the countryside (and on other towns as well, for that matter), and that was London. Because of its overwhelming size and the multi-dimensional nature of its economic, political, social, and cultural importance, London's role in the English Revolution was decisive. That London should have become Parliamentarian was by no means a foregone conclusion, as Valerie Pearl and others have demonstrated. Once identified with Parliament in the early 1640s, however, London's allegiance and backing, more than anything else, explain why Charles I lost the Civil War. The ultimate triumph of conservatism in the capital, on the other hand – a process examined in Keith Lindley's chapter below (pp. 19 – 45) – goes a long way to explain why the Restoration of the monarchy took place in 1660.[37]

Other towns, obviously, could not wield the same influence as London, and as a group they were less politically and socially distinct than towns in Scotland, which formed a concerted and influential burgh interest.[38] Towns in France were also more distinctively separate than those in England, with the result that the specifically urban contribution to the French Revolution in the late eighteenth century was greater than that made to the English Revolution.

Relations between town and countryside in the French Revolution have long been a debated issue among historians in a way that has not been seen in England; Bonald and Michelet in the nineteenth century and Cobban in the twentieth all saw the French Revolution as being energised by the tensions between urban and rural areas.[39] Recent research has reacted against some of the mechanistic aspects of Cobban's model of town/countryside conflict, recognised complementarity as well as polarisation in their relations, and has drawn attention to declining urban populations in the 1790s and to the dynamics of agrarian radicalism. The lack of linguistic conformity in France, it has been accurately observed, applied to towns as well as to the countryside. (The Abbé Gregoire estimated in 1791 that six million 'Frenchmen' – including Bretons, Flemish, Italians, Germans, patois speakers, and so on – were ignorant of the French language; for them the French Revolution was conducted in a foreign language.)[40] Nonetheless, it seems to have been the case that, apart from the initial peasant revolution in France in 1789 (which died away in most areas once the immediate objectives had been achieved), the remaining stages of the Revolution were essentially urban in nature. And the sweeping, dislodging changes of the 1790s, such as dechristianisation, the secularisation of church lands and the paper currency issued on their basis, and the Terror, all worked outwards from urban centres, especially Paris. Counter-revolution in France – formidable in regions such as the Vendée and in Brittany – was principally a rural backlash. Rural resistance to the policies of an urban-led revolution was also a characteristic of Russia in the 1920s and 1930s.[41]

Though the countryside was stirred in the 1640s and 1650s, it is clear that England experienced no large-scale rural counter-revolution of the kind which later occurred in France, partly because less happened to provoke one and also because the division between town and countryside in England was less emphatic. The gentry in England as a group had urban as well as rural foundations. French towns had a much more clear-cut political economic and social identity than their English counterparts and were much more obsessed with their separateness.[42] As we have seen, English towns had closer reciprocal links with their hinterlands and their economic and political roles in their regions rested firmly on such connections. And as they continued to grow in size and complexity such ties became even stronger. By the late seventeenth century, in any case, it has been estimated that a third of the country's population lived in provincial towns of more than 5,000.[43] In two respects at least, one largely symbolic and the other socio-political, the English Revolution helped to make the connections between town and countryside stronger still. First, the partial or complete destruction – as in the case of Coventry, Taunton, Gloucester, and Northampton – of town walls in the Civil War lessened or removed what had once been literally the dividing line between town and countryside.[44] (The wholesale destruction of Coventry's town walls in 1662, as Ann Hughes points out (p. 69), was a deliberate act of political revenge.) Second, after 1660 the gentry's presence in towns became more conspicuous than it had ever been before, both in terms of political intervention and leadership and in social terms as well, in that towns like Bath and Winchester became the gentry's leisure resorts; assembly rooms, coffee-houses, theatres and town-houses displayed the fact. What has been termed the 'the triumph of the gentry' after the Restoration was expressed in the towns no less than in the countryside.[45]

The chapters which follow explore different aspects of the wide-ranging experience of towns and the countryside in mid-seventeenth-century England. In the first part of the book five individual towns, widely separated geographically and differing in size, economies and politics, come under scrutiny.

London – vital in so many ways to the course of events between 1640 and 1660 and to the network of links between town and countryside – begins the book with Keith Lindley's reflections on its political role and political elite and detailed analysis of the signatories to three key petitions in the early 1640s. Once London's citizenry split, he argues, new opportunities lay open for radical politics, which threatened to undermine the traditional cohesion provided by wards, parishes and livery companies. Natural conservatism, however – though temporarily defeated – was never extinguished. It re-emerged in the more settled conditions of the 1650s, and clinched the Restoration.

David Scott's chapter on York – again chiefly political – considers a chronologically different and less direct urban experience of the mid-century crisis. Though cautious about ascribing too much to the direct impact of Civil War on the northern city, Scott shows how the Civil War unavoidably made urban politics and 'party' divisions more openly and permanently ideological. He goes on to demonstrate how the Parliamentarian/Puritan takeover in 1645 led on to seemingly insular politics, with no second revolution later in the decade and a pragmatic acceptance of the need for a Restoration.

Chapter Four by Ann Hughes introduces Coventry's very different economic and political circumstances. Highlighting the tensions in the relations between the town government and the Warwickshire gentry, the intermittent friction between the producers and finishers of cloth, and conflict over the use of the town's common lands, Hughes explores Coventry's reputation for Puritanism and Parliamentarianism in the Civil War period and its role as the headquarters of the County Committee. The short-term impact of economic disruption and high taxation is documented, as is the re-orientation of Coventry's relationship with the surrounding county and its gentry. Here is a town which paid a high price for its allegiance and role in the Civil War.

David Harris Sacks' study of Bristol's 'Wars of Religion', which forms the next chapter, explores the various levels of connection between religion and politics in this, the third largest town of the kingdom. Sacks shows how the question of monopoly in trade and religion became the key issue in Bristol in these years and how the Corporation, the Merchant Adventurers Company, lesser merchants and shopkeepers, conservative clergy, Puritan lecturers and (in the 1650s) Quakers, made different, but interlocking contributions to the ongoing, ideologically charged local drama.

Oxford's tensions and traumas in the 1640s and 1650s – as Ian Roy shows in Chapter Six – were of a different kind. As a market town with close links with lesser urban centres like Abingdon and Witney as well as more general connections with the surrounding countryside, Oxford – like other towns near the front-line of conflict – faced much disruption. As a seat of learning and the Royalist capital Oxford's experience of Civil War heightened the city's long-standing struggle with the arrogant university in its midst and complicated the question of political allegiance. Oxford's losses were great and its recovery slow in coming in the 1650s and beyond.

Joan Thirsk's chapter opens the second part of the book, which deals with particular themes in the experience of the countryside and its inhabitants in the English Revolution. In an incisive analysis she shows how long-standing agrarian problems connected with enclosure, the status and ownership of reclaimed coastal land, agricultural improvement, and the legal status of manorial tenants, were inconclusively handled by successive regimes in the 1640s and 50s. Attitudes and practice might change, sometimes substantially at local level, but the old agrarian framework and the principles of property (redistribution of land among the elite notwithstanding) were as entrenched under Cromwell as they had been under Charles I.

Barry Coward, in Chapter Eight, re-examines the much-debated fortunes of a major group of these property-owners – the gentry – and charts their varied political and economic experience of Civil War. He goes on to explore the processes which enabled the gentry to reunite, kept most of them from giving enthusiastic support for the republic, and which made them welcome – from self-interest, as much as anything – a Restoration in 1660 which would safeguard and complete the recovery they had already begun to achieve in the 1650s.

The extent to which Civil War, as opposed to secular change in population and price levels, affected relations between landlords and tenants is the principal question explored by Colin Phillips in Chapter Nine. Such an analysis takes stock of the evidence concerning tenants' taking up arms, the economic impact of the war on agricultural practice, estate management, capacity to pay rent and taxation, and the consequences of sequestration. Landowners and the concept of landowning may have gained something from the English Revolution but tenants, Phillips concludes, did not.

Losers as well as winners are looked at in other ways in Buchanan Sharp's study of 'Rural discontents and the English Revolution' which forms the final chapter of the book. Sharp re-examines three principal themes – the rise of a godly middling sort, the reform of popular culture, and the differences between wood/pasture and arable/fielden districts – which have emerged out of recent studies of the social, economic and religious history of local communities in this period. In particular David Underdown's model of the English Revolution as a conflict between two cultures is challenged, tested, and found wanting. Winners and losers in the English Revolution, Sharp argues, did not neatly correspond with Parliamentary/Royalist divisions.

Town and Countryside in the English Revolution thus takes the reader in a number of directions and raises questions (and suggests answers) about the nature and distribution of allegiance and neutralism in the Civil War, about religious tension and disagreement, the seriousness of the impact of the military contest, about the extent and speed of recovery, the ways in which urban and rural interests and experience were shared or remained separate and divided, and about how far the English Revolution was urban led. It raises questions (and again suggests answers) about those who gained and those who lost, and about the ways in which the political balance shifted between town and countryside, both in and after the mid-century upheavals and their eventual settlement.

Notes

1 A. M. Everitt, *The Local Community and the Great Rebellion*, London, 1969, pp. 26–7; C. Carlton, 'The impact of the fighting' in J. Morrill (ed.), *The Impact of the English Civil War*, London, 1991, p. 20. See also I. Roy, 'England turned Germany? The aftermath of the Civil War in its European context', *Transactions of the Royal Historical Society* [*TRHS*], 5th ser., 28, 1978, pp. 127–44.

2 A. M. Everitt, *The Community of Kent and the Great Rebellion, 1640–1660*, Leicester, 1966. For details of subsequent studies and the ensuing debates see R. C. Richardson, *The Debate on the English Revolution Revisited*, London, 1988, pp. 143–7.

3 M. Finch, *The Wealth of Five Northamptonshire Families 1540–1640*, Northants Record Society, XIX, 1956; A. Simpson, *The Wealth of the Gentry, 1540–1660*. *East Anglian Studies*, Cambridge, 1961; H. A. Lloyd, *The Gentry of South West Wales, 1540–1640*, Cardiff, 1968; J. T. Cliffe, *The Yorkshire Gentry from the Reformation to the Civil War*, London, 1969; B. G. Blackwood, *The Lancashire Gentry and the Great Rebellion, 1640–1660*, Manchester, 1978.

4 C. Holmes, *The Eastern Association in the English Civil War*, Cambridge, 1974; A. M. Coleby, *Central Government and the Localities: Hampshire, 1649–1689*, Cambridge, 1987.

5 M. Spufford, *Contrasting Communities. English Villagers in the Sixteenth and Seventeenth Centuries*, Cambridge, 1974; K. Lindley, *Fenland Riots and the English Revolution*, London, 1982; B. Sharp, *In Contempt of All Authority. Rural Artisans and Riot in the West of England, 1586–1660*, Berkeley and Los Angeles, 1980; D. Underdown, *Revel, Riot and Rebellion. Popular Politics and Culture*, Oxford, 1985.

6 See, for example, Joan Thirsk (ed.), *Agrarian History of England and Wales*, IV (*1500–1640*) and V (*1640–1750*), Cambridge, 1967 and 1985, and Joan Thirsk, *The Rural Economy of England. Collected Essays*, London, 1984.

7 R. Howell, *Newcastle upon Tyne and the Puritan Revolution*, Oxford, 1967: W. T. MacCaffrey, *Exeter, 1540–1640. The Growth of an English County Town*, Cambridge, Mass., 1958; J. W. F. Hill, *Tudor and Stuart Lincoln*, Cambridge, 1956; J. T. Evans, *Seventeenth-Century Norwich. Politics, Religion and Government, 1620–90*, Oxford, 1980; A. M. Johnson, 'Politics in Chester during the Civil Wars and Interregnum, 1640–62' in P. Clark and P. Slack (eds.), *Crisis and Order in English Towns, 1500–1700*, London, 1972. See also P. Clark (ed.), *Country Towns in Pre-Industrial England*, Leicester, 1981; R. Howell, 'The structure of urban politics in the English Civil War', *Albion*, XI, 1979; Howell, 'Neutralism, conservatism and political alignment in the English Revolution: the case of the towns, 1642–49' in J. Morrill (ed.), *Reactions to the English Civil War*, London, 1982; Howell, 'Resistance to change. The political elites of provincial towns during the English Revolution' in A. L. Beier *et al.* (eds.), *The First Modern Society. Essays in English History in Honour of Lawrence Stone*, London, 1989.

8 See A. L. Beier and R. Finlay (eds.), *London 1500–1700. The Making of the Metropolis*, London, 1986; E. A. Wrigley, 'A simple model of London's importance in changing English society and economy, 1650–1750', *Past and Present*, 37, 1967.

9 I. H. Adams, *The Making of Urban Scotland*, Edinburgh, 1978, p. 49.

10 See H. L. Turner, *Town Defences in England and Wales. An Architectural and Documentary History*, London, 1971.

11 On the literary motifs and practice of this period see R. Williams, *The Country and the City*, London, 1973; L.C. Knights, *Drama and Society in the Age of Jonson*, London, 1937; B. Gibbons, *Jacobean City Comedy*, 1968, 2nd edn, London, 1980; J. Turner, *The Politics of Landscape. Rural Scenery and Society in English Poetry, 1630–1660*, Oxford, 1979; See, for comparative purposes, J. Rich and A. Wallace Hadrill (eds.), *City and Country in the Ancient World*, London, 1991, which explores the ideological force of rural/urban images in the Classical period.

12 J.A. Sharpe, *Early Modern England. A Social History, 1550–1760*, London, 1987, p.79.

13 P. Clark, '"The Ramoth-Gilead of the Good": urban change and political radicalism at Gloucester, 1540–1640' in J. Barry (ed.), *The Tudor and Stuart Town. A Reader in English Urban History, 1530–1688*, London, 1990, p.249; P. Clark, 'The civic leaders of Gloucester, 1580–1800' in P. Clark (ed.), *The Transformation of English Provincial Towns, 1600–1800*, London, 1984.

14 F.J. Fisher, 'The development of the London food market, 1540–1640', *Economic History Review*, V, 1935; J. Chartres, 'Food consumption and internal trade' in A.L. Beier and R. Finlay (eds.), *London, 1500–1700. The Making of the Metropolis*, London, 1986.

15 R.B. Westerfield, *Middlemen in English Business, particularly between 1660 and 1760*, Connecticut, 1916, New York, 1969; T.S. Willan, *The Inland Trade. Studies in English Internal Trade in the Sixteenth and Seventeenth Centuries*, Manchester, 1976.

16 A.M. Everitt, 'The marketing of agricultural produce' in Joan Thirsk (ed.), *Agrarian History of England and Wales. IV: 1500–1640*, Cambridge, 1967; J.A. Chartres, 'The marketing of agricultural produce' in Joan Thirsk (ed.), *Agrarian History of England and Wales. V: 1640–1750*, Cambridge, 1985; E. Kerridge, 'Early modern English markets' in B.L. Anderson and A.J.H. Latham (eds.), *The Market in History*, London, 1986.

17 C.B. Phillips, 'Town and country: economic change in Kendal, c. 1550–1700' in P. Clark (ed.), *The Transformation of English Provincial Towns, 1600–1800*, London, 1984.

18 W. Prest (ed.), *The Professions in Early Modern England*, London, 1987; A.M. Everitt, 'The English urban inn' in A.M. Everitt (ed.), *Perspectives in English Urban History*, London, 1973; F. Braudel, *Civilisation and Capitalism. I: The Structures of Everyday Life*, London, 1981, p.481. See also A.M. Everitt, 'Country, county and town: patterns of regional evolution in England' in Everitt, *Landscape and Community in England*, London, 1985.

19 See, for example, C. Hill, *Society and Puritanism in Pre-Revolutionary England*, London, 1964 and R.C. Richardson, *Puritanism in Northwest England*, Manchester, 1972.

20 In this respect, as in others, Everitt's gentry-based model of the county community has been called into question. See, for example, C. Holmes, 'The county community in early Stuart historiography', *Journal of British Studies*, XIX, 1980, and A. Hughes, 'Local history and the origins of the Civil War' in R. Cust and A. Hughes (eds.), *Conflict in Early Stuart England. Studies in Religion and Politics, 1603–1642*, London, 1989; R. Cust 'News and politics in early seventeenth-century England', *Past and Present*, 112, 1986.

21 It is even more misleading to suggest that towns and cities were by and large Parliamentarian. (J. Kenyon, *The Civil Wars of England*, London, 1988, p.38.)

22 See Roger Howell's articles in note 7, above.

23 On Leicestershire see A. M. Everitt, *The Local Community and the Great Rebellion*, London, 1969.

24 G. N. Godwin, *The Civil War in Hampshire, 1642–45*, 2nd edn, Southampton and London, 1904, Chs. 11, 13, 23, 30, and 31; E. Broxap, *The Great Civil War in Lancashire*, Manchester, 1910, pp. 99–109, 120, 142–7; J. Eales, *Puritans and Roundheads. The Harleys of Brampton Bryan and the Outbreak of the English Civil War*, Cambridge, 1990.

25 See Ian Roy (note 1 above); M. P. Gutman, *War and Rural Life in the Early Modern Low Countries*, Princeton, NJ, 1980; M. S. Anderson, *War and Society in Europe of the Old Regime*, London, 1988; J. V. Polisensky, *The Thirty Years War*, London, 1971.

26 W. H. B. Court, *Rise of the Midland Industries*, Oxford, 1938, p. 45; Roy, *art. cit.*, p. 134.

27 P. Edwards, *The Horse Trade of Tudor and Stuart England*, Cambridge, 1988, p. 15; P. Edwards, 'The horse trade of Shropshire' in J. Chartres and D. Hey (eds.), *English Rural Society. Essays in Honour of Joan Thirsk*, Cambridge, 1990, p. 238.

28 Roy, *art. cit.*, pp. 137–40.

29 R. C. Richardson, 'Winchester and the Civil War' in S. A. Barker and C. M. Haydon (eds.), *Winchester in History and Literature*, Winchester, 1992.

30 R. Bennett, 'War and disorder: policing the soldiery in Civil War Yorkshire' in M. C. Fissel (ed.), *War and Government in Britain, 1598–1650*, Manchester, 1991, p. 258; H. Heaton, *The Yorkshire Woollen and Worsted Industry*, Oxford, 1920, p. 229.

31 See H. J. Habakkuk, 'Landowners and the Civil War', *Economic History Review*, 2nd ser., XVII, 1965; C. Clay, 'Landlords and estate management in England', in J. Thirsk, (ed.), *Agrarian History of England and Wales. V: 1640–1750*, Cambridge, 1985, and the chapters by Barry Coward and Colin Phillips below.

32 See Richardson, *art. cit.*, p. 57; Ann Hughes on the garrison in Coventry (below, p. 82).

33 R. C. Richardson, 'Metropolitan counties: Bedfordshire, Hertfordshire, and Middlesex' in Joan Thirsk (ed.), *Agrarian History of England and Wales. V: 1640–1750*, Cambridge, 1985, p. 239; Bennett in Fissel, *op. cit.*, p. 258; R. N. Dore (ed.), *The Letter Books of Sir William Brereton*, 2 vols., Chester, 1984, I, p. 191.

34 See, for example, D. H. Pennington and I. Roots (eds.), *The Committee at Stafford. The Order Book of the Staffordshire County Committee, 1643–45*, Manchester, 1957 and A. M. Everitt (ed.), *Suffolk and the Great Rebellion*, Ipswich, 1961: section 1 deals with the Committee of Suffolk.

35 See Prest, *op. cit.*, Ch. 3; C. W. Brooks, *Pettyfoggers and Vipers of the Commonwealth: The Lower Branch of the Legal Profession in Early Modern England*, Cambridge, 1986.

36 D. Underdown, 'The Chalk and the Cheese: contrasts among the English Clubmen', *Past and Present*, 85, 1979. On the Diggers see C. Hill, 'Winstanley and Freedom' in R. C. Richardson and G. M. Ridden (eds.), *Freedom and the English Revolution*, Manchester, 1986. B. Reay, *The Quakers and the English Revolution*, London, 1985. V. F. Snow, 'Parliamentary reapportionment proposals in the Puritan Revolution', *English Historical Review*, LXXIV, 1959.

37 See R. Hutton, *The Restoration. A Political and Religious History of England 1658–1667*, Oxford, 1985; P. Seaward, *The Restoration*, London, 1981.

38 D. Stevenson, 'The burghs and the Scottish Revolution' in M. Lynch (ed.), *The Early Modern Town in Scotland*, London, 1987. See also I. A. Adams, *The Making of Urban Scotland*, Edinburgh, 1978.

39 C. Crossley, 'Town, country and the circulation of Revolutionary energy: the case of Bonald and Michelet' in A. Forrest and P. Jones (eds.), *Re-shaping France: Town, Country, and Region during the French Revolution*, Manchester, 1991 and A. Cobban, *A Social Interpretation of the French Revolution*, Cambridge, 1968.

40 Forrest and Jones, *op. cit.*, pp. 1–11, 74, 137 *et seq.*, 180–81. See also G. Roupnel, *La Ville et la Campagne au XVIIe Siècle*, Paris, 1955 and P. M. Jones, *The Peasantry and the French Revolution*, Cambridge, 1988.

41 C. Tilly, *The Vendée*, London, 1964; O. H. Radkey, *The Agrarian Foes of Bolshevism*, New York, 1958.

42 P. Zagorin, *Rebels and Rulers, 1500–1660*, 2 vols., Cambridge, 1982, I, pp. 235–44.

43 P. J. Corfield, 'Urban development in England and Wales in the sixteenth and seventeenth centuries' in D. C. Coleman and A. H. John (eds.), *Trade, Government and Economy in Pre-Industrial England. Essays presented to F. J. Fisher*, London, 1976, p. 223.

44 The walls of many towns survived, it is true, as a picturesque but irrelevant anachronism until well into the eighteenth or early nineteenth century when the further demands of urban growth finally swept them away. The town gates of Salisbury and Norwich were demolished in the 1770s and 1790s respectively. P. J. Corfield, *The Impact of Towns 1700–1800*, Oxford, 1982, pp. 170–1; P. Clark, *The Transformation of English Provincial Towns, 1600–1800*, London, 1984, p. 41.

45 A. Fletcher, *Reform in the Provinces. The Government of Stuart England*, New Haven and London, 1986, pp. 351–73.

CHAPTER TWO

LONDON'S CITIZENRY IN THE ENGLISH REVOLUTION

Keith Lindley

London was to play a crucial role in the English Revolution; indeed, without the ability of Parliament to mobilise support in the metropolis, and without the later political divisions among its citizenry, there would have been no revolution. Yet as Valerie Pearl has convincingly demonstrated, the City was far from being a natural supporter of Parliament prior to 1642 and its eventual Parliamentarian alignment was the result of the seizure of power in the City by its 'Parliamentary Puritan' minority.[1] More recently Professor Pearl has sought to explain why a social revolution did not follow or accompany political revolution in London and in response to this question she has emphasised the City's basic stability and continuing sense of community. London's stability rested upon the wide availability of the freedom, a high level of participation by its citizenry in local government and a benevolent attention to poor relief. The kind of solid citizen who combined his support for Parliament with service in his parish, precinct, ward or livery company did not have the most obvious background for a social revolutionary.[2]

Explaining why London remained stable during earlier periods of rapid change and increased social tension has been the subject of two recent monographs[3] and the conclusions reached have important implications for our understanding of how radical politics were able to emerge in mid-seventeenth-century London.

Both works are concerned with explaining London's freedom from serious unrest and its essential stability in the sixteenth century, and both are in agreement with Professor Pearl in emphasising the vital part played by wards, parishes and livery companies in containing the potential for conflict. However, the more perceptive and sophisticated of the two works, that by Ian Archer focusing upon the troubled decade of the 1590s, concludes that the solidarity of the City's elite was a crucial factor in maintaining stability, for opportunities for radical politics were opened up when a divided elite was tempted to seek support from below. In the later sixteenth century the elite was not sharply divided over religious, political or commercial questions and hence the opportunities for political polarisation were absent. Dr Archer restricts his definition of the City's elite to its aldermen but it is arguable that the term should embrace its Common Councilmen as well, for they shared a close identity of interests and outlook with their aldermanic brethren and played an integral part in the government of London. Given this wider definition of the City's elite, those sources of division that were generally absent in the 1590s were clearly present in the transformed circumstances of the 1640s, as this essay will seek to demonstrate. Divisions over religion, politics and commerce combined to undermine elite solidarity and provide the opportunity for the emergence of radical politics. These divisions ran deep among the citizenry and for a time they also undermined the cohesion of the ward, parish and livery company.

This essay will examine those divisions among London's citizens by making an in-depth analysis of 450 vocal citizens who were largely drawn from the ranks of the City's rulers. These citizens are composed of the signatories of three key petitions emanating from the City at a time when the first tentative steps were being made on the road to Civil War. Two of the petitions, the petition of the 23 December 1641 to the Commons protesting against Thomas Lunsford's appointment to the lieutenancy of the Tower of London,[4] and that of the 9 March 1642 to Common Council urging them to express their support for parliament's militia ordinance,[5] brought together a number of citizens who provided some of the local dynamism that helped deliver London to the Parliamentary cause, sustained its war effort and furnished political leadership through the vicissitudes of the remaining revolutionary years. The March militia petition was a direct repudiation of the third key petition, the so-called Benyon's petition of the 24 February 1642 to both Houses opposing the recent radical change of control over the City's militia.[6] Benyon's petition was the response of a formidable coalition of wealthy, eminent and powerful citizens to the shifts in political power within the City, and the drift towards civil war, and its signatories included some citizens who were to be prominent opponents of radical counsels and defenders of a return to conservative normality in the ensuing years.

Benyon's petition bore the largest number of signatures at 351, followed by the Lunsford petition with eighty-six signatories and the March militia petition with just twenty-one. Eight of the latter had also previously signed the Lunsford petition. In what major ways, therefore, did the Benyon petitioners differ from those fellow citizens who subscribed to the Lunsford and the militia petitions? This question will be addressed by establishing the petitioners' relative economic and social standing and economic interests, their seniority and importance in the City's governmental circles, their geographical distribution, and their religious and political positions and activities both before and after the organisation of these petitions.

Contemporary observers were agreed that the Benyon petitioners were the 'Grandees of the Metropolis', men of wealth and social pre-eminence.[7] The evidence of two listings of London citizens which provide a measure of relative economic standing, the May 1640 listing of citizens judged prosperous enough to be able to contribute to a forced loan and the London tithe assessment of 1638,[8] largely confirms this view. A total of 125 future Benyonites, or over 35 per cent of them, appear on the 1640 listing. This compares with a combined total of twenty-five, or about 25 per cent, of the Lunsford and militia petitioners similarly listed. Furthermore, in those City wards where citizens were subdivided according to their wealth, Benyonites emerge as clearly superior to their Lunsford and March militia counterparts.[9] It has been estimated that valuations of £20 and above for the 1638 tithe assessment denote substantial households: 77 per cent of the Benyonites, and 68 per cent of the combined Lunsford and militia petitioners listed satisfy this criterion. If a higher valuation of £40 and above is employed, then 24 per cent of the former and over 17 per cent of the latter petitioners fall within that superior rank. Later Parliamentary assessments for the Civil War also underline the presence of men of real wealth among the Benyonites.[10]

Prime examples of wealthy Benyonites would include George Benyon himself, an extremely affluent silk mercer with an impressive City house and estates in several counties;[11] the banker-goldsmith Thomas Vyner, whose wealth enabled him to act as financier to the Commonwealth, Protectorate and the restored monarchy;[12] and the East India merchants and brothers, Daniel and Eliab Harvey, whose combined payments of Parliamentary assessments had reached £3,385 by 1646.[13] Vyner and Eliab Harvey were two of the fifty-seven Benyonites who were elected aldermen, the high property qualification for which indicated men of considerable opulence.[14]

Both the Lunsford and the militia petitions also attracted some rich supporters. A leading Lunsford petitioner, Maximilian Bard, had one of the highest tithe ratings in 1638 and owned City property and lands in two counties.[15] The prosperity of Maurice Gething and Richard Turner enabled them to lend Parliament large sums of money in the 1640s,[16] and Turner as well as Bard were amongst the thirteen Lunsford and militia petitioners wealthy enough to be elected aldermen. The signatories of all three petitions, therefore, were generally men of substance, and included within each were citizens of considerable affluence, but in comparative terms the advantage lay with the Benyonites so far as superior wealth was concerned.

A similar picture emerges when the petitioners' relative social standing is examined: one-third of the Benyonites featured in the London visitation returns of 1633–35, compared with 22 per cent of the Lunsford and militia petitioners.[17] Some of the former had relatives at senior levels within the City's government, including four recent lord mayors, and the current City chamberlain and the comptroller of the Chamber, while none of the latter would appear to have enjoyed such senior connections. Membership of one of the Great Twelve livery companies also suggests superior social standing: 81 per cent of the Benyonites and 74 per cent of the Lunsford and militia petitioners, where company membership is known, belonged to one of the Great Twelve.[18]

Economic interests and commercial connections reveal some more pronounced differences between Benyonites and the other petitioners. Overseas merchants constituted a noteworthy element in Benyonite ranks, where in percentage terms they were twice as strong as their counterparts amongst the Lunsford and militia petitioners.[19] Moreover, Benyonites enjoyed a dominant influence in the East India and Levant companies which were replacing the Merchant Adventurers as the natural wielders of power in the City.[20] Of particular note were William Cockayne, deputy-governor of both the East India and the Turkey company in 1642 (and governor of the East India company in the following year), and Andrew Riccard, a member of the court of assistants of the Levant company in 1642 and a future governor of both the Levant and the East India company.[21] In complete contrast, not one of the Lunsford or militia petitioners was to be found on the governing bodies of the great overseas companies in 1641–42.

Judging by the evidence of shares in ships and London port books,[22] much of the trade conducted by Benyonite merchants was with France, southern Europe and the East. However, a few Benyonites had interests in the colonial tobacco trade, like the tobacco importer and retailer, Toby Maidwell.[23] Two Lunsford petitioners, Peter Ducane and Edward Bellamy, were involved in the wine trade with France and Spain, alongside a number of Benyonite merchants, yet the predominant interests or connections of the merchant subscribers of the Lunsford and militia petitions lay elsewhere. Some of the leading figures had strong links with the American colonies and their trade, or were interlopers in trade elsewhere, men like Stephen Estwicke, Michael Herring, Randall Mainwaring, Lawrence Brinley and Samuel Warner.[24] Warner and two fellow petitioners, John Lane and William Underwood, were closely involved in the colonial tobacco trade,[25] while several others, including George Thompson, Richard Hutchinson, Edward Parkes and Richard Floyd, shared strong American links and interests.[26] Colonial interests in Barbados were pursued by two others: John Jurin (a later original stockholder in the Royal Africa company) and Giles Dent.[27]

Pronounced Irish interests would also be added to colonial interests: over 46 per cent of the Lunsford and militia petitioners became investors in the Irish Adventurers. Five of them were to become members of the London committee for Irish Adventurers in 1642–43, and four members of the 1647 sub-committee for Irish affairs.[28] Former Benyonites, on the other hand, showed a

very low level of direct interest in the Irish Adventurers. Only nineteen became investors, although one of these, Henry Featherston,
the stationer, made a substantial investment. Featherston was the
only Benyonite to serve on the London committee of 1642 – 43, yet
three others were to become members of the 1647 sub-committee.

Apart from sharing in some of the most lucrative and expanding
areas of overseas trade, a number of Benyonites were direct
beneficiaries of royal grants and favours. John Holloway and
several others were engaged in the operation of the customs,
Francis Hurdman enjoyed a farm of the duties imposed on sweet
wines, and George Prior had a joint interest in the farm of the
London assurance office.[29] Benyon and Richard Miller acted
as county receivers-general for Crown revenues in the 1630s.[30]
Three others, William Cockayne, Robert Charlton and William
Langhorne, were amongst the London merchants granted the farm
of the pre-emption of tin.[31] Similar recipients of royal grants and
favours included William Gomeldon (the arrears of Palatinate
donations); Francis Moss (a 1640 grant arising from the exercise
of the Crown's wardship in the town and manor of Liverpool);
Robert Oxwick (a royal protection in his dealings as a cloth
merchant); Sidenham Lukins (a fenland adventurer); Robert
Sainthill (the royal agent at Leghorn); Richard Alport (the monopoly
supplier of flags and ensigns to the Navy); Lawrence Loe (the
reversion of a surgeon's place in St Thomas's hospital); and
Edward Bradbourne (the royal family's silkman).[32]

Common interests as creditors also linked together a number of
Benyonites, including Benyon himself, who as wealthy Londoners
made loans or advanced credit to members of the peerage or
gentry. Popish recusants featured prominently in their lists of
debtors[33] and the aggressive anti-popery of the Parliamentary
leadership may have raised doubts about the security of such
loans. The small groups of Benyonite silkmen and scriveners may
similarly have been in the position of anxious creditors, with
peers and MPs possibly amongst their debtors.[34] At least two
peers, and apparently John Pym as well, had borrowed money from
Benyon.[35] The growing length of the Long Parliament seriously
affected the ability of creditors like Benyon to extract repayments
and hence his central role in the campaign against Parliamentary
protections during the summer of 1641.[36]

None of the Lunsford and militia petitioners would seem to

have enjoyed such levels of economic privilege and influence. Despite the presence of some overseas merchants in their ranks, their typical figure was the more modestly prosperous domestic tradesman with his own house and shop, and sometimes other City property, who was engaged in the retailing of textile and other goods. These two petitions drew particular concentrations of support from shopkeepers in the Cheapside area and in commercial thoroughfares running through Bridge Within, from citizens like Richard Overton, the haberdasher, and his neighbour, John Dodd, in Cheapside, or Ellis Midmor and Lawrence Warkman on London Bridge.[37]

These social and economic differences are also reflected in the relative standing of petitioners in City governmental circles. Forty-three Benyonites had been, or subsequently became, masters of their respective livery companies. The bulk of these (thirty-one) rose to the mastership of one of the Great Twelve. Yet only four of the eleven Lunsford and militia petitioners who became masters did so within one of the Great Twelve.

Although sixty-two Benyonites can be identified as Common Councilmen at some stage in the mid-century, this is almost certainly a minimum figure given the incomplete nature of our sources for Common Council membership.[38] At least one-third of the Lunsford and militia petitioners served on Common Council, thus bearing out the claim of the former petitioners to represent the views of 'divers Common Councilmen' as well as other citizens. However, as will be seen shortly, several of these were relative newcomers to that assembly.

In elections for aldermen, fifty-seven Benyonites and thirteen Lunsford and militia petitioners were chosen but in both cases most fined for office.[39] Of those who did serve, three Benyonites subsequently became lord mayors (Thomas Vyner, Richard Chiverton and Anthony Bateman), a height not reached by any of the subscribers of the other petitions. In addition, twenty-two Benyonites, and seven of the other petitioners, were elected sheriffs of London but again most fined for office. The social pre-eminence of several Benyonites is also reflected in their service as City auditors, or as presidents or treasurers of City hospitals,[40] or as officers in the trained bands. By contrast, only a small handful of Lunsford and militia petitioners served as auditors or on the governing bodies of City hospitals.

Given the circumstances of 1642, the positions of command enjoyed by petitioners in the City's militia are obviously of more crucial significance than simply indicating relative social standing. There is, unfortunately, no convenient listing of the City's militia officers below the rank of colonel prior to April 1642. Only a tiny number of Benyonites can be positively identified as militia captains prior to 1642, with the octogenarian Martin Bond undoubtedly chalking up the longest service.[41] Randall Mainwaring is the only Lunsford or militia petitioner who can be similarly identified as an earlier City captain.[42] Surprisingly few Benyonites feature in the April 1642 listing of officers under the command of Philip Skippon in the City's six regiments, suggesting that a partial purge of unreliable elements had already taken place.[43] In the White Regiment, Forth Goodday, the colonel's captain, and three ensigns were former Benyonites, and in the other regiments their presence was even thinner. By the time of the next listing of City officers, in September 1643,[44] Goodday and another senior Benyonite officer, Samuel Carleton, were no longer militia commanders, and by 1646–47 the only former Benyonite to retain a senior command was Ralph Tasker.[45] In marked contrast to this dwindling Benyonite element, a number of Lunsford and militia petitioners rose to high militia commands from 1642 onwards. The April 1642 listing included nine of the latter, made up of one sergeant major (Randall Mainwaring), four captains, the City's quarter-master, two lieutenants and an ensign. By September 1643, Mainwaring had replaced the Royalist Marmaduke Rawden as lieutenant-colonel of the Red Regiment and in subsequent years other fellow petitioners achieved senior rank in the militia or the auxiliaries, five becoming colonels, three lieutenant-colonels and two captains.[46]

The geographical distribution of petitioners in the City reveals some clear concentrations of support. Benyonites were to be found in all wards and in a majority of City parishes, yet the vast majority resided within the walls. There were distinct concentrations of Benyonites in the northern part of the City, in the adjacent parishes of St Mary Aldermanbury and St Michael Bassishaw by the Guildhall and in the ward of Broad Street; in the prosperous parishes around the Royal Exchange and in the affluent inner-City wards of Cornhill, Lime Street, Walbrook and Langbourn; in the more socially mixed Tower ward; and in the ward of Farringdon Within.[47] Those areas of the City where Benyonites were decidedly thin on the ground were the same areas where support for the Lunsford and militia petitions was strongest. The latter's supporters were especially numerous in a cluster of parishes in the centre of the City, either side of Cheapside, and in the ward of Bridge Within. Over 55 per cent of the Lunsford and militia petitioners whose ward can be traced came from the wards of Cheap, Bread Street and Bridge Within. The leading parish was that of St Pancras Soper Lane, a small wealthy inner City parish, while other parishes with a significant concentration of subscribers included St Mary Colechurch, St Peter Westcheap and Allhallows Bread Street (around Cheapside) and St Magnus the Martyr and St Leonard Eastcheap (in Bridge Within).[48] The full significance of this geographical concentration will become clearer when the petitioners' religious and political positions are examined.

Benyonites were clearly divided from Lunsford and militia petitioners so far as religious propensities were concerned. All the available evidence points to the Benyonites as being conformist members of their parish church who reacted with a cautious conservatism to the demands for change in 1641 – 42, although the tide of events was soon to oblige some of them to trim and co-operate with parish radicals they had earlier opposed. Several future Benyonites joined with fellow parishioners in denouncing to the Lords the action taken by local militants in forcibly removing altar rails from parish churches in June 1641.[49] Disputes within some parishes over the choice of minister or preacher also found Benyonites ranged against radicals. The parishioners of St Stephen Walbrook who in November 1641 opposed the attempts of a radical minority to replace their minister included three future Benyonites. The radicals were led by Samuel Warner and William Underwood, who were shortly to sign the Lunsford petition.[50] Three more future Benyonites were amongst the leading parishioners of St Christopher le Stocks who refused to contribute towards the lectureship of the Presbyterian James Cranford.[51]

Several other Benyonites had either family links or religious preferences which predisposed them to take up a conservative stance in religious matters. For example, Henry Isaacson's brother was the pluralist rector of St Andrew by the Wardrobe (who was to be sequestered in 1643), and Thomas Warren was the son-in-law of the canon and chancellor of Exeter.[52] The Bishopsgate merchant, Thomas Jeninges, had a recusant wife and he himself had been mistakenly arrested in 1636 as a suspected popish priest. A royal grant to Jeninges's wife of immunity from the recusancy laws could be expected to provide scant protection against a rising tide of anti-popery.[53] Martin Bond made his religious preferences plain when framing his will in March 1642. His choice of minister to preach his funeral sermon fell upon the rector of St Mary Woolnoth, Josias Shute, who was shortly to fall victim to the clerical purges.[54]

Their wealth and status marked Benyonites out as natural leaders of their parishes and a number of them remained active participants in parish government through 1642 and beyond. In St Michael Cornhill, for example, the parish with the largest concentration of Benyonites, most of the latter continued to attend vestry meetings in the second half of 1642, including vestries which sanctioned the construction of pews in the chancel where the railed altar had formerly stood and approved the articles against their minister.[55] Andew Kendrick remained a leading figure in St Stephen Coleman Street, where he later participated in the campaign to rid the parish of the Independent divine, John Goodwin.[56] After the imposition of Presbyterianism upon the City, several Benyonites were elected elders,[57] or came to be identified with a mainly political Presbyterianism. Amongst the later leading City Presbyterians were to be found former Benyonites like Walter Pell, Edwin Browne, John Perrin, George Wytham and Robert Thompson.[58] Yet significantly, not one former Benyonite signed the Presbyterian City petitions of the 18 November 1645 and the 11 March 1646.[59] In the changed circumstances of the mid-1640s, embracing the new religious order so as to meet the threat of Independency and the sects was a pragmatic option taken by some former Benyonites. Others, however, like Nathaniel Withers, Henry Cockson and Richard Alport, stood their ground and refused to pay tithes to Presbyterian incumbents.[60]

Whereas cautious conservatism generally characterised the stance taken by Benyonites on religious affairs, unequivocal radicalism typified the position adopted by Lunsford and militia petitioners. Several of the latter had already made their mark as Protestant zealots prior to the organisation of these petitions. John Pocock had been one of the parishioners of St Augustine's cited before High Commission in 1632 by Laud for failing to obey instructions for the removal of a pew standing above the communion table.[61] Amongst the conventiclers indicted in 1640–41 was William Shambrook, a member of Henry Jessey's congregation.[62] Others had been active in attempts to purge their churches of innovations and superstition or to remove their minister. Francis Webb and William Stackhouse had backed the removal of altar rails from St Thomas the Apostle in June 1641.[63] As junior churchwarden of St Mary Woolchurch, Michael Herring had responded over-enthusiastically to the Commons's order of September 1641 concerning superstitious images and received a rebuke from the House for defacing funeral monuments. In the following year, Herring was able to preside over a thorough purge of 'superstition' from his parish church.[64] The parish with the largest number of Lunsford and militia petitioners, St Pancras Soper Lane, had also responded enthusiastically to the Commons's order by sanctioning a comprehensive purge of images and inscriptions. Future petitioners had backed both the purge and the choice of the godly divine, Christopher Goade, as Sunday afternoon lecturer, a choice opposed by their rector.[65] In St Stephen Walbrook, Samuel Warner and William Underwood were at the head of a militant struggle to remove their minister around the time of the Lunsford petition. Most parishioners, including, as has been seen, three future Benyonites, backed the minister and at the height of the dispute the militant minority withheld their tithes pending the outcome of Chancery proceedings over the rectorship. Warner, Underwood and their allies were ultimately to secure victory in 1644 with the selection of a Presbyterian divine.[66]

Other petitioners would soon be at the forefront of campaigns to secure godly ministers or to gain control of parish government. Leonard Tillet was the moving force behind efforts to oust Robert Chestlin from St Matthew Friday Street and replace him with Henry Burton. The withholding of tithes was again a tactic used by local militants.[67] In St Dunstan-in-the-East, George Thompson joined fellow godly parishioners in urging the appointment of John Simpson as lecturer,[68] while three other petitioners followed John Venn's lead and successfully campaigned to have Lazarus Seaman appointed rector of Allhallows Bread Street.[69] Henry Allen was involved in radical manoeuvres in St Olave Southwark to transfer the choice of churchwardens from the select vestry (which included two Benyonites) to a gathering of ratepayers.[70]

Finally, the City committee that eventually presided over the systematic purge of City pulpits contained three former Lunsford petitioners.[71]

The Lunsford and militia petitions clearly attracted support from some of the leading members of the City's broad anti-episcopal alliance, which united Presbyterians and future Independents in the campaign to throw off episcopal tyranny and initiate godly reformation. Sixteen petitioners were to become prominent Presbyterians, either as signatories of the Presbyterian petitions of November 1645 and March 1646, or as leading activists in the agitation of 1646–47, or, in the case of Thomas Jackson and William Barton, as participators in Love's plot.[72] Others became active elders in the new Presbyterian order, or were named as lay tryers, or served as delegates to the London provincial assembly.[73] The kind of domestic tradesmen who constituted the petitioners' rank-and-file were doubtless drawn to Presbyterianism by its promised return to parochial discipline and the suppression of the sectarian menace. Nevertheless, a small but significant group of petitioners became equally prominent City Independents. George Foxcroft and Richard Price became members of John Goodwin's influential gathered church; William Shambrook helped organise the 1644 meeting of London separatists and Independents in his own home; and Richard Hutchinson and George Thompson became similarly notable Independents.[74] Future political Independents in the petitioners' ranks included such central figures as Stephen Estwicke, Samuel Warner and Randall Mainwaring.[75] William Underwood managed to maintain godly links with both Presbyterians and Independents,[76] while that great defender of religious freedom, and future Leveller leader, William Walwyn, was a signatory of the militia petition.

There were some equally pronounced political differences between Benyonites and the other petitioners. Two of the latter had already clashed with the Crown prior to 1640: Nicholas Clegate in 1628 over a royal loan and Stephen Estwicke over a new incorporation of silkmen and ship money.[77] The dispute occasioned by Common Hall's claim to elect both sheriffs in June 1641 found future Benyonites ranged against several citizens who were to be prominent signatories of the other petitions. Estwicke and Randall Mainwaring, for example, were two of the six representatives chosen by the citizens to discuss the matter with the lord mayor and aldermen.[78] On the other hand, exactly one half of the 170 signatories of a City petition to the Lords on the 26 July opposing Common Hall's claim subsequently signed Benyon's petition as well, including such leading figures as Thomas Keightley and Robert Gardner, and the Harvey and Bateman brothers.[79]

George Benyon did not sign the 26 July petition, for in the summer of 1641 the campaign against Parliamentary protections was monopolising his attention. During the campaign, Benyon allegedly made several inflammatory statements about the present Parliament which may have echoed the opinions of other leading City merchants. The Commons were reminded that the City was a formidable force to be reckoned with and that it would desert Parliament, as it had previously abandoned the Court, and withhold financial assistance if the protections bill were not passed. Benyon identified the failure of peers to satisfy their debts as a contributory factor in the current decay of trade and mischievously speculated about how the Lords would react when lobbied by crowds of hard-pressed clothiers as popular pressure on the Lords had only recently sealed Strafford's fate. As a portent of future political divisions, he also observed that Parliament had begun to exercise the same kind of arbitrary powers they had previously condemned in the king 'and they being many in number, being about 400, is more grievous than one.'[80]

In the final turbulent weeks of 1641, at least two Lunsford petitioners, Michael Herring and George Henley, were to the fore in the City's root and branch campaign, drumming up signatures for the petition of the 11 December.[81] The great speed with which the Lunsford petition was organised presumably owed much to the state of preparedness of men like Herring and Henley and their radical allies.[82] Drawing upon their experience of petitioning, and other forms of concerted pressure, they were apparently ready to spring into action.

The disputed Common Council elections of December 1641 resulted in the unseating of several future Benyonites. At least six of the latter can be positively identified as electoral casualties. Benyon and Thomas Lusher, both senior members of Common Council, were unseated after highly-charged meetings of their respective wardmotes and subsequent investigations by a Common Council committee set up to scrutinise the 1641 elections (on which

Stephen Estwicke and other militants sat).[83] Similarly, William Middleton, Thomas Carleton and Roger Drake either failed to secure re-election in 1641 or were subsequently unseated by the investigatory committee.[84] In each of the above cases, the unseated Common Councilmen were replaced by radical figures.[85] One other future Benyonite whose election was ruled invalid by the investigatory committee, Thomas Gee, differed from the other casualties of 1641 in that he had been the Common Council nominee of his vestry for the first time that year and was to be successfully returned in 1642–48.[86] However, the fortunes of future Benyonites in the 1641 elections were mixed. Several did secure re-election, like Francis Moss and Thomas Harris in Cornhill,[87] or, as in the case of Gabriel Newman, were returned Common Councilmen for the first time that year.[88]

During the course of 1642 a few more Benyonites were to disappear from Common Council. Robert Alden was dismissed on the 14 March, ostensibly for neglecting to take the Protestation.[89] A militant minority on the vestry of St Olave Jewry disputed the manner in which Oliver Neve was elected in 1641 by moving that the choice of Common Councilman should have been made at a wardmote and not a vestry. The militants included the future Digger leader, Gerrard Winstanley, and a prominent anti-episcopal demonstrator, Patient Wallen. Although initially unsuccessful, by the summer of 1642 the Benyonite Neve had been replaced on Common Council by a radical.[90]

While the Benyonite element on Common Council would appear to have shrunk in 1641–42, Lunsford and militia petitioners managed to consolidate and increase their strength in that assembly. At least three of the latter were long-serving members of Common Council,[91] but the largest influx of these petitioners on to that assembly seems to have taken place in the years 1640–42, with 1642 marking the peak with perhaps nine such new additions. Michael Herring and Samuel Warner, for instance, were probably first returned Common Councilmen in the disputed 1641 elections.[92] Seven of the ten Common Councilmen for Bridge Within in 1642 were Lunsford signatories, and four of these may have gained their seats for the first time in 1641–42.[93] There were three other possible newcomers chosen that year who were Lunsford petitioners, two from Bread Street and one from Cheap.[94]

The July 1642 campaign to remove Richard Gurney from the

mayoralty again ranged former Benyonites against the other petitioners. In two separate Parliamentary petitions, a number of Common Councilmen attacked Mayor Gurney. The latter's earlier manoeuvres to avert the choice of a new radical alderman for Vintry Ward were recalled in a Commons petition on the 7 July. Nominees like Samuel Warner and Isaac Penington, who enjoyed the backing of William Walwyn and his ward allies, had been rejected in favour of seasoned conservative figures, two of whom were Benyonites. Not until the spring of 1643 did Walwyn's faction finally gain an alderman to their liking.[95] The sixty-six Common Councilmen who subscribed the petition of the 9 July to the Lords (complaining about Gurney's obstruction of Common Council's vote over the disposal of the arms and ammunition brought from Hull)[96] included fifteen former Lunsford and militia petitioners. More surprisingly, however, two Benyonites, Francis Moss and Richard Bateman, also signed this petition. At Gurney's trial, several Lunsford and militia petitioners appeared to give evidence against him.[97] Former Benyonites, on the other hand, loomed large amongst Gurney's visitors whilst he was in the Tower.[98]

The advent of civil war found former Benyonites at the forefront of those citizens resisting Parliament's war preparations. At least sixty-five Benyonites can be recognised amongst those citizens who refused or evaded payment of Parliamentary assessments, and hence faced imprisonment and the distraint and sale of their goods, or eventually contributed only under heavy duress. Prosperous citizens who were failing the war effort came under intense pressure in late 1642 and early 1643, and the dominant element amongst them were former Benyonites. Of the fifty-one wealthy citizens rounded up and imprisoned on the 29 October 1642 for failing to contribute, twenty-one were Benyonites. Similarly, of the 104 citizens marked out for distraint in early 1643 for non-payment, around one half were Benyonites.[99]

Other Benyonites, however, proved less defiant and met their assessments, spurred on by a little pressure if necessary. At least twenty-nine of them proved compliant in the early stages of the conflict, and it was probably this type of citizen that the Venetian ambassador had in mind when he wrote about wealthy citizens who were cowed into conformity despite private objections to the City's mobilisation for war.[100] Amongst these co-operative Benyonites were the East India Company merchant, William

Cockayne, who advanced large sums of money to Parliament, and Samuel Mico and Thomas Man, who were commended by the committee for advance of money for the good example they had set locally.[101] Subsequent advancers of loans for the support of the City's forces, or contributors on the 'weekly meal', included some former Benyonites.[102] Conformity to the Parliamentarian regime was presumably a matter of facing up to political realities in order to survive for these compliant Benyonites who would also doubtless share in the general desire to defend the City against a possible Royalist sacking.

At the beginning of armed conflict a number of Benyonites strove hard to restore peace. Several played leading roles in the 'peace' campaigning of December 1642 or were suspected of plotting a coup in the City.[103] Some became open and enthusiastic Royalists, but most apparently baulked at the idea of abandoning London or suffering the severe penalties that an active Royalism would have invited. Royalist sympathisers attempted to smuggle funds out of the City for the king's use in the summer of 1642.[104] In the early months of hostilities, several Benyonites were accused of leaving London to lend direct assistance to Royalist forces or were amongst those 'ill-affected' citizens who were rounded up and imprisoned.[105] The active minority who joined and assisted the Royalists included the royal silkman, Edward Bradbourne; Robert Sainthill, who used his Italian contacts to raise money and arms for the Royalists; Thomas Colwell and Thomas Warren, who served in Sir Nicholas Crisp's mainly London-raised regiment of horse; William Gibson, whose conversion to Catholicism rendered him doubly culpable, and several others who were in Oxford and other Royalist garrisons at their surrender.[106] Waller's plot of March – May 1643, whose origins were traced back to the rejection of Benyon's petition, also brought together at least three former Benyonites, including a 'ringleader', Richard Chaloner.[107]

Resistance and Royalism was not the path taken by all former Benyonites. A small minority not only co-operated with, but actually rendered valuable assistance to, the Parliamentary cause. In the desperate search for ways of financing Parliament's army, assistance was welcomed from men of authority, experience and financial acumen, qualities that were strongly represented in Benyonite ranks. Four Benyonites were to serve on the committee for accounts of the whole kingdom, and one of these was later appointed a treasurer at war.[108] Richard Cranley became a navy commissioner, Francis Lenthall, a treasurer of money raised for the defence of the west, Thomas Vyner, a contractor for bishops' lands (as well as a government financier in the 1650s), and Richard Bateman and John Oldfield, commissioners for compounding with delinquents.[109] At a local level, thirteen Benyonites were named as collectors for money and plate in August 1642, and in the following December six of the local assessors and two of the collectors were former Benyonites.[110] Nevertheless, placed in context Benyonite assistance was miniscule given the numbers of citizens named as collectors and assessors, and even of these a few were to prove recalcitrant agents.[111]

There were to be no doubts about the Parliamentarian ardour of former Lunsford and militia petitioners, who in fact constituted a cross-section of the City's radical leadership. Three men in particular stand out as dynamic City Parliamentarians: Randall Mainwaring, Stephen Estwicke and Samuel Warner. All three served on the City's militia committee from January 1642[112] and remained prominent in radical politics for the rest of the decade. Mainwaring was one of the four citizens singled out by the king as being the authors of his troubles in the City. True to his reputation, he was closely involved in the radical petitions of November and December 1642, and signed the Remonstrance of the 30 March 1643. While deputising for Philip Skippon as commander of the City's militia, he took action against the 'peace' petitioners of December 1642 and rounded up suspect citizens, including several Benyonites. He employed the new regiment he had raised in October 1642 to police the capital throughout the winter of 1642–43, and played an active role in executing distraints upon the property of London malignants. A leading political Independent in 1647, Mainwaring ended his days as comptroller for the sale of Royalist lands.[113]

Estwicke and Warner were no less prominent as militant activists. One of the chief radicals on Common Council, Estwicke served on several important committees in the 1640s and was to the fore in the confrontation of 1646–47. He was one of the main suppliers of clothing and shoes to Parliament's army and also served on key committees concerned with the customs, the navy and the sale of church lands.[114] Warner was a member of the committee for the general rising in 1643 and actively opposed the City's Remonstrance of 1647. His close radical connections included his brother, John Warner, and Maurice Thompson and his family.[115]

Several other former petitioners occupied senior Parliamentarian positions. Michael Herring was joint-treasurer of the committee for advance of money and the committee for compounding until 1653,[116] and his close political ally, Lawrence Brinley, served on the committee for taking the accounts of the kingdom and, later, the committee for compounding.[117] The routine financial management of the navy in the 1640s was probably being handled by Richard Hutchinson, who finally became navy treasurer in 1651. He was also co-treasurer for maimed soldiers.[118] There were in fact few important London-based committees that did not include former Lunsford or militia petitioners in their membership during the 1640s.

When it came to providing the means with which to fight the royalists, some of Parliament's most reliable agents were drawn from amongst these former petitioners. Twenty-two of them acted as collectors under the ordinance of August 1642, and seventeen of the assessors, and five of the collectors, named in the following December were former petitioners.[119] The radical sub-committee for subscriptions established at Weavers' Hall in November 1642 included William Walwyn and Robert Sweet.[120] Former petitioners accounted for eight of the seventeen commissioners entrusted with the raising of horse for Parliament's cavalry, and four of the thirteen-man gunpowder committee.[121] Two other former petitioners were empowered to scour the City and suburbs for urgently needed arms.[122] Several more were instrumental in levying distresses upon recalcitrant citizens, including former Benyonites.[123]

By the mid-1640s, however, the fiscal and administrative burdens of war, and mounting concern about the sectarian threat, had taken its toll on the petitioners' former cohesiveness. The religious and political divisions into Presbyterians and Independents drove some of the most influential petitioners into rival camps, while at the same time some former Benyonites took advantage of the drift of opinion in the City to work for a conservative settlement.[124] The latter also resumed their positions of trust and responsibility in the City in the late 1640s and through the 1650s, securing election as aldermen, becoming masters of their livery companies or governors of trading companies.[125]

This essay has focused upon the divisions which existed within the ranks of substantial London citizens at a time of political crisis and revolution. Benyonites, it could be argued, typified the men of wealth and superior standing, the City's traditional rulers, whose strong links with the pre-1640 regime, and instinctive caution and conservatism, made them natural opponents of the advocates of radical religious and political change. The latter were to be found in strength amongst the supporters of the Lunsford and militia petitions, citizens of substance who were generally less prosperous, well-connected and powerful and without the pre-1640 links enjoyed by their Benyonite opponents. It was this kind of London citizen, working with fellow militants in his parish, ward and livery company, and ready to exert a radical influence in the City's and kingdom's affairs, who provided much of the dynamism in the English Revolution.

However, in the longer term the advantage, so far as the drift of opinion in London was concerned, lay with the advocates of conservatism. War deprived masters of the services of their apprentices, hit trade and closed shops, brought unprecedented fiscal demands and administrative burdens and failed to bring about a political settlement. The collapse of ecclesiastical coercion opened the way for the proliferation of gathered churches and threatened the unity of the parish over which London's substantial citizens presided. Godly Londoners divided into Presbyterian and Independent camps and the former came to find common cause with crypto-Royalists and peace party enthusiasts in working for a political settlement with the king. As a result, both former Benyonites and former Lunsford and militia petitioners could find themselves engaged in joint political action from the mid-1640s onwards. After the end of the first Civil War, conservative sentiment in London was so strong that it has been argued that only the action of Major-General Skippon and armed force kept it in the Parliamentary camp.[126]

The political transformation of London's previously conservative government in 1648–49 was only made possible by the disfranchisement of Presbyterians and former supporters of a personal treaty. Again both former Benyonites and former Lunsford and militia petitioners shared in this political exclusion. Yet after the failure of the Nominated Assembly power began to return into the hands of London's natural rulers and Benyonites are once again to be found in key positions of power and influence at all levels of City government. Wards, parishes and livery companies resumed their functions as stabilising agencies under the leadership of citizens who welcomed the return to normality under the Cromwellian regime and who were soon to rejoice in the Restoration.

Notes

1 V. Pearl, *London and the Outbreak of the Puritan Revolution*, Oxford, 1964.

2 V. Pearl, 'Change and stability in seventeenth-century London', *The London Journal*, V, 1, 1979; Pearl, 'Social policy in early modern London', H. Lloyd-Jones, V. Pearl and B. Worden, (eds.), *History and Imagination: Essays in Honour of H. R. Trevor-Roper*, London, 1981.

3 S. Rappaport, *Worlds within Worlds: Structures of Life in Sixteenth-century London*, Cambridge, 1989; I. Archer, *The Pursuit of Stability: Social Relations in Elizabethan London*, Cambridge, 1991. For a critical evaluation of these two works see the review article by K. Lindley, 'The maintenance of stability in early modern London', *The Historical Journal*, 34, 4, 1991, pp. 985–90.

4 House of Lords Record Office (henceforth HLRO), main papers, 23 December 1641 petition of divers Common Councilmen and others of the City of London. Professor Pearl has confused this petition with a petition of London apprentices presented on the same day (Pearl, *London*, p. 223).

5 Corporation of London Records Office (henceforth CLRO), Jor. 40, f. 25.

6 HLRO, main papers, 24 February 1642 petition of the citizens of London to the Lords and Commons now assembled in Parliament; Pearl, *London*, pp. 240–6.

7 *A continuation of the true diurnall 21–8 February 1642*, E. 201/19, p. 53; Historical Manuscripts Commission [HMC], 12th report, pt. 2, *Cowper MSS*, p. 307; J. Vicars, *God in the Mount*, E. 112/25, pp. 83–4.

8 W. J. Harvey (ed.), *List of the Principal Inhabitants of the City of London, 1640*, London, 1886; T. C. Dale (ed.), *The Inhabitants of London in 1638*, 2 vols., London, 1931. For the use of the 1638 tithe assessment to plot the distribution of wealth in the City see R. Finlay, *Population and Metropolis*, Cambridge, 1981, Ch. 4. A total of 100 Benyon petitioners, and 63 Lunsford and militia petitioners can be traced in the 1638 listing.

9 Ranking of Benyonites according to the 1640 listing with Lunsford and militia petitioners in brackets: first 18 (1); second 24 (3); third 23 (5); fourth 26 (5). In four wards future Benyonites constituted a sizeable proportion of the citizens listed in 1640. In Bassishaw six of the eleven citizens listed, in Broad Street nearly a third and in Cornhill and Langbourn nearly a quarter each of those listed were to sign Benyon's petition. The nearest that Lunsford and militia petitioners came to numerical significance was in the ward of Cheap, where eight of the sixty-seven citizens listed were to sign one of those petitions.

10 M. A. E. Green (ed.), *Calendar of the Proceedings of the Committee for Advance of Money*, 3 vols. London, 1888; PRO, SP 19/37, 38, 46. Of the seventy-six Benyonites whose assessments for the one-twentieth have been traced, well over a half were assessed at £400 and above, and eleven were rated at £1,000 or more. The assessments of only six Lunsford and militia petitioners have

been located, and of these only one was rated at £400 and the other five at £300 or less.

11 *Lords Journals*, IV, pp. 672–3; M. A. E. Green (ed.), *Calendar of the Proceedings of the Committee for Compounding*, 5 vols., London, 1889–92, I, pp. 88, 95, 233; IV, p. 2421.

12 J. R. Woodhead, *The Rulers of London, 1660–89*, London, 1965, p. 168.

13 *Cal. Com. for Advance of Money*, I, pp. 138–40.

14 Pearl, *London*, p. 60.

15 Dale, *The Inhabitants of London in 1638*, p. 174; Woodhead, p. 23; PRO, PROB 11/406/155 will of Maximilian Bard.

16 *Cal. Com. for Advance of Money*, I, p. 150; Woodhead, p. 76.

17 J. J. Howard and J. L. Chester (eds.), *The Visitation of London 1633, 1634 and 1635*, 2 vols., London, Harleian Soc., 1880–3.

18 Company membership is known in the case of 157 Benyonites (127 of whom belonged to one of the Great Twelve) and 58 Lunsford and militia petitioners (43 of whom were of the Great Twelve).

19 105 of a total of 351 Benyonites, or 30 per cent, were overseas merchants, compared with 15 of the 99 Lunsford and militia petitioners, or 15 per cent.

20 Twenty-one Benyonites can be identified as directors or leading members of the East India company; eight of these were also members of the Levant company, which had a total of eleven Benyonites at a similar senior level in the company. In addition, five Benyonites were members of the Merchant Adventurers company, two of the Eastland company, and one each of the Muscovy and Canada companies.

21 E. B. Sainsbury (ed.), *Court Minutes of the East India Company, 1635–9*, pp. 312–3; *ibid.*, 1640–3, p. 331; A. B. Beaven, *The Aldermen of the City of London*, London, 1908, II, p. 79.

22 At least twenty-five Benyonites have been identified as having shares in ships, like the *Pearl of London*, in the 1630s (*Calendar of State Papers Domestic* [*CSPD*], *1635*, p. 407; *ibid;*, *1635–6*, p. 241; *ibid.*, *1636–7*, p. 403). Eighteen Benyonites were importing wines from France and Spain in the 1630s (PRO, E 190/35/7).

23 At least seven Benyonites had interests in the tobacco trade in 1641–2 (PRO, E 122/196/24). The synchronisation of economic interests with the political and religious positions adopted by London merchants is not quite as precise as Robert Brenner suggests (R. Brenner, 'The civil war politics of London's merchant community', *Past and Present*, 58, 1973, pp. 53–107).

24 Brenner, pp. 80 note, 92 note; PRO, E 126/4, ff. 22–5.

25 PRO, E 122/196/24; BL, Harleian MS 986, f. 16.

26 R. L. Greaves and R. Zaller (eds.), *Biographical Dictionary of British Radicals in the Seventeenth Century*, 3 vols., London, 1984, III, pp. 232–3; G. E. Aylmer, *The State's Servants*, London, 1973, pp. 78–9, 97, 143, 247–50; J. E. Farnell, 'The usurpation of honest London householders: Barebone's parliament', *English Historical Review*, LXXXII, 1967, p. 28; C. H. Firth and R. S. Rait (eds.), *Acts and Ordinances of the Interregnum*, 2 vols., London, 1911, II, pp. 197–200; PRO, PROB 11/301/213 will of Richard Floyd.

27 Woodhead, p. 100; PRO, PROB 11/336/75 will of Giles Dent.

28 K. S. Bottigheimer, *English Money and Irish Land*, Oxford, 1971, Appendix A; BL, Additional MS 4771, f. 3; *ibid.*, 4782, f. 81; PRO, SP 21/26/121.

29 *CSPD, 1635*, p. 339; *ibid.*, *1635–6*, p. 316; *ibid.*, *1625–49*, pp. 650, 675; *ibid.*, *1629–31*, p. 134.

30 *Ibid.*, *1631–3*, p. 33; *ibid.*, *1635–6*, p. 326. In 1642 Benyon was accused of having abused his position by suing forth extents in the king's name to recover shop-debts (*Lords Journals*, IV, pp. 672–3).

31 *CSPD, 1639*, p. 114; *ibid.*, *1634–5*, p. 389; *ibid.*, *1635*, p. 606. The pre-emption of tin was subsequently attacked as a grievance in the Long Parliament (M. James, *Social Problems and Policy during the Puritan Revolution*, London, 1966, p. 142).

32 *CSPD, 1629–31*, pp. 59, 240; *ibid.*, *1640*, p. 200; *ibid.*, *1637*, pp. 64, 135; *ibid.*, *1625–49*, p. 396; *ibid.*, *1637–8*, p. 265; *ibid.*, *1638–9*, p. 344; *ibid.*, *1635–6*, pp. 2, 558, 565–6; *ibid.*, *1636–7*, p. 497; *ibid.*, *1639*, p. 419; *Cal. Com. for Advance of Money*, I, pp. 373–4; Cambridgeshire Records Office, R. 59/31/9, no. 1, f. 30.

33 For example, Benyon was a creditor of Lord Stafford and Daniel and Eliab Harvey were owed £10,000 by Sir Kenelm Digby by 1639 (*Cal. Com. for Compounding*, IV, p. 2421; III, p. 2173; V, p. 3296).

34 Ten prosperous silkmen and seven scriveners signed Benyon's petition.

35 *Lords Journals*, IV, pp. 672–3; PRO, SP 24/8/89.

36 Below p. 31.

37 Dale, *The Inhabitants of London in 1638*, pp. 174, 94–5.

38 The main sources used to establish the identities of Common Councilmen in mid-century are the surviving ward and vestry records which record Common Council elections, the list of Common Councilmen available in the Corporation of London Records Office (henceforth CLRO), Harvey, *List of the Principal Inhabitants of the City of London, 1640*, Pearl, *London* and T. Liu, *Puritan London*, Newark, Delaware, 1986.

39 Beaven, *The Aldermen of London*.

40 Francis Bickley, for example, had served as auditor in 1637–9 and Martin Bond was treasurer and benefactor of St Bartholomew's hospital in 1620–43 (Beaven, II, p. 71; *ibid.*, I, p. 290; *DNB*, II, pp. 802–3).

41 Bond had led his company to Tilbury in 1588 and had served as president of the Honourable Artillery Company in 1616 (Beaven, I, p. 290; *DNB*, II, pp. 802–3; *Visitation of London*, I, p. 86). Three other pre-1642 City captains were Thomas Style, Samuel Carleton and Richard Cranley (*Visitation of London*, II, p. 272; Harvey, *List of the Principal Inhabitants*, pp. 3, 16).

42 Mainwaring also served as treasurer of the Honourable Artillery Company in 1631–5 (Greaves and Zaller, *British Radicals*, II, p. 210; CLRO, Rep. 55, f. 162).

43 *The names, dignities and places of all the colonels, lieutenant-colonels, sergeant-majors, captains, quartermasters, lieutenants and ensigns of the City of London*, [April], 1642, 669 f. 6(10). Of the four City captains in note 41, only Carleton was listed in April 1642 (as sergeant-major in the Blue Regiment).

44 BL, Harleian MS 986; H. A. Dillon (ed.), 'On a MS. list of officers of the London trained bands in 1643', *Archaeologia*, LII, 1890, pp. 129–44.

45 L. C. Nagel, 'The militia of London, 1641–9', Ph.D. thesis, University of London, 1982, appendices 3 and 4.

46 Thomas Player, Martin Pindar, William Underwood, William Barton and George Thompson became colonels; Edward Bellamy, John Lane and William Shambrook lieutenant-colonels; and Peter Ducane and John Hinde captains (Nagel, appendices 3, 4 and 5; PRO, E 133/39/19; *ibid.*, E 179/252/15; Liu, *Puritan London*, p. 58).

47 The ward location of Benyonites has been established in 221 cases and the parish in 150 cases.

48 The ward location of Lunsford and militia petitioners has been identified in 81 cases and the parish in 75 cases.

49 They included Robert Rawden and Abraham Yeend in St Magnus the Martyr, George Nash and Patient Mychell in St Olave Southwark, and Henry Cockson and William Bathurst in St Thomas the Apostle (HLRO, main papers, 10 June 1641 petition of certain parishioners of St Olave and St Saviour, Southwark, and St Magnus, London, to the House of Lords; *ibid.*, 30 June 1641 petition of the parson, churchwarden and inhabitants of the parish of St Thomas the Apostle).

50 The future Benyonites were Samuel Mico, Affable Fairclough and Thomas Warren (Guildhall, MS 11588/4, ff. 36–7; below p. 29).

51 They were Thomas Culling, William King and William Middleton (Liu, *Puritan London*, p. 98 note).

52 *Visitation of London*, II, pp. 3–4, 327; A. G. Matthews, *Walker Revised*, Oxford, 1948, pp. 51–2.

53 PRO, SP 16/437/67; *ibid.*, 426/85; *CSPD,, 1635–6*, p. 329.

54 PRO, PROB 11/201/168 will of Martin Bond; Matthews, *Walker Revised*, p. 57.

55 Guildhall, MS 4072/1, pt. I, ff. 168–9.

56 Liu, *Puritan London*, p. 83.

57 For example, Francis Moss in St Michael Cornhill; William Ashwell in St Nicholas Acon; William Bowe in St Swithin; and Robert Lowther in St Margaret Lothbury (Guildhall, MS 4072/1, pt. I, f. 178; Liu, *Puritan London*, pp. 62, 82, 92 note).

58 Liu, *Puritan London*, pp. 81, 70, 165 note, 59.

59 CLRO, Jor. 40, ff. 153, 174. Yet two of the sons of the Benyonite Roger Drake, senior, were signatories.

60 BL, Additional MS 15,670, f. 216; *ibid.*, MS 15,671, ff. 210, 237, 256.

61 S. R. Gardiner (ed.), 'Reports of cases in the Court of Star Chamber and High Commission', *Camden Society*, 1886, p. 297; M. F. Bond (ed), *The Manuscripts of the House of Lords: Addenda 1514–1714*, HMC, new series, XI, 1962, p. 393.

62 Greaves and Zaller, *British Radicals*, III, p. 163.

63 HLRO, main papers, 30 June 1641 petition of one churchwarden and others of the parish of St Thomas the Apostle; *Lords Journals*, IV, p. 295.

64 W. H. Coates (ed.), *The Journal of Sir Simonds D'Ewes*, Yale, 1942, pp. 6–7; Guildhall, MS 1013/1, ff. 182–4.

65 Guildhall, MS 5019/1, f. 76.

66 The patrons of the living were the Grocers' Company and Warner was suspended from company membership for his stubborn opposition to their choice of incumbent. After the selection of a Presbyterian minister in 1644, Warner made his peace with the company and was admitted an assistant. The minister originally at the centre of the dispute left for a more lucrative (and peaceful) living in March 1642 and was replaced by another company nominee who was given an equally rough ride by parish militants (Guildhall, MS 11588/4, ff. 36–8, 41, 46, 61, 85, 91–3, 103; HLRO, main papers, 13 May 1642 petition of Thomas Warren, clerk).

67 *Mercurius Rusticus, 14 October 1643*; B. Ryves, *Mercurius Rusticus*, E 1099/1, pp. 147–53; *Commons Journals*, II, pp. 500, 510.

68 HLRO, main papers, 22 March 1641/2 petition of the parishioners of St Dunstan-in-the-East.

69 *Ibid.*, 9 September 1642 petition of the parishioners of Allhallows Bread Street; Liu, *Puritan London*, p.56. The three petitioners were John Lane, John Norwood and Maurice Gething.
70 John Harvard Library, Southwark, vestry minutes of St Olave Southwark 1604–1724, ff.82, 90; HLRO, main papers, 14 April 1642 petition of the parishioners of St Olave Southwark. The Benyonite select vestrymen were Patient Mychell and George Nash.
71 CLRO, Jor. 40, f.42. The former petitioners were John Gearing, Michael Herring and Thomas Brightwell.
72 *Ibid.*, ff.153, 174; M. Mahony, 'Presbyterianism in the City of London, 1645– 7', *The Historical Journal*, 22, 1979, pp.101–14; Liu, *Puritan London*, pp.58, 78. Lawrence Brinley, Richard Overton, Nicholas Widmerpoole and Richard Floyd are examples of former petitioners who became prominent Presbyterians.
73 John Dod in St Peter Westcheap, and Robert Sweet, Thomas Eyres and William Hubbard in St Mary Woolnoth provide good examples of petitioners who became elders (Liu, *Puritan London*, pp.71, 92 note). Ten Lunsford petitioners were later appointed lay tryers (Firth and Rait, *Acts and Ordinances*, I, pp.793–7). Nathaniel Hall was delegate to the London provincial assembly in 1650–7 (Liu, p.199).
74 E. S. More, 'Congregationalism and the social order: John Goodwin's gathered church, 1640–60', *Journal of Ecclesiastical History*, XXXVIII, 2, 1987, pp.214 note, 219 note, 220; M. Tolmie, *The Triumph of the Saints: The Separate Churches of London, 1616–49*, Cambridge, 1977, pp.40–1; Greaves and Zaller, *British Radicals*, III, pp.163, 232–3; J.E. Farnell, 'Barebone's parliament', p.28. Shambrook was one of the Independent officers purged in May 1647 (Worcester College, Clarke MS 2/3, f.161).
75 Below pp.35–6.
76 Underwod made bequests in his 1658 will to both Presbyterian and Independent ministers as well as the Fifth Monarchist, Christopher Feake (PRO, PROB 11/274/147 will of William Underwood).
77 Pearl, *London*, pp.75, 118; Liu, *Puritan London*, p.226; Greaves and Zaller, *British Radicals*, I, pp.255–6.
78 Pearl, *London*, p.120; HLRO, main papers, 16, 29 July 1641 petitions of the six persons chosen by the commonalty of the City of London.
79 Pearl, *London*, pp.120–1; HLRO, main papers, 26 July 1641 petition of divers of the commonalty of the City of London.
80 HLRO, Braye MS 25 (6 April 1642); *ibid.*, main papers, 24, 27 November 1641 affidavits of Robert Stephens; *Lords Journals*, IV, pp.673, 683–4.
81 PRO, SP 16/486/32.
82 Lunsford was appointed to the lieutenancy of the Tower on the 22 December and the petition was presented to the Commons on the following day (Coates, *D'Ewes Journal*, p.336 and note).
83 CLRO, Jor. 40, ff.21–2; Guildhall, MS 4069/1, ff.210, 212, 213, 216, 218, 220, 223, 226.
84 CLRO, Jor. 40, ff.22–3; Guildhall, MS 4384/1, f.401; 'A letter from Mercurius Civicus to Mercurius Rusticus', *Somers' Tracts*, IV, p.589; Liu, *Puritan London*, pp.79–80, 81.
85 For example, Thomas Lusher was replaced by John Bellamy in the Cornhill Ward elections. Bellamy was to be one of the signatories of the Common Council petition of the 9 July 1642 (below p.33).

86 CLRO, Jor. 40, f. 22; Guildhall, MS 877/1, ff. 92, 95, 97, 101, 104, 107, 111.
87 James Gough in Bishopsgate Without and Henry Jackson in Aldersgate Without were two other future Benyonites re-elected in 1641 (Guildhall, MS 4069/1, ff. 195–228; MS 4526/1, ff. 39, 58; MS 2050/1, ff. 40–2).
88 *Ibid.*, MS 3570/2, f. 46. John Terry in Aldersgate Without was another Benyonite elected for the first time in 1641 (*ibid.*, MS 2050/1, f. 42).
89 Yet Alden took the oath the next day (Pearl, *London*, pp. 147–8).
90 Guildhall, MS 4415/1, ff. 103–4. Wallen was one of the two demonstrators interrogated by the Lords on the 29 November 1641 (HLRO, manuscript minute books of the House of Lords, no. 8; Braye MS 22B, f. 153). Neve moved out to Hadley in 1642 where he later claimed to be confined by lameness (PRO, SP 19/63/83; *ibid.*, 37/36). Neve's replacement was William Vaughan, a signatory of the Common Council petition of the 9 July 1642 and a later elder (Liu, *Puritan London*, pp. 77, 109).
91 The three long-serving members were Randall Mainwaring, Richard Turner, senior, and Henry Allen (CLRO, List of Common Councilmen, pp. 58, 36; *Visitation of London*, II, p. 301; Guildhall, MS 3461/1, ff. 33, 39, 49, 57, 63, 72).
92 Herring was not identified as a Common Councilman in December 1641 at the time of his involvement in the City's root and branch petition yet he signed the Common Council petition of the 9 July 1642. Warner also signed the latter petition and does not appear to have been a Common Councilman before 1642 (HLRO, main papers, 9 July 1642 petition of Common Councilmen; Pearl, *London*, p. 327).
93 The four were Ellis Midmor, Laurence Warkman, Thomas Player and John Hatley. The first three could have been Common Councilmen in 1640 or 1641, as there is a gap in the wardmote records for those years, but certainly not before then, while Hatley signed the petition of the 9 July 1642 (Guildhall, MS 3461/1, ff. 63–6, 72–5).
94 Thomas Brightwell and John Gearing of Bread Street and James Rand of Cheap signed the Common Council petition of the 9 July 1642 and there is no evidence that they were members of that assembly prior to 1642.
95 HLRO, main papers, 7 July 1642 petition of divers Common Councilmen of the City of London; CLRO, Jor. 40, f. 23; William Walwyn, *A Whisper in the Ear of Mr Thomas Edwards*, E 328/2, p. 4; Beaven, *The Aldermen of London*, I, p. 209; Pearl, *London*, pp. 327–8.
96 HLRO, main papers, 9 July 1642 petition of Common Councilmen; *Lords Journals*, V, p. 197.
97 *Lords Journals*, V, pp. 239–41.
98 HLRO, main papers, 20 July 1642 a return of the names of those who visited the lord mayor of London now a prisoner in the Tower. Twenty-two Benyonites were amongst Gurney's visitors.
99 Bond, *The Manuscripts of the House of Lords: Addenda 1514–1714*, pp. 333–4; PRO, SP 19/37.
100 *Cal. S. P. Venetian*, XXVI, p. 90.
101 *Cal. Com. for Advance of Money*, I, pp. 124, 238; PRO, SP 19/1/65.
102 Thirty-two Benyonites were amongst those lending money for the City's forces, mainly in 1643–4, and at least fourteen Benyonites contributed on the 'weekly meal' (CLRO, militia accounts: money lent for the support of the City forces, accounts c. 1643–8; PRO, E 179/252/15).

103 For example, William Gomeldon, John Godsalve, Richard Chaloner, Robert Swinarton and Henry Moss (HLRO, main papers, 6 January 1643 petition of divers citizens and inhabitants of the City of London; *ibid.*, 22 December 1642 petition of divers citizens and other inhabitants of the City of London; BL, Additional MS 18,777, f. 94; *The image of the malignants peace*, E 244/12). Nine of the thirty-one citizens suspected of being involved in the planned coup were former Benyonites (*Commons Journals*, II, p. 894).

104 *CSPD, 1641–3*, p. 368; *A perfect diurnall, 8–15 August 1642*, E 239/8.

105 William Humble, Edward Trussell, Edward Bradbourne and Roger Price were said to have accompanied the king's army to Hounslow Heath on the day of the Brentford engagement, while Walter Rogers, William Langhorne and Henry Dixon were imprisoned as 'ill-affected' citizens (*Commons Journals*, II, pp. 866–7, 837, 930, 58, 78, 102).

106 *Commons Journals*, II, pp. 866–7; *Certain informations, 7–14 August 1643*, E 65/8; *ibid., 18–25 September 1643*, E 68/3; *Cal. Com. for Advance of Money*, I, pp. 373–4; PRO, SP 19/93/5–7, 9, 14, 19, 29, 11, 15–7; *ibid.*, 11/178; *ibid.*, 67/65; SP 23/1/24; *ibid.*, 2/31; *ibid.*, 3/145; *Cal. Com. for Compounding*, II, pp. 1513–4, 1565, 1571; *ibid.*, III, p. 2007.

107 Pearl, *London*, pp. 147–8; R. R. Sharpe, *London and the Kingdom*, 3 vols., London, 1894–5, II, p. 188; *Commons Journals*, III, p. 117; *Certain informations, 5–12 June 1643*, E 105/27; *Special passages, 6–13 June 1643*, E 105/32.

108 The four were Anthony Biddulph, William Cockayne, Andrew Kendrick and George Witham. Witham was also a treasurer at war (*Commons Journals*, III, p. 408; *CSPD, 1625–49*, p. 709).

109 Firth and Rait, *Acts and Ordinances*, I, pp. 27, 392, 889, 914; *Commons Journals*, III, pp. 308–9, 336.

110 HLRO, main papers, 29 August 1642, list of collectors appointed in several wards and parishes under the ordinance for raising money and plate in London; PRO, SP 19/1/37–44.

111 There were 251 collectors nominated for the City and Southwark in August 1642, and 207 assessors and 177 collectors named in the following December. Walter Pell and Edwin Browne, assessors in Bassishaw, were threatened with imprisonment before they conformed, and Walter Rogers, collector in Langbourn, was subsequently imprisoned (PRO, SP 19/1/71; *Commons Journals*, II, p. 837).

112 CLRO, Jor. 40, f. 11; Firth and Rait, *Acts and Ordinances*, I, pp. 5–6.

113 *Two speeches spoken by the earl of Manchester and John Pym*, E 85/7, p. 6; *The image of the malignants peace*, E 244/12; *The humble petition of the inhabitants of Lambeth*, 669 f. 5/138; Pearl, *London*, pp. 260–1; Nagel, 'The militia of London', pp. 85–7; Greaves and Zaller, *British Radicals*, II, p. 210; *Cal. Com. for Advance of Money*, I, pp. 13–4, 32; *ibid.*, III, pp. 1251–2; Aylmer, *The State's Servants*, p. 377.

114 Greaves and Zaller, *British Radicals*, I, pp. 255–6; Dr Williams's Library, MS 24.50, pp. 61, 78, 107–8; CLRO, Jor. 40, f. 215; Firth and Rait, *Acts and Ordinances*, I, pp. 105, 880, 990, 1007–8, 1259, 1261–2; *ibid .*, II, pp. 82, 365; *Cal. Com. for Advance of Money*, I, p. 337; *Commons Journals*, III, p. 490; PRO, SP 19/57/12–4.

115 Pearl, *London*, pp. 242, 244–5, 327; Brenner, 'Civil war politics', p. 81; *Works of darkness brought to light*, E 399/36, p. 9; *CSPD, 1625–49*, p. 652; Firth and Rait, *Acts and Ordinances*, I, pp. 990, 1007–8.

116 *Cal. Com. for Compounding*, I, pp. 10, 13, 162, 640–1; *Cal. Com. for Advance of Money*, I, pp. 105, 110.

117 Firth and Rait, *Acts and Ordinances*, I, pp. 388, 914.

118 Aylmer, *The State's Servants*, pp. 247–50; *Commons Journals*, III, p. 137; Firth and Rait, *Acts and Ordinances*, I, pp. 330, 1259; *ibid.*, II, p. 233.

119 HLRO, main papers, 29 August 1642 list of collectors; PRO, SP 19/1/37–44. Five of the seven collectors named in August in Cheap, and one half of the assessors named in December in Bread Street and Bridge Within were former petitioners.

120 *Cal. Com. for Advance of Money*, I, pp. 1–2.

121 *Commons Journals*, II, pp. 851–2; *Two orders of the Lords and Commons*, E 129/1.

122 *Commons Journals*, II, p. 857.

123 For example, William Underwood made an inventory of the goods of the Benyonite John Batty, and Thomas Player and Randall Mainwaring seized money belonging to tin-farmers, several of whom were also Benyonites (PRO, SP 19/37/125; *Commons Journals*, II, pp. 929–30).

124 For example, Richard Thorowgood, Ralph Tasker and John Graunt actively supported the City's Engagement of 1647 (PRO, SP 24/24, ff. 19–20; *ibid.*, 84 Westbrooke v. Thorowgood; *ibid.*, Westbrooke v. Tasker; *ibid.*, 3, f. 2).

125 Forty-four former Benyonites were elected aldermen in the late 1640s or in the 1650s and two of them reached the mayoralty in the 1650s. Examples of Benyonites becoming masters of livery companies or governors of trading companies during this period would include Robert Fenn, master of the Haberdashers in 1651–2, William Christmas, master of the Drapers in 1650–1, and Andrew Riccard, master of the Drapers in 1652–3 and Governor of the Levant Company from 1654 to 1672.

126 I. Gentles, 'The struggle for London in the second Civil War', *The Historical Journal*, 26, 1983, pp. 277–305.

CHAPTER THREE

POLITICS
AND
GOVERNMENT
IN YORK
1640–1662

David Scott

Recent work on the political role of towns during the English Revolution has overturned the old assumption that urban communities were naturally inclined to support Parliament and the Good Old Cause. It is now clear that many towns – the majority, according to John Morrill – did not side with Parliament and that, as Roger Howell has argued, urban political history during the 1640s and 50s was shaped as much by neutralism and the desire to preserve established privileges as by ideological commitment or 'progressive' political tendencies. Patrick McGrath, working on Bristol, found that only a tiny minority of the citizens showed more than 'minimal commitment' to either side in the war and that most leading Bristolians preferred a policy of non-involvement. Research on Worcester by Philip Styles and Shelagh Bond reveals a similar picture; though popular Royalism was strong in the city the corporation was 'at pains to avoid becoming involved' and was primarily concerned with defending its chartered privileges and asserting its independence from the county. Howell's work on Newcastle and that of A. M. Johnson on Chester also emphasise the large element of continuity in provincial urban politics during the revolutionary era. Even in strongly Parliamentarian towns such as Gloucester and Norwich, the traditional socio-political order remained firmly in place.[1]

The experience of York during the mid-seventeenth century suggests that here too, political life continued much as usual after the war. National political rivalries, particularly those which emerged after 1645, had relatively little impact on civic politics. There was no alteration in the city's constitution or in the social composition of its governors, and local concerns such as making the Ouse more navigable continued to prompt the vast majority of the city's approaches to Parliament.[2]

But whilst traditional political values and structures undoubtedly limited change in York, they could not altogether prevent it. As elsewhere, the war brought about the 'politicisation' of local government with a crude ideological divide emerging between the 'malignant' and the 'well-affected'.[3] Recruitment to high office came to be determined partly by partisan, national criteria, which in turn led to a tightening of the relationship between civic rulers and central government. Similarly, the support of leading office-holders for godly reform acquired a novel political and national dimension after the war. These were changes more of emphasis, perhaps, than of substance and there was, undoubtedly considerable continuity in post-war civic politics. However, to the extent that ideology first entered civic government on any appreciable scale after the war, the 1640s represented a real turning point in the city's political history.

York in the mid-seventeenth century was still a great city by contemporary standards. Besides being one of the largest towns in England, with a population of about 12,000 in 1640, it was the seat of royal government in the North, the hub of the Northern Province, the assize town of England's largest county and a site of considerable strategic importance, guarding major road and river junctions. Though declining as an international port, it was the focus of a thriving regional trade where country produce was exchanged for manufactured goods and services. The city was governed by a corporation which in turn was dominated by thirteen aldermen JPs, one of whom served annually as mayor. The aldermen, who were usually merchants, were elected for life from the ex-sheriffs or the 'twenty-four' and these two groups, with the mayor and acting sheriffs, comprised the upper house of the corporation and held regular sessions known as the 'mayor's court'. The lower house consisted of twelve chamberlains and the seventy-two-strong common council, which was summoned irregularly, usually to participate in municipal elections or to advise the upper house. The majority of freemen, who numbered about 1,500 in this period, had no say in civic government or indeed in parliamentary selection, even though by charter the right of election lay with the freemen.[4]

The city's political life was relatively uneventful during the early Stuart period. The corporation quarrelled with the Council in the North and with the cathedral authorities on a number of occasions, mainly over jurisdiction and precedence, but there is no evidence of factionalism among civic leaders or unrest within the freeman body. The traditional political consensus prevailed despite the spread of Puritanism among a small but influential section of the community, the merchants in particular. The programme of civic moral reform initiated by the godly in the corporation during James's reign was apparently accepted by the 'best' citizens, Puritan or otherwise, as a necessary means of preserving social order.[5]

The city remained on reasonably good if rather distant terms with central government for most of the period, although royal support for Laudian churchmen soured relations between civic leaders and the Crown during the 1630s. Archbishop Neile's campaign against what he called the 'Puritan party' in York, which involved silencing civic lecturers and questioning the city's right to appoint Sabbath searchers, was seen by many leading citizens as an attack on municipal autonomy itself.[6] This was probably the corporation's biggest grievance by 1640, but what finally caused it to lose faith in central government was the Second Bishops' War. York, as the military capital of the North, fared particularly badly during this crisis and having returned two of the Earl of Strafford's supporters to the Short Parliament, the corporation rejected his patronage in the autumn and elected the prominent civic Puritans, Aldermen Sir William Allanson and Thomas Hoyle.[7]

Civic government retained its godly bias during the early 1640s. The corporation took a keen interest in parliamentary proposals for establishing a preaching ministry and responded to the 'root and branch' petitioning campaign by drawing up a petition in February 1641 'against Episcopacy and Ecclesiastical governm[en]t as Kent and other places have done'.[8] The petition, which had the support of future Royalists as well as the godly, was framed largely in protest at Neile's aggressive prelacy and his perceived attack on civic autonomy. Some of the aldermen may have seen it in the context of a wider struggle against popery or even as a small step towards godly reformation, but there are no signs that Puritanism in York developed into a partisan movement before the Civil War, for all Neile's talk of a Puritan 'party'. There were probably very few genuinely Puritan office-holders on hand when the upper house signed a petition to Parliament from Ferdinando Lord Fairfax and other Yorkshire gentry early in 1642, requesting, among other things, the removal of the voting rights of popish peers and further reformation in religion.[9]

In the months prior to the outbreak of war the corporation tried to avoid excessive commitments to either side, a particularly difficult task in the case of the King, who made York his headquarters between March and July. In May Charles put pressure on the city to help him 'vindicate the affront to his honour' before Hull. But though civic leaders pledged to protect him as their king and guest they resisted his rather clumsy attempts to involve the city more actively, advising him to seek an accommodation with Parliament. As the fighting at Hull intensified the corporation became increasingly concerned about the city's own defences and in July it petitioned Charles that none of the trained bands be removed from the city 'upon any occasion'. It was fear for the city's safety which caused it to reject a compromising offer of protection from several local Royalist gentry a month later. The search for a safe neutrality persisted as late as November when the corporation considered the possibility of a 'treaty' with the Fairfaxes. However, the arrival of the Earl of Newcastle in December banished all thoughts of compromise and York ended the year as a Royalist garrison.[10]

Where the majority of citizens stood in the conflict is difficult to say. Although there are signs that a sizeable number of the ordinary inhabitants were Royalist in sympathy, there is no evidence of any great devotion to the King's party among the civic ēlite. According to a Parliamentarian news-sheet only the mayor and two or three of the aldermen would declare for the King in September 1642 and in October 'diverse' were imprisoned for refusing to contribute to the Royalist war-chest.[11] These reports may not be true, but even on the evidence of their opponents, those who were later removed from the bench for their alleged malignancy did little to distinguish themselves in the King's service. Perhaps the clearest examples of partisan commitment among civic leaders occurred in support of Parliament. Allanson and Hoyle remained at Westminster and became closely involved in the Parliamentary war effort, whilst Alderman John Vaux and Thomas Dickinson, Hoyle's son-in-law, withdrew to Hull. But even here it was probably self-preservation as much as positive commitment which determined their actions, York being a dangerous place for well-known Puritans by the summer of 1642. None of the aldermen went into exile after the Parliamentarians seized York in 1644, although Sir Roger Jaques and a number of other office-holders ceased to attend council meetings.[12]

The preservation of municipal autonomy remained of vital concern to civic leaders during the Royalist occupation. Indeed the corporation was prepared to defy even the King on this issue, repeatedly rejecting Charles's nominee for the post of civic lecturer in favour of the Puritan divine, John Shaw. It also protested vigorously when the Earl of Newcastle suspended mayoral elections in 1643 and 1644 in order to keep on the reliable Sir Edmund Cowper. The desire to protect York's 'ancient liberties', as well as the fact that most of the more godly office-holders withdrew from civic politics during the autumn of 1642 probably helped to maintain unity in the corporation.[13]

After the battle of Marston Moor the Parliamentarian generals presented the Royalist governor and Mayor Cowper with articles for the city's surrender which were put to the corporation and about a hundred of the 'best' citizens on 7 July and were 'well liked of it soe be my Lord Mayor and Governor assented thereunto'. With the Royalists out of the way the Puritans seized their chance. On 19 August the Commons received a petition from four godly York citizens – two of them members of the twenty-four, and one a common councillor – asking that preaching ministers be sent to York and that Hoyle be made mayor. The Commons resolved that since none of the York alderman 'were such as they could confide in, Alderman Hoyle ... should be sent down with direction from both houses [an ordinance] for him to be chosen mayor'. At a meeting late in September, which was attended *en masse* by the Puritan office-holders, Hoyle read out the ordinance which the Common Council 'very readily submitted unto and were very desirous to perform to the utmost', although it was only after 'long debate' that the councillors agreed to elect Hoyle in the customary manner. Soon afterwards, the corporation ordered that the office-holders and the 'best' citizens take the National Covenant. Remarkably for men later proscribed by Parliament as malignants, Aldermen Cowper (who had refused to participate in Hoyle's election, though he did promise to 'yield obedience to the ordinance of Parliament and all assistance in the Mayoralty'), Scott, Hemsworth and Myers continued to attend countil meetings and perform their municipal duties. Presumably they also took the Covenant.[14]

Puritan influence in civic politics increased in December with the election of thirty-six new common councillors to replace those who had died or left the city during the war. However, the initiative for further changes in the corporation came from the 'national' Parliamentarians. On 1 January 1645 Parliament issued an ordinance for the removal and disfranchisement of Aldermen Belt, Cowper, Hemsworth, Jaques, Myers and Scott as men 'much disaffected to the service of King and Parliament', having been informed of their 'several delinquencies', which appear to have been relatively minor, by Hoyle, Fairfax (the city's new governor) and the Committee for Yorkshire. This ordinance, unlike its predecessor, made no concessions to the city's charter, its main purpose being to ensure that the city was served by 'men who may more faithfully respect the Good of the Kingdom and this Place'. At a council meeting on 13 January 1645 the men were replaced by six members of the twenty-four: John Geldart, Stephen Watson (two of those who had petitioned Parliament in August), Thomas Dickinson, Leonard Thompson, Robert Horner and Simon Coulton (see Table 3.1). Although very much the community's 'natural rulers', the new aldermen were chosen primarily on the basis of their support for Parliament – Watson, Dickinson and Geldart for example had already been nominated as parliamentary commissioners. Indeed the re-modelling was shaped very much by national issues and reflected a political divide among the magistracy of only a few years' standing. This was unlike similar purges in many other towns which, it has been argued, represented the culmination of local, factional squabbles, often linked to 'protracted social and economic conflict in the decades before 1640'.[15]

The purge brought no substantial change to the social composition of the magistracy; both groups were of similar social status and

Table 3.1   *The 1645 purge*

Men installed in 1645	Purged aldermen	Survivors
Sim. Coulton* (dyer)	Robt. Belt (m)	Wm. Allanson* (dr)
Thos. Dickinson* (m)	Edm. Cowper (m)	Leo. Besson # (saddler)
John Geldart* (m)	Robt. Hemsworth (dr)	Jas. Brooke* (gr)
Robt. Horner* (m)	Rog. Jacques (m)	Chr. Croft # (mercer)
Leo. Thompson* (m)	John Myers (lawyer)	Thos. Hoyle* (m)
Steph. Watson* (gr)	Wm. Scott (m)	Jas. Hutchinson (m)
		Hen. Thompson* (m)

Notes * Presbyterians or men charged with 'Puritan' offences by the Laudians
 in the 1630s
  # ceased to attend corporate meetings by 1645
 (m) merchant
 (gr) grocer
 (dr) draper

consisted entirely of merchants or other leading wholesale traders.
The only difference between the groups in socio-economic terms
was that the Parliamentarian aldermen were largely from established
York families and were among the city's leading merchants, whereas
the Royalists tended to be of country origin and to represent the
less prosperous element in the city's mercantile community. Overall,
the Parliamentarians were probably the more powerful in terms of
wealth and strength of conviction but the most significant difference,
apart from the political one, was that of religion. All the city's leading
Parliamentarians were Puritans.[16]

However, the parliamentary re-modelling did more than merely
revive the 'civic' godliness of the magistracy in pre-war years. The
bench was now dominated by men of Presbyterian sympathies who,
whilst sharing the Calvinist ideals of their predecessors, were more
concerned with issues of national church reform and the building
of a more godly society generally. The maintenance of a preaching
ministry and the preservation of the Sabbath in York obviously
remained important to them. But as they were well aware, the success
of civic godly reform after the Civil War ultimately depended on
the survival of the Parliamentary cause and the Puritan movement
as a whole. Thus their interest in godly reform extended into the

realm of national politics and civic Puritanism after 1644 acquired novel, partisan overtones.[17]

Although the Parliamentary-Puritan take-over of York was orchestrated by national Parliamentarian figures such as Fairfax and Hoyle, it cannot simply be regarded as a case of central government imposing its will on a politically complacent or 'sub-political' local community. As the civic petition of August 1644 indicates, a number of the citizens were willing to countenance limited central government interference in municipal affairs in order to give the godly, 'honest' element the upper hand in civic politics. Admittedly, once in power the Puritans strongly resisted any further outside intervention, but this does not mean that continuity prevailed. With the civic political community divided, the relationship of the ruling group to central government became vital to its hold on power, as the Puritans themselves were to discover in the early 1660s. By destroying the traditional political consensus in the community the Civil War strengthened central government's hand in civic politics.

From early 1645 a more thorough approach to the consolidation of Parliamentarian power in York can be detected. In February the foreman of the Common Council was discharged for 'divers causes' and a more politically reliable man (in fact one of the citizens who had petitioned Parliament in August 1644) was elected in his place. On the same day the corporation ordered that two or three 'good men' be appointed in each parish to take note of those who had not taken the Covenant and it was further decreed that only those who had done so would be admitted to the Council. Even relatively minor figures in the corporation such as the city surgeon were pressed to take the Covenant.[18]

The corporation was particularly zealous in settling the city's religious life. In March 1645 it successfully petitioned Parliament for an ordinance making available the sequestered capitular revenues for the maintenance of four Presbyterian ministers to officiate in the Minster and other city churches. The Presbyterianism of the magistracy was apparently shared by the common councillors. In August 1646 the Council requested that the Minster preachers be properly provided for if the capitular revenues proved inadequate and that those in the city who had not taken the Covenant be made to do so. Later that year a county petition to Parliament for 'settling Presbeyterian Government' was approved by the house 'none contradicting'.[19]

The civic authorities also set about reforming parochial church worship. During 1645 and 1646 fonts, organs and all manner of 'superstitious pictures' were removed from the city's churches, certain 'ancient customs' were prohibited, notably perambulation, and each parish received a Directory and 'a book of the Nationall Covenant'. More sweeping reforms would undoubtedly have followed had it not been for the chronic shortage in York of godly ministers, indeed ministers of any kind, after the war. Natural wastage, the turmoil of the war years and the removal of 'malignant' and 'scandalous' ministers had reduced the number of civic incumbents to a mere handful by 1645 and some parishes would remain 'void of ministers' for the next fifteen years. The lack of pastoral supervision and the collapse of episcopal church government caused severe disruption in many parishes, particularly in the mid-1640s when there was 'great defecte' due to the failure of some congregations to elect new churchwardens. If the surviving churchwardens' accounts are any guide the traditional round of church life in most parishes contracted sharply in the period 1645–60 and much of what remained was of a distinctly unreformed character. Without the machinery of visitation the Presbyterians were unable to regulate religious observance in the city with anything like the efficiency of the episcopal authorities.[20]

Although there was no breakdown in civic government during the Civil War, the corporation's preoccupation with war measures inevitably had a disruptive effect on civic administration. Matters were made worse by the absence of several senior aldermen and members of the 'twenty-four'. Between January 1643 and April 1646 for example, there were no Quarter Sessions held in the city, probably because it was impossible to obtain a quorum. Attendance at council meetings certainly dropped during the mid-1640s, largely for political reasons, and in 1646 the Common Council demanded the removal or punishment of those councillors and members of the 'twenty-four' who did 'no service'.[21]

Political and religious loyalties were an important factor in recruitment to the Upper House after 1645. This was clearly understood at the time when 'in preparation of the Election of an Alderman', or mayor, one of the Minster preachers would be requested to deliver a sermon to the house, presumably of a suitably exhortatory nature. The predominance of the Parliamentary-Puritan element on the bench, brought about by the 1645 re-modelling, was maintained until 1662 and although wealth remained vital for political preferment the Upper House was forced to relax its financial requirements slightly in order to elect men who were known to be well-affected, or at least prepared to take the Covenant or later the Engagement. In 1656, Edward Bowles, the senior Minster preacher, lamented the fact that 'the poverty of the city and the scarcity of well disposed persons puts us upon the difficulty of choosing persons [as aldermen] whose estates are not answerable to such a charge'.[22]

In seeking to promote 'well disposed' men of sufficient wealth the Common Council (which nominated candidates) and the Upper House had no choice but to proceed in breach of the rules traditionally governing advancement in the *cursus honorum*. A number of alderman were elected to the bench within a few years and sometimes just a few months after surrendering their bonds of shrievalty; both before and after the period 1645 – 1662 it often took upwards of seven or eight years for a member of the twenty-four to gain promotion to the magistracy. Significantly, those members of the twenty-four who were appointed parliamentary commissioners nearly always secured rapid promotion. The preponderance of merchants among those who became aldermen in the 1650s (six out of eight, a higher proportion than in any other decade during the seventeenth century) is probably another indication that political considerations were affecting recruitment to the magistracy.[23]

The execution of the king and the establishment of the Commonwealth had no immediate impact on civic politics. There were no purges or resignations in the corporation, nor any serious drop in attendance at council meetings. The aldermen did not scruple at taking the Engagement which, given their Presbyterian sympathies, suggests that there was a good deal of trimming and political opportunism on the bench. Allanson and Hoyle, it is true, refused to have anything to do with the trial and execution of the king and were very late in making their dissent to the 5 December vote, but they both served in the Rump. Several aldermen were also active on the Yorkshire committee for sequestration set up on 25 January 1650.[24]

The political loyalties of the aldermen defy close analysis. Most were consistently appointed to various local parliamentary committees during the 1640s and 50s, although the proportion of active committeemen cannot be ascertained. Some aldermen may have served simply out of a desire to protect the local community or their standing within it rather than through any allegiance to the government of the day. Nevertheless, those who were politically unreliable or who were no longer active in civic government rarely seem to have been nominated. Indeed a fair amount of thought seems to have gone into the composition of some committees. The York committee for Scandalous Ministers, for example, consisted of only the staunchest Puritans, namely Aldermen Dawson, Dickinson, Geldart and Watson.[25]

Although York was left largely untouched by political developments in London after 1645, it was not therefore 'sub-political' in the sense that national issues had no defining role in civic politics. The Parliamentary-Puritan aldermen and junior office-holders formed a recognisable 'interest' within the city's political community and operated on a broadly partisan basis in local government although this is more apparent in their role as members of the York committee of the Northern Association than as municipal office-holders. Whereas the corporation was mainly concerned with the day-to-day running of the town, the role of the committee was much more 'political' in nature, involving the sequestration of delinquents' property, the tendering of national oaths, and the maintenance of local army units. The committee included eleven of the thirteen aldermen but was dominated, initially at least, by the six men installed, in 1645. Many office-holders, especially the common councillors, doubled up as collectors, assessors or sequestrators, among whom there were a number of future Quakers and Dissenters.[26]

The committee symbolised the lack of unity and consensus in the magistracy after the war. Although political differences between certain aldermen had always existed, it was only in 1645 that they acquired this formal, institutional aspect. By advertising disunity among the city's governors, the committee and the re-modelling which made it viable threatened to undermine the legitimacy of civic government and for several years after coming to power the Puritans sought to bolster municipal authority through greater attention to corporate ritual; thus the office-holders were repeatedly encouraged to attend services in the Minster as one body and fines were imposed on those who neglected to 'resort decently in their citizens gowns'. The ministry was given a more prominent role in corporate ceremonial after 1645 for partly the same reason.[27]

Although the Civil War weakened the traditional bonds of political society in York, the city was spared the factional unrest which characterised post-war politics in a number of other provincial capitals, such as Colchester and Norwich.[28] Neither the Independents nor the Royalists mustered enough support among the civic elite to compete with the Presbyterians, hence the seemingly insular character of civic politics after 1645. There was no 'second revolution' in York because there were no Independents (religious or political) in the city to mount one. The power of the orthodox Puritans in civic church life and the religious conservatism of the inhabitants prevented the emergence of an Independent congregation in York until after the Restoration.

The lack of a Royalist or conservative faction in the corporation – at least there is no evidence of such before the mid-1650s – is harder to explain. The purge of the 'disaffected' aldermen would certainly have deprived any potential Royalist faction of its leadership. However, the 'loyalist' interest in the corporation was weak throughout the later seventeenth century, perhaps because of the absence of freeman unrest and popular Puritan radicalism in the city. By contrast, popular Royalism was strong in York and according to one report the malignant element came near to overwhelming the ruling minority of well-affected citizens during the Second Civil War. Deprived of any voice in the corporation, insurrection was their only option.[29]

The relatively stable nature of civic politics after 1645 also owed much to the willingness of those office-holders of moderate or neutralist inclination to co-operate with the Parliamentary-Puritans for the 'good government' of the city. Moreover on many issues, particularly those of local interest with which the corporation was principally concerned, there was a great deal of common ground between the well-affected and their less partisan brethren. When it came to repairing war damage or the regulation and protection of civic trade for example, the house was of one mind.[30] There was also consensus regarding what Howell has termed the 'historic forms' of civic government. The one item of municipal practice which the Parliamentary-Puritan group sought to discourage was the customary obligation upon certain office-holders to provide a feast for the other members of the corporation.

The upkeep of the ministry and the reformation of popular

manners remained a high priority for all the office-holders. The corporation responded vigorously to parliamentary ordinances concerning godly reform and often supplemented them with stricter regulations of its own. The programme of moral discipline pursued in York during the 1640s and 50s was largely a continuation of pre-war measures, although support for godly reform tended to assume a more generalised form after the Civil War. Thus in 1653 the corporation petitioned Parliament 'for support and maintenance of the ministry', which was one of many from around the country in what Worden has described as a movement of 'growing Presbyterian assertiveness' urging the Rump to support the established ministry and to suppress religious radicalism.[31]

The office-holders were also united in their desire to preserve civic autonomy, although apart from the parliamentary re-modelling there is no evidence of serious intervention by the state in local government after 1645. Despite maintaining a strong presence in York, the military does not appear to have encroached on the civic authorities to any significant degree, indeed if anything the reverse was the case, with the city militia and (after a struggle) Clifford's Tower coming under aldermanic control during the 1640s. Such was the lack of military influence in civic affairs that the magistrates had no qualms about dealing harshly with the Quakers during the 1650s even though the garrison commander and town governor, Colonel (afterwards Deputy Major-General) Robert Lilburne, was reportedly sympathetic to the Friends' cause. Lilburne, for his part, doubted the loyalty of some of the magistrates and after the Yorkshire Royalist uprising of 1655, in which a number of the citizens were involved, was apparently in favour of re-modelling the bench. Fortunately for the aldermen, Lambert was one of the more moderate Major-Generals and kept his deputy on a tight rein.[32]

The only substantial changes in local government after the war occurred as a result of the setting up of the York Committee and the fall of the episcopal church, both of which served to enhance the authority of the aldermen. Control of the Committee gave them extensive new powers, particularly over civic church government which was divided up between the Committee, the corporation and the Quarter-Sessions – all dominated by the aldermen. Far from having their authority undermined by central government, civic leaders enjoyed wider powers between 1645 and 1660 than at any other time during the seventeenth century. Oligarchic rule in York was powerfully reinforced during the Commonwealth period.

Links between the city and central government, and between the city and the county, were strengthened after the Civil War, and held firm even under the Commonwealth. Hoyle and Allanson represented the city's interests on the 'Committee for Yorkshire', which sat at York, and were both trusted members of the Long Parliament and the Rump. They were followed in the mid-1650s by three more aldermen – all broadly sympathetic to the Cromwellian regime – and the city's Recorder, Sir Thomas Widdrington, who was Speaker in the Second Protectorate Parliament and highly esteemed by Cromwell. Edward Bowles, a well-known figure in Parliamentary circles, may also have played an important part in justifying the city to central government.[33]

The corporation took great care to cultivate good relations with central government and national political figures; it regularly wined and dined the Assize judges, entertained MPs and high-ranking officers whenever it got the chance, sent presents to Cromwell at Pontefract in 1648, and made Lambert Lord High Steward in 1654.[34]

Not only did the aldermen manage to retain the good will of central government during the Interregnum, some of them become closely identified with the Protector's policies, which undoubtedly caused resentment in the community. From about 1653 there are signs of growing opposition to Cromwellian rule among the freemen. The number of those buying exemption from office rose under the Protectorate, as did incidents of office-holders refusing the Engagement. The first major show of political discontent in the corporation came soon after the death of Cromwell in September 1658. Although the aldermen were quick to have 'his highnes the Lord Richard' proclaimed in the city, 'divers' of the Common Council refused to take the customary oaths at the next council meeting, apparently in an effort to distance themselves from the Cromwellian regime and its supporters on the bench.[35]

In the last year of the Interregnum a rift between the common councillors and the aldermen, largely arising it seems from a disagreement over policy rather than a clash of principles. Despite the rising tide of Royalist feeling in the city there were very few Royalists among the office-holders; there was certainly no weakening of godly zeal in the corporation. It was probably in response to the deteriorating political situation during 1659, which was keenly felt in York, that most of the Common Council moved towards a pragmatic acceptance of the need for a return to monarchy. The magistrates, however, more mindful of their office and compromised by their involvement with the Cromwellian regime, remained inclined to wait on events and keep in with the Rump and the military, hence their willingness to recognise the authority of the restored Rump in June. In fact few, if any, of the aldermen favoured the 'Good Old Cause', but as Cromwellian 'collaborators' they shared with civic leaders in Exeter, Leicester and many other towns an understandable reluctance to defy the Rump in support of the Restoration.[36]

The cautious approach of the magistracy allowed the Common Council and the 'best' citizens to seize the political initiative during Fairfax's Yorkshire Rising and to commit the city decisively to the Royalist cause. In late December the Common Council thwarted Lilburne's attempt to seize the York magazine – although Mayor Thompson was 'ready enough to deliver it' – and then invited Fairfax, who was marshalling his forces at Knaresborough, to liberate the city, which he did on New Year's Day. The aldermen appear to have remained aloof from these proceedings and even after Monck's arrival in the city and his triumphant march south they were still reluctant to declare for a free parliament. On 10 February a petition to Monck, signed by the gentlemen and Presbyterian ministers of the Fairfax group, calling for free elections or the reinstatement of the secluded members, was presented to the corporation for its endorsement. The common councillors gave it their immediate and unanimous approval but the Upper House decided that for the present it could not subscribe to the petition, the matter being one 'requiring much time and caution'. To sign the petition was a hazardous commitment – Monck himself had not yet declared for Charles and several of his officers in York were opposed to the petition. In the event the Upper House signed the petition the next day, doubtless under pressure from the Fairfax group which was virtually in armed occupation of the city centre by February.[37]

Once the Restoration was assured the aldermen joined the Common Council in welcoming in the new order. In March the corporation chose Widdrington and the Royalist Sir Metcalfe

Robinson, both supporters of the Restoration, as the city's representatives in the Convention Parliament, to which they were returned without a poll. On 9 May the king's arms were set up in the Guildhall and two days later Charles was proclaimed by the corporation and the citizens 'with the greatest Expression of Joy that possibly could be Imagined'. Although keen to ingratiate themselves with the new regime the aldermen were unwilling to abandon their public commitment to godly religion and with the capitular revenues back in the hands of the Anglicans by 1661 they attempted to maintain the Minster preachers by private subscription, though without success.[38]

During 1661 and 1662 the dominant issue in civic politics was the composition of the magistracy. On 15 February 1661 the king sent a letter to the corporation instructing it to replace 'unduly' elected and 'notoriously disaffected' office-holders, referring in particular to the aldermen installed in 1645, with 'such persons of integrity as yet remain'. A similar letter was sent to Norwich corporation and was grudgingly complied with, but in York the mayor simply argued that the aldermen had been legally elected and that those still in office were 'well affected to his Majesty' and ignored the king's orders.[39]

The corporation later claimed that the king's letter had been procured by 'discontented persons' who 'complain of their Governors and desire an Alteration on that behalf', and indeed by early 1661 a campaign was afoot in York to have certain aldermen removed from office. This received considerable support among the freemen and 'much countenance' from local Royalist gentry, although the corporation itself remained united behind the magistracy.[40] Long-standing grievances – high taxation, free-quartering, the activities of various local committees – fuelled the protest, but its immediate cause was the change in national government. As in 1644, an aggrieved group of citizens appealed to central government to make changes in the corporation.

The campaign intensified in April after the corporation 'pricked' Sir Metcalfe Robinson as city sheriff in the run up to elections for the Cavalier Parliament. Although this has been seen as an act of Presbyterian assertiveness, it actually had the support of many 'moderate' office-holders and was primarily intended to secure the re-election of Widdrington after the king's recommendation of John Scott, the commander of Clifford's Tower, forced

the corporation to choose between 'one of our own body', Widdrington, and a virtual stranger, Robinson. The king ordered the
corporation to elect another sheriff and Scott and Robinson were
returned to Parliament on a wave of popular Royalist sentiment.[41]

The virtual collapse of the municipal interest in 1661 represented
a particularly dramatic reversal of electoral fortunes in York,
for with no state interference and no successor to Strafford as
borough patron the corporation had enjoyed a free hand in parliamentary selection during the Interregnum. Before the Restoration,
the electorate, which comprised the entire freeman body by 1665,
appears to have been restricted to the corporation and a 'competent
number' of freemen, a system which gave considerable advantage
to the mayor and aldermen. During the 1660s, however, a combi-
nation of Crown intervention, Royalist fervour among the freemen,
and ambitious county gentry willing, if necessary, to contest
the seat against the corporation interest, robbed the aldermen
of any meaningful say in parliamentary selection and gave the
electorate a powerful negative voice in the selection process.
Such was the strength of Royalist feeling in the city that even
if the bench had rejected the king's nominees, none of the aldermen
had the right political credentials to compete with loyalist gentry
at the hustings. After the Restoration a candidate's politics often
counted for more with the electorate than the strength of his
local connections.[42]

The corporation suffered a further setback in April when a
group of citizens petitioned the king requesting changes in the
magistracy. Whitehall responded by having a writ of *quo warranto*
issued against the corporation which the bench decided to contest.
Because York retained its pre-war charter it was less vulnerable
to a *quo warranto* than towns whose charters had been called in
during the Interregnum, and Whitehall's main aim in bringing
the action was probably to put added pressure on the corporation
to comply with its earlier instructions.[43] Whatever the government's intention, the effect of the *quo warranto* was to unite the
office-holders behind the aldermen in defence of the charter.

The conflict entered a new phase in the summer when several
local Royalist gentry, encouraged by 'unquiet spirits' in the city,
took advantage of the community's 'distractions' to try to limit
the authority of the bench. This amounted to an assault on civic
government itself and if any freemen were involved is further

evidence of the corrosive effect of ideological loyalties on traditional political values in the city. Panic-stricken, the aldermen appealed to the Earl of Northumberland, whom they had recently made Lord High Steward in place of Lambert, and desperately pleaded the city's 'ancient privileges' to Clarendon.[44]

Although the corporation had some powerful enemies, including both the city's MPs, it emerged the victor, at least for a time. The *quo warranto* was apparently dropped, probably in anticipation of the Corporation Act, and the gentry's attack on civic liberties also came to nothing. Whitehall was more concerned it seems to put local government in 'loyal' hands than to weaken municipal authority.[45]

The Commissioners for Regulating Corporations held court in the Guildhall early in September 1662 and displaced most of the common councillors together with Aldermen Thomas Dickinson, Leonard Thompson, Robert Horner – the three surviving aldermen installed in 1645 – and Brian Dawson and William Taylor, the two staunchest Puritans. None, it seems, was given an opportunity to take the oaths. In their place, and that of the recently deceased Ralph Chaitor, the commissioners installed three members of the twenty-four, two other leading citizens and the only surviving aldermen ejected in 1645.[46]

The 1662 purge had no effect on the social complexion of the magistracy. The new men were drawn from the same group of leading traders as those they replaced. The changes in the religious temper of the magistracy were more significant, although here too there was a good deal of continuity. Inevitably, the Presbyterian old guard was removed but several magistrates of godly outlook remained on the bench; among them, ironically, was one of the men the commissioners installed, Henry Thompson, who became York's leading Whig.[47] Indeed, the 1662 re-modelling emphasises the weakness of the 'loyalist' interest among the civic elite. Most of the new aldermen had been involved in one way or another in civic politics between 1645 and 1660, though none was deeply compromised.

With the removal of the Puritan aldermen the 'discontented' citizens deferred once more to magistracy and political stability was restored. Popular Royalist feeling, however, took longer to subside and is evidence of the extent to which the cultural 'oppressions' and violation of deeply-rooted ideals of community and governance during the 'late distracted times' had politicised the ordinary people in support of the Restoration. This process, whereby local fears or grievances raised the level of popular political awareness onto a national, ideological plain occurred several times in subsequent decades, notably during the Exclusion Crisis.[48] What is interesting is the apparent non-occurrence of such a process during the Civil War. It would appear that the local impact of political developments after the Civil War, and particularly after 1649, provoked a stronger reaction from the commonalty than the war itself, which raises the question of whether the issues and events leading to civil war had any major effect on civic community life outside the corporation and the society of the godly.

One effect of the Restoration was to replace some of the old harmony and identity of interest between rulers and ruled in York which had been lost since 1645, largely due to the politicisation of local government. An inevitable consequence of placing ideological constraints on political recruitment was to render the city's leadership unrepresentative of the community as a whole. It created an 'inner ring' of Puritan magistrates whose commitment to godly reformation sometimes offended against traditional notions of civic 'good government'. Of course political tests still attached to office-holding after 1662 but these were more narrowly applied and less exclusive (particularly given the weakness of the Dissenting interest in York) than those in force during the Interregnum. Overall, civic government appears to have been less politicised and more representative after the Restoration than it had been during the revolutionary decades.

Civic political life returned to something like its pre-war pattern after 1662, at least for a decade or so, and though this doubtless encouraged some of the citizens to regard the Interregnum as just a passing phase, the unrest of the early 1660s indicates that many also saw it as a time of upheaval and 'distraction', when the natural political order had been corrupted both locally and nationally. If, as Howell has argued, the evidence for political continuity in towns during the 1640s and 50s is strong, clearly in York it is not overwhelming.[49] In many respects it was indeed 'business as usual' in post-war civic politics. But it was also during the Civil War period that the grounds for future party political conflict in the city were laid. The political associations formed during the 1640s could not be eradicated and would harden again in the 1670s and 80s; the city's Whig faction at the time of the Exclusion Crisis coalesced around a Parliamentary-Puritan core. In York, as elsewhere, the Civil War period saw the first steps towards the formation of permanent political parties and the 'divided society' of the Augustan era.

Notes

I should like to thank Claire Cross, John Morrill, Chris Webb, and Mary Heimann for reading earlier drafts of this paper.

1 J.S. Morrill (ed.), *Reactions to the English Civil War 1642–1649*, London, 1982, p. 14; R. Howell, 'Neutralism, conservatism and political alignment: the case of the towns, 1642–9', in Morrill (ed.), *Reactions to the English Civil War*, pp. 67–87; R. Howell, 'Resistance to change: the political elites of provincial towns during the English Revolution', in A. L. Beier, D. Cannadine, J. M. Rosenheim (eds.), *The First Modern Society: Essays in English History in Honour of Lawrence Stone*, Cambridge, 1989, pp. 433–55; R. Howell, *Newcastle-upon-Tyne and the Puritan Revolution*, Oxford, 1967, pp. 335–49; P. McGrath, *Bristol and the Civil War*, Historical Association Pamphlet, Bristol Branch, Bristol, 1981; on Bristol see pp. 100–29, below. P. Styles, *Studies in Seventeenth Century West Midlands History*, Kineton, 1978, pp. 213–57; S. Bond (ed.), *The Chamber Book of Worcester 1602–50*, Worcestershire Historical Society, New Series, VIII, 1974; A. M. Johnson, 'Politics in Chester during the civil wars and the interregnum, 1640–62', in P. Clark and P. Slack (eds.), *Crisis and Order in English Towns, 1500–1700*, London, 1972, pp. 204–31; J. K. G. Taylor, 'The civil government of Gloucester, 1640–6', *Transactions of the Bristol and Gloucestershire Archaeological Society*, LXVII, 1946–8, pp. 58–118; J. T. Evans, *Seventeenth-Century Norwich: Politics, Religion and Government, 1620–1690*, Oxford, 1979.
2 For civic politics during the Civil War see G.C.F. Forster, 'York in the seventeenth century' in P. M. Tillott (ed.), *Victoria County History: The City of York*, Oxford, 1961; B. M. Wilson, 'The Corporation of York, 1580–1660', (unpublished M. Phil. thesis, University of York, 1967).
3 A. Hughes, *Politics, Society and Civil War in Warwickshire, 1620–1660*, Cambridge, 1987, p. 289.
4 Forster, 'York in the seventeenth century', pp. 162–70; Wilson, 'The Corporation of York', Ch. 2.
5 Forster, 'York in the seventeenth century', pp. 186, 196–8, 202–3; York City Archives house book [YCAH] 35, ff. 302, 336; *Historical Manuscripts Commission: Manuscripts of the House of Lords*, New Series, XI, Addenda, 1962, p. 400; P. Slack, *Poverty and Policy in Tudor and Stuart England*, London, 1988, p. 150.
6 M.C. Cross, 'Achieving the millenium: the church in York during the commonwealth', *Studies in Church History*, IV, 1967, pp. 122–33.
7 A. R. Warmington, 'The corporation of York in peace and war, 1638–1645', *York Historian*, IX (1990), p. 17; *Calendar of State Papers Domestic [CSPD] 1640–1*, p. 158; F. Drake, *Eboracum*, London, 1736, p. 231.

8 YCAH 36, ff. 52, 53, 55.
9 York Minster Library [YML] Civil War tracts, P1807A, *The Petition of the Knights, Gentlemen, Freeholders, and others* ... *of the County and City of York*, London, 1642.
10 YCAH 36, ff. 70–2, 74–5, 77; Warmington, 'The corporation of York', pp. 18–19.
11 Wilson, 'The Corporation of York', p. 246; *Calendar of State Papers, Venetian*, 1642–3, pp. 29, 37; BL Thomason tracts, E239(17), *A Perfect Diurnal*, (5 Sept– 12 Sept 1642); YML Civil War tracts, K23, *Terrible Newes from York*, London, April 1642: D1383, *The Last true Newes from Yorke*, London, Sept 1642: T773, *Terrible Newes From York*, London, Oct 1642.
12 M. F. Keeler, *The Long Parliament, 1640–1641: A Biographical Study of its Members*, American Philosophical Society Memoirs, XXXVI, Philadelphia, 1954, pp. 83–4, 224–5; *CSPD* 1655–56, p. 389; Warmington, 'The corporation of York', p. 19; BL Thomason tracts, 669 f. 6(44), *Newes from Yorke*, London, July 1642; York produced only a small number of delinquents – M. A. E. Green (ed.), *Calendar of the Proceedings of the Committee for Compounding*, 5 vols., London, 1889–92, I, p. 113.
13 *Ibid.*, p. 268; YCAH 36, ff. 81, 83, 85, 86, 94; Warmington, 'The corporation of York', p. 20.
14 YCAH 36, ff. 102, 105–6, 110; *Journals of the House of Commons*, III, pp. 597, 612, 613; BL Additional MS 31116, f. 310.
15 YCAH 36, ff. 118, 119; Bodleian Library, Tanner MS 60, f. 125; *Commons Journals*, III, p. 719; IV, p. 5; *Journals of the House of Lords*, VII, pp. 119–20; C. H. Firth and R. S. Rait (eds.), *Acts and Ordinances of the Interregnum, 1642–1660*, 3 vols., London, 1911, I, pp. 230, 544; Evans, *Seventeenth-Century Norwich*, pp. 138–9.
16 Wilson, 'The Corporation of York', pp. 278–9.
17 See B. Manning, 'Parliament, 'party' and the 'community' during the English Civil War, 1642–46', *Historical Studies*, XIV, 1981, pp. 107–12.
18 YCAH 36, ff. 123, 124, 190.
19 *Ibid.*, ff. 129, 149, 190, 192, 197; Firth and Rait, *Acts and Ordinances*, I, pp. 669–70.
20 D. Scott, 'Politics, Dissent and Quakerism in York, 1640–1700', (unpublished D. Phil. thesis, University of York, 1990), Ch. 3; YCAH 36, f. 178.
21 Forster, 'York in the seventeenth century', p. 189; YCAH 36, f. 105; York City Archives [YCA] Quarter Sessions Book, F/7, ff. 175–7.
22 BL Additional MS 21424, f. 173.
23 Scott, 'Politics, Dissent and Quakerism', p. 263.
24 D. Underdown, *Pride's Purge: Politics in the Puritan Revolution*, Oxford, 1971, pp. 138, 217, 251, 366, 376; *Commons Journals*, VI, pp. 153, 165; J. H. Morehouse (ed.), *Yorkshire Diaries and Autobiographies in the Seventeenth and Eighteenth Centuries*, Surtees Society, LXV, 1877, pp. 145–6; PRO SP/215, *passim*; the Presbyterian aldermen of Exeter, in contrast to those at York, refused to recognise the Republic – W. Cotton, H. Woollcombe, *Gleanings from the Municipal and Cathedral Records Relative to the History of the City of Exeter*, Exeter, 1877, pp. 141, 144.
25 Firth and Rait, *Acts and Ordinances*, II, p. 970.
26 YCA E/63, Proceedings of the Commonwealth Committee for York and the Ainsty, f. 1; Scott, 'Politics, Dissent and Quakerism', pp. 22, 162.
27 YCAH 36, ff. 120, 125, 208.

28 J. H. Round, 'Colchester during the Commonwealth', *English Historical Review*, XV, 1900, pp. 641–4; Evans, *Seventeenth-Century Norwich*, pp. 151–222.

29 C. H. Firth (ed.), *The Clarke Papers*, Camden Society, New Series, LIV, 1894, pp. 8–10.

30 York, particularly the suburbs, suffered extensive damage during the siege and the cost of repairs imposed a heavy financial burden on the corporation. The city's population dropped sharply after the siege, mainly due to an outbreak of plague in 1644–65, and did not regain its pre-war level for many years. The impact of war, high taxation and the general disruption to trade during the 1640s brought to an end the period of modest economic growth York had enjoyed since the 1560s and plunged the city into a severe economic recession, which lasted at least until the 1660s – Wilson, 'The Corporation of York', pp. 281–3, 300; C. Caine (ed.), *Analecta Eboracensia*, London, 1897, pp. x–xi; D. M. Palliser, 'A crisis in English towns? The Case of York, 1560–1640', *Northern History*, XIV, 1979, pp. 108–25. Several towns in the Midlands suffered a similar fate to York, see Hughes, *Politics, Society and Civil War*, p. 258.

31 YCAH 36, f. 149; 37, ff. 30, 31, 54, 60, 125; A. B. Worden, *The Rump Parliament*, Cambridge, 1974, p. 322.

32 *The Clarke Papers*, Camden Society, NS, LXIX, 1891, pp. 121–2, 163–7; Scott, 'Politics, Dissent and Quakerism', Ch. 1; Friends' House Library, London, Swarthmore MS I 373; W. C. Braithwaite, *The Beginnings of Quakerism*, 2nd edn, Cambridge, 1955, p. 450; R. Howell, 'The army and the English Revolution: the case of Robert Lilburne', *Archaeologia Aeliana*, Fifth Series, IX, 1981, pp. 299–315; BL Lansdowne MS 988, ff. 320–1; T. Birch (ed.), *A Collection of the State Papers of John Thurloe*, 7 vols., London, 1742, III, p. 360.

33 P. A. Bolton, 'The Parliamentary Representation of Yorkshire Boroughs, 1640–85', (unpublished MA thesis, University of Leeds, 1966), pp. 315–7, 322–5; R. Spalding (ed.), *The Diary of Bulstrode Whitelocke, 1605–75*, Oxford, 1990, pp. 226, 227, 285, 410; *State Papers of John Thurloe*, V, p. 711.

34 YCA Chamberlains' Account Book 24, 1646, f. 33; 1648, F. 17; 1649, f. 19; YCAH 36, f. 201; 37, f. 56.

35 Old Parliamentary History, 20 vols., London, 1763, XX, pp. 276–9. YCAH 37, ff. 50, 55, 59, 60, 61, 70, 75, 90, 116, 117.

36 *Ibid.*, f. 127; BL Additional MS 21425, f. 45; Cotton, Woollcombe, *Gleanings from the Muncipal and Cathedral Records of Exeter*, p. 183; H. Stocks (ed.), *Records of the Borough of Leicester: Being a series of Extracts from the Archives of the Corporation of Leicester, 1603–1688*, Cambridge, 1923, p. 459; R. Hutton, *The Restoration*, Oxford, 1985, p. 92.

37 For Fairfax's Rising see A. Woolrych, 'Yorkshire and the Restoration', *Yorkshire Archaeological Journal*, XXXIX, 1956–8, pp. 483–507; HMC Leyborne-Popham MSS, III, London, 1894, pp. 147, 148; BL Additional MS 21425, f. 204; YCAH 37, f. 134.

38 *Ibid.*, ff. 137, 139, 147; B. D. Henning (ed.), *The History of Parliament: The Commons, 1660–90*, 3 vols., London, 1983, I, p. 489; YCA ACC 104 Ant/3, 'Hammond's Diary' (unfoliated).

39 YCAH 37, ff. 149, 150; Evans, *Seventeenth-Century Norwich*, pp. 230–2.

40 YCAH 37, ff. 155, 165.

41 *Ibid.*, ff. 150, 152, 153, 154; Hutton, *The Restoration*, p. 153; Leeds Record Office, Newby Hall MS 2848.

42 See M. Kishlansky, *Parliamentary Selection: Social and Political Choice in Early Modern England*, Cambridge, 1986, pp. 225–30.
43 YCAH 37, ff. 155, 157; J. Miller, 'The crown and the borough charters in the reign of Charles II', *Transactions of the Royal Historical Society*, 5th Series, 33, 1983, p. 57.
44 YCAH 37, ff. 155, 159, 160, 165, 168.
45 Miller, 'The crown and the borough charters', p. 56.
46 YCAH 37, f. 177; YCA 'Hammond's Diary'; only one of the new aldermen, John Taylor, had been adjudged a delinquent and was never sequestrated – *Calendar of the Committee for Compounding*, IV, p. 2760.
47 Scott, 'Politics, Dissent and Quakerism', pp. 297, 319–20.
48 See R. Howell, 'Newcastle and the nation: the seventeenth-century experience', *Archaeologia Aeliana*, 5th Series, VIII, 1980, pp. 18, 30.
49 Howell, 'Neutralism, conservatism and political alignment', p. 85.

CHAPTER FOUR

COVENTRY
AND THE
ENGLISH
REVOLUTION

Ann Hughes

In August 1662, James Earl of Northampton, Lord Lieutenant of Coventry and Warwickshire, rode to the city with a party of the Warwickshire militia, accompanied by his deputy lieutenants and other leading county gentlemen. He headed the commissioners who were enforcing the Corporation Act, but had an additional pressing purpose. On the king's order he was to ensure that Coventry's proud walls, three miles in circumference, its four great gates and fortifications were 'razed and demolished' so that the city could never be used as a stronghold by 'mutinous and turbulent spirits'. The immediate context of this act was the panic-stricken aftermath of Venner's Rising but it had a clear connection with Coventry's past reputation as a committed Parliamentarian and puritan city: the same punitive action was taken against Taunton, Gloucester and Northampton, three other towns seen as heroic (or shameful) opponents of Charles I. In the rubble of its walls, condescendingly returned to the corporation for the use of the poor by county gentlemen from whom Coventry citizens had habitually kept aloof, can be seen the most obvious and most humiliating aftermath of the years of civil war and republic for the city.[1]

A major city has a twofold, sometimes contradictory character: first as an enclosed stronghold, legally and physically defined through its charters and its walls, with much autonomy from outside authority, but also as a focus for that same outside world, a nodal point in a series of economic, political and cultural networks.[2]

The contrast should not be overstated for inside and outside factors are obviously interrelated, but the distinction between internal developments and outside influences was often made by citizens in the mid-seventeenth century, as we shall see, and is a useful way of analysing the experience of Coventry in the 1640s and 1650s. This essay seeks to capture something of the double nature of the city looking at both the impact of civil war and revolution on the internal political, religious and social character of Coventry, and also at the ways in which Coventry's links with the outside world were affected: the role of the city in its region and the connections between national events and developments within the city. Transformations in the relationship between the city and outsiders were perhaps more drastic than any internal changes.

Coventry, with a population of some 7,000 in the seventeenth century, was no longer the proud regional capital of its medieval heyday, but it remained a substantial provincial city of the second rank, an important manufacturing and commercial centre for the West Midlands and a major road-hub, on the main road from London to Chester and thence to Ireland. A slow decline brought about by restructuring in the textile industry culminated in a severe crisis or 'desolation' in the early 1520s when heavy taxation, epidemics and dearth intensified underlying problems. Recovery was underway by the 1570s but it remained slow and partial. The textile industry regained something of its previous strength and weaving was still the most common trade in the mid-seventeenth century. One expanding, but very risky, sector in the city's immediate hinterland was coal-mining: the city's own mines rarely brought profits to their lessees, but coal provided a stimulus to Coventry's trading role. Grain and wool were brought to the city by the inhabitants of Leicestershire, Warwickshire, Northamptonshire and Oxfordshire, while coal and cloth were taken away in return.[3]

Mid-seventeenth-century Coventry was no Norwich or York, ranking rather with county towns like Oxford, Nottingham or Worcester (although it was itself emphatically not a county town for Warwickshire). It was, however, sufficiently prosperous to support a powerful, self-conscious elite, closely bound by kinship, economic ties from apprenticeship onwards, and shared administrative experience. Coventry clearly demonstrates those tendencies towards oligarchy which have been seen as typical of English towns in the sixteenth and seventeenth centuries. Drapers, dyers and mercers, from the companies that controlled the finishing and marketing of cloth, dominated the city's power structures, providing seventeen out of twenty-three mayors between 1620 and 1642. Characteristically, under Coventry's 1621 Charter, the first or mayor's Council recruited itself; in the first half of the seventeenth century it numbered about fifteen, including the mayor and ten Aldermen. Mayor and Aldermen were ex-officio JPs and the members of the Council usually headed the grand inquest jury at the twice yearly Leet court, whose function by the seventeenth century was confined mainly to the formal election of officials (in practice chosen by the First Council). The grand inquest was made up of thirty-one men in all, freemen who had all served as mayor, chamberlains or wardens. A second or Common Council of twenty-five was supposed to advise on matters referred to it by the First Council but it did not operate like this in our period, although individual Common Councillors were invited to council meetings when difficult issues were on the agenda (such as the problems of providing for the city's ministers in the 1650s). The council minutes provide occasional lists of Common Councillors but it seems to have had a largely formal existence. For some, especially younger members of leading families, it provided an honorific stepping-stone on the way to membership of the First Council, but for most it gave an abstract title, parallel it seems to junior membership of the Leet's grand inquest. Only seven of the men listed as Common Councillors in 1640 were ever admitted to the First Council, all but one of these were succeeding or joining a father or brother. There was no connection between length of service as a Common Councillor and procession to the First Council: many of the 1640 men who were passed over had already been Common Councillors in 1636.[4]

A succession of Davenports, Barkers, Snells, Jessons, Hopkins, Clarks, Leggs, Smiths and Nortons were thus prominent in city administration before the Civil War. The draper John Barker, one of Coventry's Long Parliament MPs and the Civil War governor entered the Council in April 1632, joining his Alderman father. Within months of his father's death, Barker junior was appointed as an Alderman. The two Short Parliament MPs, Simon Norton and William Jesson, both wealthy dyers and both members of office-holding families, had entered the Council House together in 1629 and both became Aldermen in 1634. Jesson's 1650 will shows the elaborate links that bound together the leading families: he left tokens to his 'cousins' Thomas Norton (Simon's son) and Henry Smith, and to his kinswomen Joan Snell and Sarah Rogerson, all from Aldermanic families, and to his cousin Humphrey Burton, Coventry's town clerk. Jesson's son-in-law was Richard Hopkins, a successful Coventry lawyer, the son of Coventry's 1621 MP and brother of an Alderman. Thomas Jesson, William's elder brother, made a fortune in London and left £2,000 to his native city in 1634; a younger brother Richard entered the Council House in 1645 after a decade as a Common Councillor.[5] Economic interests created other links, although these by no means implied shared political and religious attitudes. Alderman John Clark and Alderman Thomas Basnet had succeeded each other as apprentices to the mercer and Alderman William Hancock at the turn of the sixteenth century; forty years later they took diametrically opposed stances on the Civil War. Future Aldermen were in turn amongst Basnet's and Clark's own apprentices: Julius Billers, Basnet's; George Earle, Clark's.[6]

This was a distinctively and self-consciously urban and mercantile elite. When a substantial clothier, Christopher Davenport, endowed a charity to provide loans for 'young beginners' of the weavers and clothiers company, 'to the end I may in some sort express my thankfulness to Almighty God and my affection and good will towards the city and place wherein I live', he cited the inspiration of 'other cities and towns corporate'. Coventry's leaders were aloof from, even suspicious of the gentry. In 1624 and 1625 their Recorder, Sir Edward Coke, was made one of Coventry's MPs and in 1628 local gentry opponents of Charles I's 'forced loan' were returned in a contested election; otherwise the Parliament men were chosen from the leading men of the Council House. Coventry was not a social focus for the Warwickshire gentry, who gravitated instead towards their administrative centre, Warwick. The mostly minor gentry from Coventry's rural parishes played little part in city life; the one significant gentry family resident in the city itself, the Hales of Whitefriars, played an equally minor role, to the complete approval of the citizens as we shall see. After the dissolution, Coventry was not an ecclesiastical centre. Although it had titular priority in the diocese of Coventry

and Lichfield, Lichfield was the headquarters of episcopal administration, and no clerical establishment vied with the Aldermen
for influence in Coventry.[7]

The suspicion of outsiders was intensified by the elite's enduring
consciousness of the city's comparative decline, and by social
threats within Coventry. It was directed especially at Coventry's
nearest outsiders, the Warwickshire gentry. Since 1451 Coventry
had been a county in its own right, with a hinterland of rural
parishes, and there was bitter resentment of any suggestion that
it was part of Warwickshire for fiscal or military purposes. Such
resentment was voiced most strongly when the financial and
military demands of central government were most irksome, but
it was nonetheless genuine for that. A protracted ship money
dispute with Warwickshire in 1635 was written up by Humphrey
Burton in a dramatic narrative, preserved in a bound volume.
The most serious occasion of dispute was over the proportion of
the assessment Coventry should pay but profound offence was
taken at the claims of Warwickshire's sheriff to rate the city.
In subsequent writs, the sheriffs left the city well alone. In the late
1630s Coventry refused to train its two horse with the Warwickshire
militia and Aldermen refused to respond to their Lord Lieutenant's
demands for men or money if he mentioned Warwickshire only.
William Jesson claimed his oath to 'maintain the customs, liberties,
franchises and privileges' of Coventry prevented him paying
coat and conduct money for troops going to the Scots war for
the same reason.[8]

It is paradoxical but unsurprising that conflicts with local
rivals were often conducted through appeals to the more distant
authority of central government. The Coventry elite did not
seek influence in Warwickshire any more than they wanted its
gentry involved in their city, but they were capable of sophisticated
lobbying of the Privy Council through friendly lawyers and officials.
This, combined with zealous soliciting of the Bishop's favour,
was to win them victory in the ship money dispute. The title
page of the ship money narrative declared that 'the city of Coventry
and the county thereof is to be rated but at a fifteenth part of
Warwickshire ... and that it is so ordered by the right Honourable
Privy Council for the future quietness of that city in all such
services and assessments whatsoever'.[9]

Divisions within the city also prompted appeals for outside

support. The increasing concentration of economic and political power in Coventry was a response to the elite's perception of their own vulnerability to attack from their poorer neighbours, but oligarchy in itself exacerbated social tensions. The councillors tended to favour their own whether in nominations of their sons to university places sponsored by the city, in allocating charity monies, or in advantageous leases of city lands.[10] Two sources of social tension in particular were evident in the early seventeenth century. There were frequent clashes of interest between the producers of cloth, weavers and spinners, and the more powerful companies concerned with its finishing and marketing. Here the 'poor weavers' of the city more often solicited the help of the Privy Council to ban or limit the import of Gloucester cloth into Coventry for finishing. Their attempts to protect their livelihood were much repeated in the 1620s and 1630s and it seems that the drapers, dyers and mercers were able to use their political power within the city to ignore the Privy Council's attempts at compromise.[11]

The second flashpoint was the use of the city's common lands. Part of the commons, the manor and park of Cheylesmore, was acquired and retained through outside favour. In the mid-sixteenth century the city was granted a long lease of this royal land on the intercession of the Earl of Leicester and on condition the poor were allowed common pasture. In the early seventeenth century Henry Prince of Wales successfully claimed the manor was part of his inalienable Duchy of Cornwall, but shorter leases were nonetheless obtained up to the Civil War. The loss of Cheylesmore was to be a further blow to Coventry at the Restoration. The Lammas and Michaelmas lands where common grazing was supposed to be available after hay-making and after harvest had been much enclosed from the sixteenth century and ploughing often prevented the exercise of grazing rights. The city elite argued that the rents received from leasing closes benefited the commoners and poor of the city and tried intermittently to limit autumn ploughing and sowing through ordinances of the Leet. The commoners themselves resorted to more direct measures, throwing down hedges and burning crops. Lammas day was intended as an exhibition of civic ceremony and a celebration of urban solidarity as the chamberlains rode the boundaries of the commons, confirming general access, and then threw a public feast. This interpretation was often overturned by the commoners. who seized the opportunity to exercise through riot the privileges they believed were being withheld. The commons rose repeatedly in the first decade of the seventeenth century while nearby rural areas were engaged in the 'midland rising' against enclosures. Lammas day 1639 saw hedges destroyed and the five people arrested quickly released by 400 who came to the jail 'with crows of iron'. The council needed two quarts of canary sack to sustain them 'at their meeting to suppress the rioters'.[12]

In 1640, then, Coventry was a substantial city with a proud but troubled ruling elite, anxious to preserve their independence from interfering neighbours, but always conscious of the need for outside support in local conflicts. By this time it was not a city with much enthusiasm for the government of Charles I. Coventry, one of several towns decried by Laudian churchmen as a 'second Geneva', had a tradition of zealous reformist Protestantism going back to Elizabeth's reign when it had been one of the centres of Presbyterian organisation. The 1621 Charter had been granted only after James I had been reassured about the city's conformity, while Charles I began *quo warranto* proceedings against the charter after it gave an enthusiastic welcome to the mutilated William Prynne passing through Coventry on his way to prison. The city's religious and social practices were threatened in many other ways during the personal rule. Post-Reformation Coventry had only two parishes, whose clergy were both nominated by the Crown. The corporation sought to supplement the religious, particularly the preaching, provision in the city, and acquire some influence on the character of the clergy, by the regular appointment of lecturers. Their priority was clearly to acquire effective, godly preachers and they were less concerned about lecturers' conformity to all the practices and ceremonies of the established church. Pre-Civil War lecturers included a veteran Presbyterian Humphrey Fen and the young Samuel Clarke, later a prominent London Presbyterian and a prolific biographical author. Tensions with the parochial ministers and with the 1630s Bishop, Robert Wright, were the predictable result.[13]

As Peter Clark has shown for Gloucester in this period, godly reformist Puritanism had social as well as religious dimensions for a corporation conscious of the problems of poverty and division. Exhortatory sermons denouncing sin were matched at Coventry also by attempts at the regulation of alehouses, and surveys of the needs of the poor. The suspicion of sermons, which led to an order after the 1635 metropolitical visitation that sermons in Coventry's churches be delivered at the same time, whereas previously 'sermons were at such times as that everyone might be at both if he pleased', had broad and alarming implications. So did other Laudian measures to bring greater order and decorum to parish churches and to replace communion tables with altars. In 1636 the diocesan authorities cleared many of the pews at St Michael's and sought to prevent the corporation and city companies from having substantial pews in both churches. There was bitter resentment at this ecclesiastical interference with one of the most visible representations of the social and poliical hierarchy.[14]

The king's religious policies were the most obvious cause of alienation but equally resented were the ham-fisted interventions in the cloth trade, the threat to the city's liberties represented by the *quo warranto*, and, as elsewhere in England, the bungling demands for the Scots wars, exacerbated in this case by jurisdictional rivalries between the counties of Coventry and Warwickshire. We should not exaggerate this vision of Coventry as an embattled godly stronghold. A visiting Puritan lawyer, Robert Woodford, was sadly disappointed in the religious commitment of the city, 'oh, Lord restore and establish thy gospel in that city' he exhorted in his diary after Arminian doctrines had been defended at a dinner with the corporation. The city rulers were never sufficiently committed to godly preaching to overcome the admittedly serious problems of securing an adequate maintenance for their ministers and lecturers.[15] Furthermore, the cohesiveness of the elite, their sense of shared urban traditions and experiences, and their perceptions of the threats to their position from outsiders and from the commons – all these militated against any dynamic initiatives in national politics. The city's parliament men in the Short and Long Parliament were, as usual, chosen from the leading members of the Council House, rather than for any particular political stance. The city's Recorder and Lord Lieutenant, the courtier second Earl of Northampton, apparently had little influence; Barker and Jesson in the Long Parliament both supported the measures against the personal rule although their paths diverged after 1642.[16]

Between 1639 and 1642 Coventry was clearly well-informed

about political events; there is little sign of open division within the city or of any great impact on its internal affairs, apart from the removal of the altar rails erected in 1636. The usual courtesies of bell ringing and gifts of wine and sweetmeats were granted to Lord Deputy Wentworth as he came from and returned to Ireland for the Short Parliament; royal proclamations against 'slanderous papers concerning Scotland' were succeeded by 1641 official condemnations of the army plotters, and there was 'ringing at both parishes on the 17 of February 1640 [i.e. 41] for the news that the king's Majesty had assented unto the Act of Parliament for a triennial parliament as London did for joy'. As the crisis deepened, especially after the Irish rebellion and Charles's attempt on the Five Members, the corporation took measures for the city's defence. In December 1641 all householders were ordered to provide muskets and in January 1642 procedures for watch and ward were tightened up because of 'the present troubled and dangerous times' and so 'that the delinquents shall be severely censured and punished, as enemies to the state'. Common watchmen were to be replaced 'by able men both of estate and persons' under the supervision of Common Councillors and other corporation officials. As early as March William Jesson was arranging for four pieces of artillery to be sent up from London.[17]

Two months of confused jockeying for power in Warwickshire and Coventry in the summer of 1642 ended in triumph for the Parliamentarians led by Lord Brooke. The city of Coventry played a crucial part in this triumph. On 20 August Charles I came in person to the city and demanded admission for himself and his army. He was denied however, and the city held out against a substantial army until the morning of 22 August when Brooke brought relieving forces up from London, thus forcing a general royalist withdrawal by the king and the local leader, Northampton. Coventry became the headquarters of the powerful county committee that held Warwickshire for the Parliament throughout the Civil War, and a garrison of regional significance. The siege of Coventry, like the later resistance of Gloucester, was a vital event in the course of the Civil War; it had also a defining impact on Coventry's experience up to and beyond the Restoration. Some aspects of Coventry's earlier history, as described here, make its Parliamentarian heroics unsurprising: its dominant religious affiliations, its resentment of royal policies, its early military preparations.

In many other ways, however, August 1642 was an unlooked
for and unwelcome climax. Coventry's dramatically transformed
role in the outside world, in Warwickshire and beyond, was achieved
in a very real sense by delivering the city up to outsiders, albeit
with the enthusiastic co-operation of many (although not most)
of the population.[18]

Both Charles and Parliament had their partisans among the
city elite in 1642, but the corporation as a whole sought, vainly,
to offend neither side. John Barker, Alderman and MP, worked
hard to execute Parliament's militia ordinance although William
Jesson remained in London and voiced in the Commons his
disquiet at the resort to arms. Barker openly defied the Earl of
Northampton when he attempted on 25 June to execute Charles's
commission of array: 'I answered his Lordship that I was a member
of the House of Commons and sent from the Parliament to see
the ordinance of both houses concerning the militia put into
execution and according to the trust reposed in me would oppose
the said commission of array'. This clear sense of responsibility
to the Parliament was shared only by Alderman Thomas Basnet,
also a militia commissioner; most of the council gave priority
to the liberties of the corporation. Thus when Northampton
appealed to the corporation as its recorder, he was granted a
meeting with the whole council and accorded the usual civilities
of eminent visitors (as Brooke was a week later). The Earl failed,
however, to win support for the commission although the Mayor,
Christopher Davenport, refused to execute the militia ordinance.
Northampton withdrew in disarray after a bungled attempt,
aided by Aldermen John Clark and Henry Million, to seize the
Warwickshire county arms which were stored in Coventry.[19]

Amongst the broader population of the city, there was more
support for Parliament and Brooke seized control of the county
arms, and finally executed the militia ordinance in early July.
Barker was busy arming Parliamentary supporters, while Million
and Clark, apparently with less success, rallied support for the
king; rival parties were identified by different coloured ribbons,
so that 'nearest neighbours were in great fear of each other'.
The corporation's quest for peace was thus compromised by the
party commitments of a minority amongst its own membership,
and sabotaged by popular Parliamentarianism. When Charles
summoned the Mayor and sheriffs to attend him at Leicester to

explain the failure to execute the commission of array, the council resolved on 24 July that they should go, 'to give satisfaction to his Majesty that so no prejudice shall happen against the city or the liberties thereof'. However, as they set off on the Lord's day (a tactless move in a godly city) 'some that favoured the parliament' – a 'rabble' according to one hostile witness – 'compelled them to stay at home'.[20]

As Charles approached the city a crowded meeting of the council made arrangements for his entertainment, borrowing £200 from their steward John Whitwick and £100 from Mayor Davenport. Whitwick was with the king's army and appealed to his 'Gentlemen and neighbours' to admit the king in a letter which poignantly displayed the rhetoric of urban privilege and solidarity. Whitwick referred to his own oath to the city, 'and in that respect tied to a more than ordinary care thereof, besides the bond of love which is inseparably united between it and me ... incites me to move, persuade and for god's sake, your own sakes, and your wives', children's and mine and your servants' sakes, with whom we are trusted ... that you embrace peace and quietness speedily whilst it may be had ... if you have for the present suffered the government of that city to be transferred into other hands, that it be reduced presently into your own power'.[21] The defiance of Charles despite the corporation's arrangements suggests that the council had indeed been bypassed. In June, Barker had been commissioned by Brooke as a colonel of a foot regiment and Governor of Coventry, and some thousand men were raised from early August. Hundreds of volunteers came from the city itself: Barker listed 207 in his own company, Samuel Ward, a minor city merchant, captained a company of 116, three-quarters of whom were still serving in the autumn.

Despite some historians' scepticism about the popularity of Parliament's cause in 1642, it is clear that in Coventry Parliamentarianism had wide appeal; it was popular in two senses, in that Parliament could raise numbers that the king could not match and in that these men came largely from outside the ruling elite of Coventry. Systematic demonstration of these points is difficult, but a mass of anecdotal evidence is available from musters, military accounts and taxation material. The Coventry men who provided the officers in Barker's regiment were small merchants or professional men: Major Robert Phippes, who played an important role in the siege, and Captain Matthew Randall were both physicians; Randall's lieutenant was a felt-maker from Cross Cheaping ward, paying tax at about a quarter of the rate of leading merchants and Aldermen. These were men of some substance but not hitherto central figures in the city. Independent craftsmen, including weavers and tylers along with some labourers filled the ranks. A strong sense that they were fighting the Lord's battles was fostered by rousing sermons and the radical Puritan leadership of Lord Brooke, a charismatic, popular figure. He stressed also the collective, participatory elements in Parliament's cause and many men who had some capacity for independence and initiative in their own lives seem to have been attracted to his army. By late August, as described by Nehemiah Wharton, a Londoner in the relieving army, Coventry was in a high state of godly excitement where ministers denounced malignants and pilloried vice, in a divisive language alien to the council's style. Throughout the Civil War, eminent Puritan ministers like Richard Baxter and Richard Vines 'kept by turns' a daily lecture to the troops and inhabitants while 'weekly days of fasting and prayer' were kept with a solemnity that was still remembered seventy years later.[22]

Coventry's transformation into a godly stronghold of zealous Parliamentarianism was not the work of its own citizens alone. Barker's regiment was raised from communities throughout north and east Warwickshire and volunteers from Birmingham were especially prominent in the siege. The city's own identity was diluted in a very direct way by the incursion of outsiders, a process that accelerated after August 1642 when Coventry, as one of the very few secure Parliamentarian cities in the region, was a refuge for those who feared royalist attack. The council's anxiety about this influx was demonstrated in an order to the Aldermen in July 1644 to count the numbers of strangers in their wards, especially single women 'that work at their own hands' and 'separatists that come not to church' so that 'such of them as shall be thought fit may be expelled the city'. Coventry's population was swollen by some 2–3,000 in the mid-1640s; most of this increase was presumably soldiers and refugees rather than independent women and radical sectaries.[23]

A militant and determined county committee based in Coventry held Warwickshire for the Parliament throughout the Civil War.

Coventry men were crucial to its work: Barker as Governor was very active, Alderman Thomas Basnet was an indefatigable treasurer and the clerk was Abraham Boune, a lawyer from one of the rural parishes of the city and county. They were, however, a minority among Warwickshire gentry and refugees from Staffordshire, Herefordshire and Shropshire. For most of Coventry's pre-Civil War elite the committee represented an imposed, outside authority – 'the committee of the parliament residing in the city' as the council minute book had it in 1643, not an opportunity for influence in a wider world. Coventry was further disadvantaged in the long term for the established Warwickshire gentry opposed the *prominence* of Coventry merchants in their affairs and would not forget their discomfiture at the Restoration.[24]

The events of August seem to have produced a form of corporate paralysis: no council meeting is recorded between 17 August and 1 October 1642 when Barker, speaking on behalf of the council of war, induced his 'brethren' to hand over to him the money borrowed for Charles's entertainment for the city's defence. Attempts were made to domesticate the changes military rule brought to the city government: assessments for parliamentary taxation were carried out by a committee that at least sat under a distinct heading, and Barker and Basnet were consistently used as intermediaries between the committee and the Council. When the committee wrote with a most drastic request, the city's Mayor Nicholas Rowney, an ex-officio committeeman, headed the list of signatories. Perhaps this did help the council acquiesce in the physical destruction of part of their city: their co-operation was sought in pulling down many houses outside the walls to improve defences. Inevitably there were sinister dislocations, some symbolic (although nonetheless real for that), others of the crudest practical impact; moves to normalise war may in fact have served to highlight its effects. In 1644 Parliament would not allow George Monk to serve as Mayor 'being disaffected', so the familiar figure of John Barker replaced him. But the 'Governor ... wore a sword and a buff coat under his gown and was attended by military as well as civil officers and when he proclaimed the great fair he had a troop of horse to attend him'.[25]

Although accounts of civil war losses survive for nine out of ten of Coventry's wards, few generalisations can be made about the financial impact of civil war taxation and other military exactions.

Only a minority of taxpayers seem to have reported on their losses, some of them could not remember what they had paid, and the major levy, the weekly pay, was distributed in very complex ways between owners and tenants. Furthermore, people were assessed on all of their property and it is impossible to know if returns are complete, especially for the more prosperous. In February 1648 the corporation claimed to their MPs that national taxation amounted to 18*d*. in the £1 of rents and as rents were 'extremely racked', taxation was 'an unsupportable burthen because of so many thousands of poor lying on the inhabitants for present relief these hard times and the great decay of trade with us'. It is likely that the corporation was exaggerating their plight (they were seeking a reduction in levies) but they were writing at a time when taxation was already much lower than it had been at the height of the war. The taxation of the 1640s was unprecedented in both the amounts required and the numbers expected to pay. Alderman John Rogerson of Smithford Street ward paid £3-4*s*. for the subsidies of 1640–41; his civil war taxation in three and a half years came to £40. Prominent merchants paid at least 4*s*. a week; on the other hand even labourers, smiths, poor weavers and tailors, were expected to find a few pence each week to pay the troops. Then there was free-quarter, especially heavy in the winter of 1642–43 before the committee sorted out regular pay for its troops, and again in the winter of 1643–44 when the regional commander, the Earl of Denbigh, kept his ill-paid troops in Coventry during a struggle for power with the county committee. War was a disaster for a trading community: Julius Billers, a mercer of Cross Cheaping, paid about £13 in tax over two and a half years but claimed £248 of goods had been 'lost on the road at several times'; a Smithford threadmaker paid £6 in tax, but had lost £67 through Royalist plunder. A widowed innkeeper in Broadgate was excused taxation, 'in regard of the shutting up of Grey Friars gate through which great store of travellers formerly used to travel to and from her house.' Many were even more unfortunate, for their houses no longer existed, sacrificed to the imperatives of defence: inhabitants all over the city reported the destruction of their property 'beyond Spon gate', 'beyond Bishop gate' and so on.[26]

After the first winter of war, Barker's regiment was reduced in size to some 750 men, half countrymen and half from the city. They were mostly well paid from 1643; in a garrison town there was little alternative for taxpayers but to pay up as required. Captain Matthew Randall's company received some 80 – 90 per cent of the sums due from Coventry, and were only two weeks in arrears for the period December 1642 – March 1645. These were part-time soldiers, young men who lived at home and undertook one or two watches per week. They were collecting their pay from their neighbours for clearly defensive duties. The Coventry regiment in general did little fighting, although companies that helped in the sieges of Banbury and Dudley found it harder to maintain their pay. Good pay ensured reasonably good behaviour except in the winter of 1643 – 44 when the local troops came into conflict with Denbigh's disorderly rival forces.[27]

The efficiency of the Coventry committee's military organisation did not endear it to Coventry corporation. City notables were active with Warwickshire men in successive campaigns to limit the powers of the militant committee, first by supporting the moderate regional commander Denbigh, and then by encouraging the supervision of the war effort by a pernickety committee of accounts which sat in Coventry from the autumn of 1644. The moderate MP William Jesson, in whose house Denbigh stayed while in Coventry, was a crucial figure who nominated the accounts committeemen; among the five members of Coventry's council chosen were the 1642 Mayor Christopher Davenport and the 'disaffected' George Monk. In part these men simply had different political positions from Thomas Basnet, for example, but there were also contrasting priorities. Jesson and the seven Aldermen and ex-sheriffs who signed a petition in favour of Denbigh were engaged in the strategy familiar before the war of using outside bodies to reinforce an internal position – here to restore the pre-war urban status quo. A radical like Basnet, a close associate of the militant Warwickshire county boss William Purefoy, and one of the small minority of Parliamentarians prepared to serve the restored Rump in 1659, saw Coventry as an integral part of a general struggle; city resources and reliability were more important than its privileges and autonomy. John Barker, the military Governor who was also an Alderman, a Mayor who was armed as well as gowned, uneasily straddled these two positions, attempting to serve both city and Parliament. Hence the corporation promoted an unsuccessful petition to retain him as Governor after the self-denying ordinance, and he worked with Jesson to lessen the taxation imposed on Coventry after the war was over.[28]

National developments necessitated changes in the honorific and technical offices of the corporation. Adroit choices of Recorder mark the external political climate of the 40s and 50s. In 1642 the Royalist Northampton was replaced by Parliament's commander, the Earl of Essex; on his death the Earl of Denbigh took over, but his lukewarm attitude to the Republic prompted the city to pick William Purefoy in his place in 1651. On Purefoy's death in autumn 1659, Chief Justice Oliver St John held the post briefly until at the Restoration the circle was completed with the choice of Northampton's son. The Royalist steward also had to go: during the war years the post was held by Humphrey Mackworth, a Shropshire 'stranger' on the county committee; thereafter a city man, Richard Hopkins, was steward.[29]

The corporation's own membership provides a contrast. A city corporation had a strong collective identity in which a crucial element was its chartered privilege of choosing its own members. It was much harder for outside political change to have an impact here than it was in county commissions of the peace, because JPs were directly appointed by the central government. Urban privileges encouraged resistance to changes in the personnel of rulers, even where councillors disapproved of the political attitudes of their 'brothers'; the use of familial language in the Council House reinforced this antipathy to purges. The position of Mayor was a sensitive one: George Monk was nominated as the next mayor in August 1642 but the more reliable Nicholas Rowney (who had made money selling ribbon to John Barker) ultimately served. When Monk was picked again, the county committee ordered his replacement as we have seen. But throughout the 1640s the only changes in the actual membership of the First Council were due to illness or death, not political affiliation. The open Royalist sympathisers Million and Clark continued to act, even after Clark was forced to compound in 1645 and Million was denounced to the Indemnity Committee in 1647. Clark rarely attended the council except in the summer of 1644 and the winter of 1646–47, but he was always among the notables who audited the chamberlains' and wardens' accounts, and usually at the Leet. Million too was prominent as an auditor and as a member of the Grand Inquest, indeed he headed the jurors' list in October 1649 and October 1650. Both men were added to quorum of the city commission of the peace in April 1644, in a small house of six Aldermen, including Clark and Million themselves but not Barker or Basnet.[30] It was not until 6 July 1651 that the two were removed, along with William Jesson who had been secluded from Parliament in December 1648. The council did their best to disassociate themselves from the purge by stressing that it was 'in obedience to the said order' of Parliament, and Million and Clark were entertained in the Mayor's parlour at the city's expense in the following spring.[31]

There is clear evidence of dislocation and demoralisation in the work of the corporation: meetings of the Council were much reduced in the war years as Table 4.1 shows; there was some recovery from the mid-1640s but problems emerged again in 1653–54 and in 1659, both periods of national political crisis.

Table 4.1 *Meetings of the First Council, 1641–62*

Calendar year (Jan–Dec)	Number of meetings	Months when no meetings took place
1641	26	Feb, Nov
1642	15	June, Sept, Nov, Dec
1643	17	May, Oct
1644	15	Jan, Feb, Mar, June, Oct
1645	21	Jan, June
1646	24	–
1647	22	June, Aug
1648	29	–
1649	27	–
1650	21	–
1651	22	–
1652	22	July, Dec
1653	16	Jan, Sept, Oct, Nov, Dec
1654	20	Feb, April, June, Dec
1655	15	Feb, July, Sept
1656	18	May, June
1657	23	–
1658	20	May, Oct
1659	15	Feb, May, June, Dec
1660	15	June, Sept, Dec
1661	7	Mar, Apr, June, July, Sept, Nov, Dec
1662	17	Mar, April, May

Equally ominous are the long periods when no meetings at all were held – none between December 1643 and April 1644 or between August 1653 and January 1654 (although an account of problems over the elections of officials in October 1653 is included in the council minute book). Attendance at the First Council also declined: six to seven members was the normal Civil War attendance; ten, the pre-war average, became an absolute maximum. Political hostility to Parliament was one factor: Clark was most often absent, Samson Hopkins was at only one meeting between August 1642 and April 1646 but once the war was decided he attended regularly until his death in 1652; Henry Smith was missing for long periods; Christopher Davenport attended intermittently. Demoralisation is shown also in the lack of the new entrants to the house: the aged and ill were replaced only in May 1645 when five new men, an unprecedented number, were recruited on the same day. Financial difficulties added to the problems of office-holding: Richard Jesson, chosen Mayor in October 1645 'on a sudden reason', was given a subsidy of £20 because he had received no present from the departing Mayor Barker. But then the new chamberlains refused to take office because the profits of the Little Park of Cheylesmore had been allotted to the Mayor: 'they would rather pay that £40 [fine] than accept of the place upon those conditions'. Only after much persuasion did they take their oaths. Reluctance or refusals to serve occurred intermittently throughout the Interregnum whereas Coventry seems to have been little troubled with such problems in the 1620s and 1630s.[32]

The late 1640s saw some recovery in corporation morale as William Jesson promoted a reaction against committee and army dominance. In March 1647 Jesson was teller for the ayes in a successful but close Commons vote to 'disgarrison' Coventry; militant members were clearly opposed and over the next weeks a series of letters and petitions were sent to the Parliament. One of the ministers and 'divers well-affected citizens' wanted the garrison retained, 'other well-affected citizens' thanked the two Houses for their favour in laying it down. The rival factions went up to lobby the Commons committee established to consider the city's military role and to explore the possibility of some compromise. A vivid letter from Jesson gives his view of the points at issue. Jesson and his allies bitterly resented the attempts to keep the garrison; they wanted the committee removed from the city and a united campaign in the Commons to put the city militia 'in the hands of citizens and freemen', and to obtain satisfaction, 'for all the houses, barns and stables pulled down and grounds trenched upon without the walls of the city which (as I understand) was not only promised by the committee, but published by proclamation made by the then Governor'. Purefoy, Barker and Basnet wanted county gentlemen joined with citizens in control of the militia, promoting the claims in particular of John Hales, esquire, who was a resident of Coventry but was clearly seen by Jesson and his allies as an outsider. Hales, they pointed out, was also a Deputy Lieutenant for Warwickshire and 'he could not be a fit counsel for both but we were sure he would always be leaning to the greater place' if the usual conflicts between Coventry and Warwickshire developed. But, 'their next demand, more unreasonable than that in my opinion ... was that Mr Clark, Mr Million, and Mr Monk must be made uncapable of sitting in the house or bearing any office in the city, but the consequence of that (if this be granted) would be to let Mr Alderman Legg, Captain Hopkins, Mr Love and my cousin Snell to sit in the house upon their good behaviour so long as they did please Alderman Basnet, Mr Snell the weaver and Mr Samuel Gilbert his brother'. Jesson urged his colleagues, 'let not any slavish fears come upon you to destroy your own liberties', and stressed that it was not in his, or the Parliament's power to expel from the Council House, 'for that was a business that did concern the Mayor and the whole house or twelve at the least of the house.' He could not see the grounds for suspicion of Million and Monk and though he tacitly accepted Clark's Royalism, 'I did not hear of any hurt he had done the city but good'. The eclipse of moderate Parliamentarians in London in 1647 ensured the survival of the Coventry garrison but Jesson's doughty commitment to urban liberties and unity delayed and limited any purge of the corporation, as we have seen.[33]

Despite clear resentment of the disruptions of the war years, there is little sign of pro-Royalist feeling in Coventry and the city co-operated in the defensive measures taken during the second Civil War. The garrison was finally removed in November 1648 prompting the council to order that it had been 'very inconvenient to have any main guard constantly kept at the Mayor's parlour in Cross Cheaping ... in case any future garrison be kept in

Coventry then the committee to be desired to keep their main guard in some other place'. National political changes – the purge of Parliament, the regicide, and the imposition of an Engagement of loyalty by the new republic – did force changes in council membership, but in other ways Coventry experienced a process of readjustment and gradual acquiesence in the 1650s. For the most part the council met regularly and attendance was at pre-war levels; new men were admitted to the House. Except during the Worcester campaign in 1651 and the various crises of 1659, there was no longer a garrison in Coventry, removing the obvious domination by outside powers. Certainly Jesson's allies of 1647, Hopkins, Love, Legg and Snell, did continue to work with Basnet, who was the dominant city figure throughout the 1650s, consistently heading the Grand Inquest. The routine leasing of city lands returned to dominate the council's business and if Basnet, along with other enthusiastic Parliamentarians like Alderman Robert Bedford, was a noted beneficiary, so were the unenthusiastic Thomas Love, Richard Jesson, Joseph Chambers and Godfrey Legg. One notable absentee from city affairs was John Barker who resigned from the council in April 1655, apparently exhausted and impoverished by his war-time labours.[34]

Signs of strain occasionally disrupted this apparent return to normal. No council meetings seem to have taken place as the Nominated Parliament failed and gave way to the Protectorate. At the Leet in October 1653 one sheriff refused to serve until pressure was put on him while Thomas Hobson, an ex-soldier, a Baptist and a committed republican, refused the office of chamberlain. Difficulties were also caused by the refusal of the ex-sheriffs, both connections of Thomas Basnet, to pay their fees to the steward Richard Hopkins. The political implications, if any, of these events are unclear; certainly there is no pattern in the later careers of the men involved.[35]

It was hard to find men willing to bear the expenses of the Mayoralty and in October 1656 an allowance of £44 was granted to Mayors. Office was also more politically contentious than it had been in the 1620s and 1630s and the political elite of the 1650s was, presumably for this reason, more of a mixed bag, less obviously a mirror of the social hierarchy of the city. Only twelve of the twenty-three mayors who served between 1643 and 1665 were drapers or mercers; there were no dyers at all, while clothiers, and the occasional baker or apothecary were much more prominent. For those who were willing to serve, the time taken to reach the First Council was often much shorter than before the war: very few of the admissions to the First Council in the 1650s are listed as Common Councillors in 1647. This was no social revolution, rather a shift away from the greatest merchants to some of the second rank. Only one Alderman, Robert Beake, admittedly a very influential figure, was a 'new man' who had come from obscure origins to political power through local military service. Beake settled in Coventry after rising from Lieutenant to Major in Barker's foot regiment; he rapidly became prominent in the draper's company and as a city officer, serving as sheriff in 1650–51, a member of the Council from March 1652 and Mayor in 1655–56. He was also the city's MP in all the Protectorate Parliaments, sitting with the Recorder William Purefoy. As an MP he was noted for his tactless but striking oratory supporting the moves to restore kingship and the Lords in 1656, and opposing republicans in 1659; his adherence to the more conservative trends in the Protectorate led to a civil service post in the Admiralty from 1656. In Coventry he could be equally tactless in his enthusiasm for godly moral reform, as we shall show.[36]

In an important article, Ian Roy has suggested that many corporations, without sympathising with the regicide, found non-monarchical governments congenial allies and to that extent encouraged the Anglican Royalist stigmatising of factious towns at the Restoration. There was an affinity between the habits of corporations and the more collective nature of 1650s central government; through the purchasing of Crown lands and the removal of episcopal authorities, cities acquired greater control over their own affairs.[37] The experience of Coventry corporation suggests the impact here was in some ways more ambiguous but the 1650s did bring benefits. After long negotiations and the crucial help of Purefoy, a leading Rumper, Basnet and Burton arranged for the corporation to buy the fee farm rents previously paid to the Crown for the city lands. It cost £1,443; to raise money the city borrowed £1,100 and was forced 'to let at long leases, to make sale of some of the city's lands and tenements and to use other means contrary to some orders heretofore made'. Nonetheless the corporation welcomed a purchase which reduced the city's dependency; Richard Jesson and Thomas Love, as well as Basnet and Robert Bedford were amongst those who bought land, took long leases, and arranged loans. After inconclusive negotiations to purchase outright the Crown manor of Cheylesmore, the city continued to occupy it even after their lease expired in 1659.[38]

Changes in Coventry's broader political culture after the Civil War suggest an acceptance of many national changes, but also a reluctance to forget some of the monarchical past. It was not until December 1650 that the arms of the new republic replaced those of the 'late king'. The public calendar, as defined by ringing in the city churches, was but partially transformed: after 1643 the bells did not ring to mark Charles's coronation day but Elizabeth's accession was celebrated every year except possibly for 1649; Christmas and other 'superstitious' feasts were no longer marked. Celebrations for victories in the first Civil War were rare, but ringing welcomed the 1648–49 victories in Ireland and Scotland, and the eclipse of the Royalist cause at Worcester in 1651. Similarly, few visitors were entertained by the corporation during the war but thereafter the traditional courtesies were granted the newly powerful. Candied oranges, perfumed comfits, claret and 'high country white wine' were purchased for Lieutenant General Cromwell when he dined at the Mayor's and at Basnet's house in July–August 1648. Less lavish arrangements were made for military commanders like Lambert and Harrison in the summer of 1651, for the local Major General Whalley between December 1655 and April 1656 and for Lord Henry Cromwell on his way to Ireland. The victims of national change were not, however, ignored: wine was provided for the Leicestershire gentlemen held as prisoners after Penruddock's rising.[39]

In the 1640s and 1650s the Coventry elite could influence the city's religious character in a manner not possible in the 1630s. As before the Civil War, there are qualifications to the stereotype of a zealous, godly city but nonetheless Coventry was noted for a broad, genuine committment to orthodox Puritanism. Ornaments such as eagle lecterns were removed from the city churches and two highly qualified preaching ministers were appointed, Dr John Bryan at Trinity and Dr Obadiah Grew at St Michael's. These men were 'Presbyterians', active in Warwickshire's small Kenilworth classis, but they worked well with Samuel Basnet, son of Thomas, who was appointed by the corporation as lecturer in 1653 and was pastor of an Independent congregation, despite wrangles over maintenance. All three men opposed the radical sects, and supported an educated, maintained ministry in some form of national church, even if they differed over details of church government. In Coventry such a ministry was widely accepted. Richard Baxter's comment on the garrison troops of the 1640s, 'the most sober, staied men that I ever met with', could stand for most of the city. Orthodox preaching prevented Baptist ideas becoming widespread while the more enthusiastic sectaries got nowhere; as the Quaker George Fox wrote of Coventry, 'there they was closed up with darkness'. Neither is there any evidence of Anglican traditionalism, although the problems over ministers' maintenance persisted despite repeated orders of the council from 1647, an act of parliament in March 1651, and an elaborate rating of the inhabitants in March 1653. Bryan and Grew resorted to pained letters elaborating on the biblical precedents for supporting ministers, ending plaintively in May 1653, 'Truly ... we are afraid we have laboured amongst you in vain for did our ministry effectually work upon your hearts they could not be so straightened towards our persons'. Bryan was persuaded with difficulty from accepting a Shropshire living in 1652.[40]

In the 1650s, Coventry was again compared with Geneva, but this time with approval, for the co-operation of magistrates and ministers, whether Presbyterian or Independent, in promoting true religion and godly reform. The elite were not unanimous; while Major General Whalley was charged with the supervision of local government and the encouragement of reform in Coventry and Warwickshire, he claimed the city was divided between wicked and godly magistrates and he forced the removal from office of Joseph Chambers, a 'faithful friend' of William Jesson in 1647, but accused of opposing Whalley's campaign against alehouses in 1655. The council characteristically signified its disapproval of this interference by making no mention of it in its minute book, but the majority of the corporation co-operated in the drives against 'sin and wickedness'. Certainly, Robert Beake, Mayor between 1655 and 1656, worked enthusiastically with the Major-General, once he was reassured that Whalley did not intend to ride roughshod over the city's privileges. Beake initiated drives by the constables against alehouses and idle rogues, not always with success, and was a fanatical sabbatarian, sending troops to seize unwary travellers and going in person to the park to 'observe who idly walked there'. Beake could be over-zealous even by godly standards: Samuel Basnet and Obadiah Grew talked him out of prosecuting a gentlewoman's servant who travelled to Coventry to arrange a funeral. Nor were Beake's victims always co-operative: on 25 January 1656 the Mayor provoked a riot when he went to investigate the unlicensed alehouses in Much Park Street, Gosford and Jordanwell wards, and the diary records much recidivism. Some of the campaigns were self-defeating, as ex-alehouse-keepers became indigent seekers of poor relief. Beake's commitment to the regulation of Coventry life, which extended to weekly reports from the constables on the cleanliness of the streets, was greater than most of his brethren's, but his basic attitudes were widely shared in what was by the 1650s a sternly disciplined city.[41]

A remarkable petition from 1657 or 1658 signed by 1,100 Coventry men (in a city of some 1,400 households) demonstrated widespread support for the religious and moral character of the Protectorate. All three ministers and most of the corporation, from the moderate Love to the anabaptist Hobson, signed in support of Oliver Cromwell's balance between liberty and discipline. The petition urged Cromwell, 'to curb and restrain more and more all prophaneness and ungodliness on the one hand, so also discriminate a true stated christian liberty from the practice of damnable errors and blasphemy', and concluded 'we judge that our weal and happiness, lives, religion and the interest of the Protestant cause lie greatly wrapped up and folded in the safety of your highness' person and the success of your counsels'.[42]

This sense of accommodation or even satisfaction with affairs by the later 1650s was probably encouraged by economic recovery after the disruptions and burdens of the war years. The accounts of the city wardens suggest increasing stability in Coventry's economy. In 1648 the wardens paid out more in charity moneys than they received in rents but by the mid-1650s rent arrears were tiny. The corporation had over-extended itself in buying the fee-farm rents; its debts reached £1,500 by October 1659 and more land had to be sold. The continuing capacity of leading members of the corporation, of all political affiliations, to lend money or buy city land indicates considerable resilience amongst the leading merchants. Not everyone was lucky: several of the citizens whose houses had been destroyed in 1643 were still petitioning for compensation in 1654.[43] Despite political tensions the Coventry elite were more secure in social terms in the 1650s, acquiring a closer control over their poorer neighbours than they had had before the war. Moral reform was one aspect of this, while the purchase of the fee farm rents and the unfettered possession of Cheylesmore park encouraged the exploitation of the common lands. In 1661 a disgruntled ex-office-holder accused the corporation of ploughing the commons and there are almost no Leet orders for the late 40s and 50s to restrict ploughing or protect commoners' rights. The poor commoners, on the other hand, seem to have had less access to outside support than before the war. They could still resort to riot and there were serious disturbances in spring 1657 when the Mayor, Aldermen and sheriffs were pelted with stones, and again in spring 1659. In May 1660 the Leet again banned ploughing after Lammas and Michaelmas; this revival of social traditionalism at the Restoration was not simply coincidence.[44]

As city and corporation accepted or even supported the Protectorate so the period of national crisis that followed Cromwell's death was matched by renewed demoralisation in the corporation. Council meetings were again intermittent and there was unusual turnover in the membership of the Leet's grand inquest. Of the thirty-one members present in October 1659 only eleven were nominated in May 1660. Only seventeen of the May 1660 jurors served in the autumn while fifteen of the October 1660 jurors continued to October 1661. Leading Interregnum figures were prominent in the moves towards a Restoration that was to prove calamitous both for their own political careers and for the city itself. In December 1659 Beake raised a volunteer militia to secure Coventry against the army and in support of the return of Parliament. The Mayor who had to proclaim Charles II king was Thomas Basnet, and the corporation lost no time in surrendering its fee-farm rents and organising gifts of plate for the new monarch. Ringing in the city churches marked Charles II's return to England in May 1660; the new Recorder Northampton and soon the Bishop too were honoured visitors to Coventry.[45]

Significant changes took place in the corporation. Chambers lost no time in reclaiming his place: 'it is not unknown to you the wrongs I sustained by Whalley ...', he complained to Mayor Basnet, 'what calumnies and unjust aspersions were laid upon me ... when ... there was a door open for every inconsiderable, ill-conditioned fellow to throw dust in the face of authority'. Julius Billers, who had succeeded Chambers, finally resigned the ward in February 1661 after Chambers had petitioned the king. Beake and Basnet decided not to wait for a purge, and resigned for 'divers causes moving them' in February 1662. Thomas Hobson was nominated as Mayor in October 1661 but Northampton complained about the choice of an 'anabaptist' and Hobson gradually stopped attending the House. The 'purge' under the Corporation Act was thus deceptively limited: Robert Bedford of the First Council and one of the sheriffs only were removed.[46]

The initial transformation in the religious atmosphere was more dramatic. In 1660 some citizens erected a maypole, as in many parts of England, but it was promptly pulled down again on the orders of the corporation. In 1662, however, it was the Mayor himself who provided the maypole; Thomas Pidgeon, who had only entered the Council House in February 1661 replaced Hobson, and also 'put a stop to the weekly lecture ... he frowned upon pious good ministers'. Pidgeon may therefore have been one of the few Coventry men to welcome the Act of Uniformity which removed both parish ministers and the lecturer. These sober Puritans were described by the new bishop as 'two seditious preachers', but a grateful corporation paid gratuities to Bryan and Grew more willingly than they had paid their official salaries in the 1650s.[47]

Most serious of all, however, was the reorientation of Coventry's relationship with the outside world as the local gentry sought revenge for the 1640s. One of the most overt examples of this revenge is found in an order of the Warwickshire Quarter Sessions in Epiphany 1662, an order which some, at least, of the justices present must have known to be untrue. Coventry they declared had 'anciently and heretofore' paid a seventh or eighth part of all levies imposed on Warwickshire and the city and county, until the proportion was altered to a fifteenth during 'the time of the late wars and distractions within this kingdom ... the citizens of the said city, having the power in their hands (by reason of a committee of Parliament ... there sitting)'. Parliamentary elections revealed a changed world. In the 1660 election to the Convention the city steward, now Sir Richard Hopkins, was chosen along with Beake; when Beake's return was challenged William Jesson, son of the Long Parliament MP, replaced him. These were all city men but in the 1661 contest two gentlemen were returned: Thomas Flint was from one of Coventry's rural parishes but the Royalist Sir Clement Fisher was a North Warwickshire figure with no previous city connections.[48]

In October 1659 Thomas Basnet's power in Coventry and beyond was recognised in the grant for life of the office of chief bailiff of the manor of Cheylesmore. It is not clear how the city acquired the power to grant this honour in a previously royal manor; in any case the loss of any rights in Cheylesmore was one of the more serious blows of the Restoration. The city's use of the park had been acquired through royal favour and the intercession of a local notable in the sixteenth century; a hundred years later it was to be lost in a parallel fashion. In September 1660 the city petitioned Charles for the renewal of the lease, collecting the signatures of 832 men, over half the adult males of Coventry. Knowing this would not be sufficient they also took the humiliating step of persuading several leading Warwickshire peers and gentlemen to intervene with the king on their behalf in January 1661. In the city's support it was urged that the park was vital for the poor of Coventry but a local Royalist, Sir Robert Townshend, accused the corporation of diverting its profits to their own end, an accusation that had at least some plausibility. Coventry's Parliamentarian past was held against it and in March 1661 Townshend was granted a lease that remained in his family until the eighteenth century. Ironically, the loss of a substantial part of the city's common rights brought a new unity between corporation and commoners for in the 1660s the elite were accused of fomenting riot; they were no longer the objects of it.[49]

The sober, disciplined Presbyterian city of the Protectorate – the 'populous and arrogant city' of government informers in the 1660s – could not be transformed overnight and Coventry remained into the eighteenth century a 'fanatic town', where some 40 per cent of the population were dissenters, predominantly Presbyterians as they had been in the 1650s. Occasional conformity ensured that men sympathetic to dissent served on the Council and as Mayor, although fewer dissenters were among the younger men elected annually as sheriffs or wardens. Coventry was bitterly divided internally over politics and religion in the 1670s and 80s as elsewhere in England, but by the end of the century 'Whigs' were in control, and the urban elite had regained some of its former autonomy. Only some, however, for the Coventry of the Restoration period was a diminished, threatened city in comparison with the regional stronghold of the 1640s or the aloof, independent city of the pre-war years. It was at the mercy of the country gentry for the first time and prey to the royal interference that culminated in the loss of its charter in 1683. This new vulnerability to the outside world was clearly revealed, in symbol and in practice, in the traumatic destruction of its walls.[50]

Notes

1 *Calendar of State Papers Domestic* [*CSPD*], 1661–62, pp. 423–4; Coventry City Record Office [Cov CRO] A79, P250 (Coventry Corporation Letter collection). Some of the corporation archives have been renumbered in recent years but I have continued to use the 'A' numbers which were used when I first worked on the collections and which are used in older guides to the city records. Full cross-referencing of numbering systems is provided in the record office.

2 P. M. Hohenberg and L. Hollen Lees, *The Making of Urban Europe*, Cambridge, Mass., 1985, pp. 4–5 for a general discussion; R. Howell, 'Newcastle and the nation: the seventeenth century experience' in J. Barry, (ed.), *The Tudor and Stuart Town*, London, 1990, for a discussion of the links between internal and external political change in one English city.

3 A. Hughes, *Politics, Society and Civil War in Warwickshire*, Cambridge, 1987, pp. 12–15; C. Phythian-Adams, *Desolation of a City: Coventry and the Urban Crisis of the Late Middle Ages*, Cambridge, 1979, pp. 33–61, 281; A. W. A. White, *Men and Mining in Warwickshire*, Coventry and North Warwickshire History Pamphlets, 7, 1970, pp. 6–8; A. Everitt, 'The marketing of agricultural produce' in J. Thirsk, (ed.), *The Agrarian History of England and Wales*, IV, Cambridge, 1967, pp. 492, 534; *Victoria County History of Warwickshire* [VCH, *Warwicks*], (1904–69) VIII, pp. 167–8.

4 P. Clark and P. Slack, (eds.), *Crisis and Order in English Towns*, London, 1972, pp. 16, 21–2. Analysis of office-holding is based on the Council Minute Books: Cov CRO A14(a), A14(b) and on the Leet Book: A3(b). Lists of the Common Council are available for September 1636, December 1640 and September 1647: A14(a), f. 340fr, A14(b), ff. 7r, 66r. For an example of Common Councillors being consulted by the First Council: A14(b), ff. 110v–111r, 20 July 1653. For the 1621 Charter: F. Smith, *Coventry: Six Hundred Years of Municipal Life*, Coventry, 1945, pp. 88–91; A. A. Dibben, *Coventry City Charters*, Coventry City Papers 2, 1969.

5 A14(a), ff. 295v, 323v, 328v, 333v; Public Record Office [PRO] Prob 11/219, f. 215; A14(b), f. 45r.

6 I owe the information on the mercers to the kindness of Professor Ronald Berger.

7 Hughes, *Politics, Society and Civil War*, pp. 16–17; A14(a), f. 290v, March 1628; for opposition to Hales in 1647 see below.

8 Hughes, *Politics, Society and Civil War*, pp. 15–17, 105–6, 114–15; 'This book touching Ship Money' is Cov CRO A35. In October 1635 Burton was granted a gift worth £50 'in recompense of his labours' over it: A14(a), f. 333r. Military protests: A79/P167, 184, 185; PRO SP16/459/99, for Jesson's protest.

9 Hughes, *Politics, Society and Civil War*, pp. 87–8; A35; A14(a), ff. 331r, 334v for grateful presents to the Bishop and his wife.

10 Much of the business of the mayor's council concerned leases of the city lands, and many leases were to members of the council or their families: A14(a) and (b) *passim*; the first nominees for Davenport money were three young members of leading families: A14(a), f. 290v.

11 Hughes, *Politics, Society and Civil War*, p. 14.

12 VCH, *Warwicks*, VIII, pp. 19–20, 199–204; A3(b), pp. 147, 154, 161–2, 167–8 for Leet orders forbidding ploughing without the consent of the mayor and council, 1633, 1635, 1638, 1640. Cov CRO A48, City Annals, ff. 33r–34v, 41r; A7(c), Chamberlains and Wardens Accounts, p. 63.

13 Hughes, *Politics, Society and Civil War*, pp. 81–2; PRO PC2/48, pp. 185, 359, 373–4; A14(a), ff. 271r, 273r, 291r, 318r, 354r; Samuel Clarke, *The Lives of Sundry Eminent Persons in this Later Age*, London, 1683, pp. 5–6. Clarke was only appointed after several Aldermen had heard him preach in his father's nearby parish.

14 P. Clark, ' "The Ramoth-Gilead of the Good": Urban change and political radicalism at Gloucester 1540–1640', in P. Clark, A. G. R. Smith and N. R. N. Tyacke, (eds.), *The English Commonwealth 1547–1640*, Leicester, 1979, now reprinted in Barry, (ed.), *The Tudor and Stuart Town*; A14(a), ff. 278v, 279r, 341v; SP16/293/128, f. 10r; SP16/218/77, 229/122, 330/40.

15 New College Oxford MS 9502, ff. 50r, 86v, 125r. I am grateful to Dr John Fielding for this reference. The Council Minute Book records frequent attempts to solve problems and divisions over ministers' and lecturers' remuneration, and in 1638 they fought a tithes suit against William Panting, the minister at St Michael's: Cov CRO, A14(a), ff. 318r, 322r, 335v, 337v, 356r, 365; Corporation Ecclesiastical Records, Box 2.

16 Hughes, *Politics, Society and Civil War*, pp. 117, 129.

17 Hughes, *Politics, Society and Civil War*, p. 86; Cov CRO A7(c), pp. 61–3, 74, 77, 88–9; A14(b), ff. 23v, 24v–25r, 26v.

18 Hughes, *Politics, Society and Civil War*, pp. 136–58, for a full analysis of the coming of war. The siege of Coventry is described in A48, f. 42v and in many contemporary pamphlets and newsletters: *A True Relation of his Majesties Coming to Coventry*, London, 1642, British Library [BL] Thomason Tracts, E114 (1); *Speciall Passages*, 23–30 August 1642, E114 (36) are particularly useful. The king's forces are variously assessed at 1,500, 6,000 and 11,000 men. The relieving army was made up of 4,800 foot and 11 troops of horse: *Commons Journals* [*CJ*], IV, pp. 724, 735, printing errors for pp. 720, 731.

19 *Lords Journals* [*LJ*], V, pp. 163–4, Barker to Lord Brooke; A7(c), p. 100; A48, f. 41v.

20 A48, f. 42v; Barker's accounts record extensive purchases of ribbon from Coventry drapers: PRO SP28/136, accounts of Colonel John Barker, August 1642–November 1643. A79 P206, for the summons from Charles which was sent through the city's steward, John Whitwick. A14(b), f. 28v; A48, f. 41v; Staffordshire CRO Leveson MSS D868/5/66, Samuel Hinton, Archdeacon of Coventry to Sir Richard Leveson.

21 A14(b), f. 30v, fourteen councillors were present including Barker and Basnet; A79 P208, for Whitwick's letter from Kenilworth, the king's headquarters, 20 August.

22 The latest important works on the social appeal of Parliamentarianism are D. Underdown, *Revel Riot and Rebellion, Popular Politics and Culture in England 1603–1660*, Oxford, 1985 and the introduction to the new edition of B. Manning, *The English People and the English Revolution*, London, 1991. The Warwickshire military and the popularity of Parliament are discussed in Hughes, *Politics, Society and Civil War*, pp. 150–3, 194–205; for specific detail on the Coventry forces: BL Additional MS 35,209, SP28/136, accounts of John Barker; SP28/131/Part 15, accounts of Matthew Randall; SP28/121A, 122, 123, musters of Coventry forces; SP28/201, accounts of the losses of Cross Cheaping Ward; SP28/203, losses in Much Park Street ward. SP16/491/138 is a good example of Wharton's letters. Hughes, *Politics, Society and Civil War*, p. 311 for the Civil War sermons.

23 The city Annals record an influx of 400 men from Birmingham on 19 August and city accounts include claims for payment of their freequarter: A48, f. 42v; SP28/201; A14(b), f. 40r; VCH, 8, p. 5.

24 Hughes, *Politics, Society and Civil War*, pp. 170–84 for a full account of the Coventry committee (i.e. the Warwickshire county committee); A14(b), f. 34r.

25 A14(b), ff. 34r, 35r–36r; A48, ff. 43r–44v.

26 No return has been found for Gosford Street. Those available are: Cross Cheaping, Jordanwell, Earl Street, SP28/201; Much Park Street, SP28/203; Bayley Lane, SP28/185, f. 420r; Spon Street, Bishop Street, Smithford Street, SP28/182/31–2, 34; Broadgate, SP28/136. Bishop Street's return lists fifty-seven taxpayers and Cross Cheaping fifty-nine, but this must represent little more than a quarter of households. Those omitted are not necessarily too poor to pay: some returns are for labourers and craftsmen paying 3*d* a week. A79 P216 for the committee's claims.

27 Hughes, *Politics, Society and Civil War*, pp. 196–7, 200–1; SP28/131/15 for Randall's men. Married men with children were disbanded. A less favoured company was that of Major Robert Phippes, commanded in practice by his Lieutenant Thomas Hobson, a radical and apparently dishonest officer who was a Coventry butcher.

28 Hughes, *Politics, Society and Civil War*, pp. 228, 238–46; A7(c), pp. 127–8, for Denbigh and Jesson; House of Lords, Main Papers, 21 August 1644 for the petition in favour of Denbigh signed by 2,000 men from Coventry and Warwickshire. A36(a) Treasurer's accounts, April 1645; A14(b), f. 44r for the petition to retain Barker. He was in fact succeeded by Thomas Willoughby, a minor Warwickshire gentleman.

29 A3(b), pp. 176, 187, 195, 217, 223.

30 Hughes, *Politics, Society and Civil War*, p. 274; A14(b) *passim* for attendance at the Council, ff. 29v, 38v, for Rowney and the April 1644 meeting; A7(c) for the auditors; A3(b) for the Leet, pp. 193–4 for 1649–50.

31 A14(b), f. 99v; A7(c), p. 272.

32 A14(b) *passim* and ff. 45r, 56v, 57v–58r for May 1645 and October/November 1646.

33 A79, P214, Jesson to the Mayor etc. of the 'suffering city of Coventry'; *CJ*, V, pp. 104, 110, 122, 250.

34 A14(b) *passim* and ff. 75r, 79r, 118v; A3(b) *passim*; Hughes, *Politics, Society and Civil War*, pp. 270, 274, 298 for the garrison and for Barker's impoverished old age.

35 A14(b), ff. 111v–112r, 113r, 124v, 128r, 131v, 133v–134r; A3(b), p. 207; Hughes, *Politics, Society and Civil War*, pp. 196, 275, 330–1 for Hobson's career. The reluctant sheriff, Richard Baron also refused to enter the Council House in September 1659, whereas Hobson served as sheriff in 1656–7 and entered the Council House in September 1658. John Crichlow, one of the 1652–53 sheriffs, served on the restored Rump's militia commissions of 1659, usually a sign of political radicalism, but he only took his oath as a member of the Council House some nine months after he was first summoned.

36 A14(b), f. 124r; Hughes, *Politics, Society and Civil War*, pp. 270, 291–4 for Beake's origins and national career; A3(b), p. 194; A14(b), f. 103v for his City office-holding.

37 I. Roy, 'The English Republic, 1649–1660: the view from the Town Hall', in *Republiken und Republikanismus im Europa der Fruhen Neuzeit: Herausgegeben von Helmut Koenigsberger*, Schriften des Historischen Kollegs Kolloquien II, Oldenburg, 1989.

38 A14(b), ff. 88v, 92v–94v; A79, P219, P220b, P221–3, January–October 1650; P233B, VCH *Warwicks*, VIII, p. 19 for Cheylesmore.

39 D. Cressy, 'The Protestant calendar and the vocabulary of celebration in early modern England', *Journal of British Studies*, XXIX, 1990; A7(c) *passim*, and pp. 200, 256 for Cromwell and the removal of the king's arms.

40 Cf. Roy, 'The English Republic', p. 233; Hughes, *Politics, Society and Civil War*, pp. 311–13; VCH *Warwicks*, VIII, pp. 325, 350; R. Baxter, *Plain Scripture Proof of Infants Church Membership and Baptism*, 1651, sig B4; N. Penney, (ed.), *The Journal of George Fox*, Cambridge, 1911, I, p. 36. On the problems caused by ministers' maintenance: CJ, 6, pp. 443, 458, 551; A14(b), ff. 69r, 108v, 110r, 123v, 130v; A79 P227–P231 for indignant letters from Beake, Grew, Bryan, Purefoy and Thomas Basnet on his son's behalf 1653–56; A40 for the assessment.

41 *Thurloe State Papers*, 7 vols., (1742), IV, pp. 273–4, 284; 'The Diary of Robert Beake', in Robert Bearman, (ed.), *Miscellany*, I, Dugdale Society Publications, 31, 1977; A3(b), p. 205; Hughes, *Politics, Society and Civil War*, pp. 283–4 for a fuller discussion.

42 PRO SP18/158/114.

43 A7(c) *passim*; A14(b), ff. 134v–137r; SP18/69/21; cf. I. Roy, 'England turned Germany? The aftermath of Civil War in its European context', *Transactions of the Royal Historical Society*, 5th series, 28, 1978.

44 PRO E134, 13 Charles II, Easter 25; A7(c), pp. 337, 359; A48, f. 47r; A3(b), p. 222.

45 A3(b), pp. 216–27; SP25/99/, pp. 5–6; A48, ff. 47r–v; A14(b), f. 139r; SP29/1/27; A7(c), pp. 369–94.

46 Hughes, *Politics, Society and Civil War*, p. 275; SP29/13/98; A79 P241, 242a; A14(b), ff. 143r, 144v, 145r. CSPD, 1661–62, pp. 90–1 for Hobson.

47 A37, no pagination; A14(b), f. 140r; F. J. Routledge, (ed.), *Calendar of the Clarendon State Papers*, 5 vols., Oxford, 1970, V, pp. 254, 259.

48 S. C. Ratcliff and H. C. Johnson, (eds.), *Quarter Sessions Order Book*, Warwick County Records, IV, 1938, p. 175; Hughes, *Politics, Society and Civil War*, pp. 336, 338; A48, ff. 47v–48r.

49 SP29/17/28; A79 P240, P242B, 243–4; A14(b), ff. 141r, 147v; VCH *Warwicks*, VIII, pp. 19–20, 204–5.

50 *CSPD*, 1661–62, p. 145; J. J. Hurwich, ' "A Fanatick Town": the political influence of dissenters in Coventry, 1660–1720', *Midland History*, 4, 1977.

CHAPTER FIVE

BRISTOL'S 'WARS OF RELIGION'

David Harris Sacks

Every effect necessarily has its cause. But, as Conrad Russell reminds us, just what kind of causes we should seek depends upon the effects we wish to explain.[1] In an influential article on the religious context of the English Civil War, John Morrill set out to explain what 'drove minorities to fight and forced majorities to make reluctant choices' for the king or Parliament in 1642. He finds the cause in religion. Only the religious perception of misgovernment or mode of opposition, he says, had 'the momentum, the passion, to bring about the kind of civil war which England experienced after 1642'. He sums up this argument in a sentence that has been a rallying cry for much revisionist scholarship: 'The English civil war was not the first European revolution: it was the last of the Wars of Religion'.[2]

Morrill is concerned to limit the range of subjects requiring explanation. His subject is the outbreak of hostilities, the beginning of the Civil War, not the 'English Revolution' in any of its accepted meanings.[3] At issue is an event or sequence of events leading to the opening of war in 1642. But does the explanation of 'events', even if concentrated only on those of a single year, necessarily preclude the possibility of revolution? Lawrence Stone thinks not and in his own influential study of the causes of the English Revolution, he also looks to religion to explain the occurrences which came to a head in 1642. Religion plays a prominent role for him not only because it was one of the main sources of legitimation for the governing institutions of society, but also because a 'true revolution needs ideas to fuel it'.[4]

Religion, it seems, can explain both narrowly circumscribed political events and broadly construed socio-political processes. It can be understood as an arrangement for regulating devotional observances or as a system of beliefs about the nature of God and the Church. It can equally well be viewed as a symbolic code or vocabulary for understanding the temporal as well as the spiritual world; or as the ground for a person's or a group's sense of identity, or as the ethical foundation for social and political action. For this reason thinking of the events of the 1640s as a 'war of religion' poses just as many problems of interpretation as it purports to solve. On narrowly institutional definitions, these events might be seen as amounting to a self-interested contest for power and influence among the members of a secular-minded and propertied elite, clerical as well as lay. On strictly doctrinal definitions, they look more like a clash between conflicting theological schools striving for control of dogma and the means to salvation. In the first instance we would understand our war of religion to be a sort of rebellion; in the second, it would appear as a kind of crusade. In neither instance, however, do we capture the genuine power of religion to engage men's and women's passions and to motivate them to concerted action in their public and private lives.

A more broadly framed cultural approach has greater explanatory possibilities. Religious symbols, ideas and practices, it has been argued, 'synthesize a people's ethos – the tone, character and quality of their life, its moral and aesthetic style and mood – and their world view – the picture they have of the way things ... are, their most comprehensive ideas of order'. These two sides reinforce one another. They depict 'moral and aesthetic preferences' as 'unalterable' features of 'life implicit in a world with a particular structure' and support these 'received beliefs ... by invoking deeply felt moral and aesthetic sentiments as ... evidence for their truth'. They 'formulate a basic congruence between a particular style of life and a specific ... metaphysic, and in so doing sustain each with the borrowed authority of the other'.[5] This congruence makes religion a powerful force in politics, potentially the source of contested opinions as well as undisputed truths. It opens the possibility that opposing religious views will lead to violent confrontations across the social field.[6]

The history of early modern Bristol offers a good opportunity to test this hypothesis, even though it is very far from being a

typical town. Situated near the confluence of the Severn and
Avon rivers, at the head of the Bristol Channel, it was England's
second port in the sixteenth and seventeenth centuries and the
dominant town in the West. Its population at the start of the
Civil War approached 15,000, which made it perhaps the third most
populous urban centre in England after London and Norwich.[7]
What happened in it, therefore, did not represent the common
experiences of towns in this era. But its importance in the nation's
urban hierarchy also gave it a prominence, often unwanted, in
the great matters that stirred church and state from the Reformation
to the Restoration and after. In the Civil War itself, it was so
significant strategically that it twice suffered sieges, once in 1643
when Prince Rupert captured it for King Charles I and again in 1645,
when Fairfax and Cromwell recaptured it for the Parliament.[8]
Hence, it could not help but be a testing ground for political
and ideological conflict in this era. In what follows, I want to
use this history to understand what it might mean to speak of
England's wars of religion in the seventeenth century.

Let us begin with the period of the Bishops' Wars, since 'there
is no doubt', as Russell has said, 'that they started the immediate
sequence of events which led to the English Civil War'.[9] Although
Bristol is distant from Scotland, events there were a great deal
on the minds of Bristolians around 1640. William Adams, Bristol's
seventeenth-century chronicler, gave special notice to them in
reporting the occurrences of 1638 – 39. Despite the many favours
granted Scotland by Charles and his father, Adams said, this
year the Scots 'moved great rebellion there ... under colour'
of religion, which served as 'a cloak for their mischievous intent'.[10]
Within a year, however, Adams changed his view in the light of
further information garnered at the outbreak of the Second Bishop's
War. Looking back to earlier events, he now said that the Scottish
forces 'came not as rebels', but in defence of true religion.[11] In a
subsequent narrative, he tells us that at 'their front marched many
learned Divines in humble manner, with papers and petitions in
their hands challenging to dispute against our bishops'. The
Parliament called at the Scots' behest, Adams says, 'brought to
light much treason, and sundry wicked plots of great men, as
well in the Parliament house as others in which some Judges were
taxed for corrupt judgement'.[12]

How had he become so certain of the righteousness of the Scots and the beneficence of their influence in England? What new insights and information had came to him after he wrote his initial account of the First Bishops' War? We cannot give a complete answer to these questions, since we are aware of only a small fraction of the sources Adams used in his writing. He may have been familiar, for example, with the Scots' defences of their position, which according to Charles I were in wide circulation in England in the winter and spring of 1640.[13] But we do not know for certain whether copies came into Adams's hands. Adams may also have learned something of the Scottish cause from Mathew Hazard, minister in St Philips, who in 1640 openly challenged royal propaganda against the Scots when in response to a nation-wide order to pray for the welfare of the king 'against the Rebels of Scotland', he declaimed instead against 'all those Traitorous enemies in this Kingdom that disturb the Peace of the Realm and that vex and molest the hearts of thy Church and faithful people'.[14] But again we have no direct evidence that Adams heard Hazard in person or learned of his prayer when it came to the attention of the magistrates.

Nevertheless, there can be no doubt that Adams was in sympathy with Hazard's view, especially as regards the bishops. He quotes at length from Richard Bernard's systematic critique of episcopacy, published early in 1641.[15] Bernard, minister of Batcombe in nearby Somerset, based his attack on Chapter 34 of the Book of Ezekiel, condemning those shepherds of Israel who 'feed not the flock', but only themselves, and who 'with force and with cruelty' ruled over their charges.[16] He challenged the participation of the bishops in Parliament and royal councils, cried out against their courts and their use of *ex officio* oaths, complained of their upholding popish ceremonies and superstitions and their suppression of lectures and sermons. He accused them of raising 'a *bellum Episcopale* to dash two Kingdoms one against another, to the shedding of much blood'. He was particularly scornful of the numerous, meddlesome under-officials – 'swarms of wasps', Bernard called them – whom the bishops employed to do their dirty work and who added so greatly to the financial burdens of the realm.[17] Most of all Bernard condemned the bishops for bearing 'up themselves mightily by their Revenues and Baronries, strengthening themselves in their pomp, and in their pride to overtop whom they list'.[18] By the Church, Bernard argued, the bishops understood only the clergy; they debarred even 'the Nobles and Gentry, the whole house of Parliament, the Upper, and Lower' from membership. 'The Church of *England* now so called', he complained, 'is the Church of our Prelates ... received from *Rome*, the seat of *Antichrist*, and set up here ... for it is framed of Prelates ... and only ruled by them'. Bernard insisted, however, that according to Scripture 'the title of Church (monopolized now to themselves)' belonged either to 'the Ministers and the people together' or to 'the people distinct from Ministers'.

Use of the term 'monopoly' reveals Bernard's central idea. 'There is much complaint touching Monopolies in another nature and justly', he argued. Nevertheless, the monopoly of the bishops and clergy 'is a mystery of mischiefs; for by this name of the Church assumed to themselves' the episcopacy had corrupted the church at its very heart. 'They dignify very greatly their Prelatical power ... They decree what they please without control ... They strike an awefulness in all sorts under the sacred name of Church'. Bernard concluded, therefore, that 'the Church representative ought to be gathered of both sorts (as they now be distinguished) of the learned and godly Laity as well as of the Clergy' instead of being engrossed into clerical hands.[19]

This critique of English episcopacy helps explain Adams's change of mind about the Scots. Adams was a godly man, who took his Protestant convictions with utmost seriousness. In his *Chronicle*, for example, he organised his account of the Reformation as a story of 'the furtherance of God's word and true religion', and the spreading of 'the true and unfeigned worshipping of God in heart and mind' against the thrall of 'superstition'.[20] He looked upon Prynne, Bastwick, and Burton as 'champions' of the faith and greatly lamented the unjust punishments they had received at the hands of illegitimate clerical authority and the state.[21] He also held a providentialist view of history, in which God intervened directly in the world to reward the faithful and punish sinners, even kings.[22] These views disposed him to search for the sources of sin that had led to calamity and to condemn wrongdoing where he found it, whether among princes or bishops.

Adams tells us in the introduction to his *Chronicle* drafted in 1625, that he wrote in the service of God and the commonwealth especially to pass 'unto posterity' the story of England's liberation, 'to show God's great love and blessings bestowed upon us in freeing us' from barbarousness, 'to the great comfort of all godly and true hearted subjects that now can enjoy the benefit of their labours in peace and quietness every man under his own vine'.[23] The reference here is to the beneficent rule of King Solomon,[24] but Adams was also endorsing the regime of James I, who identified himself and was often identified by others with King Solomon.[25]

Adams implicitly accepted the argument that the godly rule of righteous monarchs guaranteed the liberties of the subject. History conceived in this way could not readily promote resistance to duly constituted authority. Instead, in Adams's view, it served 'to teach us, having good and godly sovereigns, to acquit them with true obedience, love, and prayers; if otherwise to pray heartily for their conversion, that under them we may live in a godly and peaceable government'.[26] Even the most egregiously sinful actions of rulers did not warrant the making of war against them. King James I himself could not have made this point more succinctly.

But Adams was also a shopkeeper in Bristol, a draper and retailer of small wares and imported finery. As such, he was closely associated with those groups in the city that most felt the dangers of monopoly in trade and that most ardently condemned it as a social, political and moral evil – a hindrance to members of the commonwealth in the proper performance of their personal obligations and public duties. It is perhaps no wonder that he found wisdom in Bernard's critique of episcopacy as a pernicious form of monopoly; prelatical power threatened to put souls in bondage by much more direct and damaging means.[27]

There was no more divisive issue in early modern Bristol than monopoly. By the time Charles I set up his standard at Nottingham in August 1642 it had been a recurring cause of factionalism and dissension within the city for a hundred years or more. The focus of the controversy was the claim of the city's major overseas merchants, made on numerous occasions and in differing institutional settings, to an exclusive right to trade with foreign markets from the port of Bristol.[28] By the 1540s it was already widely argued among the citizenry that handicraftsmen should refrain from engaging in any form of commercial enterprise. According to Roger Edgeworth, a conservative minister who preached in the city at the end of Henry VIII's reign, each man was morally obligated to remain within the vocation to which he had been called, '[f]or when a tailor forsaking his own occupation will be a merchant, venturer, or a shoemaker to become a grocer, God send him well to prove'.[29] The aim was to protect those occupations having significant trading functions, which were heavily dependent upon personal reputation and good credit, from encroachment by manufacturers, whose competition it was believed would undermine the traders' ability to work the market for a profit.

In keeping with this view, the merchants in 1552 acquired a royal charter creating a Society of Merchant Venturers in Bristol with exclusive rights barring 'men of manual art' from overseas trade from the port.[30] By the beginning of Elizabeth I's reign, the target of these monopolistic aspirations shifted to include retailers, whose competition in luxury items threatened the profits of the wholesale traders, the so-called 'mere merchants' of the city.[31] To protect themselves further against this competition, the merchants acquired a parliamentary act in 1566, prohibiting the middling tradesmen of the town – the retailers of luxury imports, such as grocers and mercers, and the manufacturers of goods for national and international markets, such as clothiers and soapmakers – from engaging in overseas commerce.[32] The retailers and craftsmen thus excluded from foreign trade determined to have the new statute quashed whenever the next parliament was convened. The result was a bitterly contested election for the 1571 Parliament, ultimately won by the anti-monopolists.[33] In Parliament, they succeeded in repealing the 1566 statute and ordering full restoration of 'the wonted liberty of the said citizens ... to traffic for merchandise beyond the Seas'.[34] But it left the original charters intact, 'to have their validity according to the laws'.[35]

By the end of the sixteenth century alternative concepts of the urban community thus had found particular expression in Bristol. The Merchant Venturers envisioned a society in which specialised economic functions were arranged in hierarchical order, with foreign commerce at the pinnacle. The retailers and manufacturing entrepreneurs saw all freemen of the city as members of the same undifferentiated legal and economic group, each possessed of equal rights to trade abroad. The struggle between these views, which previously had coexisted in the city's culture of community and authority, remained the recurring theme of local politics in the period that followed. The issues came to a head at the end of the 1630s when, with the aid of the Bristol Common Council, the Society acquired a new royal charter and drafted new by-laws restricting membership. Once again the Society enjoyed the secure legal position and effective monopoly it had achieved in 1566.[36] The results of this apparent victory were immediate. Within weeks of receiving the new charter in 1639, the Society's Court of Assistants was meeting to enforce its new powers on those who had been resisting the Merchant Venturers in its various capacities. On two days, twenty-nine individuals were summoned to the Merchants' Hall to pay fines and settle accounts. Twelve of them were not members of the Society at the time.[37] This new power in turn had an effect upon the size of the Society's membership, since it was now not only more difficult for non-members to engage in foreign commerce, but also more beneficial to be a member. Within three years, fifty-one overseas traders entered the fellowship, including five of the twelve men previously chastised for failing to pay their debts to the Society. During the twenty-one years between 1618 and acquisition of the new charter in 1639, only sixty-three members had been added to the Society.[38] As we shall see, this triumph soon became its own source of dissension in the city.

What made possible the Merchant Venturers' resurgence in the early seventeenth century and ultimate victory over their enemies in 1639 was the close association of their Society with the Bristol Corporation. This body was never intended to be a cross-section of civic society. It was rather an organisation of the community's social and economic leaders, chosen primarily because their personal fortunes could bear the costs of service. In consequence, the make-up of the Common Council tended to reflect the distribution of wealth in the city. In the sixteenth century, and probably for much of the fifteenth, the Common Council was dominated by men in trading occupations. Between 1500 and 1600, almost 80 percent were either overseas merchants or major retailers or soapmakers, but this proportion was on the increase – under 70 percent in the first fifty years, over 85 percent in the second. Among the grocers, drapers, mercers and vintners, morever, many had abandoned their retail shops to deal exclusively by wholesale as 'mere merchants'.[39] The pattern is much the same in the early seventeenth century. For the period from 1605 to 1642, over 80 percent of the Common Councillors came from the ranks of the city's leading entrepreneurs. Not surprisingly, the role of the Merchant Venturers was also very large.[40]

The exclusivity of Bristol's governing body was reinforced by close personal ties among its members, based on marriage alliances, neighbourhood associations and credit relationships. These ties in turn increased the possibilities for deep factional division within the council and between the dominant figures on it and their rivals in the city at large. The result was recurring political conflict within Bristol in which rival groups not only struggled for domination of the city's institutions but contested its traditions as well.[41]

When the Merchant Venturers succeeded in advancing their monopolistic claims in 1639, this same rivalry resurfaced, this time however in the heated climate of Long Parliament politics and civil war. The first signs came in 1640 in an unsuccessful attempt by some of the freemen to win the franchise in the October parliamentary elections, which renewed the efforts of 1571 and 1625 made in similar circumstances.[42] Further evidence of trouble appears in the fate of Aldermen Long and Hooke, prominent Merchant Venturers and Bristol's MPs in the Long Parliament. In 1642, both were ousted from their seats for participating along with many other Merchant Venturers in Alderman Abell's wine licence. In 1645 the Long Parliament removed them from the municipal office as delinquents.[43] Their replacements, elected in 1642 under the same franchise as Long and Hooke, also had similar histories. John Glanville, the City Recorder, and John Taylor, a Merchant Venturer and Alderman, shared the same conservative social, economic and political vision as Long and Hooke and the other leaders of the Merchant Venturers. Taylor went to Oxford when the king set up a Parliament there, and died in Bristol in 1645 defending the city against Fairfax and Cromwell. Glanville, who had been Speaker of the Commons in the Short Parliament, also joined the King in Oxford in 1643, was disabled from future service by the Long Parliament and was imprisoned for a time in the Tower before compounding for his delinquency. He was purged as Bristol's Recorder in 1646.[44]

Roger Howell has observed that a 'considerable volume' of seventeenth-century commentary on urban politics during the

Civil War views 'the King's cause' as 'favoured by the social extremes in the town[s], while Parliament and godly religion drew their support from the solid "middling" sort'.[45] John Corbet, minister in the city of Gloucester and ardent supporter of the Parliamentary cause in this period, is a case in point. According to him, Bristol at the outbreak of Civil War was 'much distracted' between the 'well-affected and malignant parties', with the 'basest and lowest sort' together with 'the wealthy and powerful men' supporting the 'King's Cause and Party', while 'the middle rank, the true and best Citizens', were on the Parliamentary side. '[T]he present state of things', he says, 'had taught men to distinguish between the true Commons of the realm and dregs of the people, the one the most vehement assertors of Public Liberty, but the other the first rise of Tyrannical Government and the foot-stool upon which Princes tread when they ascend the height of Monarchy'. The shortcomings of 'the needy multitude' he attributed not only to 'their natural hatred of good Order', but also to the fact that they 'were at the devotion of the rich men', whom, he tells us, were 'disaffected to reformed Religion' and 'conscious of delinquency' and therefore 'did much distaste the wares of the Parliament'. By implication he saw the virtue of the true Commons resulting from their support of 'good Order' in civic affairs, their independence from the patronage of the powerful, and their affection for 'reformed Religion'.[46] Howell has expressed considerable scepticism regarding this class-oriented interpretation.[47]

In offering this analysis, Corbet refers specifically to events in December 1642 when Bristol was garrisoned by Parliamentary forces under the command of Colonel Essex. Fearful that a garrison would make Bristol the target of attack from the king's forces, the city government, already committed to the Western Association in support of Parliament, sought to man the fortifications on its own. As Corbet tells the story, Essex found himself blocked 'by the multitude' at one of the gates and had to force his way into the city at a less well-manned place to which he received direction 'from a Party within'.[48] But Corbet may also have been thinking of the events of the following spring when a band of Bristolians, including the two sheriffs for the year, organised a plot to reverse these events by opening the city's gates to Prince Rupert. The attempt was thwarted when a considerable number of sailors and portside labourers along with many of the leading merchants were arrested by Colonel Nathaniel Fiennes and his soldiers. Although there were certainly men of 'the middling sort' in this conspiracy,[49] its leaders, including both Robert Yeamans and George Bowcher, who were executed for their complicity in the plot, came from that very same group of leading Merchant Venturers who long had supported its claims to monopoly.[50]

Many of these very men had also been behind the effort in the spring and autumn of 1642 to send petitions to both the king and Parliament urging an 'accommodation' of their differences. At first glance, this petition campaign appears to support the claim that a large number, if not most, Bristolians preferred a form of neutrality to partisan commitment in the Civil War.[51] But a closer look shows that even neutrality had its partisan edge. Only the city's petition to the king has survived.[52]

The petitioners put special emphasis on the disastrous toll on trade created by the outbreak of war. '[I]stead of the continual and gainful trade and commerce, which all maritime towns, in especial this City of *Bristol* had into foreign parts', they said

Our ships lie now rotting in the Harbour without any Mariners or freight or trade into foreign parts, by reason of our home-bred distractions, being grown so contemptible and despised there, that our credits are of no value, we being (through the misfortune of our nation) reputed abroad as men merely undone at home.

At the same time, the petitioners complained, citizens were 'enforced to their great and infinite expense, to maintain garrisons and courts of guards for their security'. In consequence, 'no man enjoys his wife, children, family or estate in safety this day ... so that unspeakable is our misery, unutterable our grievances, fathers being engaged enemies against sons; and sons against fathers'.[53]

But the Bristolians also had more general concerns. In keeping with many similar petitions for accommodation issued in this period, they lamented that the realm was now 'as full of horror and wrath as any object which can encounter human eyesight, appearing merely the Ghost of that *England* which it was so lately'. They protested that they were 'overwhelmed with an increasing perpetuity of cares and troubles, such as not time nor history has scarce mentioned in this Kingdom, neither in the Barons nor any other civil wars: Your Majesty being, as it were divorced from those husbands of the Common-wealth, the honourable the high Court of Parliament'. And they spoke bitterly of the 'strange and uncouth distractions that have lately broken forth into the Church of *England*'. They were especially pained by the 'too much power of the Prelacy in forcing new Canons and unheard of doctrines upon us'. They saw the bishops as 'the immediate and efficient causes of the many dissensions and troubles now reigning in the realm, no oppression being so forcible or oppressive to mens' consciences, as that which is intruded on them concerning their Belief and the worship of God'.[54] Hence they sought the restoration of peace between king and Parliament, with due recognition for the principle of hierarchy and the honour and authority of each.

The 1643 plot in Bristol to turn the city over to Prince Rupert similarly linked support for the Crown with the defence of liberty and church.[55] The plotters' motives were heavily coloured by the economic and financial burdens imposed upon the city by the war, the blame for which was placed by the conspirators squarely on the shoulders of the Parliamentary forces resident within their walls. As an anonymous pamphleteer said in commenting on the Royalist martyrdom of Yeamans and Bowcher, 'it is no wonder ... that a city thus robbed of its wealth and liberty, groaning under the insupportable yoke of bondage and tyranny should endeavour by restoring the king to his rights, to restore themselves to their former freedom', which could be done only by breaking the bonds and casting off the chords in which the Parliamentary garrison had ensnared them.[56] According to one source, the plotters considered themselves as standing for 'the King, the Protestant Religion, and the Liberties of this City'.[57] Yeamans said as much in his own defence. His commission from the King, he argued, was

for the maintenance of the true Protestant Religion established in the Church of *England*, the King's Prerogative and safety of his Person, Privileges of Parliament, and the liberty and propriety of the subject, and the defence of the City against all forces without the joint consent of the Mayor, Aldermen and Common Council amongst whom there was some difference at that time concerning the admission of any Forces.[58]

This identification of local liberties of self-rule with the more general liberties of the subject offers an insight into the inherent royalism of Yeamans' position. Serving as members of the Corporation meant to Yeamans, Bowcher and many of their colleagues on the Common Council being a royal officer, acting according to the city's charters for the mutual benefit of the urban community and the kingdom at large. Any action that threatened the political role of the Mayor, Aldermen and Common Council as the proper agents of royal authority in the city would be met with resistance, whether it came from the King's principal officers, as had been the case in the late 1620s and 1630s,[59] or from the Parliamentary army, as in 1642 and 1643. Since their own position in Bristol, and more generally in the English polity, depended in large measure upon their relationship to the Crown, preserving the 'liberties' of the city in the 1640s required restoring the king to his proper place at the head of the state.[60] In their religious beliefs, however, they were moderate Anglicans, earnest supporters of 'the religion of Protestants' to adopt Patrick Collinson's term, not advocates of Laudian reforms or of Arminianism.[61]

Most of the Bristol magistrates in the early days of the Civil War strongly desired social and political unity. They desired 'to be in love and amity one with another' and to form 'a friendly association together in all mutual accommodation', as they said in a Common Council motion in November 1642.[62] But these Bristolians were neutralists only in a tactical sense; their hierarchical vision of the social order, which made them desire peace within their community, also allied them with the King as the one force ultimately able to bring harmony and proportion to the body politic.

Despite its shortcomings, therefore, Corbet's analysis of the politics of Bristol in the early 1640s has much to commend it. Like the ancient writers from whom he derived his social categories, Corbet's understanding of the concept of class was never exclusively economic, but involved the intertwining of political power, personal honour, and private wealth. On this analysis, a person's political outlook was not simply the consequence of his social position, but an expression of his cultural identity. The Bristol evidence lends credence to this idea. Precisely because the possession of wealth typically carried with it the obligation of service and the capacity to command, the majority of Bristol's merchants conceived of themselves in the king's party when events forced them, sometimes against their wills, to decide where they stood. As magistrates and Merchant Venturers, they served as the Crown's lieutenants in the city, exercising power in his name, and they enjoyed privileges and franchises that could come only from princely benevolence. They lived according to a vision of public order that depended for its coherence on their connection with royal authority.

Corbet was also right in thinking that many of the most ardent supporters of the Parliamentary cause during the Civil Wars came from the ranks of the city's shopkeepers and craftsmen.[63] Given the links between the leading mere merchants and the Crown, it is hardly surprising that many men and women in these middling ranks were filled with zeal for significant changes in church and state. By the early 1640s, as we have seen, there was already a rich legacy of antagonism, sustained for almost a century, among the retailers and craftsmen of Bristol towards the Merchant Venturers. But many of these same figures also had a deep faith in the ideal of reciprocity in social and political life, according to which the better and the meaner sort, the rulers and the ruled, necessarily worked together for the common good. They looked to their city as a moral community of brothers, each justly and proportionally enjoying the benefits and bearing the burdens of membership in the commonweal. They opposed the Merchant Venturers not simply out of envy or pure class hatred, but because they saw them as the enemies of this ideal.

In the early modern period political ideology normally was never very far from religious outlook. Were there then religious dimensions to the socio-political factions we have been discussing? Did the rival groups ally themselves with different religious parties? If we are seeking evidence of the segregation of Bristolians into warring confessional camps, each committed not only to a unique social programme but to a corresponding sectarian vision, we must give a negative answer. In the later sixteenth and early seventeenth centuries, when controversy over the monopolistic pretensions of the Merchant Venturers frequently disrupted civic life, there seems to have been little religious factionalism within the city, especially in the Common Council, which was dominated by godly men of a moderate Calvinist outlook.[64] Even in the 1630s, when a Laudian party rose to influence among the civic elite, and the possibilities for a link between religious views and socio-economic outlooks grew commensurately greater, this potential for conflict seems to have been largely contained, at least within the membership of the city government, as we can see from the religious programme it followed. For example, the Common Council appointed Richard Standfast and Richard Towgood to city lectureships in the 1630s, men who appear to have been open, though not vituperative, critics of the Puritans among the city clergy; both were certainly ardent supporters of the royalist cause in the 1640s. At about the same time, however, they appointed Mathew Hazard as minister in St Philips, the advowson of which the city had acquired in 1627 along with those for six other parishes. As if to signal their desire for evenhandedness, the committee of aldermen and former sheriffs, appointed in 1636 as feoffees to oversee the management of these seven parishes, seems to have been chosen because its twenty-two members represented a cross-section of religious views among the civic elite.[65] The result was an avoidance of extremes in the selection of ministers, even in the case of someone as vocal as Hazard turned out to be.[66] Little in these facts suggests that differences over the Merchant Venturers' monopoly had become systematically conjoined in Bristol to differences over religious doctrine or policy.

However, if we think of the contribution of religion to ideology in broader cultural terms, our rather artificial distinction between religious and social thought begins to dissolve. For conservatives there was always a strong link between God-given skills and divinely ordained authority. According to Edgeworth, this connection was no less apparent in the priesthood than in any lay occupation. 'I have known many in this town,' he said, 'that studying divinity, hath killed a merchant, and some other occupations by their busy labours in the scriptures, hath shut up the shop windows, fain to take Sanctuary.' Christ had distributed his gifts 'as doth please his goodness ... to some more of them, to some fewer and not so many'. To some God had given 'knowledge and cunning in spiritual causes, to some in temporal matters, to some learning in physical, to some in surgery, to some in handicrafts, to some in merchandise or in such other occupying'.[67] Among each craft, moreover, there were those more fit to lead than others.

As if there should be a matter of the trade of merchandise to be entreated of among the merchants of this city, if there came in a merchant of grave and long experience, all the others would give ear and listen to his talk, and would be glad to follow his counsel ... Even so it is in matters of higher learning pertaining to our souls' health.[68]

Without the existence of such authority there would be nothing but disorder. Hence, on Edgeworth's interpretation, those in Bristol who believed in the priesthood of all believers were as wrong in their outlook as those who interloped on the trade of the Merchant Venturers.

In Edgeworth's theory of society, to have peace with one another required each man 'to do his office to his degree'.[69] A century later, Richard Standfast argued in the same vein, citing St Paul's first letter to the Thessalonians:

Let it be your ambition to be quiet; and how should this be done, but by doing your own business? Breach of ranks disorders an Army; and to be medling in things beyond our bounds disturbs the Peace. This was that bred such division among the People, and such confusion ... *they took too much upon them.*[70]

But this commonplace of early modern English social thought had deep political significance. Richard Towgood, preaching in 1643 against 'disloyalty of language' in Bristol, took the same text of St Paul to make his point:

Let us study to be Quiet and do our own Business, namely those Duties that do *concern our selves*; Let us not be Eagle-eyed abroad, especially above us, and not discern what faults are great at home; Let no evil words against Sovereign Authority upon any either suspected or known error drop from thee, seeing by that very act thou doest attract upon thy Soul that very thing which so eagerly thou reprehendest, even the guilt of no light Transgression; *for to speak bitterly and reproachfully of supreme authority is a very unwarrantable and unlawful thing.*[71]

On this theory, only those with duly granted magisterial authority had the God-given right to exercise governing power in the realm; they enjoyed a monopoly, as it were.

Those in Bristol and elsewhere who opposed this line of argument did so by stressing the freedoms held by christians in God's commonwealth and the obligations these freedoms entailed. For them, freedom meant the ability to respond to God's will, for the good of all, without 'Favour to any person, Fear to displease great ones, Rancour or malice, Love of money', or hindrance from any group or individual. It was the freedom to choose 'God's choice', to have our 'love oversway'd by His'.[72] Samuel Kem, who briefly succeeded to Standfast's city lectureship after the victory of the Parliamentary army at Bristol in 1645, argued in a sermon at the time of the so-called Recruiter elections to Parliament in 1646 that 'prosperity' came to a city only 'when righteous men have freedom of goods, of mind, body and providence'. The 'Goods of Providence', he said, are 'wealth, worth of Birth, reputation and credit, friends'; and of the body, 'health, strength, grace of person'. But the 'goods of the mind to complete this Prosperity are Wisdom to judge, Will to choose what we have judged, Power to prosecute what we have chosen, Ability to order'. The achievement of these benefits depended first on 'self denial and meekness', since a 'man that loves self cannot love God, nor Christ nor Nation, nor Neighbours: It is a self denying man [that] is for Jesus Christ and his people'.[73]

Self-denial, in Kem's terms, referred to the outlook of men who had done away 'with all private interests' and devoted themselves 'for the public and righteous cause'. They were men free of jealousies and darkness, in 'fellowship one with another', always eyeing 'God's choice'. Once they had found such 'a new Charter' among themselves, 'complete with Privileges, new Habitations, new company, all friends', 'a new Society' would emerge in their midst, 'and with their Society new Language, new walking, new Trading, new Blessings, new Providences, new Experiences, even such Blessings of God as make [men] rich'. Because righteous choices 'must relate eminently to God's choice', Kem argued, human beings must forego all personal advantage and act only for the common good.[74] They must be free, therefore, of the burdens of monopoly in all its forms, as William Adams had learned from Richard Bernard. As we know, anti-monopolists in Bristol and elsewhere had been arguing much the same since Elizabeth I's day.[75]

These religious and ideological differences lurked beneath the surface of civic controversy in Bristol throughout the later sixteenth and early seventeenth centuries. By the 1620s and 1630s the city's socio-political factions had taken on some characteristics of this rivalry. We can see it surface, perhaps, in the contested election for mayor in 1626. Robert Aldworth and some of his supporters favoured the Laudian party in the church as well as the social conservatism implicit in the Merchant Venturers' monopolistic claims. Aldworth himself was a distant kinsman of Archbishop Laud.[76] In the 1630s, he and some of his allies favoured church beautification and church music in their wills.[77] Unfortunately we know nothing directly about Christopher Whitson's religious views, although the use of the word 'punctual' to describe him may hint that his enemies viewed him as a Puritan, overly precise in his morality and public observances.[78] It is also possible that his cousin and apparent patron, John Whitson, was favourably disposed to Puritan views, at least at the end of his life. The moral and religious reflections he left behind and his charitable bequests conform nicely in thought and action to many teachings of Puritan divines.[79]

Rather more is known about Christopher Whitson's brother-in-law, Matthew Warren, who when he stood for election as mayor in 1633 was also opposed by Robert Aldworth. Warren had a rich anti-monopoly heritage behind him. As a young man in Queen Elizabeth I's reign, he served his apprenticeship with William Tucker, clothier, who as mayor in 1571 had led the fight against the Merchant Venturers' monopoly.[80] Warren's wife was almost certainly active in Rev William Yeamans' circle of the godly in St Philip's parish. Like Dorothy Hazard and others from this group, she became a sectary after 1640 and later was among early members of the Quakers in Bristol. Warren was also closely connected to George Bishop, one of Bristol's leading sectaries of the 1640s and 1650s.[81] The members of Yeamans' group were primarily small shopkeepers and craftsmen, just those most likely to see injustice in the Merchant Venturers' monopolistic pretensions. But since they were not Common Councillors, their role in disputed municipal elections was at most indirect.[82] Although we have no evidence of Warren's own involvement in Yeamans' meetings, we can see that in his relations with his family and with the city's craftsmen in the cloth industry he lived in intimacy with some of its most faithful attenders. As a vestryman in St James parish in the mid-1620s, he was active in acquiring the right of advowson for the parish; in 1627 he had played a similar role on behalf of the city itself in purchasing the advowsons of all seven parishes which had been appurtenances of St James priory in the city.[83] St James's parish, like the neighbouring St Philips, was a significant home for religious dissension and sectarian sentiment in seventeenth-century Bristol.[84]

The careers of several leading supporters of the Long Parliament in Bristol also illustrate the connection between religious and political radicalism and opposition to the Merchant Venturers' monopoly. One of them is Richard Vickris, who was one of

William Adams's closest friends in the 1630s.[85] Vickris served on the Commission appointed by the Long Parliament in 1645 to purge Bristol's government of 'delinquents' after Prince Rupert had been ousted from the city and to settle affairs in the interests of the Parliamentary side. He became the city's mayor in 1646 in the aftermath of this purge. Although trained as a fishmonger, he joined the Society of Merchant Venturers in the 1630s. Nevertheless in 1638–39 we find him openly resisting its authority to collect payments owed to it.[86] During the 1630s he also traded regularly in partnership with non-merchants in violation of the Society's strict ordinances forbidding this practice. So had another ardent Parliamentary supporter, Richard Aldworth, cousin to Robert. Although a member of the Merchant Venturers, he had been trained as a mercer, maintained a shop in Bristol's High Street in partnership with the mercer John Young, and kept up close ties with other retail mercers throughout the 1620s and 30s. Aldworth was one of the Recruiter members of the Long Parliament added in 1646. In the religious politics of the 1640s, he was probably a Presbyterian. Like Vickris, and perhaps John Whitson before him, he seems to have viewed the Merchant Venturers as a useful institution for commercial regulation but not as an exclusive organisation for promoting the interests of only a few. The other Recruiter member for Bristol was Luke Hodges, a grocer and sometime partner of Vickris, though never himself a member of the Merchant Venturers. In 1635, he had fallen foul of the Bristol Corporation and was threatened with a heavy fine when he resisted election to the Common Council. He was probably an Independent in his political and religious affiliations in the 1640s. While neither Aldworth nor Hodges was an extreme radical, both were politically committed members of the Long Parliament who conformed themselves to the revolution as it unfolded in the late 1640s and early 1650s. Hodges eventually became an Excise Commissioner for the Commonwealth in 1652.[87] The experience of opposing the Merchant Venturers' monopolistic claims and practices in the 1630s helped shape the outlooks of these three men and accounts in part for their alignment with Parliament in the 1640s.

The history of the Society's relations with its opponents after the Parliamentary army's victory in 1645 also reveals how much Bristol's politics in the mid-seventeenth century turned on attitudes towards the Merchant Venturers' monopoly. The purge of the

Common Council in that year removed ten men for their military service in the Royalist cause and for other forms of 'delinquency'. Eight of them were Merchant Venturers, drawn from that very same group of Spanish and Mediterranean traders who in the 1630s had looked to Robert Aldworth for leadership. In the years from 1645 to 1650, eighteen men were either restored to or newly elected to the Common Council. Only eight were Merchant Venturers. One of these members of the Society was Richard Vickris, who had been ousted from his Council post by the Royalists in 1643. A second was his son Robert, who was probably an early sectary in his own right and who later married the daughter of George Bishop, one of the city's leading radicals and a founding member of the Society of Friends in Bristol.[88] Two more were among the large throng of interlopers who joined the Merchant Venturers after the crackdown on illicit trade that followed the grant of new letters patent in 1639. A further two became members only after 1645 when the Society markedly relaxed its old standards of admission.[89] In other words, there was not only a significant drop in the proportion of Merchant Venturers added to the Council, from about 75 percent in the 1620s and 30s to about 45 percent in this period, but even among the Merchant Venturers on the Council there was no longer the same support for the old monopolistic policies and practices.

What the victorious party desired in Bristol was an end to the monopoly of the Merchant Venturers. They did not resist the idea of regulation in economy and society; far from it. A godly city was an orderly city, and for most of them the maintenance of order demanded strong government lest civil peace and social harmony be undermined by the depraved self-wills of the sinful. But they wanted all the city's occupations to be on an equal footing in the enjoyment of the city's privileges and immunities. They envisioned Bristol as a harmonious community of separate but interrelated parts each serving the larger good, a place where every head of household was able to pursue his duties to himself, his family and the commonwealth as his conscience dictated. Hence they did not wish to crush the Merchant Venturers outright, only to assure that membership in their Society would be open to all those who wished to submit themselves to its discipline, and that others would nonetheless be free to conduct overseas trade if they chose.[90] Although this programme had many shortcomings as an economic policy, it united a wide group of Bristolians in political opposition to the great merchants. Many of these same anti-. monopolists had religious outlooks that emphasised their individual relationship to God and the religious and ethical obligations that arose from their callings.

Only in the 1650s was this coalition permanently fractured as the centripetal forces inherent in what Collinson has called 'voluntary religion' became manifest.[91] But even in that over-heated climate of dissension, the deep ideological and cultural rivalry of the monopolists and their opponents is apparent enough. The year 1654 brought many of these issues of economics, politics and religion to a head. According to James Powell, Bristol's Chamberlain at the time, there were two causes for the 'distempers' of that year: the dispute over the parliamentary election and 'the coming of the Quakers'. The election, he said, 'bred an extreme feud' between the magistracy and the two defeated candidates, Colonel Haggatt and his cousin, Captain George Bishop. These men looked upon their opponents as Cavaliers; they accused Alderman Miles Jackson, one of the newly elected MPs, of royalism, made similar charges against those electors who voted for Jackson, and accused the Sheriffs and their fellow Common Councillors of complicity in a plot to defeat 'the godly party' in the town. Afterwards, Powell continues, 'they waited occasions to blast the city by all possible means'.[92]

Although Powell does not tie the arrival of the Quakers explicitly to the election, in truth they were closely connected. The Quakers first came to Bristol in the spring of 1654; by June they already had won some important converts. Moreover, John Audland and John Camm made one of their initial visits to the city at the time of the poll itself, although for what reason we cannot tell. Many of their early converts appear as parties to the election squabble. George Bishop soon became one of Bristol's most out-spoken Quakers, his tireless pen turning out pamphlet after pamphlet for the cause from 1655. Haggatt never went so far, but his family allied him with many of Bristol's first Friends, his wife among them. Their supporters too appear connected to the Quaker movement. A third of them became Friends in the first waves of conversions following the visits of Audland, Camm and other first publishers of Truth.[93] In Powell's view the 'frantic doctrines' of these Quakers had not only 'made ... an impression on the minds of the people of this city' but also had 'made such a rent in all societies and relations which, with the public affront offered to ministers and magistrates, hath caused a division, I may say a mere antipathy amongst the people, and consequently many broils'.[94]

As a result, these events ushered in a period of nearly unprecedented dissension within the city. Haggatt and Bishop, using their allies among the Bristol garrison, mounted a concerted attack on the loyalty of the Bristol Common Council. A broad body of their supporters petitioned the Lord Protector to quash the election results, and George Bishop filed informations accusing the magistrates of complicity in Royalist plots. By the end of 1654, the effects of the Quaker conversions had become all too apparent to the civic authorities. Individual Quakers began disrupting religious services in the city's churches and resisting the authority of the Aldermen to punish them for their breaches of the peace. At the same time large public meetings were held, some recording over one thousand participants. As the movement grew, fear of Quakerism also grew in many quarters. Riots ensued in which bands of apprentices assaulted Quakers on the streets and threatened their public meetings. Moreover, George Cowlishay confirmed the worst suspicions of many Bristolians by spreading a rumour that he had picked up from an Irishman. The Quakers, he charged, really were Franciscan and Jesuit subversives, in England to undermine Protestantism. Many Baptists, their ranks severely depleted by losses to the Quakers, accepted the story as Gospel.[95]

These developments certainly did not grow only from seeds planted by economic divisions within the city. The election and its aftermath hardly reveal a clear-cut conflict between the mere merchants and their rivals. Differing views on the constitution and on religious settlement lay at the bottom of the troubles. Nevertheless, the two political factions do show some interesting socio-economic differences. Although many of Aldworth's and Jackson's supporters had interests in trade, just like Haggatt's supporters, the latter consisted much more heavily than the former of men in the lesser crafts and in the shipping industry. Only seven of Haggatt's votes came from merchants, and only five in total from Merchant Venturers. Although both factions in the election found considerable support among soapmakers, grocers and other major retailers and entrepreneurs, a higher percentage of Aldworth and Jackson's votes came from this quarter. In addition, twenty-six of their backers were merchants and the same number of Merchant Venturers, most of them older members of the Society.[96] Jackson himself had been a member since at least 1618, and Aldworth, a lawyer by profession, was the son of a Merchant Venturer of the 1620s and 1630s.[97] The impression is strong, therefore, that Aldworth and Jackson's supporters on the whole came from the richer segments of Bristol's population and were closely tied to the Merchant Venturers.

These supporters of monopoly had not only experienced a significant decline in their ability to control the economy through their Society, but they had also lost effective control of trade in two vitally important luxury items, tobacco and sugar. Where previously the problem of interloping had been contained by the need for established financial and commercial ties in specialised markets, the rapid rise of colonial enterprise in the 1640s and 50s had provided new openings for small shopkeepers and artisans to enter into overseas commerce. In the early 1650s, hundreds of townsmen, some of them not even sworn burgesses of the city, engaged freely in dealings with the Chesapeake region and the West Indies, shipping small wares and indentured servants in return for the tobacco and sugar their overseas customers produced. A number of these figures had a history of political support for Parliament and the New Model Army; many too were members of the sects.[98]

It would be a mistake to think that all those who sided with the Parliament in the Civil War or with the sectaries in the 1650s did so because of their grievances against the mere merchants or that those who supported the King or the Protectorate were all favourably disposed to monopoly. Most Bristolians acted from deeply-held religious and ideological convictions, not narrow self-interest. But those convictions had taken shape in the context of long-standing rivalry between the Merchant Venturers and their opponents. Among the supporters of monopoly, there was a profound sense that only the due exercise of skill and authority in public and private life could guarantee the obedience and deference deemed essential to the preservation of order. The opposition of the anti-monopolists was grounded as much on their deeply held beliefs about the demands of conscience on them as Christians and the requirements of justice owed them as freemen of Bristol as on the actual damage monopoly had caused to their social prospects and material welfare. These views in turn helped define what it meant for them to live in a properly ordered and godly community.

The power of religion to promote rebellion has always been great. As Richard Towgood said, 'the conceit of ... religion' can easily draw a person into 'transgression', for 'pride and self-conceit' – 'the principal actors in sedition and Rebellion' – are often mistaken for true piety.[99] Religion could also advance the spirit of crusade in which the godly, using their God-given 'zeal and courage', struggled against sinfulness in the world. 'This was Christ's own mark' according to Samuel Kem, 'though the priests [were] in authority, and multitudes of their associates; yet ... [Christ's] zeal feared not their power, nor started at any opposition'.[100] But just who were God's saints? Religious claims sometimes masked hypocrisy and self-interest, as Richard Standfast made clear. '[T]is no great matter to *seem* Religious', he said,

... but to *be* religious, that's a matter both of difficulty and consequence, and hereunto there is more required than a form of Godliness. If the *outward performance* of religious duties were enough to make a man a sincere Christian, it were an easy matter to be religious ... [T]herein the *grossest Hypocrite* may go as far as the *devoutest Saint*. But this we know, that if the heart be not sound, and perfect towards God; all outward performances, are but *bodily exercise*, and that profits not.[101]

Hence he urged his listeners 'to labour also for the power of godliness'. Following this advice, however, meant bringing body and soul in conformity with God's will, which did not necessarily guarantee the preservation of the existing social and political order. It could just as easily move the professors of piety from resistance to what they deemed the illegimate demands of false authority to the affirmation of a new way of life in which it would be possible to live as God demanded.[102]

Religion could change the outlooks and consciences of believers, and thereby challenge, alter, and even overturn the existing order of things. Considered in this light, the events of the 1640s and 50s appear as a confrontation of forces, each struggling to bring institutions and practices into conformity with its most deeply-felt ideas and beliefs. Instead of being focused, as in the case of a rebellion, primarily on gaining control of political institutions, or being centred, as in the case of a crusade, mainly on advancing a theology and ecclesiastical regime, they amount to a contest to determine the character of authority and community in the nation. As is shown by the recurring battles over monopoly in sixteenth- and seventeenth-century Bristol, there was much confusion, considerable debate, and no firm consensus about these difficult issues. The resulting clashes were rooted in the language and ideas of Protestant dialectic as well as in legal, political and constitutional discourse. They depended from the start on differing understandings of obedience and calling and differing senses of justice and personal identity. In a way, therefore, they made the struggles over monopoly 'wars of religion' of their own.

Notes

1 C. Russell, *The Causes of the English Civil War*, Oxford, 1990, p. 2.
2 J. Morrill, 'The religious context of the English Civil War', *Transactions of the Royal Historical Society* [*TRHS*], 5th series, 34, 1984, pp. 157, 178; see also J. Morrill, 'Rhetoric and action: Charles I, tyranny, and the English Revolution', in G. Schochet, (ed.), *Religion, Resistance, and Civil War*, Washington, DC, 1990, pp. 91 – 113. Recently Russell has offered related, though somewhat more complex, accounts: see Russell, *Causes*, pp. 20 – 2, 58 – 82, 83 – 130, 210, 216 – 17, 220 – 6; Russell, *The Fall of the British Monarchies, 1637 – 1642*, Oxford, 1991, pp. 14 – 26, 526 – 32; Russell, *Unrevolutionary England, 1603 – 1642*, London, 1990, pp. xxi – xxvi.
3 Morrill, 'Religious context', p. 178; see also pp. 157, 168, 170, 174, 175; see also Russell, *Causes*, pp. 6 – 8; Russell, *Unrevolutionary England*, pp. ix – xxx.
4 L. Stone, *The Causes of the English Revolution, 1529 – 1642*, London, 1972, pp. ix, xii, 48, 57, 79, 98.
5 C. Geertz, 'Religion as a cultural system', in C. Geertz, *The Interpretation of Cultures: Selected Essays* , New York, 1973, pp. 89 – 90; see also P. Bourdieu, *Outline of a Theory of Practice*, trans. R. Nice, Cambridge, 1977, pp. 164 – 8.
6 See Bourdieu, *Outline*, pp. 168 – 71.
7 D. H. Sacks, *The Widening Gate: Bristol and the Atlantic Economy*, Berkeley and Los Angeles, 1991, pp. 353 – 5; see also D. H. Sacks, *Trade, Society and Politics in Bristol, 1500 – 1640*, 2 vols., New York, 1985, I, pp. 204ff.
8 See S. Seyer, *Memoirs Historical and Topographical of Bristol and its Neighbourhood, From The Earliest Period Down To The Present Time*, 2 vols., Bristol, 1821 – 23, II, pp. 401ff.; J. Latimer, *The Annals of Bristol in the Seventeenth Century*, Bristol, 1900, pp. 177 – 84, 196 – 205; C. V. Wedgwood, *The King's War, 1641 – 1647*, New York, 1959, pp. 232 – 6, 484 – 8.
9 Russell, *Causes*, p. 11.
10 Bristol Record Office [hereafter BRO] MSS, *Addames Chronicle*, unpaginated, entry for 1638 – 39; William Adams, *Adams' Chronicle of Bristol*, ed. F. F. Fox, Bristol, 1910, pp. 261 – 2. Two different version of *Adams' Chronicle* survive.

One, which Adams began in 1623, was used by Fox in his edition. The other, started in 1625, contains entries for the years 1640–45 not available in the Fox edition, and in a few instances is somewhat fuller in the materials offered for earlier years.

11 BRO MSS, *Addames Chronicle*, entry for 1639–40.

12 *Ibid.*, entry for 1641–42.

13 J. F. Larkin (ed.), *Royal Proclamations of Charles I, 1625–1646*, Oxford, 1983, pp. 704 and 704n. Charles refers explicitly to *Information from the Estaits of the kingdome of Scotland to the kingdome of England* (n.p., 1640). But by the late 1630s there were a large number of Scottish writings circulating in England, many of them explictly attacking the tyranny of the English bishops; see P. Donald, 'The Scottish National Covenant and British politics, 1638–1640', in J. Morrill (ed.), *The Scottish National Covenant in its British Context, 1638–51*, Edinburgh, 1990, pp. 97–8.

14 PRO, SP 16/467/147; see also Russell, *Fall*, pp. 163–4. It may be that Hazard knew the Scottish counter-propaganda, even if Adams did not; compare Hazard's prayer to *Information from the Estaits*, p. 12.

15 [Richard Bernard], *A Short View of the Praelatical Church of England*, London, 1641.

16 Ezekiel 34:3, 4, 10, as cited in [Bernard], *Short View*, title page; for Bernard's biography see 'Richard Bernard', *DNB*.

17 *Ibid.*, pp. 5–12, 15, 26–7, 34–40. Adams picks up explicitly this theme in his *Chronicle* entry for 1641–42. There he praises the Scots for demanding the suppression of 'the superstition and unjust proceedings of the foresaid bishops, and the swormy droves of their adherents and dependents, which so long time by usurping authority had blinded mens eyes, and hindered Parliament meetings', BRO MSS, *Addames Chronicle*, entry for 1641–42.

18 [Bernard], *Short View*, p. 34.

19 *Ibid.*, pp. 1, 3–4; cf. BRO MSS, *Addames Chronicle*, entry for 1640–41.

20 Adams, *Adams' Chronicle*, ed. Fox, p. 98; see also pp. 102, 105–6, 176–8.

21 BRO MSS, *Addames Chronicle*, entry 1640–41.

22 *Ibid.*, Introduction; see also Adams, *Adams' Chronicle*, ed. Fox, pp. 227–8.

23 BRO MSS, *Addames Chronicle*, Introduction.

24 1 Kings 4:25.

25 See for example John Donne, 'Sermon preached at Denmark House, April 26th, 1625', in J. Donne, *The Sermons of John Donne*, eds. E. Simpson and G. Potter, Berkeley, 1953, pp. 290 ff.; S. Orgel, *The Ilusion of Power: Political Theater in the English Renaissance*, Berkeley, 1975, p. 73; G. Parry, *The Golden Age Restor'd: The Culture of the Stuart Court, 1603–42*, Manchester, 1981, pp. 21, 22, 24, 26, 29–30, 35, 59–60, 240, 248.

26 BRO MSS, *Addames Chronicle*, Introduction.

27 For early instances of the rhetoric of complaint against monopoly, see the debates against monopoly in 1601 in Heyward Townshend, *Historical Collections; or, an Exact Account of the Proceedings of the four last Parliaments of Q. Elizabeth of famous memory*, London, 1680, pp. 224 ff. and in Simonds D'Ewes, *The Journals Of All Parliaments During the Reign of Queen Elizabeth*, London, 1682, pp. 644 ff. These arguments are given additional authority in the reports of *Darcy v. Allen* in 11 Co. Rep. 84b–88b in *English Reports*, vol. 77, pp. 1260–6; Noy, 173–85 in *English Reports*, vol. 74, pp. 1131–41; Moore, 671–75 in *English Reports*, vol. 72, pp. 830–2; PRO, SP 12/286/47; British Library, Add. MSS 25, 203 ff. 543v and ff.; see also Edward Coke, *The Second part of the Institutes*

of the lawes of England, London, 1642, pp. 46–7; Edward Coke, *The Third Part of the Institutes of the Laws of England*, London, 1644, pp. 181–2. For discussion see D. H. Sacks, 'Parliament, Liberty, and Elizabeth I to the Civil Wars', in J. H. Hexter (ed.), *Parliament and Liberty from Elizabeth I to the Civil Wars*, Stanford, 1991, pp. 85–121; D. Sacks, 'Private profit and public good: The problem of the state in Elizabethan theory and practice', in G. Schochet (ed.), *Law, Literature, and the Settlement of Regimes*, Washington, DC, 1990, pp. 121–42.

28 The following account is based on Sacks, *Trade, Society and Politics*, II, Chs. 12–13; Sacks, *Widening Gate*, Chs. 3, 7–8.

29 Roger Edgeworth, *Sermons very fruitfull godly and learned*, London, 1557, f. 43v. For an effort in 1500 to impose this view as policy in Bristol, see J. Latimer, *The History of the Society of Merchant Venturers of the City of Bristol; With Some Account of the Anterior Merchants' Guilds*, Bristol, 1903, pp. 26–35.

30 Latimer, *Merchant Venturers*, p. 96.

31 Sacks, *Trade, Society and Politics*, II, pp. 550–7; Sacks, *Widening Gate*, pp. 73–6.

32 Latimer, *Merchant Venturers*, pp. 47–50.

33 Seyer, *Memoirs*, II, p. 243; J. Evans, *A Chronological Outline of the History of Bristol*, Bristol, 1824, p. 149; see also Adams, *Adams' Chronicle*, ed. Fox, p. 112.

34 Stat. 13 Eliz. I, c. 14, printed in Latimer, *Merchant Venturers*, p. 57.

35 T. E. Hartley (ed.), *Proceedings in the Parliaments of Elizabeth I: 1558–1581*, Leicester, 1981, p. 211.

36 For discussion see Sacks, *Widening Gate*, Ch. 6.

37 Society of Merchant Venturers of Bristol [hereafter SMV] MSS, *Hall Book*, I, p. 2.

38 McGrath (ed.), *Records*, pp. 29, 261.

39 See Sacks, *Widening Gate*, pp. 162–5; Sacks, *Trade, Society and Politics*, II, pp. 694–8; D. H. Sacks, 'The demise of the martyrs: The feasts of St Katherine and St Clement in Bristol, 1400–1600', *Social History*, 11, 1986, pp. 156–65; D. H. Sacks, 'Celebrating authority in Bristol, 1475–1641', in S. Zimmerman and R. F. E. Weisman (eds.), *Urban Life in the Renaissance*, Newark, Del., 1989, pp. 202–4.

40 Sacks, *Widening Gate*, pp. 164–8; Sacks, *Trade, Society and Politics*, pp. 699–706; D. H. Sacks, 'The corporate town and the English state: Bristol's "Little Businesses" 1625–1641', *Past and Present*, 110, 1986, pp. 87–91.

41 Sacks, *Widening Gate*, pp. 167–70; Sacks, *Trade, Society and Politics*, II, pp. 706–8.

42 BRO MSS, *Common Council Proceedings*, III, f. 198r; Sacks, 'Corporate town', pp. 104–5.

43 M. F. Keeler, *The Long Parliament, 1640–1641; A Biographical Study of its Members*, Philadelphia, 1954, pp. 220–1, 255–6; *CJ*, II, pp. 415, 567; C. H. Firth and R. S. Rait (eds.), *Acts and Ordinances of the Interregnum, 1642–1660*, 3 vols., London, 1911, I, pp. 797–8.

44 Latimer, *Annals*, pp. 157, 158, 181, 189, 205, 210, 214; 'Sir John Glanville, the younger', *DNB*.

45 R. Howell, 'Neutralism, conservatism and political alignment in the English Revolution: The case of the towns, 1642–9', in J. Morrill (ed.), *Reactions to the English Civil War, 1642–1649*, London, 1982, p. 76; see also Howell, 'The structure of urban politics in the English Civil War', *Albion*, XI, 1979, pp. 114–15.

46 John Corbet, *An Historical Relation of the Military Government of Gloucester*, London, 1645, p. 14.

47 Howell, 'Structure of urban politics', pp. 114–21; Howell, 'Neutralism', pp. 75–7.
48 *Ibid.*, p. 14; see also Latimer, *Annals*, pp. 164–5; Howell, 'Structure of urban politics', p. 118.
49 This point has been emphasised by Howell, 'Structure of urban politics', p. 115; see also Howell, 'Neutralism', p. 76.
50 Bodleian Library, Portland MSS, *Nalson Papers*, N. XIII, 151, 155–71, 190.
51 See Howell, 'Structure of urban politics', p. 118; see also Howell, 'Neutralism', p. 72.
52 *The Humble Petition of the Citie of Bristoll, for An Accommodation of Peace between His Majestie, and the Honourable the High Court of Parliament*, Oxford, 1643.
53 *Humble Petition*, pp. 4–5.
54 *Ibid.*, pp. 4–5. For the history of related petition campaigns in this period see A. Fletcher, *The Outbreak of the English Civil War*, London, 1981, pp. 192, 264–82. The Bristol petition is most closely connected to the London petition of October, 1642, *The Petition of the Most Substantiall Inhabitants of the Citie of London*, Oxford, 1642; see also Sacks, *Widening Gate*, pp. 239–40.
55 For a somewhat different interpretation of this material see Howell, 'Structure of urban politics', p. 119; more generally see Howell, 'Neutralism', pp. 67–87.
56 *Two State Martyrs* in Seyer, *Memoirs*, II, p. 373.
57 J. Toombes, *Jehovah Jirah, or Gods Providence in Delivering the Godly*, London, 1643, sig. A4b.
58 Clement Walker, *The Severall Examinations and Confessions of the Treacherous Conspirators against the Citie of Bristol*, London, 1643, p. 12; see also Bodleian Library, Portland MSS, *Nalson Papers*, N. XIII, 151, 155–71, 190, 210.
59 See Sacks, 'Corporate town', pp. 76–105.
60 *Two State Martyrs* in Seyer, *Memoirs*, II, p. 373.
61 P. Collinson, *The Religion of Protestants*, Oxford, 1982.
62 BRO MSS, *Common Council Proceedings*, IV, pp. 5, 6; see Howell, 'Structure of urban politics', p. 118; Howell, 'Neutralism', p. 76.
63 See, for example, William Prynne and Clement Walker, *A True and Full Relation of the Prosecution, Arraignment, Tryall, and Condemnation of Nathaniel Fiennes*, London, 1643, pp. 16, 179, 42, 44 and the appended *Catalogue of Witnesses*, pp. 21, 27, 28, 32, 33; R. Hayden (ed.), *The Records of a Church of Christ in Bristol, 1640–1687*, Bristol Record Society, XXVII, 1974, pp. 17–19.
64 Sacks, *Widening Gate*, pp. 183–5, 190–2, 235–7.
65 See BRO MSS 01075(1) (1627); BRO MSS, 01075(2), (1636); Latimer, *Annals*, pp. 95–6.
66 On Hazard see Hayden (ed.), *Records*, pp. 293–94, see also pp. 13, 18, 85, 87, 88, 90, 93. On Standfast see Richard Standfast, *A Little Handful of Cordial Comforts*, London, 1639; Richard Standfast, *Clero-laicum Condimentum*, Bristol, 1644; on Towgood see Richard Towgood, *Disloyalty of Language Questioned and Censured*, Bristol, 1643 [1644]; 'Richard Towgood', *DNB*. Standfast was the grandson of William Adams, BRO MSS, 09467(13)a (1638); BRO MSS, *Addames Chronicle*, entry for 1635–36.
67 Edgeworth, *Sermons*, ff. 43v–44r, 266r.
68 *Ibid.*, f. 279v.
69 *Ibid.*, f. 265v.
70 Standfast, *Clero-laicum Condimentum*, p. 30.
71 Towgood, *Disloyalty of Language*, pp. 57–8.

72 Samuel Kem, *The King of Kings His Private Marks For The Kingdoms choyce of new Members*, London, 1646, pp. 5, 9.

73 *Ibid.*, pp. 3, 14, 15; for Kem's career see 'Samuel Kem', *DNB*.

74 Kem, *King of Kings*, pp. 9, 10, 14–15, 22, 27, 36.

75 See n. 27 above.

76 See W. Laud, *The Works of the Most Reverent Father in God, William Laud, D.D.*, ed. W. Scott and J. Bliss, 7 vols. in 9, Oxford, 1847–60, VII, p. 31; E. E. Salisbury, *Family Memorials: A Series of Genealogical and Biographical Monographs on the Families of Salisbury, Aldworth-Elbridge, Sewall, Pyldren-Dummer, Walley, Quincy, Wendell, Breese, Chevalier-Anderson and Phillips*, 1 vol. in 2, New Haven, 1885, I, pt. 1, pp. 103–21 and 'Pedigree of Aldworth-Elbridge', facing p. 142.

77 See, for example, 'Will of Alderman Robert Aldworth', BRO MSS, *Great Orphan Book*, II, ff. 16r–17r; 'Will of Alderman Henry Yate', *ibid.*, II, ff. 21r–24r. Aldworth's own funeral monument is itself an example of the high baroque style favoured by many of the followers of Laud in this period; for a photograph see J. W. Damer Powell, *Bristol Privateers and Ships of War*, Bristol, 1930, facing p. 72.

78 PRO, SP 16/41/80; C. Hill, *Society and Puritanism in Pre-Revolutionary England*, London, 1964, pp. 13–29.

79 See J. Whitson, *The Aged Christians Final Farewell to the World and its Vanities*, Bristol, 1729; 'Will of John Whitson', BRO MSS, *Great Orphan Book*, II, ff. 244v–250v; W. K. Jordan, *The Forming of the Charitable Institutions of the West of England: A Study of the Changing Pattern of Social Aspirations in Bristol and Somerset, 1489–1660*, American Philosophical Society, Transactions, new series, I, pt. 8, 1960, pp. 23–4, 30, 33, 38, 39. But see also J. Aubrey, *Brief Lives*, ed. O. L. Dick, Harmondsworth, 1974, pp. 366–7; P. McGrath, *John Whitson and the Merchant Community of Bristol*, Historical Association, Bristol Branch, Pamphlet no. 25, 1970, pp. 1–22.

80 BRO MSS, *Common Council Proceedings*, III, ff. 44–5; 'Will of William Tucker', in T. P. Wadley (ed.), *Notes or Abstracts of the Wills Contained in the Volume Entitled the Great Orphan Book and Book of Wills in the Council House at Bristol*, Bristol, 1886, pp. 245–6; 'Will of Christopher Whitson', BRO MSS, *Great Orphan Book*, II, ff. 100v–103v.

81 'Will of William Yeamans, gent.', PRO, PROB 6/17 Essex; 'Will of Mathew Warren', *BRO MSS, Great Orphan Book*, II, ff. 36v–39v; George Bishop, *A Relation of the Inhumane and Barbarous Sufferings of the People Called Quakers in the City of Bristol during the Mayoralty of John Knight commonly called Sir John Knight*, London, 1665, p. 75; see also R. Mortimer (ed.), *Minute Book of the Men's Meeting of the Society of Friends in Bristol, 1667–1686*, Bristol Record Society, 1970, XXVI, p. 220.

82 For the early history of the group, see Hayden (ed.), *Records*, pp. 13, 17, 19, 84, 88.

83 BRO MSS, 01075(1) (1627).

84 On the socio-cultural history of this district see Sacks, *Widening Gate*, pp. 146–52, 356–7; see also Hayden (ed.), *Records*, pp. 14–18, 105, 133; Mortimer (ed.), *Minute Book*, pp. xxi–ii; M. Caston, *Independency in Bristol*, London, 1860, pp. 39–88; J. Barry, 'The Parish in civic life: Bristol and its churches, 1640–1750', in S. Wright (ed.), *Parish, Church and People: Local Studies of Lay Religion, 1350–1750*, London, 1988, p. 153; J. Barry, 'The politics of religion

in Restoration Bristol', in T. Harris, P. Seaward, and M. Goldie (eds.), *The Politics of Religion in Restoration England*, Oxford, 1990, p. 165.

85 BRO MSS, 09467(13a) (1638).

86 SMV MSS, *Hall Book*, I, p. 2.

87 On the politics of these men in the 1640s see D. Underdown, *Pride's Purge: Politics in the Puritan Revolution*, Oxford, 1972, pp. 366, 376, 393; J. R. MacCormack, *Revolutionary Politics in the Long Parliament*, Cambridge, Mass., 1973, pp. 328, 335; R. Zaller, 'Richard Aldworth' in R. L. Greaves and R. Zaller (eds.), *Biographical Dictionary of British Radicals in the Seventeenth Century*, 3 vols., Brighton, Sussex, 1982–84, I, p. 5; M. J. Brown, 'Luke Hodges', *ibid.*, II, p. 97.

88 See Hayden (ed.), *Records*, p. 103; Mortimer (ed.), *Minute Book*, pp. 58, 133, 218.

89 These conclusions are based on analysis of McGrath (ed.), *Records*, pp. 27–30, 261; A. B. Beaven (ed.), *Bristol Lists: Municipal and Miscellaneous*, Bristol, 1899, pp. 119 and 185–315 *passim*.

90 Sacks, *Widening Gate*, pp. 246–8.

91 Collinson, *Religion of Protestants*, Ch. 6; see Sacks, *Widening Gate*, Chs. 8–10.

92 J. Thurloe, *A Collection of the State Papers of John Thurloe, Esq.*, ed. Thomas Birch, 7 vols., London, 1742, III, p. 170.

93 Henry Fell to Margaret Fell, 11 August, 1656, Friends' House Library, London, Swarthmore MSS 1/81. On the Quaker missions to Bristol see John Camm and John Audland, *The Memory of the Righteous Revived*, ed. by Thomas Camm and Charles Marshall, London, 1689; see especially Charles Marshall's *Testimony* published as an appendix; Friends' House Library, London, MSS, *A Book of Letters which were Sent to G. F. from John Audland and John Camm*, pp. 7–12, 26–7; George Bishop *et al.*, *The Cry of Blood*, London, 1656, pp. 2–14; [Robert Purnell], *The Church of Christ in Bristol Recovering her Vail*, London, 1657, pp. 1–2. Of the 128 men who supported Haggatt and Bishop with their votes or in petitions, 41 were Quakers by 1665 or if deceased had close kin who were Quakers by this time.

94 Thurloe, *State Papers*, III, p. 170.

95 PRO, SP 18/75/14i; Thurloe, *State Papers*, III, pp. 117, 153–4, 161, 165–9, 172, 176–8, 181, 183–4, 191–2, 223–5, 242, 248–9, 259–60, 268; Bishop *et al.*, *Cry of Blood*, *passim*; Hayden, (ed.), *Records*, pp. 105–14; BRO, MS 04417(1), ff. 18v, 27v, 28r–v, 29r. In this period Bishop was identified with Wildman's plot; see Thurloe, *State Papers*, III, pp. 147–8; on popular fear of the Quakers in this period see Reay, *The Quakers and the English Revolution*, Ch. 4.

96 Sacks, *Widening Gate*, p. 272.

97 SMV MSS, *Hall Book*, I, pp. 187, 249.

98 Sacks, *Widening Gate*, Ch. 8.

99 Towgood, *Disloyalty of Language*, p. 87.

100 Kem, *King of Kings*, pp. 8–9, 15–16.

101 Standfast, *Clero-laicum Condimentum*, pp. 15–16; see also Towgood, *Disloyalty of Language*, p. 87.

102 For a discussion as regards Bristol, see Sacks, *Widening Gate*, pp. 307–29, 339–43, 357–62.

CHAPTER SIX

THE
CITY OF
OXFORD
1640–1660

Ian Roy

In a celebrated phrase the great Victorian populariser of English
history, J. R. Green, once wrote: 'The University found Oxford
a busy, flourishing borough, and reduced it to a cluster of lodging
houses'. In its quarrel with the town, which is one of the themes
to be explored here, the university in the 1640s had said much
the same: 'The Towns of Oxford lies out of the road; and is in
no way useful to the public by any trade or manufacture. It
serves only for the entertainment of Scholars, and the Townsmen
have no possible means of subsistence but by the University'.[1]
Both statements are at best half-truths. The town, more ancient
than the university, had for centuries been an important place
in its own right, and far from being bypassed its central location,
on a river and road crossing, in the more prosperous half of
England, had long ensured that its markets would flourish, and
also that teachers and their students would find it a convenient
home. It was the trading centre for a rich agricultural region.
It had been a Saxon capital, and was the county town; from 1542
it was a cathedral city, the centre of a new diocese. The early
seventeenth century witnessed the steepest rise in population,
much new building, and the making of fortunes. It was no coincidence that this occurred when the university was rapidly
expanding, for it was undeniable – and here the scholars had a
point – that townsmen and academics were dependent on each
other for their livelihood, indeed survival. The fact that they were
indissolubly yoked together gave a greater edge to their historic

quarrel. The university's success in attracting 'a great part of the flower of the youth of this Kingdom both of the Nobility and Gentry', meant that Oxford's economy, supplying the needs of a captive, luxury market, was diversified and consumer-oriented. Almost a hundred different trades can be identified in the mid-seventeenth century.[2] It possessed drawing, dancing and fencing schools, bowling greens and tennis courts, many fine inns and quality wine importers. The opening of the Thames to navigation as far as Oxford, in 1635, furthered this trend, bringing goods from the Continent to the city. If the ancient colleges, largely the work of the sixteenth and seventeenth centuries, are today the main attraction of the city as a tourist centre, we should not overlook the surviving listed buildings of the same period which bear witness to the former wealth and self-confidence of the town.[3]

Relations between the city and the surrounding countryside were close. Oxford, like many towns of its size, was primarily a rural centre. The main markets on Wednesdays and Saturdays offered all kinds of agricultural produce, and the fairs held in the city, though in decline, were of long standing. Expensive gloves were its most famous product, and it was customary for distinguished visitors to be presented with a pair, but beer, bread and clothing were basic to the town's economy. Boatloads of grain, malt and firewood were landed at the wharves and stored in the warehouses that lined the banks of the streams and water-courses at the south and west ends of the city. Woods at Eynsham belonged to the city, and many leading tradesmen were the owners of houses, farms and pasturge, and had a vote as freeholders, in the shire. The whole body of freemen had important grazing rights on the town common, Portmead, and cattle cropped the grass, as they still do, on Christ Church meadow.[4]

As the county town Oxford housed the shire court, the half-yearly assizes and the county gaol. Only the latter still functioned in the precincts of the ruinous old castle: since the mid-sixteenth century the assize judges and county justices had used the town hall. By charter of James I Oxford itself had acquired county status. Its leading councillors were magistrates with their own courts, held in the Guildhall, which housed the many functions the city's government: it was arsenal, record office, courtroom (on Mondays and Fridays), temporary prison, solicitor's office for the registering of deeds and all manner of business transactions;

its lower hall served as meeting place for the city's main trade guilds, its upper for the council. Oxford had a range of skills and services which was unrivalled beyond the confines of a larger regional capital like Bristol or Norwich. Local landlords made extensive use of its commercial facilities: when Nathaniel Fiennes, the eldest son and heir of the influential North Oxfordshire family headed by Lord Say and Sele, lent the heirs of Sir John Eliot of Cornwall, the Parliamentarian 'martyr', £4,000 in 1636, he sealed the bond in the Oxford town court.[5] With these connections to the neighbouring nobility and gentry the town had no difficulty gaining the patronage of the great. The Howards had replaced the Knollys family as the city's High Stewards in the 1630s. The town shared in the honour of a royal visit, in 1636, when Archbishop Laud, Chancellor of the university since 1630, set the seal on the transformation of his *alma mater*.[6]

Early Stuart Oxford took pride in its reputation for prosperity, and even, at times, relative healthiness, so important in the business of attracting students, and apprentices, from far and wide. But it had its fair share of the problems common to urban communities of the period. Partly these were the result of rapid population growth: in most years baptisms outrun burials in all parishes where records survive. By 1640 the city had between 7 and 8,000 inhabitants, to which must be added a further 2,000 or more attributable to the university. Historic Oxford, its centre at Carfax crossroads (quatrevoix: four ways), was hemmed in by rivers on three sides. On his annual beating of the bounds the mayor travelled mainly by boat. Expansion was difficult, once the open spaces in the wealthier central area, visible in the Elizabethan map of the city, had been filled up, and it was in the poorer western and northern parishes, some parts of which were subject to flooding, that cheap housing was constructed, to receive an influx of poor migrants, in the two decades before the Civil War. 'Inmates', of no fixed address, abounded. Multitudes of poor roamed the streets, begged at college gates and pilfered the houses of the respectable. It was matter of complaint by the university that cottages and 'squabs' were being 'erected upon the town ditch and the town wall', and that their thatched roofs constituted a fire hazard.[7]

Neither the old streets nor the ancient drainage system could cope. Open sewers, like Canditch, were 'floundered by houses of office', choked by the deposit of offal and ordure, and eventually filled up and built over. Paved in 1674, it became the Broad. Oxford's narrow town gates, and its town walls, in an advanced state of disrepair, impeded the flow of goods and traffic. Removing 'the dirt at the Northgate' was a perennial concern, and after rain that main entrance to the town was often flooded and impassable.[8] The city of dreaming spires was stuck firmly in the mud. It still boasted lanes, redolent of medieval squalor, such as Slaying or Slaughter, Shitebarn and Grope, slum dwellings nicknamed 'the Seven Deadly Sins' (next to the Star Inn, a well-known galleried hostelry), and 'a ditch called the Dung'. Bocardo, the celebrated town lock-up ('put Duns in Bocardo' was the watchword of critics of scholastic learning; it had been the prison of the Oxford martyrs), probably derived its name from 'bog', meaning privy. It was equally possible for children to die in an accident on a hayrick within the city boundaries as for others to be killed 'by the fall of the town wall'.[9]

The structure of politics at Oxford was oligarchic, though less than it had been in the medieval past; its reputation for political corruption was still in the future. The common council, from 100 to 140 strong, was drawn from the whole body of freemen, adult males who had, either by, prenticeship, patrimony or purchase, gained the right to practise a trade within the city. As about 800 men had this right, and it might be estimated that there were 1,200 male heads of household within the city limits, the pyramid, which describes the city's government, had a broad base. Laud accused the baker and the brewer, who were candidates for mayor in 1638, of employing strong beer in the competition for the votes of councillors. This was denied (the beer and wine flowed at the dinners that always followed the elections), and the considerable work-load and expense of being mayor was not always desired, in spite of the £40 salary: in 1633 five men in turn had declined the honour.[10] The election of the two burgesses to Parliament was popular, but one candidate was normally chosen by the High Steward, the other by the mayor's council. The latter, thirteen strong, consisted of the mayor, three or four aldermen, and eight 'assistants'. In effect they were the ruling elite, and entry was by co-option. If this was the executive the common council was the legislature, made up of three groups: in ascending order the twenty four, who were held to represent 'the commons', the chamberlains, and the bailiffs. Each year, to assist the executive, two chamberlains (who accounted for the city's finances) were selected from the twenty four, and from the chamberlains two bailiffs, who assisted the mayor's brethren. Most members of the common council did not aspire to enter the inner circle; that as many as forty-six men entered the thirteen between 1635 and 1665 was an indication of the exceptionally turbulent character of those years. On average it took them sixteen years from their first entry into the council.[11]

The ruling elite was also an elite of wealth. The major trades in Oxford were those connected with the supply of basic necessities to the colleges, food, drink and clothing: mercer/draper, brewer, baker and tailor; to these may be added those innkeepers or victuallers who possessed one of the three wine licenses: most of the city's executive body were drawn from the most prominent members (very often the masters) of these guilds. It was in their interests, as substantial property owners and producers of consumer goods, to have a say as magistrates in the granting of city leases, commercial dealings with the university, and – if brewers – the licensing of alehouses. They lived mainly in the central parishes with the highest taxable value, or, if they headed a brewing interest, close to the many branches of the Thames and its tributaries on the southwest side of the city, where access to water and riverborne fuel and grain supplies was easiest.

There was a concentration of wealth in certain families, and so of high office in the town. From 1614 to 1666 the Wright family supplied mayors on no less than five occasions. The Smiths of St Aldate's, brewers, provided four mayors in the first half of the seventeenth century, over three generations. Their kinship circle was wide, connected as they were by marriage to other prominent and wealthy families. Thomas Smith, whose father had been mayor in 1631, himself held the highest office in 1638; he was succeeded by his brother, John, whose father-in-law, perhaps in his day the wealthiest brewer and maltster in Oxford, had been mayor in 1625–6, and who became MP for Oxford in 1640. Their townhouse was the splendid Old Palace, opposite Christ Church, with its frontage of five gabled bays, decorated with the arms of the Smiths. They owned what would now be called tied pubs within the city, and several profitable freeholds in the rich farmland outside. When members of this family and others comparable came to compound for their property after the war they paid as much as untitled country gentry elsewhere.[12]

Two other noteworthy councillors were of the wealthy guild of mercers and drapers, which had an important role in converting textiles from clothing centres like Abingdon for the increasingly sophisticated Oxford market. Neither was the offspring of an old Oxford family. Thomas Dennis was from Ingatestone in Essex; he was first apprenticed in the city in 1617 and entered the common council in 1633. He grew rich supplying the most costly materials to the university, and was of the thirteen in 1640, becoming mayor two years later.[13] John Nixon, the son of a Bletchingdon yeoman, entered the council in 1622 and was first elected mayor in 1636. For thirty years he rented a large house opposite St Mary the Virgin's (the university church) in the High Street, and it was in association with three other prosperous tradesmen in the same neighbourhood (one of them privileged of the university) that he acted as banker for those requiring loans in the 1630s. He and his business partners shared the same political and religious outlook, for they were joined, in one such transaction, by John White, 'the Patriarch of Dorchester', and Henry Wilkinson, Rector of Waddesdon, Buckinghamshire, two celebrated 'old Puritans'. Did this amount to a local 'network of the Godly', unknown to Laud, which combined commercial enterprise and religious zeal, of the kind now uncovered by historians in other areas? Nixon, his associates and customers, were to play an important role in the years to follow.[14]

Towns like Oxford, medium-sized and enjoying a degree of autonomy under their charters, returning their most respected citizens or the kin of their noble patrons to Parliament, could not conceive of challenging the authority of the crown. Their representatives, however, would win respect and a renewed mandate by gaining concessions, especially at the expense of a rival authority. In many cathedral cities disputes broke out between the city fathers and the dean and chapter, or with the bishop, especially if, in the 1630s, he was a reforming Laudian. Oxford, however, had no quarrel with its bishop, whose presence is seldom referred to in the city archives, and who probably spent most of his time at his newly built palace at Cuddesdon. It was in its historic quarrel with the university that the city fathers might build their reputations as friends of the populace and defenders of their ancient liberties. Among many other irritants, but possessing symbolic importance, were the ancient ceremonies in which each new mayor was obliged to participate every year: the oath, taken before the barons of the Exchequer at Westminster, the oath he took in St Mary the Virgin's church to safeguard the university's rights, and the service held in the same place on 10 February, St Scholastica's day, when the town made offerings for the scholars killed in the famous affray of 1356. Those councillors taking part found this humiliating, and complained that they were often, in going to St Mary's, jeered at by the young scholars.[15]

Laud, with the enthusiastic support of his sovereign, wished to bring the ideals of 'good order and decency' to the university where he had first risen to prominence. He turned it into a model of Laudian practice and belief, censuring and expelling all those who were deemed nonconformists. His reform programme was substantial; the statutes promulgated in 1636, after years of work, remained those in force until the nineteenth century.[16] But as the laity was in some cases antagonised by reforms which maximised the rights of the clergy, so the city of Oxford found Laudian reinvigoration of their neighbour uncomfortable. In most matters the university had legal and historical justification for its claims, so supportive had the monarchy and the royal courts been in the past. But now Laud was waging nothing less than a campaign, which ignored the grievances of a town which was itself enjoying rising prosperity and enhanced self-esteem, but needed all its resources to combat growing social problems.

The university's privileges had been granted over the centuries to ensure the survival of a band of poor clerks who were dependent on lay charity and royal protection. Matters appeared somewhat different when the much enlarged student body contained the 'flower of the gentry'. It possessed an independent jurisdiction, its own courts and means of law enforcement, through the activities of the proctors in suppressing night walking ('noctivigation'). The setting of prices, the assize of bread and beer, the clerkship of the market, at times the taking of tolls, were in the hands of the university officials, who also had first choice of all commodities within a five-mile radius of the city, where, for instance, the royal rights of purveyance were suspended, and within the same area the university and the city jointly could raise money for the maintenance of roads.[17] The university was able to grant privileged status to its main suppliers, which removed from the jurisdiction of the town over 200 tradesmen (and taxpayers), and it licensed victuallers and vintners, the better to control undergraduate drinking. Laud waged war against the proliferation of alehouses, of which there were 300 (a figure which would indicate that every fifth house in Oxford sold beer) before his purge of the late 1630s. Even the paving and cleansing of the city streets was its responsibility.[18]

The late 1630s saw a number of challenges to the most irksome rights of the academics. In 1640 the town set a watch, which clashed with the proctors. When these cases were brought before the Privy Council the town's Steward, the Earl of Berkshire ('his interest and reputation less than any thing but his understanding'), was no match for the Archbishop. He accused the well-to-do, sobersided aldermen of disorder in a recent mayoral election, in which, he said, wine had flowed in 'pails and kettles'. He scolded them for corrupting the morals of 'the commons' in order to buy votes. When they objected to the curfew policed by the university – the watch it kept at night – Laud gave a warning, no doubt laced with sarcasm, to those who were returning late to Oxford after the Privy Council hearing: 'Ye were best to look to your hours, else the proctors are too blame if they do not lay ye by the heels'.[19] This may have been one of the Archbishop's weak jokes, like his remark about the townsmen, in one case, 'whistling up' their recorder (John Whistler, a London lawyer), but it does not seem like it, and may not have seemed like it to them. The city fathers were Cinderellas in their own home.

While Laud undoubtedly exacerbated old grievances it would be wrong to conclude that, by 1640, the hostility of town and gown was absolute. College members, privileged tradesmen, and citizens were often friends as well as neighbours. Several councillors in our period were the fathers of well-known Oxford academics. Some dons made charitable bequests to the city for the sole benefit of the citizens, although this could be unpopular with their colleagues. The city appointed university divines as Sunday lecturers, and, where the colleges owned the livings, the parish clergy were often college men. Householders were often the tenants or leaseholders, as well as the suppliers, of the academic societies. Tradesmen pursuing members of the university for debt, a common occurrence, had no objection to using the Chancellor's court.

Equally, and in spite of Laud's best efforts, it cannot be concluded that by 1640 most of the townsmen were Puritan and the academics Arminian. A principled minority of anti-Laudians, among both lay and clerical Oxonians, was soon to emerge into the open, as the divisions in the nation worsened, but most of those in the common council supporting the city's case against the university would have rejected the label Puritanism with scorn. Giles Widdowes, accused of Arminianism, was rector of the city church, St Martin's, for twenty-five years and was paid as lecturer by the city in the 1630s. If he was heckled during a service it was by students, not his usual congregation at Carfax.[20] It was All Souls College, known for its Laudian sympathies, which appointed as curate of St Ebbe's, a poor parish, a strict precisian who soon fell foul of his flock: among those who apparently still wished for cakes and ale was a woman parishioner who 'called him a Puritan dog to his face'.[21] Even the new 'popish' images and ornamentation of Oxford's churches were not necessarily unpopular with the locals. When war broke out it was Parliamentarian troops from London and Buckinghamshire who attacked them, and the townsmen, led by Nixon, no doubt for prudential reasons, who protected them.[22]

Under Laud, Oxford politics had become closely meshed with politics at the centre. With the opening of the Long Parliament and the downfall of the Archbishop apprehension in the academic establishment was balanced by excitement and heightened expectations among the townsfolk, who gathered nightly at Carfax to hear the news from London. The city immediately began to take advantage of the changed political situation. In January 1641 it took over the right to levy a toll on corn sold in the market (a long disputed point) from the university.[23] The popular association of Laudianism with popery was made to discredit the university, and the heads of houses were forced to investigate and disprove the rumour that the mass was commonly celebrated at Oxford.[24] A scare about the Catholic owner of the Mitre, Charles Greene, and arms left by 'Cavaliers' at the Star Inn, caused a local panic. Divisions could no longer be easily contained within the local community. Greene had presumably lived in peace with his neighbours for many years, but was now expelled the council. The arms were those of a neighbouring gentry family, the Spencers, with whom the city had good relations, but they were reputed 'malignant', and the arms were seized for the use of the town.[25] The Howard family, which despite the political ineffectiveness of its head in the 1630s, had long enjoyed a leading role at Oxford, was no longer able to maintain its position. It was symptomatic of change that when Berkshire's son, one of the town MPs, was elevated to the Lords, the council chose one of their own members to replace him: John Smith of the brewing family, who had been mayor in 1639.[26]

The King had to give way to political pressure, in Oxford as elsewhere, in 1641–42. Charles I conceded, upon the petition of the city fathers, that the new mayor should in future take his oath of office at Oxford, not in London. In February 1642, for the first time, the mayor refused to do penance at the university church. Such ceremonies could be attacked as 'superstitious', a view which would find a ready response in Parliament, and the university no longer had powerful friends at court to enforce obedience.[27] The Long Parliament's reforms had an immediate impact locally. The Clerical Disabilities Act (February 1642), which excluded the clergy from secular office, made it uncertain whether academics in holy orders could accept even university offices; the leadership was weakened at the time when it needed to be strongest. Leading dons had been named to the commission of the peace for Oxford before the war; those who were clergymen were now disabled from sitting.[28]

By the summer of 1642, however, the political climate had changed again, and nowhere more obviously than at Oxford. The King, having sacrificed Strafford and Laud, sent the Queen abroad and abandoned London, built up a strong position, based on his acceptance of Parliament's reforms, and the admirably reasoned defence (in the arguments penned by Edward Hyde) of the established church and constitution. To all those who held political responsibility, who had taken the oath of allegiance, this was a powerful appeal. At Oxford his declarations were publicised by the university, and well received. There were distinct signs, such as the guying of Puritans at the Holywell maypole, that Parliament was being blamed for the growing divisions in the nation, and London crowds for disorder and iconoclasm. It was now the turn of those labelled Roundheads to feel the weight of popular disapproval. Some collusion by Oxford citizens and their leaders was probably needed to ensure that the university's magnificent gift of £10,000 safely reached the royal war chest in June 1642, and that the 'delinquent doctors' responsible escaped Parliament's vengeance.[29]

At the moment when the taking of sides could no longer be postponed, September 1642, a remarkable snapshot of shifting allegiances in the city is provided by the 'distracted thoughts' of one of the bailiffs, George Heron. A friend of Parliament, he was 'much distempered' by the warm welcome given to a party of Cavaliers sent by Charles to Oxford, not only by the university but by some leading councillors. His impressions, though confused and panicky, are candid and revealing: they show a close-knit urban community, anxious to preserve at least the outward appearance of civic unity, breaking up under the pressures generated by the coming conflict. Heron was shocked, as were the town's MPs, at the hatreds unleashed among the citizens; 'Mr Smith hath received some blows for no other reason but because he is of the Parliament'. Heron and his supporters were assaulted in the street, had their windows broken, and received some shots in their 'backsides', at the hands of what a later generation would recognise as a 'Church and King' mob.[30] When he attempted to rally resistance he found that most of his neighbours preferred to remain 'discreet cowards'. Some of those who had taken a leading part in the quarrel with the university and clashed with Laud, such as Alderman Thomas Smith, were now active for the King. On the other side John Nixon and his associates, and some like-minded academics, fled to Abingdon, a Puritan clothing centre in a different and more friendly county, or to London. But even in these extreme circumstances many avoided a commitment to one side or the other as long as possible: the common council postponed a decision to ally with the university in aid of the King's men, and later expunged any record that it had met for that purpose.[31] When, briefly, Roundhead troops under Lord Say in turn occupied Oxford, the council refused to accept his nominee for mayor, Nixon, as someone too obviously partisan and who had abandoned them in their hour of need. Instead they elected Thomas Dennis, who was less heavily involved, at this stage, with either side.[32]

The forward policies of the university on behalf of the King, its critics had warned, would make Oxford the seat of war. In late October 1642 this prediction came true, as the triumphant Royalist army, bearing before it sixty or seventy colours captured at the first major encounter of the war, the battle of Edgehill, entered the city. For almost four years Oxford served as the Royalist capital, the King's military headquarters and principal garrison, and 'the common asylum of afflicted Royalists', those Cavalier gentry and clergy (including displaced Cambridge academics) who had fled or been driven from enemy quarters. Inevitably, the life of the citizens was to be transformed, as, once again, Oxford politics became national politics.[33]

Conflicting pressures on the inhabitants, and the conflicting signals they gave to either side at the start of the war, were early apparent. They had refused to make common cause with the university in support of the first Cavaliers, but they had rejected Nixon's leadership. Dennis appears to have been reassured by the King's celebrated statement of political moderation at Wellington in Shropshire, of 'his Majesty's princely truth and goodness', but he led the town in building defences 'to keep out Prince Robert'.[34] Hyde, who knew Oxford politics well, believed that of all the corporations in England it was the only one 'entirely at his devotion', and the London troops were said to have been disappointed at their reception there.[35] The King had commended the mayor for protecting the university but had not included any townsmen in the Commission of Array for the shire of July 1642; on the Royalists' entry their arms were transferred from the Guildhall to one of the new arsenals set up on university premises. On inspecting the defences being hastily constructed, Charles I 'took notice' that far fewer citizens than scholars and countrymen were working.[36] The treatment of the city's MPs (John Whistler, the recorder, and John Smith), reflected these contradictions. Disabled by the Long Parliament for their attendance at the King's Oxford assembly, they nevertheless endured spells of imprisonment at the hands of the Royalists.[37]

Whatever the Cavaliers' private views of their hosts, or the citizens' of their guests, they were now forced into a close if uneasy partnership by the circumstances of war. It was no doubt flattering for townsmen to have the King's 'sacred person', and the glitter of his court, in their midst, and to be asked to play a crucial role in the defence of his cause. If the minority of students before the war who could be described as the 'flower of the gentry' had provided a good living for Oxford tradesmen, what rich pickings might there be in supplying the needs of the households of the

King, the Queen and their offspring, the greatest royal servants and wealthiest noblemen?

The King and his council of war, meeting in Christ Church, had overall charge of his headquarters; he appointed a Governor and a board of civilian administrators, known as the Lords Commissioners, manned by several of his leading councillors and courtiers, to take charge of the day-to-day running of affairs. It was this committee which negotiated with the mayor and the vice-chancellor when the co-operation of the city and university was required, and in the last two years of the war it supplemented the stream of royal proclamations on Oxford matters with its own printed orders. Under its guidance many of the gentry followers of the King at Oxford – of whom there was a superfluity – were provided with jobs as commissioners, assisting parish officials in the listing and taxing of the inhabitants, and the fortifying, cleansing and victualling of the city. Such an arrangement reflected the fact that the city was now home to several different classes; soldiers, civilian 'strangers', royal servants, the lords and commons of Parliament, academics, as well as the resident population. Churchwardens and constables found themselves being joined in their work by eminent refugees: in All Saints Lord Chief Justice Heath, in St Clement's Sir Henry Mainwaring, onetime pirate and ex-master of Trinity House.[38]

The first requirement of the occupying forces was billets, and, as well as the half-empty colleges (the students having 'fled home to their mothers'), citizens' houses were requisitioned for the use of the King's military or civilian followers. Rooms were assigned according to the status, vocation and family or other connections of the lodger. Alderman Thomas Smith was no doubt honoured to receive the Lord General Forth into his house in St Aldate's. A prominent officer, Sir Richard Cave, was billeted on his brother, the brewer Walter Cave, in the same parish; the Lord Keeper lodged with a wealthy lawyer in St Mary's parish.[39] Several substantial houses, like those of Nixon and his associates, who had fled the city for the second time, were no doubt quickly seized, stripped of anything of value and crammed with lodgers.

The pressure on accommodation in the city was severe, and good rooms were prized possessions. As well as private houses the city's Bridewell, prison and almshouses were soon full of soldiers; for a time they were used as military hospitals, to which wounded soldiers from Royalist quarters elsewhere were sent. Thirty-one shrouds had to be provided for those who died in the almshouses opposite Christ Church in the weeks after Edgehill. The city's churches were used as emergency prisons for the Roundhead soldiers taken in early campaigns, and much damaged.[40] Courtiers, royal servants and Lifeguardsmen flocked to the bigger houses in St Aldate's, close to the King's presence in Christ Church. By early 1644 408 'strangers' were lodging in seventy-four houses there (including two inns). It was a well-to-do area, and each household would normally have contained, on average, from five to six persons. The war had effectively doubled their number. One house contained, in addition to the family and servants of the owner, twenty-two lodgers, and two small cottages, leaning against Christ Church wall, contained eight Lifeguardsmen and two royal pastrycooks.[41]

The population of temporary migrants was a constantly shifting one (few of the 'strangers' listed in January 1644 had been in the same billet six months earlier), and some large houses were underused. It was impossible to make the distribution of quarters equitable, and intrigues and quarrels over accommodation between potential lodgers were frequent. One Royalist captain complained that he had been used by a nobleman to stake a claim to desirable lodgings, but that on his return the peer had 'turned him and his horse out of doors'. Other Cavaliers, however, more or less set up home in the city for the duration of the war, and can be found paying rates for the houses they occupied. Wealthy lodgers may well have spent heavily to secure the best rooms, and to obtain luxuries for their families, and some citizens may have benefited from private trade of this kind. The majority of householders, however, were forced to provide bed and board in return for paper 'tickets', promissory notes redeemable at some future date, but which were not even accepted as part payment of the contribution laid on Oxonians for the upkeep of the soldiery.[42]

The numbers involved in the military occupation of Oxford fluctuated as the tide of war ebbed and flowed around the walls. It was strategically placed at the centre of the area used as winter quarters by the infantry of the main field army. Some 3,000 Foot were mustered in New Parks in January 1643, and again in the following year, and this was considered the ideal number to provide a 'settled garrison' for the spring. Temporary sheds had to be erected in the northern suburbs to relieve the pressure on private accommodation in town of penniless soldiers. Later the size of the army's contribution to the garrison declined. In the turbulent last few months of the siege, before the surrender of the city, the number of troops, including disbanded officers and men, inflated by the drawing of the net around Oxford, may have swelled again.[43] The influx of civilian migrants probably reached a peak in the winter of 1643–44, with the first sitting of the King's Oxford Parliament. The numbers of those temporarily within the defences of the city more than made up for the absence of students; at its maximum Oxford may have contained half as many inhabitants again as before the war. While courtiers, major office-holders and high ranking army officers favoured larger houses, as in St Aldate's, and the best college rooms, and found the space – and the money, or credit – to keep their families and servants with them, the common soldiery and menial servants were packed into those areas of Oxford which already had pressing social problems – slum housing, subdivided dwellings, transient 'inmates' and large numbers of the very poor – before the war.[44]

The expense of maintaining so many fell heavily on a town the size of Oxford. Parliament had the advantage of a populous and prosperous base area, in London and the Southeast of England, which was not seriously threatened or disrupted by invasion during the war. The King was forced to rely on Oxford and its hinterland, and this was an area always at risk from enemy forces. Much of Buckinghamshire, and in the last two years of the war, Abingdon, was in Parliamentarian hands, and each year, at the beginning of the campaigning season, hostile armies penetrated the ring of strongholds and garrison towns which protected the royal headquarters. The demands made by the King's men were therefore, and inescapably, heavy, at a time when normal trading was often dislocated. They were also unprecedented. Civil War payments may be compared with the normal annual tax yield at Oxford before the war of £170, and the ship money payment, at its greatest, of £100.

At his first entry Charles had been presented with £250, which could only be found by borrowing from Mrs Bosworth, the rich widow of a former mayor. But in common with other captured towns Oxford was quickly educated in the ways of contemporary warfare: a larger sum had to be paid the occupying forces lest they exercise their right to plunder and fire the place. The gift was doubled by means of further loans raised from over a hundred citizens (and the Tailors' guild), led by Mayor Dennis. The scale of military taxation imposed on the resident population, and the size of the forced loans frequently demanded, in the years of Royalist occupation, were crippling. In the spring of 1643, £2,390 had to be raised to pay for the fortifications, and the ordnance and ammunition with which they were armed, the making of drawbridges, the treatment of wounded soldiers, and the sheds for those on sentry duty. The first of several large loans, of £2,000, coincided with these demands. A further expense, then and later, was the public provision of foodstores for every class of inhabitant, against a possible siege. Mayor Dennis led the way in raising taxes, in every parish, to buy 'corn and victual' for the inhabitants, and contributed himself to the cost. As a concession to the city, on which they so much depended, the Royalist authorities allowed the mayor to tax privileged persons, the many college servants and suppliers who would normally claim exemption as members of the university. All householders except the poorest, and 'mere scholars', had to pay.[45]

In addition, and in the same way that the county had agreed to maintain troops of horse, the 'Contribution' was introduced in the city for the upkeep of the garrison, at £450 a month. The tax returns from the parishes show the significant contribution made by some academics (and a few 'strangers') whose houses were rated, and the shortfall caused by the absence of prominent citizens, like Nixon and his friends, marked 'gone'. The military were brought in to assist in the work of collection, in which they had such a direct interest, and provost marshals were ordered to deal with defaulters, 'by some exemplary punishment'. In spite of the use of force arrears rapidly escalated. The financial burden could only be contained by introducing payment in kind requiring the citizens to work themselves in the defences and to raise their own regiment for home defence. Even so the credit of the city could scarcely be maintained, by constant borrowing on the city seal, the loan of the city plate, and, as we shall see, the personal efforts of Dennis and Smith.[46]

The King ordered all adult males, aged sixteen to sixty, whether academics, citizens or 'strangers', to work one day a week, or pay a shilling. In a six-day working week the parishes, where 3,320 men were listed for this purpose, were to provide labour for four, the colleges (1,500 men) for two days. Every day, it was hoped, 800 would be working, on a designated section of the line. The cost was £240 weekly. The service was unpopular, and in spite of the best efforts of the commissioners appointed, the numbers who either worked in person, or paid in lieu, declined rapidly; both in summer 1643 and spring 1646, where the returns survive, only a fraction of the available work-force regularly attended. Harsh measures were used: workmen had at first been discouraged, it was said, 'by cutting and beating from the engineer', and in the later stages of the war the parishioners of St Martin's complained that they had to compel their neighbours to work, or face imprisonment themselves.[47]

Nevertheless Oxford was transformed, from a city with decayed medieval walls, to a stronghold with extensive earthworks of the modern kind, eventually judged by the King himself, Sir William Waller and Sir Thomas Fairfax to be incomparably stronger than it had been in the early stages of the war. A line three miles in circumference, fully enclosing both city and suburbs, made full use of the rivers which were Oxford's natural protection on three sides. Wet ditches and flooded fields (such as Christ Church meadow) protected the earthen walls, which were surmounted by numerous cannon; from outlying ravelins on all sides the countryside was kept under constant observation. Booms were laid on the river, new drawbridges ('parting arches') made, and channels cut to allow the water supply to continue to reach the mills, some of which had been converted to wartime use. Inevitably the locks on the Thames, so recently and expensively constructed for the navigation of the river, were lost, and some of the river-borne trade stopped. The vulnerable north side was under almost continuous reconstruction during the war, and the whole strengthened by palisades. The most substantial single work, which entailed the destruction of some housing, was the fortress at St Clement's, built to guard the east bridge. It enclosed the parish church. It was later said that Oxford's defences as a whole cost £33,000 in Sir Arthur Aston's time as governor, 1643 – 44.[48]

The Royalist high command had been at first content to disarm the citizens (in spring 1643 a further 1,000 pieces of arms and armour had been handed in to the royal magazine at New College), but in July decided to raise a regiment recruited from the inhabitants which would release units of the marching army from garrison duty. Somehow more arms were found from their own resources, the King again allowed the privileged to be taxed for this purpose, and 600 men were listed in six companies, each recruited from a particular section of the city.[49] The mayor and his brethren struggled hard to gain control of this regiment for themselves: Alderman Thomas Smith was made second in command, and bore on his colours the arms of the city, and other companies were given in the main to prominent citizens (and a servant of the city's Steward, the Earl of Berkshire, an indication of his presence and renewed importance in the city). But despite their complaints they were forced to accept as colonel a courtier and gentleman pensioner, Sir Nicholas Selwyn. Apart from being a 'stranger', he proved contentious and was soon highly unpopular. When his pay fell into dispute he obtained the support of the King, the Council of War and the equally unpopular Governor, Aston, and relations between the military and civil authorities rapidly deteriorated, as we shall see. Later the regiment became that of the Governor in 1645, William Legge. With others raised by the scholars and 'strangers', it at least had the desired effect of reducing the numbers of the regular troops in the garrison.[50]

Crucial to the continuing credit-worthiness of the city was the financial support of leading figures like Thomas Dennis and Thomas Smith, who succeeded Dennis as mayor in 1643, serving in this post for the second time. Already heavily involved on their own account in the city's finances before the war they provided loans now, and persuaded others to lend. As Oxford was fortified and armed, and turned into a centre of munitions production, their example was crucial not only in underpinning regular military taxation but in paying or providing credit for local suppliers. Drawbridges, ironwork and other materials for the defences, and arms, ammunition and armour for the main magazine in New College, were made in the city and the surrounding villages, and the makers were in a stronger position to demand payment than most. They organised the contribution by citizens of private weapons and armour, brassware, shovels and sheds, all of some military value.[51] They were also instrumental in the success of the scheme to raise money for the King in October 1643, known as the Oxford Engagement. Wealthy dons, rich widows, their fellow councillors, and Oxfordshire and Berkshire clothiers – drawn in no doubt partly through Dennis's pre-war contacts as a mercer – lent cash, on the security provided by the King's most prominent supporters, who themselves had grants of Crown land for this purpose. On his own account Dennis even lent money to hard-up Cavaliers, billeted in the city, which were recorded in the town court.[52]

If some leading citizens, and the city itself, were running into debt, there were opportunities for others to make profits, as some must have hoped at the start. There were many more customers for Oxford's basic products, beer, bread and clothing, and even, among the better-off lodgers in the colleges and wealthier parishes, for luxury goods. The city's brewers and bakers were seldom cut off completely from their sources of supply, the grain producers, maltsters and woodmongers of the surrounding countryside; Alderman Smith had several thousand bundles of faggots in store at any one time, shipped from the city's woods at Eynsham. Despite the conversion of some mills to military production the city's own mills at the Castle continued to operate. Silks could be obtained for the household of the Duke of York. Even the vintners stayed in business. It was a measure either of the Royalists' desire to maintain high standards against all the odds, or their inability to order their priorities, that wine from Spain and France was expensively procured and sold at Oxford.[53]

An indication of the flourishing state of the markets for much of the war was the severe overcrowding in the space reserved for the sale of farmers' produce at Carfax – where a gibbet for military executions had been placed near the conduit – with consequent traffic jams, problems of waste disposal, and the usual accusations that 'hucksters' were forestalling the market. Indeed it was felt by the Royalist authorities that the soldiery were being unduly enticed by the array of fruit and vegetables on offer. The years of civil war were not ones of harvest failure. When Mayor Dennis bought in supplies of wheat for the public magazine he paid less than he would have done in most years of the pre-war decade.[54]

One reason for the low prices of some commodities was that the King abolished the usual restrictions on trade in the interest of supplying so many, even permitting outsiders, such as refugee Londoners, to trade in their calling. No doubt he wanted to demonstrate publicly the strength and prosperity of his cause. In the same spirit the city brewers' monopoly was broken, and a free market in beer was established in order to increase production. Only the strength of the beer brewed was restricted. At the end of the war beer was being brought in from Abingdon. In these circumstances it was difficult to regulate drinking, limit the number of alehouses and combat drunkenness. The strict regime established by Laud at Oxford was laid in ruins, as his dreams had foretold.[55]

As the war progressed and conditions worsened, however, the incursions of enemy troops, the threat of encirclement, the interruption of trade caused by blocked roads and rivers, the destruction of locks, boats and wharves, grew more frequent. For their part the Royalists exercised an imperfect control over their own troops, principally because their pay was uncertain, and the plundering of even friendly territory – especially the seizure of goods on their way to market – was frequently condemned by royal proclamations. Heavy taxation may have driven buyers away, and according to the council's petition of 1644 the imposition of an excise spelled doom. But in the final year of the war loans could still be raised on the security of this tax. More important for the longer term profitability of suppliers, however, was the failure of customers at the end of the war to pay their bills. Colleges went bankrupt, some had been 'dissolved', and contracts made by their servants with local suppliers were (after the purge that followed Parliament's victory) often repudiated. Most notoriously, many Royalists fled to escape their creditors even before the surrender of the city. After 1646 the King and his followers were in no position to settle the accounts of those to whom they owed money for services rendered in the war. Most Oxford tradesmen and householders ended up with worthless paper tickets.[56]

The wartime crowding of the markets, public spaces and private houses exacerbated problems with which Oxford had long contended: blocked drains, narrow streets and flooded gateways. The temporary migrants – especially, one imagines, the poor, 'foreign', country-bred soldiery, unused to city living – lived in insanitary conditions. A royal edict, in Latin, complained of the number of pigs and pigsties fouling the highway, 'horror abominabilis', and ordered the scavengers paid double to remove the unprecedented mounds of dirt, particularly at the Northgate. Slaying Lane remained a notoriously foul passageway. The alteration of the watercourses to flood the wet ditches protecting the defences, and the appalling state of the water itself, polluted 'by the casting of Dung, and other filth thereinto', and the presence of 'dead hogs, dogs, cats, and well flayed carrion horses', led to the spread of water-borne diseases. These were the streams the brewers drew water from to make beer.[57]

'Casualty of fire', as we have seen, had always been a possibility in early seventeenth-century Oxford: it was even more likely given the overcrowding, squalor and disorder of the military occupation. A fire began outside the city walls, beyond the Northgate, on the afternoon of Sunday, 6 October 1644; driven by a high wind, it 'raged through' and over the wall, and did not stop till it had reached the river on the southern limits of St Aldate's parish, a distance of a thousand yards. It laid waste a segment of the west end of the city between the castle and the main road from south bridge. Some 2–300 houses in its path were destroyed, much of it cheap housing in the poor parishes of St Ebbe's and St Peter's in the Bailey, and the notorious 'Seven Deadly Sins' in St Michael's. It devastated the local food and drink industry, for ten bakehouses, eight breweries, 'many malthouses' and grain and fuel stores, on the riverside frontages, and all containing highly combustible material, were burned down. Miraculously it spared all five churches of the parishes through which it spread (although the lead roof of St Peter's melted), and Pembroke College. At the Restoration £43,000 was voted by way of compensation for the sufferers. The rehousing of those made homeless, and the loss of income and resources suffered by those affected, worsened conditions in the city.[58]

The coming and going of troops from all parts of Royalist Britain, their presence in the winter months in the poorest and most crowded western and northern suburbs (a Welsh prayer book was employed in services at St Giles, the garrison church) made it likely that diseases, long associated with the passage of armies, would be rapidly disseminated in the city. Oxford had prided itself before the war on its general healthiness and freedom from plague, but with the opening of the campaigning season in 1643, a 'new fever' quickly spread among the ranks of the opposing forces in the field, and in the garrison itself. An outbreak of 'gaol fever' had driven the assize judges from the castle to the town hall in the mid-sixteenth century. The poor living conditions under which soldiers existed in the field, and in overcrowded billets in Oxford (many observers commented on their lousiness), were similar to those in contemporary gaols: the sickness was no doubt a form of typhus, re-christened 'morbus campestris' from its military associations.

Soldiers, 'strangers', and their families, were buried, very often, from the citizens' houses where they lodged. Soon the resident population itself was experiencing a period of crisis mortality, which lasted from May to October 1643. Parliamentary spies reported that at its height, in August, twenty a day were dying. Deaths in aggregate during this year climbed to over six times the pre-war annual average in those parishes where the burial registers survive. From a third to a fifth of all the burials were of outsiders, and a few were of the surviving academic community. But the majority were townsmen, and it may be estimated that over a thousand, an eighth of the population, died in 1643. Twenty-four of 123 councillors, almost a fifth of their number, fell victim.[59]

Plague came to the city in June 1644. The following month the London news-sheets reported it was prevalent in such spots as the 'Seven Deadly Sins'. The usual orders on quarantine, burials at night and not in the churchyards, the killing of cats and dogs, and the imposition of special taxes on the parishes, were issued in August by the Royalist authorities; the pest house to the east of the city was reopened, and some cabins were hastily set up in Holywell. Collections for 'the visited' appear to have begun even before the publication of the orders. A surviving printed bill of mortality, for a week in October 1644, when the epidemic was abating, recorded nineteen plague deaths out of a total of thirty-one. But the plague was not as fatal as the previous year's typhus outbreak. The number of burials was about three and a half times the pre-war figure, in a year when the population of the city was probably at its maximum. Thereafter the mortality rate declined, though remaining well above average: it is probable that at least a further thousand citizens succumbed to plague, typhus, smallpox and other diseases in the last two years of the war, before the surrender of the city in June 1646.[60]

The authorities, already hard pressed, were overwhelmed by the scale of the disaster. Most of the soldiers buried by the parish officers were not even given names, and some were interred not in the overfull churchyards but in the hillocky waste land, once the bailey of the castle. There was growing disorder and violence in the city, as well as sudden death, and the parish records tell their own tale: 'a stranger lying dead in the street' buried 18 September 1643; 'for burying a woman shott – lay dead three days ... and making her a grave at Bally hills'; 'for a soldiers grave that was murdered & burying him at Bally hills'; 'for drawing a dead horse out of the churchyard'.[61]

In any case the needs of the military could not easily be met by the operation of the normal civic government, far less with the preservation of the privileges of the rival corporations, town and gown, at Oxford. There was bound to be contention over billeting of troops, raising the contribution, conscripting labour for the works, and the place of a city regiment in a royal garrison; even the repair and cleaning of waterways and streets when vital to military supply. Although the King respectfully asked permission of the council for the hay from Port Meadow, the property of the townsmen, for his stables, and maintained the concessions he had made to the mayor before the war, a governor like Aston, arguing military necessity, was able to force obdurate parishioners to unblock a main road. The raw Cavalier element in the King's army could go much further. Within a week of the first occupation of the city two senior officers, one of them, admittedly, a Lunsford, demanded money with menaces from an elderly rent collector, privileged of the university, and relieved him of a large sum.[62]

Although he did not legislate, as did Parliament, on the political qualifications for membership of town councils under his control, the King was naturally concerned with the reliability of the rulers of his wartime capital. He wrote from his campaign headquarters, in September 1643, to recommend the removal of those councillors absent and in rebellion. Six councillors, headed by John Nixon, and including some of his old associates, and seven prominent freemen, were expelled the city. Their importance was recognised by Parliament also. Some were present with the forces close to Oxford, for three were actually captured in arms during the Chalgrove raid. So long as the Royalist occupation of Oxford continued there was a Parliamentarian government in waiting, ready to take over when the city fell, and co-operate with the county committee based on Banbury. Nixon spent part of his exile in London testifying, at the trial of Laud, to the activities of the former Chancellor of the university at Oxford.[63]

In the summer of 1643 and again in September 1644 the university attempted to regain for its members the age-old freedom from taxes laid on the city. There was no redress, either from the royal judges, who issued a most uncertain judgement on the matter, or the Lords Commissioners. For its part the city council felt that the 'pressures and grievances' of the city had grown insupportable by October 1644. It drew up a petition to the Lords Commissioners under twelve heads, which set out the full burden of the exactions so far imposed on the city, and the impossibility of finding any further sums. The behaviour of the city's colonel, Selwyn, was particularly resented: he had recently brought his already poor relations with the city fathers to a dramatic climax by assaulting Mayor Smith in his place in the Guildhall. The city could find no more because, they explained, the debts already incurred could not be fully secured on citizens' property, 'stranger' soldiers living in Oxford were trading in competition with freemen, some of the richest inhabitants were either dead or fled, many families which had formerly paid taxes were shut up as infected, and the recent fire had destroyed a major part of the brewing and baking industry. Householders enlisted in the city regiment, overtaxed and lodging 'foreign' officers and their men, their wives and children, some of whom were, by trading, destroying the livelihood of their hosts, were 'the most miserable of his Majesty's soldiers'.[64]

But the Royalists had a short way with dissent of this kind. They had already imprisoned the city recorder (and MP) and one alderman for unspecified reasons. They now threw into prison three of the mayor's brethren (including Dennis), and kept them there until they agreed to pay the sums demanded. The act of council containing the petition was erased from the official record, and new taxes were raised to pay Selwyn. Military rule in Oxford was being tightened. An oath of loyalty to the King was imposed on all classes in March 1645 and rigorously enforced. When the Governor claimed that *his* pay was running short three more leading councillors were held to ransom, and Dennis went further into debt to secure their release. The desperate plight of the city in the last year of the war is shown by the sale of the food in the public magazines to the parish overseers of the poor, to keep the destitute from starving, and the loans levied on the better-off inhabitants to pay the garrison, lest the 'mutiny or violence of the soldiers', already in evidence, reach new heights.[65]

A London newsbook may for once have been accurate in saying

that there was considerable disillusionment and discontent at Oxford long before this. The bells and bonfires which had welcomed the Royalists' victories, and other days of celebration, were a thing of the past. Smith, it reported, had had enough of the Cavaliers, and would be willing to come off with the loss of £2 – 3,000. This is not an unreasonable estimate. He had lent large sums, and issued pledges, to a losing cause, and fire and 'foreign' competition had damaged his brewing monopoly. At his death in April 1646 he left little but debts. Equally, at the start of the war, Dennis had been convinced of the King's political moderation and 'princely goodness'. He had since striven hard to aid the royal cause, and, like Smith, invested much of his own personal fortune. By 1646 he was ready to welcome a new regime.[66]

Oxford had endured the horror of seventeenth-century warfare in all its guises. It had suffered the loss of about a fith of its original population, the same fraction of its housing stock, severe damage to its basic industries and the roads and rivers by which they were supplied. Its capital assets were diminished. There had been invasions of its privileges and attacks on the dignity of its councillors. The ruling elite of 1642, some of whose families had been associated with the government of the city for generations, had suffered more grievously than most ordinary citizens. Their political prominence and personal wealth made them more vulnerable to the depredations of the occupying force, and would render them liable to punishment at the hands of the triumphant Parliament. Several were, like the families of Smith and Dennis, virtually bankrupt. The university, on which for so long Oxford tradesmen had depended for custom, was equally destitute, its coffers as empty as those of the city chamberlains. It would take some years and much effort before the city could recapture its pre-war prosperity.

John Nixon returned to the city, from which he had withdrawn at the beginning of the war, in the baggage of the New Model Army. Like those elsewhere intruded into high places by the new authorities, as the only men on whom they could rely, he would depend on a trusted handful of friends, neighbours and business associates, who shared the same outlook and the same wartime experience. They had been expelled the city at Charles I's behest in 1643. That act of council was reversed immediately after the city's surrender, and he, five other councillors, and five of the seven freemen formerly debarred, were restored to their places. A few months later he was elected mayor, and took his oath in the Guildhall, not at Westminster, although the way to London was now open. The other ceremonies associated with the start of the new mayoral year were postponed, however, because they fell on the day which since 1642 had been kept as a monthly fast in Parliamentarian quarters. It was no doubt hoped that, as Oxford's duties were brought into conformity with the new dispensation, its rights would be equally respected. Representation at Westminster was urgently required. The Recruiter elections, held in those areas which were now falling to the forces of Parliament, gave the council the chance. Nixon and John Doyley, a local gentleman, were elected unopposed as MPs in December 1646.[67]

The military presence in Oxford continued to be obtrusive, even after the city's surrender and the end of the war. Although the Parliamentarian garrison was much smaller than the one it replaced, it registered some of the violent political changes of the post-war years. The seizure by some soldiers of the train of artillery, lodged in Oxford, and of money sent for the disbandment of others, which led to a skirmish outside All Souls in June 1647, was second in importance only to the capture of the King himself by the army.[68] In September 1649, in the wake of the suppression of the Leveller mutinies at Burford, part of the garrison revolted and seized New College as a stronghold, before order was restored. The 'new works' – especially the strong defences on the northern side – were ordered slighted, and the Castle was instead designated as a 'citadel', in the approved modern manner; but when 'the Scots King' and his forces got as far as Worcester in 1651 the small number of Parliamentarian troops withdrew to the safety of New College.[69] Thereafter the garrison was withdrawn and both the old and new fortifications round the Castle levelled, the demolition aided by student volunteers.[70] The drain on the local economy, and the potential for disorder, of mutinous or unpaid soldiery, were removed for the first time since summer 1642, and the 1650s were marked in this respect, as in others, by a return to peacetime normality. The remains of the Civil War earthworks, still visible in Loggan's map of 1675, stood as a reminder of what had been.

While Nixon and his friends had been added to the council in 1646, there had been no immediate purge. But as Parliament authorised Visitors to undertake a thorough reformation of the university so it passed measures, in time for the elections of Michaelmas 1647, to ensure that those suspected of being 'delinquents' would be ineligible for civic office. At Oxford this had the desired effect. Twenty-eight 'well affected' citizens petitioned the House of Commons to overturn the election of the new mayor and bailiffs, as men who had taken the 1645 oath to the King and adhered to the enemies of Parliament. The petitioners were headed by Thomas Wickes (a prosperous brewer and maltster, and one of Nixon's old business partners), Walter Cave, the brewer who had housed his brother, the Royalist officer, in 1643, and George Potter, a wealthy draper, and included seven who had been disfranchised in 1643. The House responded immediately, ordering Nixon and the bailiffs of the previous year to continue in office, despite the rule that required three years to elapse before any man could be re-elected mayor. Aided by the work of the county committee, meeting at Oxford, in identifying thirty-five delinquent citizens, a wider purge followed: some 17 per cent of the membership departed the council in 1648, mainly for political reasons. This, and the previous high mortality among councillors, reduced the council to scarcely more than a hundred. It ensured the dominance of the new men around Nixon. Five of the petitioners, including Wickes, Cave and Potter, replaced those accused of Royalism, including John Smith, on the thirteen. All three then served in succession as mayor, 1648–51. While the circle of Oxford's governors was widened, as a result of these changes, most of the ruling elite remained men of wealth and status; some, however, were enabled to advance to the thirteen in fewer years than normal.[71]

The wounds inflicted by the war were long lasting, and political and personal antagonisms boiled over on occasion in the post-war years. Tale-bearing and ill-feeling flourished in a town where, because it had been the King's headquarters, so many of the ruling elite were politically compromised, and where the process of establishing delinquency encouraged informers. Following the extensive purge of 1648, however, the new rulers of Oxford tried hard to patch up these quarrels, in the interests of civic unity and the restoration of peace. When another 'great difference between divers members of this house' arose, the leadership called for 'a reconcilement of love and unity one to another ... for the general good of this city'.[72] There is no evidence that subscription to the Engagement, to uphold the new republic, was rigorously enforced at Oxford. When two aspirants for city office used the 1652 Act of the Rump, directed against ex-Royalists holding place, to demand further removals, the council deplored this further politically-inspired purge. As the city had been under military occupation, it was argued, Oxford citizens had been given no choice but to collaborate with the prevailing power, serve in the city regiment, and take the oath of loyalty to the King: the government of the city could not be carried on if all those who had been so compelled were declared unfit to serve. When the government suggested that the council's choice of mayor in 1658 had been a Royalist, and so was disabled, a powerful delegation was sent to London and successfully argued the case for his retention.[73]

That many on both sides had suffered greatly in the war exacerbated the continuing political differences. Sequestration of property, as well as exclusion from office, awaited those who had most heavily backed the losing side. The principal victims were the former MPs, Smith and Whistler, uniquely unfortunate in being imprisoned by the Royalists and then declared delinquents by Parliament. Whistler, the city recorder since 1627, was disabled and would have been fined had he not died in the following year. John Smith, though much indebted, and unable to recover the loans he had made to his late brother Thomas, paid £216, the largest fine of all Oxford citizens. Thomas Smith's death in 1646 thwarted the sequestrators, but he left liabilities estimated at over £2,000. His widow and son were dragged through the courts by their creditors and forced to sell the family property in St Aldate's and outside the city. The Smiths were ruined: they played no further part, for the first time for half a century, in the government of the city.[74]

But most Oxford citizens condemned for Royalism were not wealthy enough to be sequestrated, and those who were benefited from the articles of surrender, which set the fine at no more than a tenth of the value of the estate. The case of Thomas Dennis, as heavily in debt as Thomas Smith, shows how the new regime in the city tried to restore harmony and preserve continuity after the war. Dennis had spent £1,600 on the King's behalf, according to his family, but he had altered his political stance, as we have seen, and this helped, eventually, to lift the threat of sequestration. He continued as a member of the thirteen, and became mayor again in 1657. Several others, including the head of the long-serving Wright family, who had been uncontroversial members of the council during the war, were permitted to stay. Dennis's estate, however, had been critically damaged by the war; like others who had subscribed to the Oxford Engagement he lost his investment, and was harried by those to whom he owed money. He scarcely escaped bankruptcy before his death. After the Restoration his son quietly disappeared from the council, and later still his daughter was reduced to beggary.[75]

Under Nixon's leadership the city maintained, so far as possible, strong links with central government, of whatever political complexion, in the turbulent years that followed. He himself had been allowed by the House of Commons, in 1648, to return to Oxford to attend to the affairs of the city; his fellow MP was secluded at Pride's Purge, so that the city was unrepresented during the trial and execution of the King, and the creation of the republic. The city required, in order to navigate these dangerous political rapids, a weighty patron and protector at the centre of events. It was Nixon who persuaded Bulstrode Whitelocke, MP for Great Marlow, Buckinghamshire landowner, and soon to be the republic's chief law officer, to replace Whistler as the city's recorder. This was an admirable choice: Whitelocke was well known and respected locally, and could alert the city to any actions of the government which affected it. When in 1649 he was elected unanimously High Steward in place of the elderly earl of Berkshire, disabled as a delinquent, he obtained the recordership for his protégé and old family friend, Bartholomew Hall, who played an active part in preserving good relations between the locality and the centre.[76]

That there was a military dimension to the new regime was not forgotten. A succession of influential army officers was honoured by the council, some even taking their seats as councillors. The corporation earned the thanks of the government by its loyal actions in moments of crisis, among them the mustering of the militia by some of Nixon's supporters during the invasion scare of 1651, and help with the local forces raised to suppress the

Cavalier plots of 1655. While Oxford no longer possessed a garrison, and the defences had been torn down, security remained a priority. The Cromwellian Protectorate saw something of a recrudescence of power in the hands of the old Parliamentarian gentry, still militarily serviceable. In Oxford this meant the Crokes, of St Aldate's and Marston, who won the favour of Oliver himself. When in 1656 Whitelocke ('Lord Whitlock') preferred to sit for Buckinghamshire rather than Oxford in the first Protectorate Parliament, the corporation chose Richard Croke, already deputy recorder. Members of this family continued to be of political importance in the city during the rest of the Interregnum, and after the Restoration. It is significant that Nixon, although he stood, was not elected.[77]

His hold on the city was nevertheless unmatched. He was chosen mayor in 1654, for the fourth time, at the age of sixty-five, and two years later selected Mathew Martin, the young man he treated like a son (the Nixons were childless), as the new town clerk. They, with the aid of Whitelocke and Hall, dominated Oxford politics, ensuring that the city would benefit from the opportunities presented by the republic. When, as a result of the dispersal of Crown revenues, the fee farm rents were sold, the council bought them. The peculiar position of the cathedral, as part of the university, meant that the corporation did not profit from the sale of the property of the church in the way that other cities did. But when the university itself, remodelled by the Parliamentary Visitation, revived the old quarrel and questioned anew the rights of the city in the usual matters, the council was strong enough to see off the challenge. Its appeal to Parliament struck the right note, referring to the supremacy of the civil magistrate over privileges 'founded upon superstition or Tyranny'. Those tradesmen privileged of the university did not regain their independence; the market and its tolls, the setting of the night watch, the licensing of alehouses, even the meeting of the university's court leet in the Guildhall, remained for the duration of the 1650s in the hands of the city. Needless to say there was no revival of the ancient ceremonies at St Mary's church.[78]

On the other hand there was a genuine attempt to make peace between the ancient rivals, comparable to the patching up of quarrels, left over from the war, in the council chamber. Twenty 'solemn debates' were held between town and gown, over two years, and articles of agreement were drafted by both sides.[79] While in the end no peace treaty resulted, there was a good deal of co-operation between the two in other fields. For one thing the university was in an exceptionally flourishing state in the 1650s, with more students than ever before, a fact which materially aided the recovery of the city's economy in the same period. The laudable aim of bringing about a 'godly reformation' was common to both Puritan magistrates and Cromwellian heads of houses. As before, political and religious controversy did not preclude good relations at the personal level between academics and city councillors. Several handsome benefactions by collegians for the relief of the poor were received by the corporation in these years. For his part Nixon made two prominent university clerics trustees of his new school, and the son of his old business associate, Dr Henry Wilkinson, was now a canon of Christ Church and Professor of Divinity.[80]

There were important areas where the union of magistracy and ministry was required. Although little is known about the process of uniting the many poor parishes in the city, the better to provide for a preaching and adequately paid ministry, in the Puritan manner, the city's JPs used their enhanced powers to deal with the old problems: the influx of poor migrants, the existence of bad housing and filthy streets. In the records of the magistrates' sessions, and the comments of their critic, Anthony Wood, a rigorous Puritan regime can be detected at work. Discipline and good order were emphasised – the old Laudian ideals, though now in very different hands. 'Slovens Hall', an annual revel held in the lower part of the Guildhall, was abolished. After-hours drinking and immoral conduct were severely dealt with; instruments of correction were repaired and no doubt put to good use, and the Bridewell was enlarged. In all of these the co-operation and exhortation of preachers supplied by the colleges would be essential. Some actions were harsh, and controversial. A young woman, accused of killing her baby and hanged, was revived by university physicians. The bailiffs bore the brunt of popular disapproval when they insisted on hanging her again.[81]

Unlike some towns Oxford was not unduly troubled by radical political or religious activity. There was no possibility, after 1651, of a sympathetic garrison commander encouraging the setting up of conventicles: a residual Royalist-episcopalian party was more in evidence than the 'swarms of sectaries' noted in other places. Nor was there, under the Nixon regime, much chance of a movement from below to change the oligarchic constitution of the city; nor of a big dispute breaking out, and involving freemen as well as council members, of the kind which unsettled Colchester and High Wycombe, and perplexed the Cromwellian government. Some novelties were brought to Oxford, however: Jacob, a Jew, opened a coffee-house, and some Quakers made their appearance in the Seven Deadly Sins; two Quaker women were set upon and nearly killed by students.[82]

Civic unity and the co-operation of the university were needed if the great task of post-war reconstruction was to proceed. As well as the defensive earthworks other impediments to trade were removed as quickly as possible. The booms which had been laid across the Thames were dismantled, and the repair of the 'turnpikes' (locks) on the river was undertaken at the joint cost of university and city. Larger boats were soon bringing trade back to Oxford's wharves. Plague and other epidemics subsided in 1647, and the death rate returned to normal. The rebuilding of the area destroyed in the great fire of 1644, and the improvement of others, was well under way by the mid-1650s.[83] Leases of city property, at a low ebb during the war, were, by late 1646 and thereafter, at a higher level than in the 1630s. The numbers of apprentices enrolled, which had reflected the dangers of coming to or residing in wartime Oxford, were 30 per cent higher in 1647 than they had been before the war: thereafter the numbers returned to the old level. This was comparable with other towns, such as those in the Severn valley, which recorded a dramatic increase immediately after the war, then a more gradual improvement at a lower rate. There were, literally, signs of economic revival: licences to hang out signs, for shops as well as inns, were much in demand from the autumn of 1646. As the university expanded the tradesmen engaged in Oxford's basic industries resumed their important place in the city's economy: maltsters were accused in 1649 of making undue profits selling to the London market.[84]

The city's own finances had been devastated by the war, as the corporation acted as surety for the loans made to the King and others. The defects of civic finance were such that leading citizens needed to help: councillors, taking up city leases and contracts, and issuing licences, helped themselves as well as the corporation. The city debt amounted to over £2,000, and in 1647 Nixon, in a strong position to recover the rents owing him during the war, came to the rescue, with the aid of a close associate, one of his fellow mercers. In return Nixon gained valuable concessions from the city, which allowed him in due course to found the school for the sons of freemen, in the town hall yard, for which he was long remembered in Oxford. The portraits of Nixon and his wife, commissioned in 1659, remain to this day in the Guildhall.[85]

As the ruling elite in Oxford had taken no hand in the abolition of the monarchy there is no reason to suppose that it would not welcome the Restoration of the King in 1660. A full council took the necessary oaths in 1660, and sent a loyal address, no doubt as fulsome as that sent to Richard Cromwell the year before. There was a general restoration of those councillors who had been ejected after the war, and Whitelocke and Hall, the recorder, too close to the old regime, were immediately asked to resign; but Nixon and his friends remained in office. When the ceremonies to be performed by the city, in obedience to the university, were required by the new authorities, the council supported the mayor's polite refusal. It prudently invited representatives of the neighbouring gentry and their clients to become freemen and, in some cases, councillors. The Howards returned to high office. The head of the Oxfordshire gentry family whose arms had been impounded by the city in 1642, Sir Thomas Spencer, was given a bailiff's place on the council.[86]

Nemesis, however, was not long delayed. The old Royalist nobility and gentry had been defeated and humiliated in the 'broken times', as Wood called the years of war and revolution, and by 1661, having recovered their property and influence, they proceeded to reassert their control over those aspiring urban communities which had sought to benefit from the political opportunities created by the unprecedented conditions of the Interregnum. They were appointed to the commissions which imposed the severest tests of loyalty, under the terms of the Corporation Act. Thirty-one councillors, including four who had been mayor in the 1650s, and Nixon's protégé as town clerk, were removed. John Nixon himself narrowly escaped humiliation in the city which he had ruled for so long, and for which he had given much, by dying in April 1662. In all a quarter of the council departed, for whatever reason, a larger number than during the wartime mortality crisis, or the post-war purges. The council was as small as it had been in 1648. The city's government was weakened in every way. In 1662 it was obliged to undertake once more the traditional rituals at Westminster and St Mary's church. When the university reopened the case for the restoration of its rights, in a now much more favourable climate, Charles II, that former resident of Christ Church, pronounced for the academic cause. The university was to retain its ancient privileges thereafter, without further serious challenge, into the nineteenth century.[87]

The history of Oxford city, from the dominance of Laud to the Restoration of the King, was not untypical of the experience of other urban communities in those 'tumultuous times'. The city had suffered in the war, with the loss of population, the destruction of property, accidental and deliberate, the interruption of trade and industry; the ruling body had suffered as much as any, for the leaders had been obliged to aid the King and his supporters, and financial loss and political discrimination were inevitable with the downfall of the Royal cause. Some families never regained the positions they had once held. Nevertheless, as we have seen, there was a strong economic recovery, aided by the revival in the fortunes of the university, which had to accept some diminution of its privileges. Where so much in these years was unprecedented and uncertain the city government attempted to preserve civic unity, restore peace to the community and provide the means for a moral reformation. It was successful in some of these endeavours. It sought the protection of men who were close to the centre of events, and co-operated, without giving away the concessions it had recently won, with the rival corporation of the university. At the Restoration, however, the neighbouring nobility and gentry resumed their reign, and the university, continuing to attract 'the flower of the kingdom', became once more the dominant partner in town-gown relations.

Notes

1 W. A. Pantin, *Oxford Life in Oxford Archives*, Oxford, 1972, pp. 96–7, 118.
2 Oxford University Archives [OUA], SP E 9(5). I am grateful to the Keeper of the Archives, University of Oxford, for permission to quote from the records in his keeping. *Oxford Council Acts, 1626–1665*, ed. M. G. Hobson and H. E. Salter, Oxford, 1933 [*OCA*], pp. xii–xiv: 86 are mentioned in the council acts, but to these can be added college servants, and others known

from a wider range of sources. Victoria County History, *Oxfordshire*, IV, *City of Oxford*, 1979 [VCH, *Oxford*], p. 107.

3 *OCA*, pp. ix–x; P. Manning, 'Sport and pastime in Stuart Oxford', in *Surveys and Tokens*, ed. H. E. Salter, Oxford Historical Society, LXXV, 1920, pp. 109–23; I. G. Philip, 'River navigation at Oxford during the Civil War and Commonwealth', *Oxoniensia*, II, 1937, pp. 152–65. Imported goods have left an archaeological deposit in the city ditch area: B. Dunham *et al.*, 'Oxford's northern defences: archaeological studies, 1971–1982', *Oxoniensia*, XLVIII, 1983, pp. 13–40; Royal Commission on Historical Monuments [RCHM], *An Inventory of the Historical Monuments in the City of Oxford*, 1939.

4 *OCA*, pp. xvi, 27; VCH, *Oxford*, pp. 104–10, 113–4; letter of Lord Say on freeholders, 1660, Oxford City Library [OCL], F 5.2, f. 102.

5 VCH, *Oxford*, pp. 121–2; *Oxford Council Acts, 1583–1626*, Preface; OCL, A 5.4, f. 284.

6 *OCA*, pp. xvii–xix; A. J. Taylor, 'The royal visit to Oxford in 1636', *Oxoniensia*, I, 1936, pp. 151–8.

7 *Surveys and Tokens*, pp. 184, 215; OUA, WP R.10 (2); VCH, *Oxford*, pp. 75–6.

8 OUA, SP E 9 (5).

9 OCL, F 5.2, f. 105; Oxfordshire Record Office [ORO], St Michael's parish burial register, 1 April 1624.

10 *OCA*, p. 47.

11 Matters were brought to a full council after consideration in the smaller council: Historical Manuscripts Commission [HMC], *House of Lords*, XI (new series), p. 328, makes this clear.

12 VCH, *Oxford*, p. 138 on Smith family; M. Toynbee and P. Young, *Strangers in Oxford. A Sidelight on the First Civil War, 1642–1646*, Oxford, 1973, pp. 122–3, 136–42; OCL, A 5.4, ff. 53–4, 60; RCHM, *Oxford*, pp. 173–5.

13 Vice-chancellor's accounts, A. Wood, *Life and Times*, ed. A. Clark, Oxford Historical Society, 1895, IV, pp. 57–8.

14 OCL, A 5.4, f. 282; F 4.1, f. 1.

15 Mayor's oath in the Exchequer, undated, OCL, F 5.2, f. 56; VCH, *Oxford*, pp. 159–60; *OCA*, p. 112.

16 K. Sharpe, 'Archbishop Laud and the University of Oxford', in *History and Imagination*, ed. H. Lloyd-Jones, V. Pearl and B. Worden, London, 1981.

17 Bodl., Top Oxon, c. 275, f. 23.

18 VCH, *Oxford*, pp. 161–8; *OCA*, pp. xiv–xv, 63, 373–6, 171–4.

19 Clarendon, *History of the Rebellion*, ed. W. Macray, II, p. 533; HMC, *House of Lords*, XI (n.s.), pp. 404, 413–14, 416, 417.

20 *OCA*, pp. x, 413, 422.

21 *OCA*, pp. 360–1; Wood, *Life and Times*, I, p. 48.

22 *Ibid.*, I, p. 63.

23 *OCA*, pp. 362–3; OUA, SEP T 9 (14).

24 OUA, WP.A.ii(1), f. 1; certificate that they know no papists, 14 December 1640.

25 *OCA*, pp. 104, 107, 363–5.

26 *Ibid.*, pp. 97–8.

27 OCL, K.12.2, Commission of Charles I, 16 March 1642; *OCA*, pp. 105–6.

28 OUA, SP F 15, list of *c.* 1639.

29 See the chapter on the university in the 1640s by T. Reinhart and I. Roy in the forthcoming *History of Oxford University*, IV.

30 HMC, *Portland*, I, pp. 56–8, 59–60; HMC, *House of Lords*, XI (n.s.), pp. 324, 326, 329; 'backsides' are back gardens.

31 *Ibid.*, pp. 330, 332; OCL, A.4.3.

32 Wood, *Life and Times*, I, p. 63.

33 A. Wood, *Fasti Oxoniensis*, II, p. 81.

34 *OCA*, pp. 367–8; Wood, *Life and Times*, I, p. 67.

35 Clarendon, *History of the Rebellion*, II, p. 375; Wood, *Life and Times*, I, p. 63.

36 *Ibid.*, pp. 70, 72; OCL, E 4.5; *Strangers in Oxford*, pp. 208–9; *Royal Letters Addressed to Oxford*, ed. O. Ogle, Oxford, 1892, pp. 260–2.

37 Wood, *Life and Times*, I, p. 73; OCL, F 5.2, f. 58; *Strangers in Oxford*, pp. 142–3; Bodl., Add. D 114, f. 15, 5 June 1643; OCL, A 5.7. For both see M. F. Keeler, *The Long Parliament*.

38 BL, Harleian MS 6802, ff. 162–4; Bodl., Add. D 114, ff. 5, 10, 15, 28–9, 73, 77–8; W. H. Black, *Docquets of Letters Patent . . . of King Charles I at Oxford*, 1837, pp. 30–1, 121, 220, 236.

39 *OCA*, p. vii; *Strangers in Oxford*, pp. 122–4, 150–3; Bodl., Twyne-Langbaine MS 2, f. 37 [January 1643].

40 ORO, DD Par. St Aldate's, b 17/27; 'Oxford Church Notes, 1643–44', in *Collectanea*, IV, Oxford Historical Society, 1905, pp. 99–134.

41 Bodl., Add. D 114, ff. 17, 24–6, 46–9, 81; *Strangers in Oxford*, pp. 6–12, 53–9, 154–5, 231–2. The two St Aldate's lists of June 1643 and January 1644 (Add. D 114, ff. 24–6, 46–9) form the basis of the study by M. Toynbee and P. Young, *Strangers in Oxford*, which is a mine of information on householders and their Royalist lodgers. Regrettably, however, they do not transcribe, edit or otherwise analyse the texts themselves.

42 Only those having the extra expense of stabling horses as well as soldiers could pay in tickets. Kent Record Office, Bath Letters, C 283/1; ORO, DD Par. St Aldate's, d. 3, ff. 6–10.

43 *The Royalist Ordnance Papers, 1642–1646*, ed. I. Roy, Oxfordshire Record Society, XLII, XLIX, 1964, 1975, pp. 174–5, 186–7, 188–9, 465, 469–70; Wood, *Life and Times*, I, pp. 81–2; BL, Harl. MS 986, f. 75; Bodl., Add. D 114, ff. 80–1, 94; Bodl., Twyne-Langbaine MS 2, f. 37; W. Dugdale, *Life, Diary and Correspondence*, p. 86; *A Full and True Relation*, 1 July 1646, BL, E 342(9).

44 The Council of War decided in January 1643 not to remove the sixteen Irish wives of Lifeguardsmen from their lodgings, but clearly this was exceptional: BL, Harl. MS 6851, f. 95. The January 1644 census of 'strangers', in St Aldate's, and in two colleges, Pembroke and Lincoln, may be used to calculate probable totals: Bodl., Add. D 114, ff. 17, 18, 46–9, 81.

45 *OCA*, pp. 111, 129, 369–71, 373–4, 379, 390, 394; OCL, E 4.5, ff. 51–2; F 5.2, f. 91; A 4.3, unnumbered folios at end of volume; Bodl., Add. D 114, ff. 80, 99; OUA, SP F 1, the 1643 assessments, and SP F 40 (14); ORO, DD Par. St Aldate's, ff. 6–7; Bodl., Twyne-Langbaine MS 2, ff. 37–8, 47; *A Narrative by John Ashburnham*, 1830, II, Appendix, pp. v, vii, xxxii; *Royal Letters*, pp. 262–3.

46 Bodl., Twyne-Langbaine MS 2, f. 38; OUA, SP F 1 (1–24); *OCA*, pp. 113, 371–2, 373–4, 457; Bodl., Add. D 114, ff. 20, 80.

47 *OCA*, pp. 113, 117, 373–5, 381; OUA, SP F 1(1–23) and 40 (21); OCL, F 5.2, ff. 60–3; Bodl., Add. D 114, ff. 15–31, 80; R. R. Martin, *The Church and Parish of St Michael*, Oxford, 1967, pp. 38–40.

48 *Royalist Ordnance Papers*, pp. 186–7, 468–9; BL, Harl. MS 6852, f. 82; F. J. Varley, *The Siege of Oxford*, Oxford, 1932, pp. 106–21; BL, Harl. MS 986, f. 77.

49 *Royalist Ordnance Papers*, pp. 34, 69, 434 etc; *Royal Letters*, pp. 264–6; *OCA*, pp. 117, 123, 126, 376–8, 380–3; *Stuart Royal Proclamations*, ed. J. Larkin, II, Oxford, 1983, 412 (citation will be by item number unless otherwise stated).

50 BL, Harl. 986, f. 76; *Royalist Ordnance Papers*, pp. 208, 495; *OCA*, pp. 117, 123, 126; *Royal Letters*, p. 268.

51 *OCA*, pp. 367–72; *Royalist Ordnance Papers, passim*.

52 *OCA*, p. 373; OCL, A 5.1, f. 292; E 4.6, f. 44, F 5.2, ff. 65, 91 and F 4.1; ff. 37, 42; *Calendar of the Committee for Advance of Money*, pp. 998–9, 1120–1; PRO, SP 19.125, nos. 158, 182; Dennis himself raised £500.

53 *OCA*, p. 120; OCL, A 5.1, f. 279; Wood, *Life and Times*, I, p. 84.

54 The order for hucksters, 4 October 1644, OUA, SEP T 6 (17); ORO, Hardy MS 1/5.

55 The brewers' petition to the Marquess of Hertford, Chancellor of the university, May 1644, Bodl., Twyne-Langbaine MS 2, f. 119; Larkin, 423.

56 F. Madan, *Oxford Books*, II, Oxford, 1693 (citation by item number); Larkin, 508, 518; OCL, F 5.2, ff. 66.

57 *Royal Letters*, pp. 263–4; OUA, SP F 40 (45), order of 5 June 1643 on scavengers; Bodl., Twyne-Langbaine MS 1, ff. 264–6, 269, 272; Larkin, pp. 908–9.

58 S. Porter, 'The Oxford Fire of 1644', in *Oxoniensia*, XLIX, 1984, pp. 289–300.

59 The registers of St Michael's, St Ebbe's, St Mary Magdalen's, St Martin's, St Peter's (East): ORO, originals or t/s copies; *Journal of Sir Samuel Luke*, ed. I. G. Philip, Oxfordshire Record Society, XXX, 1951, p. 130; Wood, *City of Oxford*, III, pp. 233, 245.

60 ORO, St Ebbe's burial register, June 1644, and St Aldate's parish accounts, d 3; *A Diary, or an exact Journal*, 4–12 July 1644, BL, E 254 (1); Madan 1671, 1673: also 1775 (May 1645); Bodl., Wood 514 (15a), Madan 2062; burial registers as note 59: St Michael's gives cause of death in several cases from July 1644 to August 1646.

61 ORO, St Mary Magdalen's, c 1, burial register; R. R. Martin, *The Church and Parish of St Michael*, pp. 38–40; ORO, St Peter's (East), d 1, churchwardens' accounts, 1645–6.

62 *OCA*, pp. 118, 129, 133, 394–5; Bodl., Twyne-Langbaine MS 1, ff. 264–6, 269, 272; ORO, Hardy MS 1/5; Toynbee and Young, *Strangers in Oxford*, pp. 208–9.

63 *OCA*, pp. 123–6.

64 Bodl., Twyne-Langbaine MS 2, ff. 38–40; *OCA*, pp. 123–7, 374–8, 388–90.

65 *OCA*, pp. 126–7, 129, 427, 452–8; OCL, F 5.2, f. 91; oath administered to Oxford, BL, Harl. MS 6852, ff. 263–4; Madan 1764.

66 BL, TT, E 19(4): *Mercurius Civicus*, 79, 21–28 November 1644. For the later history of the Smith and Dennis families' fortunes see below, pp. 157–8.

67 18 November 1646, warrant for new elections at Oxford, *Commons Journals* [*CJ*], IV, p. 724; *OCA*, pp. 134, 137, 141.

68 *OCA*, pp. 396–7; A. Woolrych, *Soldiers and Statesmen. The General Council of the Army and its Debates, 1647–1648*, Oxford, 1987, p. 106.

69 C. H. Firth, 'The mutiny of Colonel Ingoldsby's regiment at Oxford in September 1649', *Proceedings of the Oxford Architectural and Historical Society*, new series, IV, 1884, pp. 235–46; *OCA*, pp. 401–2; *Calendar of State Papers*

Domestic, 1650 [*CSPD*], pp. 127–8, 144, 187, 411, 547, 578; *CSPD, 1651,* pp. 202, 295, 336–7, 343, 408, 416.

70 *Ibid.*, p. 416; *OCA*, p. 180; Wood, *Life and Times*, I, p. 170.

71 C. H. Firth and R. Rait, *Acts and Ordinances of the Interregnum*, I, pp. 1009, 1025; *CJ*, V, pp. 318–21; Bodl., MS Wood F 35, f. 13; OCL, A 5.7, ff. 161–2; F 5.9, ff. 101–3; *OCA*, pp. 150–2, 155–7. Anthony Wood, that inveterate snob, and bitter critic of the changes now taking place at Oxford, records their lineage and coats of arms, and their daughters' marriages (often to prominent academic and local gentry families), with appropriate deference: Wood, *Life and Times*, I, pp. 127, 198, 231, 238, 255.

72 OCL, F 5.9, ff. 101; *OCA*, pp. 152–3, 432.

73 Petition, 15 February 1653, PRO, SP 24.13, f. 38v; *OCA*, pp. 41, 72, 89, 231–2, 412; Wood, *Life and Times*, I, pp. 101, 183, 266; OCL, A 4.3, f. 275.

74 *CJ*, V, p. 52, VI, p. 33; *Calendar of the Committee for Compounding with Delinquents*, pp. 945, 1563; *Strangers in Oxford*, pp. 122, 158, 218; OUA, Chancellor's Court Papers, 27; OCL, A 5.4, ff. 48–9,53–5, 61–2; *OCA*, p. 317. Thomas's son Oliver was granted a place on the council in 1662, but he does not appear to have taken it up, *OCA*, p. 292.

75 OCL, F 5.9, ff. 101–3; F 5.2, f. 65; E 4.6, f. 44; A 5.1, f. 292; *Calendar of the Committee for Compounding with Delinquents*, pp. 945, 1550, 1563–4, 3257; Dennis was freed from sequestration in May 1650, *Calendar of the Committee for Advance of Money*, p. 1001; *CJ*, V, p. 313; *OCA*, pp. 198, 200, 223, 314, 431; *OCA, 1666–1725*, pp. 2, 5; Bodl., G. A. C 250, petition of Anne Dennis, *c.* 1698.

76 *CJ*, V, p. 52; *OCA*, pp. 143–4; Longleat House, Whitelocke MSS, IX, f. 123, Nixon to Whitelocke, 1 February 1647. His family stayed with Thomas Dennis, 'who kindly intertained them, & would take no money for it': *The Diary of Bulstrode Whitelocke*, ed. R. Spalding, Oxford, 1990, p. 197.

77 *OCA*, pp. 164–6, 202–3, 207, 213, 237; *CJ*, V, p. 544, VII, p. 373; *The Diary of Whitelocke*, pp. 502–3. For the Croke family in Oxford see *Strangers in Oxford*, pp. 138–9, and Wood, *Life and Times*, I, pp. 195–6.

78 *OCA*, pp. 137, 150, 163, 171–4, 209; OCL, C 6.1a; E 4.3, ff. 30–3, city petition of April 1649; Madan 2011; admitted by the House of Commons, 6 April 1649, *CJ*, VI, p. 180.

79 *OCA*, p. 169; OCL, E 4.3, ff. 58–66, 75–6; F 5.2, f. 95.

80 *OCA*, pp. 168, 180, 246; OCL, E 4.3, f. 44; Bogan's benefaction, E 4.2, f. 20; Nixon's will, PCC 1662, f. 52 (PRO, PROB 11.307, p. 414).

81 *OCA*, pp. 142, 155, 186; Wood, *Life and Times*, I, pp. 250–1; Sessions of the Peace, Oxford, from 1657: OCL, O 5.11, f. 12, April 1658.

82 S. R. Gardiner, *History of the Commonwealth and Protectorate*, IV, Ch. 43; Wood, *Life and Times*, I, pp. 188–91, 201.

83 Butcher Row was rebuilt at the considerable expense of the city in 1656. *OCA*, pp. 212–3; Wood, *Life and Times*, I, p. 210; Wood, *City of Oxford*, II, p. 483; ORO, CH/N lx.1, f. 24.

84 OCL, D 5.5 and D 5.6, lease books; L 5.2 and L 5.3, registers of apprentice enrolment; *Oxford City Properties*, p. 340; I. Roy, 'England turned Germany? The aftermath of the Civil War in its European context', *Transactions of the Royal Historical Society*, 5th series, 28, 1978, pp. 143–4; OUA, WP.C 16.1 (34)(38), Carpenter to Langbaine, May 1649.

85 *OCA*, pp. 152, 227–8, 230, 236–7, 242–3, 432, 436; OCL, A 4.3, f. 275;

E 4.2, f. 19; F 2.12a, articles of agreement, January 1659, between the city and Nixon; H 37.3 f, g, i, j; Wood, *Life and Times*, I, pp. 245–6.

86 *OCA*, pp. 107, 236, 255, 259–60, 267, 272, 276; OCL, E 4.3, ff. 81–2; F 5.2, f. 101.

87 *OCA*, pp. 293, 305–6; OCL, E 4.3, ff. 82–9.

CHAPTER SEVEN

AGRARIAN PROBLEMS AND THE ENGLISH REVOLUTION

Joan Thirsk

Many revolutionary changes occurred in English life during the Civil War and Interregnum, but how did they alter agriculture and rural society, and how permanent were they? All wars enforce a fundamental reappraisal of food supplies, and all wreak damage upon the land that has to be repaired as quickly as possible. But they may also precipitate unavoidable, or deliberate, structural changes of greater long-term significance, and, in any case, they impose new experiences which colour the outlook of the whole population for at least a generation. The long-term economic and social consequences of the Russian Revolution were radical indeed, but in the English case they were far less so, for the old agrarian framework was conserved. Nevertheless, perceptions of the kingdom's agricultural needs, its agricultural potential, and its social goals underwent fundamental change as a result of experiences during the war and after. Many attitudes and practices were significantly modified, while the debates on long-standing agrarian problems also moved forward, and took a fresh direction. So although a different atmosphere was restored at the Restoration, not all the new viewpoints and aspirations emerging since 1640 were immediately abandoned. A notable interest in agricultural innovation survived, though that will not form the theme of this essay, for it has recently been discussed elsewhere.[1] Here attention is concentrated on older structural problems which rumbled on throughout the seventeenth century and beyond. Were they solved, and if not, was their complexion altered as a result of insights achieved in the years of revolution?[2]

In order to judge the novelty of events in the years between 1640 and 1660, it is necessary briefly to survey the agrarian scene in the 1630s, and observe the preoccupations of that decade. In the first years a run of wet seasons, ruining grain harvests and spreading livestock sickness, caused grievous hardship throughout the kingdom. When inviting reports from the counties, the Privy Council received plentiful evidence of rural poverty aggravated by depopulating enclosure; indeed, it was generally considered that the prevailing grain scarcity had been much worsened by enclosure. Hence a first enquiry into enclosure was launched in 1632 followed by two more in 1635 and 1636. Commissioners assiduously gathered information against enclosers, and fined them, in some cases heavily. As chairman of the Commission Archbishop Laud was alleged to have had an almost fanatical prejudice against enclosers, and even though the rigours of the punishments seem to have been alleviated between 1632 and 1635 – 36, gentlemen were still paying fines in 1639. The evils of depopulating enclosure remained in the forefront of public debate on the eve of the Civil War.[3]

Another issue high on the agenda at the same time was the king's claim to own all coastal land then being recovered from the sea.[4] He did not need to own the adjacent manors to protest his claim; all land which had once lain under the sea but was now retrieved was said to be his by royal prerogative. The legality of this assertion was contested, and was even contemptuously dismissed in 1640, but, if it ever should prevail, it was well understood that the Crown would be in a position to dispossess the inhabitants of coastal parishes of hundreds of acres recently acquired, and to bestow the land elsewhere.[5] In places where this had already happened (on manors owned by the Crown), the grantees of this so-called 'surrounded ground' were courtiers without local affiliations, and the inhabitants seethed with resentment.

At the same time the Crown was supporting the policy of improving common lands. The right to improve all waste land that was deemed in excess of the needs of manorial tenants was a statutory enactment from the Middle Ages, and was re-enacted with minor revisions in 1550. This had the effect of underlining, even recommending, the principle of improving the commons, and in Elizabeth's reign it was discreetly put to use on Crown lands in moorland country. It was far from becoming a forgotten statute, for in common parlance in the early seventeenth century it was called the Statute of Improvement.[6] Under its provisions, both James I and Charles I supported fenland drainage schemes, claiming the right to appropriate thousands of acres of common land, partly for the profit of the Crown, and partly to reward the drainers. The Crown was also in the process of disafforesting some forests in the 1630s, in order to allow agricultural improvement and industrial development. All this formed part of a larger programme to reform the management of the Crown's estates, and had been under way since at least Elizabeth's reign, but it was clumsily handled in the second half of James's reign, and expanded under Charles into yet wilder realms of fantasy. One of its most significant consequences in the 1630s was to draw ever more attention to tracts of land in the kingdom which might be, or perhaps ought to be, differently, or more intensively, farmed in the future. It did not make the monarchy popular.[7]

A fourth prominent concern of the 1630s, which had been running on from the beginning of the century, was the legal status of manorial tenants on both Crown and lay estates. For financial reasons in a period of price inflation, lords were calling the customary status of their tenants into question. This bred much uncertainty. Settlements were achieved either by confirming established customs (at a price, of course) or by enfranchising copyholds (at a still higher price). The Crown had embarked on a deliberate policy of enfranchisement on its own estates in 1603–04, but was thwarted by its tenants' resistance. It had settled in many cases for the confirmation of manorial customs, and then, at the end of James's reign, had abandoned the programme altogether.[8] Among private lords facing the same alternatives, however, enfranchisement did not become a dead issue; we shall see the current of debate flowing on, and some modest changes achieved, during the Interregnum.[9]

Yet another tenurial uncertainty entangled tenants who held Crown land directly from the king, and who were charged with holding it by defective titles, or with 'concealing' land from the authorities, and failing to pay the due rents and charges to the Exchequer. The right to search could not justly be contested, but the method was. Searchers for 'concealed' land were such a plague in the countryside that a storm of protest erupted in Parliament in 1621. It was assuaged by royal promises of reform. Yet the procedure of granting to individuals rights of search continued furtively in use throughout the 1630s, and although it did not feature among complaints in the Grand Remonstrance in 1640, it remained in some districts of the country a festering grievance.[10]

Thus the agrarian scene in 1640 was littered with unresolved conflicts between the Crown and the people. Nor were these conflicts confined to tenants of the Crown. The relations of private lords with their tenants were also affected, for landowners had been much influenced by the Crown's policies on its own estates. The Crown, in fact, set an example, which encouraged lay lords to follow suit, and the repercussions were already conspicuous with regard to the improvement of commons. All in all, then, the rural scene at the end of the 1630s was far from peaceful, and much of the unrest sprang from clumsy governmental mishandling of delicate situations. Mounting pressure of population on the land necessitated changes, but the cautious policies of Elizabeth had been abandoned for an entirely different style; in breaking long-standing conventions, the Crown nurtured among all classes of tenants a deep sense of grievance and injustice, and caused special hardships among the poor. The Commonwealth had to face every one of these issues in turn.

Finally, we should not ignore another disruptive feature of the decade namely, the sharp rise in the cost of living which occurred in the 1630s, and which marked a notable break in the trend of the previous twenty years. Counting from a base of 100 in 1600–09, average food costs in the years between 1610 and 1630 had hovered between 115 and 116, but in the 1630s they rose sharply to 137.[11] In other words, another problem loomed, that of protecting consumers of food against producers. Considerable efforts were made, on the orders of the Privy Council, to provide cheap bread for the poor, but ministers saw the long-term solution in using the land more intensively to grow more food, mainly by accelerating the drive to improve commons, but also by allowing enclosure, though strictly without depopulation. All this might have been possible through a cautious, slow-moving programme. But in 1640 the king's subjects were far from reconciled to the methods which the government chose to achieve this goal. The Grand Remonstrance, drawn up in 1641, voiced clear protests at the King's policy towards the forests, fen drainage, newly inned coastal marshland, the improvement of commons, and enclosure and depopulation.[12]

All continuity in government policy was abruptly broken by the rupture between king and Parliament and the consequent Civil War. When peace was restored, agrarian problems loomed large because of the damage done to land, and to the routines of the food producers. But the measures that were taken were not planned in a cool and considered manner. They were forced on Parliament by the crises of the moment, and most of all by the heavy burden of debt with which it was now laden. Its shortages of funds to pay for the war obliged it in November 1646 to sell all the lands of the bishops, in April 1649 the lands of deans and chapters, in July 1649 the lands of the Crown, and in 1651–52 the lands of Royalists whose estates had been sequestrated but who refused, or were not allowed, to compound. Social relations in villages were much disturbed in consequence, and to a less extent so were farming regimes.

A small number of tenants, sometimes acting as a group, seized the chance to buy their properties.[13] But most purchasers of confiscated land were gentry, merchants, or soldiers returning to civilian life, and some radical changes in land use were, therefore, inevitable. Land once held by a bishop, for example, was not likely to be used in the same way by a Parliamentary officer turning to farming and a gentlemanly lifestyle. In any case, some new owners had high hopes of experimenting on fresh lines.[14] Land was thus put to different uses, thereby affecting the community at large, while many farmers experienced a change of landlord, or had to accommodate to new neighbours.

In some communities where former Royalist landlords retained the loyalty of their tenants, new purchasers had to establish peaceable relations under delicate circumstances. One Royalist observer saw nothing but scenes of bitterness: tenants of former church and crown lands, he maintained, hated new purchasers as 'the greatest tyrants everywhere as possibly men can be. They wrest the poor tenants of all former immunities and freedoms they formerly enjoyed'.[15] But this was only one view of the uneasy scene. Tenants with Parliamentary sympathies suffered, in their turn, from the oppressions of 'malignant', i.e. Royalist landlords. In fact, so grave were these accusations that Parliament under the new republic promised in June 1649 to legislate in their defence. Judges on their circuits publicly proclaimed that an act to protect the tenants of malignant landlords would follow. The Commons were reminded again and again of their undertakings, and a direct appeal was made to Cromwell in 1654 from tenants in Lancashire and Cheshire.[16] But other business constantly intervened, and no act or ordinance was ever passed.

While many tracts of country were beset with social tensions, directly caused by the war, the economic consequences raised other difficulties. Landlords of all persuasions had suffered damage to their properties and income, and somehow had to make up their losses. The pressing need for food to feed the army, and for horses to equip it, made unprecedented demands on farmers throughout the forties. The protests of the Clubmen resisting damage to their farmlands reflected their struggles to survive and supply the market,[17] as did the complaints of the rural population against the demands for free quarter for soldiers.[18] The difficulties were made much worse for all by a run of bad weather and disastrous harvests which started in 1646 and did not end until 1652. Yet the only positive action taken by Parliament and the Council of State before 1650, which helped to overcome these many short-term agrarian problems, was to check grain exports.[19] In short, agrarian problems generally ranked low in the list of priorities.

After 1650 the supporters of the new republic took stock of the agrarian situation in the liberated, optimistic mood of planners surveying the scene with fresh eyes.[20] Some well-intentioned preliminary moves were made to resolve short-term difficulties, but most were endlessly delayed, either by more pressing debates, or by changes in Parliament. As a result, they finally ran into the sand. Thus the relief of the poor was reported and considered in September 1648, and February 1649. London's poor were promised action in May 1649, but none followed.[21] A committee to revise the whole body of poor laws and devise means of setting the poor to work throughout the Commonwealth was named on 1 March 1650, and an act hoped for in May 1650. It was still awaited in October 1650, but it never came.[22] In February 1651 the wild suggestion was made that superfluous cathedrals be pulled down and sold, and the profits used to buy work stocks.[23] In April 1652 measures to provide work for the poor were again called for, and this time the resulting bill seems to have included some reference to the growing of hemp and flax. It was on the brink of acceptance in February 1653, but faltered with the expulsion of the Rump Parliament in April, and a fresh start was made by Barebones Parliament in July. Again nothing passed.[24] Three years later the Committee for the Poor was revived, and ordered to revise the statutes concerning vagrants and raising stocks for the poor. It produced a bill in June 1657, and was considering yet another in August 1659. But finally the republic's time ran out.[25] Yet another failed scheme was intended to look at the laws concerning the wages of artificers, labourers, and servants. A bill was ordered 'for further redress' in October 1656, though we are given no clue whether it would have raised or lowered wages. It too slipped from sight.[26]

The one decisive and constructive measure to assist farmers in the 1650s was taken as a result of falling food prices, which presented a dramatic contrast with the situation in the 1630s and 1640s. From 1653 prices fell so low that farmers feared ruin. An ordinance of 1656, therefore, (coming three years after it was first called for) allowed the export of grain. It explained the necessity for this remarkable change of policy as a consequence of the improvement of fens, forests, chases, and other lands, whereby an excess of corn, cattle, butter, cheese, etc., was being produced; these foodstuffs, it explained, were needed by nations abroad and in the plantations. Thus was inaugurated a fundamental reversal of policy, which proved to be of long-term importance. Prices continued low after the Restoration and Parliament was subsequently obliged to go still further to dispose of surplus foodstuffs; it actually paid bounties from 1674 onwards to farmers who managed to export.[27]

Decisions on agrarian matters did not come easily either in Parliament or the Council of State. Good intentions were frustrated by the failure to agree or by preoccupations with other matters. But decisions to relieve financial problems were much more urgent, and one of these, involving the future of the forests, not only profoundly affected the woodland communities; it had consequences which reverberated over a far larger territory.

In particular, it introduced fresh nuances into the debate on the improvement of commons, and the effects lasted well after 1660.

Charles I had outraged opinion by his grotesque manoeuvres for raising revenue from the forests, by disafforestation and then by his extension of forest rights into much larger areas beyond the existing boundaries. When once Parliament declared England a Commonwealth, prerogative laws were considered no longer to be in force, and hence it was assumed that forest law was suspended.[28] This, in effect, gave the forest inhabitants free rein to exploit and despoil woodland timber. Not all blame for the ensuing destruction should be laid at their door, however, for Parliament itself enacted ordinances in 1643 to allow fuel to be taken from church and delinquents' estates within sixty miles of London. This relieved the immediate problem of supplying the needs of Londoners when Newcastle fell into Royalist hands and coal could no longer be despatched south.[29] In 1644 Parliament issued another order, requiring timber for the navy to be felled in Waltham Forest and on certain delinquents' estates.[30] Again the urgent needs of the moment dictated these decisions, and the long-term supply of forest timber was still not considered.

Glimmerings of a larger responsibility began to be shown when the Crown's lands were put up for sale in 1649, and Parliament omitted the forests in order to preserve naval timber.[31] But even then the consequences of former neglect were not fully realised, and it was not until 1651 when Parliament considered the need to build more ships for the navy, that the Council of State was earnestly warned to look at the state of the forests.[32] Alerted to consider their long-term future, it at last ordered an enquiry into the New Forest, which was then broadened to other forests, including the Forest of Dean.[33] A Committee for Forests and Preservation of Timber sprang into being, which was kept busy throughout 1652 hearing many petitions. By November it had assembled various alternative proposals for preserving timber, the urgency of the matter being reflected in one expensive suggestion for obtaining masts and tar, if need be, from Scottish woodlands.[34]

The wording of the Parliamentary instructions to the Committee for Forests was now, however, significantly different from that which would have been used in the 1640s. It reiterated the need to improve the forests not only for the advantage of the commonwealth, but having 'special regard to the poor and to the just rights of all persons claiming anything therein'.[35] Recent events had shifted the viewpoint from which the matter was now being observed. Doubtless, the memory of Charles's forest policies, and the fury of the foresters, had not faded, but much more prominent in the minds of MPs were the recent reminders of the Levellers, the Diggers, as well as some Parliamentarians that the common people had been the loyal supporters of Parliament, and had made victory possible. Their rights had to be regarded.

Nevertheless, the prospective improvement and partial sale of the forests were inseparably linked with the need to pay off the army. Hence soldiers were prominent among the MPs to whom the Parliamentary bill for sale was committed in January 1653. Still, a reluctance to act may be read into its sluggish progress, even though other matters of greater moment also intervened: the Rump was expelled in April 1653, and Barebones Parliament replaced it. So fresh petitions were needed, from the army for pay, and from the navy for money, to stir the issue again. In November 1653, terms for the disafforestation, sale, and improvement of the forests seemed to be complete. But even then, in March and April 1654, the details were still being altered. Finally, in the same year four forests reserved as security for the payment of soldiers' arrears of pay were ordered for sale.[36]

Far from being the end of the long forest saga, this was only the end of the beginning. Now officials appointed to improve or sell the forests confronted the practicalities, and the true scale of their daunting task. They had been reminded many times to satisfy the poor, and pay heed to all commoners' claims. When these were satisfied, they had to choose the parts of each forest which were to be conserved by the state for its timber and let on lease, and allot other parts for sale. The whole scheme quickly became bogged down in surveys, the investigation of documents, arguments with the forest inhabitants, and, even worse, controversy within the circle of officials carrying out the decisions.[37]

In the end some pieces of the forests, which were not reserved to pay off the soldiers, were, indeed, sold, but in general these sales attracted few buyers. In the Northamptonshire forests, an account prepared in 1662 names only four purchasers, paying £773 18s. 4d.[38] As for the four forests intended to raise money to pay off the soldiers, matters never reached that advanced stage. The sales were thwarted by a multitude of other problems on the way, including disputes among the surveyors about the fees which they would be paid.[39] These uncertainties delayed the start of the surveys, but more problems loomed when the surveyors confronted the forest inhabitants. Battles with them are graphically portrayed in the Needwood forest, Staffordshire, and, better than any other examples, these illuminate how new perceptions of commoners' rights, and fresh nuances of understanding glimmered as Parliament strove to 'improve the commons' and raise money at the same time.

When news of the prospective sale of Needwood forest reached the inhabitants, twenty forest villages combined to prepare a weighty petition against it. It was worded with great skill, and plainly had been phrased by astute lawyers. Ten parks had already been taken out of Needwood by former kings, it declared, yet now Parliament was choosing to reduce the forest further. Some inhabitants held charters dating from before the time when the Duchy of Lancaster was annexed to the Crown, while some had 'common of estover in gross and common of pasture in gross', which the lawyers assured them precluded any improvement of the soil. The foresters pronounced confidently that compensation would leave little to be sold for the benefit of the soldiers, and boldly asked that those, whose claims might in the end be disallowed, should still be given the right to pursue them in the lawcourts. More conditions in the document led up to the final withering reminder: Parliament already owed the county of Staffordshire (of which Needwood was 'no small part') nearly £8,000 spent on the soldiers. Sheets of signatures, ranged in three and four columns on a page, contained 834 names, and ran to nine pages.[40]

The organisation lying behind this document can be imagined. Those living on the north side of the forest especially had rallied whole families of 5, 6 and 8 people to make their marks on the petition: in Marchington, for example, 134 out of the 165 signatories signed with a mark, representing 35 different surnames. The Grand Jury had carried the protest to Quarter Sessions, expressing its own cogent support for the Needwood foresters, to which the JPs of the county had added their own remarks. The projected sale was, they maintained, an affront to 'the rule of reason and proportion'. Why should the army of the whole commonwealth be paid for by a few poor townships, while the great and rich townships 'did not pay or sustain a farthing loss'? Why not sell all the King's and Queen's commons, so that all shared the cost?[41]

Zachariah Babington, one of Staffordshire's JPs zealously fighting the foresters' cause, carried his influence to Westminster. He won the ear of Sir Charles Wolseley, who was an MP for the county as well as a member of the Council of State. The ground was thus well prepared when Needwood's impressive bundle of documents was thrust into the hands of John Thurloe, who showed them to Cromwell. Cromwell passed them for deliberation to the whole Council of State.[42]

The Needwood forest battle was a superlative example of the tussle between high principles and expedient practice which so often divided opinion in Parliament and thwarted decisions on agrarian matters. Whenever the sale of the forests was discussed in Parliament MPs underlined their desire to deal justly with the poor, with commoners, and with all their loyal supporters, who had helped them to victory against the King. Yet their actions were at variance with their words. For their part, the commoners adopted a much bolder posture, and engaged in far more outspoken and logical debate with their masters than ever occurred under the first two Stuarts.[43] In short, the issues raised by 'the improvement of the forests' were now discussed at Westminster on a different plane from before. If it was to be implemented, the procedures had to be far more circumspect.

Cromwell soothed the petitioners of Needwood with promises that the commoners would be justly compensated, and that the forest would not be sold if too little remained to yield the necessary cash. A long enquiry plainly lay ahead.[44] Battles broke out whenever the surveyors appeared in the forest, and in May 1657 the commissioners for sale appealed desperately for a troop of horse to defend them while they collected rents, sold fallen wood, and fined offenders.[45] The sales had originally been ordered in 1654, but renewed instructions in June 1657 showed that little progress had yet been made.[46] Indeed, even some of those closely involved in the sale had lost all faith in their power to raise much money by such efforts. Colonel Sydenham, one of the administrators, warned the Commons in debates in 1657 that, when once claimants and commoners had been compensated, the sales would yield much less than MPs hoped.[47] In the event, all the delays gave the foresters victory, for with the return of Charles II the sale of Needwood was abandoned.[48] After 1660 the Crown emphatically retreated from any aggressive policy to sell or raise revenues drastically from its forests. A radical review was not undertaken until the 1780s, and only then, under quite different economic circumstances, was Needwood (in 1801) finally enclosed.[49]

Another series of battles raged around the draining of the fens, which had been closely associated with the former king. Parliament in 1640–42 had encouraged the protests of the fenlanders, but during the war, as the drainers maintained their pressure on Parliament for support, notably in the Great Level, a more ambivalent attitude was adopted towards the obstinate inhabitants.[50] Then at the birth of the republic, Parliament granted its approval unusually promptly to the drainers in the Great Level, in spite of the fenlanders' plea for the poor to be delivered out of the hands of their rich neighbours, and 'enjoy their own'.[51] The drainers were allowed to complete the work already begun, and their final objective was approved in the judgment that it would be 'of great advantage to the Commonwealth'.[52] The drainers of the Lindsey Level appealed for similar support, but were given a committee to investigate, which clogged the machinery in argument and counter-argument and delayed any report until 1652. In 1653 Cromwell was said to have mixed feelings on the merits of that project, and it made no further headway.[53] In Axholme the fenlanders went on the offensive against the drainers, with the help of experienced attorneys and political support from the Levellers.[54]

The battle in the fens divided opinion into two camps, as in the forests. On the one hand, draining the fens would create more arable land to grow more food, and yield more farms for husbandmen. Many gentlemen had vested interests in this purpose, being investors or landowners. On the other hand, it was recognised that the fenlanders had valiantly contributed to the defence of Parliament against the king, and did not deserve to see their livelihood altered out of recognition, even destroyed, by the drainage. The fenlanders recognised clearly that drainage would undermine their pastoral economy, whereas those in authority without personal knowledge of these regions were deaf to arguments in favour of a stock-grazing, fishing, fowling economy. The official viewpoint was deeply entrenched, at least until 1653, that grain growing should be extended wherever possible.

Yet as a result of experiences in the 1650s, opinions shifted more than once, and the balance of opinion was far from clear at the Restoration. Walter Blith, for example, writing on the improvement of agriculture in 1649, bitterly opposed drainage. But, wanting to see things at first hand, he went into Lincolnshire, and by 1652 had changed his mind. He now wrote enthusiastically in favour. Among Parliamentary soldiers who were put to work in the fen, and might have been expected to sympathise with the fenlanders, some were sufficiently persuaded of the fine prospects ahead that they took land there.[55] Some Parliamentary officers also acquired estates around the Wash which they transformed into experimental farms, growing new crops, and attracting special admiration from William Dugdale. At the same period, 1652–54, the pronouncements of government and others in official circles showed increasing impatience with the hostile fenlanders and stronger support for the drainers.[56] By 1656 the opinion was publicly purveyed in an ordinance that the surplus of foodstuffs, driving down prices, was due to the new productivity of the fens and the forests.[57]

After 1656, however, some of the belligerent determination to push ahead with drainage schemes evaporated, and approval for drainage schemes everywhere could not be taken for granted.[58] In 1656 Parliament faced a plan to revive an old scheme involving drainage in King's Sedgmoor, Somerset. We do not know the full content of the debate that followed, but one MP reported that the tenants and freeholders did not consent, and Parliament rejected the scheme. Experience had shown how much clamour, besides crops, was raised by improving waste lands, and for other reasons too, the advantages were no longer clear-cut.[59]

The success of some of the new fenland crops like rapeseed and onions was unquestionable, and was achieved in no small measure by the experience of foreign settlers, who had cultivated these crops in the Netherlands and France, and who now demonstrated what could be grown on fertile, drained soils. But at the same time plentiful grain and falling grain prices weakened the argument in favour of drainage. Thomas Fuller in 1655 poured scorn on the opponents of drainage, whose worst complaint now must be of 'an inundation of plenty, all commodities being grown so cheap', but when cheapnes continued it did become a valid farmer's complaint. Moreover, some persuasive arguments began to be assembled in the 1650s on the superior advantages of pasture, because it yielded products that enjoyed more stable prices, and ultimately gave more work, not only in the textile and leather industries, but also in dairying.[60] At the Restoration the merits of pasture farming weighed more heavily still, as grain prices continued low. Moreover, a certain shift of emphasis to livestock-keeping occurred on arable farms through the introduction of clover, lucerne, and sainfoin into arable rotations. These new crops had received much attention from experimental farmers during the Interregnum, and bore a rich harvest after 1660.[61] Consequently, drainage projects for more grain slid from their high place on the agenda of agricultural improvement.[62] Economic conditions after 1660 further relaxed the pressure on the fenlanders, slowed down drainage operations, and gave some of the inhabitants the chance to preserve the old fenland economy for some decades longer. Drainage schemes were not revived with the old enthusiasm until the later eighteenth century.[63]

Outside the fens and the forests the Crown had favoured a larger programme to improve the commons on its own estates and had encouraged other landowners to follow suit. Events in the 1650s showed that the desirability of improving the commons aroused little disagreement among landowners, so long as the process was held firmly in their control. But Parliament's victory against the king also aroused hopes among commoners that they too might benefit from the new freedom that dawned. The plan to improve the commons now took a new turn. As Gerrard Winstanley pointedly noted in his *New Year's Gift for the Parliament and Army* in 1650, whilst the king reigned 'all sorts of people complained of oppression, both gentry and common people, because their lands, enclosures and copyholds were entangled'. Now he reminded the gentry: 'when you were assembled in Parliament, you called upon the poor common people to come and help you and cast out oppression. And you that complained are helped and freed'.[64] It was now the turn of the commoners to share some of the fruits of victory.

Gentlemen could not deny that 'there is land enough and more by half than is made use of'; they had repeatedly asserted this themselves when pressing their own schemes of improvement.[65] They also recognised the dependence of the poor on the commons; whenever improvement and enclosure were debated, the need to protect the poor was reiterated. Winstanley was but logical in asking, in the light of the new political situation and the current moves to improve the commons, that the poor should be granted a more active role, and share in the benefits. Under his plan the poor would be the improvers of the waste and common land. They could then 'live in peace, freed from the heavy burdens of poverty. For hereby our own land will be increased with all sorts of commodities ...' The very words were the same as had been used by the gentry in their tracts and treatises.[66]

Winstanley not merely claimed for the poor their right 'to dig and freely plant the waste and common for a livelihood', he implemented the right with action. The digging up of commons took place at St George's Hill, Surrey, in 1649, where it lasted a full year, and by 1650 had spread to seven other known places in the Home Counties and East Midlands, and to other places unknown in Nottinghamshire, and Gloucestershire.[67] Winstanley argued the legal claims of the commoners thus: it was an ancient custom 'bred in the strength of kingly prerogative' that allowed lords of manors to lay claim to commons, and that right was 'of no force now to bind the people of England since the kingly power and office was cast out'. England could not claim properly to be called a Commonwealth unless the land of England were 'a free land and a common treasury to all her children'.[68]

Landlords, of course, were alarmed, and the humble improvers of commons were promptly prosecuted for trespass, and forcibly driven out. The Digger movement subsided within two years, but it does not belong to the footnotes of history.[69] It has been described as the culmination of a century of squatting on forests and wastes,[70] but in fact, discerning contemporaries recognised a different parentage. It was the offspring of the programme for improving commons, one of the prominent items in the Stuarts' reform of Crown lands, and named as a grievance in the Grand Remonstrance. The Diggers had elevated it into a respectable goal for the common people, who would carry it out in the name of the Commonwealth. Not surprisingly, it was not acceptable to landowners in this altered guise. During the war gentlemen had already expressed alarm lest 'the necessitous people of the whole kingdom' should 'set up for themselves, to the utter ruin of all the nobility and gentry'. Now that prospect threatened indeed, and the Diggers could not expect to enlist wholehearted support even from their fellow commoners. Both small and large farmers must have looked on with misgiving, as their commons were diminished by the new allotments.[71] But the stronger cry which defeated the Diggers was that which drove more plans than this into the ground. Landowners would not tolerate a threat to property rights.

Enclosure was another such issue, in which Parliament declined to meddle for the same reason. Charles I had set up vigorous commissions against depopulation in the 1630s. But after thirteen years of neglect it demanded attention again. The Committee for the Poor was asked in July 1653 to look at a proposal to check depopulation and the decay of tillage.[72] The deprivation of commoners plainly lay behind this move, for otherwise it would not have been deemed a concern of this committee. Two years passed without further action, but in the provinces, notably in the East Midland counties, lively discussions continued on the way to effect enclosures fairly. To many contemporaries, the true centre of the debate in these years was the means to achieve a fair division of the commons.[73] Ensuing debates, and the requirements of particular enclosures, often shifted the ground to tithes, or to the geographical location of the new lots in common fields, but the main anxieties centred on justice to the poor and the commoners. This was made clear when Parliament finally agreed to hear some petitions from Leicestershire, and Major-General Edward Whalley brought in an enclosure bill in 1656. It was described as 'concerning the dividing of commons', and although its contents were nowhere made clear, it seemed designed to ensure that three commissioners and a jury supervised every enclosure, and gave full compensation for lost common rights. But members of Parliament declared such a bill to be 'most mischievous' for it 'destroyed property', and they refused it a second reading.[74] So ended all official attempts under the Commonwealth to seek legislation on enclosure.

The burdens of copyhold tenure were another problem inherited from the past, which republicans repeatedly discussed, though not in Parliament, in the hope of finding a solution under the new Commonwealth. Copyhold services and obligations to attend courts baron, act as jurors, pay arbitrary fines, heriots, and quit rents, were frequently referred to in the writings of Levellers and Diggers, and were always deemed 'the ancient and almost antiquated badge of slavery'. Disputes about uncertain fines, determined by the will of the lord, rankled most, and as early as 1647 1,200 inhabitants of Hertfordshire had reminded the

Parliamentary party that the suffering copyholders were a large proportion of the population, who had been loyal to Parliament while lords had not.[75] Security and independence for copyhold tenants were their goals, but these did not remain simple slogans demanding the abolition of servile tenures. Hard proposals also featured in the tracts. The Levellers' *New Engagement or Manifesto* suggested that one rate be fixed at which all copyholders might buy their freeholds. A version of *The Agreement of the People*, amended by Lieutenant Colonel Jubbes, suggested a price of not more than twenty years' purchase, noting that this was the figure that had been arrived at 'upon a conscientious computation of profits' in James's reign.[76] This was a clear reference to James's short-lived scheme in 1603–04 to enfranchise copyholds on Crown estates. Because tenants had resisted, it had been abandoned, but significantly the memory survived.[77] Further knowledge of past endeavours surfaced in a lawyer's *Experimental Essay touching the Reformation of the Laws of England*, which cited Coke and Bacon, and recommended that base tenures be bought out. On some manors, it observed, the freehold had been sold to copyholders at thirty years' purchase.[78]

Yet the copyhold issue was never deemed important enough to reach the top of the agenda under the Commonwealth. Even among the Leveller leaders, H. N. Brailsford noted the lack of vital interest in the matter: though some Leveller petitions and proposals included it, it was left out of the amended versions. In the Putney debates Cromwell had tentatively suggested the enfranchisement of some copyholders by inheritance, but this was a thoroughly conservative proposal, for such copyholders were already virtually freeholders. In 1652 a bill was drafted to limit arbitrary fines on inheritance and alienation to one year's rent, but four Parliaments came and went and it did not pass. Even though all base tenures were abolished in Scotland by the Act of Union in 1654, MPs, as English landowners, were unwilling to liberate their constituents from the same yoke.[79]

The Stuarts' search for concealed Crown lands had aroused contention about governmental procedures, rather than about principle, while the search for reclaimed marshland had engendered controversy on both counts. Since the Stuarts engaged its searchers to look for both kinds of land at the same time the two procedures became associated, and so they remained under the Commonwealth.

At no stage after 1640 was it necessary to debate the principle. The need to search for the concealed lands of delinquents, the Crown and the church was accepted without question, as their owners were the state's enemies. Nor were republicans disposed to revive, with fresh arguments, royal claims to own reclaimed marshland, however urgent their need to raise cash. But memories of the means used by the Stuarts to search for concealed land, and to discover and dispute the ownership of marshland did not lie dormant in the 1650s. Despite the known evils of the devices used to search for concealed land, Parliament did not manage to avoid using them. After first making concessions to delinquents themselves who confessed to concealments, the government encouraged individuals, sometimes army officers, sometimes speculators, to discover them. After July 1654, discoverers of concealed church lands also had the first right to buy.[80] Those who discovered concealments were allowed to buy the land at twenty years' purchase, using public faith bills, though they were not allowed to buy on behalf of tenants, auditors, or surveyors. In the event, many discoveries were made by Parliamentary soldiers, doubtless grateful to redeem public faith bills in this way. And though we have no clue to the means by which they found such lands, it is unlikely that they managed without the help of professional searchers.[81]

More memories from the past stirred when the Exchequer instituted county-wide searches for 'concealed lands'. One search for Crown land was instituted in 1651 by means of Exchequer commissions, but it does not appear to have yielded a rich harvest. The concealed lands of Royalists and Papists did not prompt debate in the Commons until 1656, when it was evidently deemed that the Exchequer had lost touch with the day-to-day lettings of sequestered estates that had not been sold. Formal county-wide enquiries were launched in 1657 and the commissioners were authorised to issue new leases.[82] Did John Pym smile benignly from his grave? At least these searches had the merit of being conducted according to correct Exchequer procedures. Serving in the Exchequer in the early 1620s, Pym had sought out in some detail the crimes of Giles Mompesson, a corrupt private searcher for concealed lands, holding a patent from James I; nearly twenty years later Pym had been the leading compiler of the Grand Remonstrance, protesting at such abuses. Now in the later 1650s, the correct, official procedures were being followed in a public manner, and many 'good and lawful men' were enrolled as jurors. Here and there the enquiries dragged on into 1659 but they did not stir the waters, and the Restoration brought them to an end.[83]

Echoes of Charles I's claim to coastal marshlands also reverberated faintly in the later 1650s. They prompted two very different responses, but both showed that old resentments simmered still. In the first case, a private individual asked in 1656 for a patent, though he did not call it such, and received a prompt official rebuff: John Osborne requested a warrant to search for concealments, including reclaimed marshlands, desiring for himself a grant of one-third of the lands discovered, and 50-year leases of flooded land. This savoured too much of Charles's corrupt grants, and was summarily dismissed with the retort that such commissions were illegal.[84] But another Exchequer enquiry was launched in 1655 into marshland won from the sea in the vicinity of Deal in Kent, calling for information about cottages built on the marsh. This time it was the inhabitants who gave robust answers, in a thoroughly recalcitrant frame of mind. They noted that a survey of all the Deal manor lands had already been conducted in 1650, resulting in a document twenty pages long. The committee of Parliament, they declared, had resolved that the houses on the marshland 'properly belonged to the Commonwealth of England'. Nevertheless, under this new threat, they took more resolute action: they sought the help of two admirals of the fleet, opportunely lodging on ships lying at anchor off Deal. These influential gentlemen sent their own letter to the Council of State.[85] Considered at this high level, and with sound evidence of the republic's earlier decisions, the dispute was doubtless settled in the cottagers' favour. But it demonstrated how poor men had learned to make their voices heard in high places. They were not prepared to stand weakly by and suffer, their boldness being encouraged by the examples of their peers in fens and forests, and the known sympathy that poor men's causes elicited in Parliament.

Many hopes of positive action to achieve agrarian change were disappointed during the English Revolution. Plans were discussed, and much thought went into considering practical ways of implementing them, but in Parliament the majority vote in favour failed to emerge, and one after another proposal fell by the wayside, either rejected outright, or squeezed out by other business or indifference. For the most significant changes, we have to look not to the actions of Parliament at Westminster, but to the efforts of individuals, effecting changes locally even if they could not be achieved nationally. The 1650s gave some landowners, especially those acquiring confiscated land, new opportunities and new arguments for changing agrarian relations, and although the majority of English parishes were untouched by any subsequent revolution, a careful reading of their histories yields evidence, or at least hints, that some opportunities were seized, perhaps even some idealist aspirations put into practice.[86]

Some purchasers of confiscated estates proceeded to sell off small parcels to tenants and local buyers, mostly yeomen and husbandmen, which effectively enfranchised copyholds. Major-General Philip Skippon did this on Winslow, Whaddon, and Bletchley manors, Buckinghamshire, for example, and his action leaves a lurking suspicion that he acted on principle. Samuel Chidley re-sold many parcels of the Crown manor which he bought at Greensnorton, Northamptonshire, and as he was a Leveller, may we not believe that some ideals underlay his actions?[87]

Some of the enclosures completed in the 1650s, though doubtless mooted earlier, and perhaps in a different political climate, showed a marked concern to divide commons and fields agreeably and equitably, and provide for the poor. Were they responding to new aspirations for the commonweal? They certainly seem conspicuous at Clifton-upon-Dunsmore, Warwickshire in 1648–50.[88] They also seem to underlie a division of the commons at Sheene in Staffordshiire where 800–1,000 acres were distributed among commoners between 1649 and 1659. It is true that this matter took ten years before all objectors were satisfied, and the final agreement was imposed in the Court of Chancery, yet the circumstances suggest a care to deal justly with everyone in a way that faithfully mirrored current concerns. The move in this case had been initiated much earlier, but long-drawn-out wrangles, and then, doubtless, the Civil War had obstructed its completion. Sir Henry Montagu, the first Earl of Manchester, a lawyer and chief justice of the King's Bench, had agreed to enfranchise the copyholds of the manor and divide the common between the commoners in 1629.[89] He died in 1642, but the copyholds were nevertheless enfranchised without trouble. Dissent obstructed the division of the commons and it was still unsettled in 1649. In that momentous year a fresh survey was instituted, and 'a great deal of pains' were taken to measure the ground, and then to arrange for four gentlemen, nominated by the tenants, to supervise the allocation of land with the surveyor. Even when the final partition was published seven years later in 1656 five freeholders still dissented, and the four referees resigned. Finally, the judges in Chancery were asked to settle the dispute, and they now appointed four new referees. We cannot pass judgment on the equity of the final agreement in 1659, but we have to recognise the prolonged efforts to achieve it; in the mood of the age, it was probably the fairest settlement that could be hoped for.[90] The same pains appear at East Knoyle, Wiltshire, where a lowland common in the vale of Wardour was divided. Enclosure had been agreed in 1636, at a time when enclosers were already on their guard, since Charles's depopulation enquiries were actively under way. Due caution was taken in the allotment of pieces to commoners and cottagers by appointing ten lottsmen 'of good condition and quality, against whom there shall be no just exception taken by any main party of those interested in the enclosure'. The settlement was still in dispute when Edmund Ludlow bought this confiscated bishop's estate, and attempted in 1651 to end the wrangles amicably.[91] Six years later in the manor court it was agreed to seek a settlement in the Exchequer court.

In this case Exchequer Commissioners were appointed, who held several meetings and spent many days in the parish, examining grievances. They decided that the stumbling block was recent purchasers who unreasonably quarrelled with the partition of the commons, which they had accepted at purchase. Even their suggested settlement still did not pacify, and the commissioners resigned. This finally brought matters to a head, and the judges were called on to give the final verdict. This they did, evidently on much the same basis as the original one in 1636. It did not long benefit Edmund Ludlow, for his estate was restored to the bishop at the Restoration, but the story, so far as it can be uncovered, suggests that while public opinion moved steadily towards the view that enclosure was a desirable objective, the practical measures to achieve it now included some long-drawn-out, painstaking reviews. Exchequer and Chancery decrees were not always rubber stamps upon an agreement arrived at elsewhere. Sometimes agreements were, indeed, reached amicably, but in other cases decrees ended persistent attempts to enclose with the consent of all, and had required repeated investigations by more than one group of referees, before a decision was finally made by the judges.[92] Thus, although Parliament rejected legislation, public concern for the claims of commoners was now so cogent that infinite time and care was taken to satisfy claimants. The final solution, using private Parliamentary acts and enclosure commissions, was not yet recognised as a less expensive alternative. But experience in the 1650s had clarified and reinforced the need, in long-running disputes, for the courts to provide independent arbitrators to remove the last and most intractable remnants of dissent.

The long-running agrarian problems of the seventeenth century discussed here have concerned the movement of food prices, which always required government watchfulness to balance the interests of producers and consumers, the enfranchising of copy-holders, enclosure, the improvement of commons, including those in fens and forests, the search for concealed Crown lands, and the Crown's legal claim to own marshland recovered from the sea.

The single positive measure taken under the Protectorate allowed the export of foodstuffs and proved so beneficial in giving farmers more outlets for their produce, that it remained in operation after 1660 and was even strengthened by more generous incentives to export food later in the century and beyond. Good harvests during the rest of the 1650s ensured that the towns received sufficient grain, while prices continued low. Indeed, the policy commanded agreement for nearly a hundred years, for although bouts of grain shortage returned, they were few and far between until after 1750 when changing conditions called the policy into question again.[93]

None of the other long-running agrarian problems of the seventeenth century, however, were solved by government during the Revolution. The royal claim to own recovered marshland, having hardly stirred the waters between 1640 and 1660, was revived at the Restoration as though no Interregnum had intervened, and remained an unresolved dispute, wearing down the resistance of coastal landowners, yet leaving them continuously in doubt, throughout the nineteenth century.[94]

The enfranchising of copyholds received no assistance from the state in these years of revolution, though in tracts and public speeches it had received more open discussion than ever before. Some little progress with enfranchisement was made here and there by private effort, but it did not command sufficient interest or approval for copyhold tenures to be abolished in 1660, even though the occasion offered when the gentry briskly abolished knight service. The omission of copyhold from the 1660 statute was criticised as unfair by Roger North in the later seventeenth century, but the interests of the gentry were then aggressively held uppermost, and while landowners were resolved to remove royal abuses which weighed on them, they were careless of the burdens they laid on lesser men. However, the actual progress of enfranchisement calls for more investigation by local historians before its progress between 1640 and 1660 can be judged against earlier and later years. It was hardly noticeable nationally, but where success was achieved locally, the circumstances deserve the same close examination as enclosure to discover the personalities involved. After 1660 the preference for turning copyholds into leaseholds may, on balance, have been stronger than the move to enfranchise, and it was not until 1832 that a fresh review was undertaken by the Real Property Commissioners. Even then no outright abolition was recommended. Only by slow attrition was the scale of the problem worn down in the next hundred years, until in 1922 copyhold was abolished.[95]

Other problems which failed to secure agreed government action during these twenty years were at least seen in a fresh way as a result of public discussion and the agitations of small men. An improvement in enclosure procedures was achieved, by trial and error, by individuals negotiating under the influence of republican sympathies, and showing concern for the commoners and the poor. A number of the schemes to improve commons, fens, and forests, were also delayed, modified, or halted by the same considerations, and even after 1660 the rights of small men were not forgotten. Economic conditions generally did not strongly spur enclosers or improvers of commons to resume old schemes after 1660, and this was assuredly the main reason for the subdued pace of their ventures. But the interests of commoners were on occasion brought into the discussion to good effect. When yet another effort was made to resume fen drainage in the Lindsey

Level, Lincolnshire, in 1701, the scheme was attacked, and defeated because 'it invaded the properties of thousands of people'. Since arguments in defence of private property had enabled the gentry to withstand agrarian reforms during the Interregnum, it was at least a small measure of progress when the concept of property rights was enlarged to admit some reference to small owners and commoners. In this case, moreover, the reminder was effective enough to cheat the gentry of victory.[96] In fact, for about a century after 1660 small men and commoners in many quarters won a breathing space. They would not, however, hold back the tide after 1750, when a rising population raised the urgent need for more food, new economic circumstances encouraged fresh speculative ventures, and all the long-running agrarian problems came to the fore again.

Notes

1 See Joan Thirsk (ed.), *The Agrarian History of England and Wales*, V, 2, Cambridge, 1986, Ch. 19.

2 I wish to thank Christopher Hill and Richard Hoyle for their helpful comments on this essay.

3 E. M. Leonard, 'The inclosure of common fields in the seventeenth century', *Transactions of the Royal Historical Society* [*TRHS*], NS. XIX, 1905, p. 129; A. E. Bland, P. A. Brown, and R. H. Tawney, (eds.), *English Economic History. Select Documents*, London, 1914, pp. 276–7, n. 1; also *Calendar of State Papers Domestic* [*CSPD*], *1636–7*, p. 257. This subject is newly surveyed in Joan Thirsk, 'Changing attitudes to enclosure in the seventeenth century', in *Festschrift for Professor Ju-Hwan Oh*, Taegu, Korea, 1991, pp. 517–43.

4 Joan Thirsk, 'The Crown as projector on its own estates, from Elizabeth I to Charles I', in R. W. Hoyle (ed.), *The Estates of the English Crown, 1558–1640*, Cambridge, 1992, pp. 302, 310–14, 332–3, 336–7, 341–2, 348, 350.

5 Three grantees of marshland (including the Earl of Carlisle) reported in 1640 'the common outcry' that the royal claim was unlikely to prevail, *CSPD, 1639–40*, p. 479.

6 *Statutes of the Realm*, IV, 1, pp. 102–03 (1549–50). This statute recites the Statute of Merton, 20 Hen. III, c. 4 and of Westminster, 13 Ed. I, c. 46, and makes further changes.

7 Thirsk, 'The Crown as projector', *op. cit.*, pp. 304–5, 316–9, 343–4.

8 R. W. Hoyle, ' "Vain Projects": the Crown and its copyholders in the reign of James I', in J. Chartres and D. Hey (eds.), *English Rural Society, 1500–1800*, Cambridge, 1990, pp. 73–102, but especially pp. 77–8, 87, 89–91. A last vestige of James's scheme appears in Exchequer Commissions in 2 Chas. I (1626) when, at Wokingham, Berks., the costs of enfranchisement were apportioned between tenants (PRO E178/5148).

9 This large subject is broached for the northern Yorkshire dales in R. W. Hoyle, 'Lords, tenants, and tenant right in the sixteenth century: four studies',

Northern History, XX, 1984, pp. 38–63. See also E. Kerridge, *Agrarian Problems in the Sixteenth Century and After*, London, 1969, pp. 53–8.

10 Thirsk, 'The Crown as projector', *op. cit.* For an example of the intensity with which Charles pursued claims concerning concealed land and defective titles, and also regained marshland, see the case of Gedney, Lincs., in CSPD, 1635–6, p. 294. For disputes on many fronts in 1636, see PRO SP16/339, *passim*.

11 P. Bowden, Statistical Appendix, in Thirsk (ed.), *The Agrarian History of England and Wales*, IV, Cambridge, 1967, p. 862.

12 S. R. Gardiner (ed.), *The Constitutional Documents of the Puritan Revolution, 1625–60*, 3rd edn., Oxford, 1979, pp. 211–12, clauses 21, 25, 26, 31, 32.

13 I. Gentles, 'The purchasers of Northamptonshire Crown lands, 1649–60', *Midland History*, III, 3, 1976, p. 210; *idem*, 'The sales of Crown lands during the English Revolution', *Economic History Review*, 2nd Ser., XXVI, 4, 1973, p. 623.

14 I. Gentles, 'The management of Crown lands, 1649–60', *Agricultural History Review*, 19, 1971, pp. 37–40.

15 C. Hill, *The Century of Revolution, 1603–1714*, London, 1969, p. 132.

16 *Commons Journals [CJ]*, *1648–51*, indexed under tenants; *CSPD, 1649–50*, p. 199; *CSPD, 1650*, pp. 24, 39, 149, 442, 480; *CSPD, 1651*, pp. 16, 269; PRO SP18/74/35 and 35 I; SP 18/74/33, reprinted in Joan Thirsk and J. P. Cooper, *Seventeenth-Century Economic Documents*, Oxford, 1972, p. 142.

17 *CSPD, 1645–7*, pp. 30, 200, 146, 147, 148; J. S. Morrill, *The Revolt of the Provinces*, London, 1976, pp. 197–9.

18 See, for example, *CSPD, 1649–50*, pp. 60–61, 64, 94, 113.

19 *CSPD, 1649–50*, pp. 35, 108, 121, 472; Thirsk, *Agrarian History*, V, 2, *op. cit.*, p. 305.

20 W. Lamont, 'The Left and its past: revisiting the 1650s', *History Workshop Journal*, 23, 1987, p. 143.

21 *CJ, 1648–51*, 24 May, 9 Oct, and 18 Feb, 1650/51. For earlier permissive legislation in 1647, affecting country parishes, but evidently producing no action, see C. H. Firth and R. S. Rait, *Acts and Ordinances of the Interregnum*, London, 1911, I, pp. 1042–5; II, pp. 104–110.

22 *CJ, 1648–51*, pp. 2, 137, 160, 201, 374, 416, 481.

23 *Ibid.*, p. 535.

24 *CSPD, 1651–2*, p. 210; *CJ, 1651–9*, pp. 127, 129, 259, 287, 294. An Act for the Poor is referred to in Samuel Hartlib's Journal, *Ephemerides*, in February 1653, reporting a visit from Mr Dormer, 'a Parliament man' who failed to get his clause inserted in the act, 'for transplanting the worst persons to become better in another soil' (Sheffield University Library, Hartlib MSS, *Ephemerides*, 1653, GG-GG3).

25 *CJ, 1651–9*, pp. 439, 766.

26 *CJ, 1651–9*, p. 435; *The Diary of Thomas Burton*, ed. J. T. Rutt, London, 1828, I, p. clxxxii. The same Parliamentary committee was ordered to consider the habits and fashions of servants and labourers, and prepare a bill to remedy abuses.

27 Thirsk, *Agrarian History*, V, 2, *op. cit.*, pp. 305–8, 328–34, 334ff.

28 *CSPD, 1653–4*, p. 10; *CSPD, 1654*, pp. 9–11. The end of forest law is explained by Winstanley in *A Watchword to the City of London and the Army*, reprinted in C. Hill (ed.), *Winstanley. The Law of Freedom and other Writings*, 1973, pp. 132–3.

29 Firth and Rait, *op. cit.*, I, pp. 303–5.
30 *Ibid.*, I, pp. 422–3, 571.
31 S. Madge, *The Domesday of Crown Lands*, London, 1938, pp. 90, 102, 107–8.
32 *CSPD, 1651*, pp. 63, 151.
33 *Ibid.*, p. 151; *CSPD, 1651–2*, pp. 461, 501.
34 *CSPD, 1651–2*, pp. 103–4, 495; *CSPD, 1652–3*, p. 178.
35 Madge, *op. cit.*, p. 109.
36 *Ibid.*, pp. 109–19; *CSPD, 1653–4*, p. 264; *CSPD, 1654*, pp. 97–8.
37 For the scale of the documentary investigation alone, see *CSPD, 1653–4*, p. 133, concerning 102 documents of title and patents going back to Edward II.
38 Madge, *op. cit.*, p. 388; P. A. J. Pettit, *The Royal Forests of Northamptonshire. A Study in their Economy, 1558–1714*, Northants. Record Society, XXIII, 1968, p. 70.
39 *CSPD, 1656–7*, p. 78; *CSPD, 1658–9*, p. 19.
40 PRO SP 18/94/56.
41 PRO SP 18/94/57.
42 G. Mosley, *History of the Castle, Priory, and Town of Tutbury in the County of Stafford*, London, 1832, pp. 289–90.
43 As Henry Robinson reminded the House when opposing the sale of the forests in December 1656, 'We promised Englishmen freedom, equal freedom ... Did we not make the people believe that we fought for their liberty? Let us not deceive them of the expectation.' (*Diary of Thos. Burton, op. cit.*, I, p. 228).
44 Mosley, *op. cit.*, p. 289.
45 PRO SP 18/155/18. See also Thirsk, 'Horn and thorn in Staffordshire: the economy of a pastoral county', in *idem, The Rural Economy of England*, London, 1984, pp. 167–8.
46 *CSPD, 1657–8*, p. 16.
47 *Burton's Diary, op. cit.*, II, p. 241. Enclosure and sales were somewhat more advanced in Enfield Chase than in Needwood, but in 1659 violent protests by the commoners were still in progress, and the Restoration, which restored these lands to the Crown, seems to have brought the enclosure to naught (D. Pam, *The Story of Enfield Chase*, Enfield, 1984, pp. 66–89). See also Bucharan Sharp, below, pp. 267–8.
48 Thirsk, 'Horn and thorn', *op. cit.*, p. 168.
49 *Commissioners ... to enquire into the ... Woods, Forests, and Land Revenues of the Crown*, Seventeen Reports, 1787–93.
50 Clive Holmes uses the words 'passively condoned' to describe the attitude of the Long Parliament towards the fenlanders, in his *Seventeenth-Century Lincolnshire*, History of Lincolnshire, VII, Lincoln, 1980, p. 208.
51 K. Lindley, *Fenland Riots and the English Revolution*, London, 1982, p. 143.
52 Holmes, *ibid.*
53 Holmes, *ibid.*, pp. 208–9; H. C. Darby, *The Draining of the Fens*, Cambridge, 2nd edn., 1968, pp. 80–81.
54 Holmes, *op. cit.*, pp. 210–11.
55 Joan Thirsk, 'Plough and pen: agricultural writers in the seventeenth century', in *Social Relations and Ideas*, (ed. T. H. Aston *et al*), Cambridge, 1983, pp. 309–11; Lindley, *op. cit.*, p. 144.
56 Thirsk, *Agrarian History, op. cit.*, V, 2, p. 323; Holmes, *op. cit.*, pp. 211–12.
57 Firth and Rait, *op. cit.*, II, p. 1044. See also Hartlib's Diary, Sheffield University Library, Hartlib MSS, *Ephemerides*, 1653, 00–004; Sylvanus Taylor, *Common*

Good or the Improvement of Commons, Forests, and Chases by Inclosure . . ., London, 1652, p. 33.

58 Holmes, *op. cit.*, pp. 228, 254–5.

59 *Burton's Diary*, *op. cit.*, p. 259.

60 S. Hartlib, *His Legacie*, London, 1652, pp. 8, 5, 42–3.

61 J. Broad, 'Alternative husbandry and permanent pasture in the Midlands, 1650–1800', *Agricultural History Review*, 28, 2, 1980, pp. 77–89.

62 Holmes, *op. cit.*, pp. 211–12, 226–8, 254–5; Thirsk, *English Peasant Farming*, *op. cit.*, pp. 126–7.

63 H. C. Darby, *The Changing Fenland*, Cambridge, 1983, pp. 80–91, 94ff.

64 L. Hamilton (ed.), *Selections from the Works of Gerrard Winstanley*, London, 1944, p. 82.

65 *Ibid.*

66 *Ibid.* Plans for the poor to enjoy the commons prompted more than one suggestion that the state should take them over, and let them out. See *Waste Land's Improvement* . . ., *1653*, BL Thomason E715 (18), reprinted in Thirsk and Cooper, *Seventeenth-Century Documents*, *op. cit.*, pp. 138–9, and Peter Chamberlen, *The Poor Man's Advocate, 1649*, cited in Hill, *Century of Revolution*, *op. cit.*, p. 135. See also C. Hill, *The World turned Upside Down*, London, 1972, pp. 43–4.

67 C. Hill (ed), *Winstanley. The Law of Freedom and other Writings*, London, 1973, pp. 26–31.

68 *Ibid.*, pp. 132–3. See also M. James, *Social Problems and Policy during the Puritan Revolution*, London, 1966, pp. 98–9.

69 Hill, *Winstanley*, *op. cit.*, p. 33; Hill, *The World turned Upside Down*, *op. cit.*, pp. 90–91.

70 K. V. Thomas, 'Another Digger broadside', *Past and Present*, 42, 1968, p. 58.

71 Hill, *Winstanley*, *op. cit.*, pp. 22–3. See also Hill, *World turned Upside Down*, *op. cit.*, pp. 90–91. At Wellingborough, Northants, however, some rich men gave up their commons to the Diggers, other farmers gave seed, and the Diggers' own Declaration claimed that 'hundreds more' gave their consent. Wellingborough was seemingly overwhelmed with hungry poor in the harsh years of food shortage, 1649–50. (BL Thomason, E669 f. 15 (21).)

72 *CJ, VII, 1651–9*, p. 287; *Burton's Diary*, *op. cit.*, I, p. xiv. This committee was probably the one on which Dormer sat (see above, note 24).

73 In an idealist, but also practical essay by Sylvanus Taylor (see n. 57) on the enclosure of commons, he recognised 'the petty tyranny' exercised by those with the longest purse over commoners. Idealism was reflected in the hope that 'the many thousands unborn may bless God for the change he hath wrought for us by putting the opportunity of doing good in our hands'. His proposed practical measures began with a division of the commons into four parts, one part being reserved for the poor (Taylor, *op. cit.*, pp. 10, 24, 34ff).

74 *CSPD, 1655–6*, pp. 9, 21; *Burton's Diary*, *op. cit.*, pp. 175–6; *CJ, VII, 1651–9*, p. 470.

75 H. N. Brailsford, *The Levellers and the English Revolution*, ed. C. Hill, London, 1961, discusses this subject in most detail. See pp. 328–31, 437–43, 190. See also Margaret James, *op. cit.*, Chapter 3. The Royalist, Sir Richard Weston, referred to the inconvenience of ill tenures, including copyhold and knight service, which the husbandman had to live with, but which he hoped 'we shall see . . . remedied'. (Hartlib, *His Legacie*, *op. cit.*, p. 58.)

76 Brailsford, *op. cit.*, pp. 328–31, 449, 437–43, 453, n. 24.

77 Hoyle, 'Vain projects', *op. cit.*, pp. 73–101.
78 Brailsford, *op. cit.*, p. 453, n. 24.
79 *Ibid.*, pp. 449–50, 349–50, 287, n. 11, 442–3. The wrangling seemed to turn on the level of fine. Voting started at two years' rent, then 1½ years. Finally a majority favoured 1 year, but subsequently, on a technicality, the whole bill was rejected. (*CJ 1651–9*, pp. 121, 130, 433).
80 C. Hill, *Puritanism and Revolution*, London, 1969, p. 177.
81 Madge, *op. cit.*, pp. 339–42.
82 *Burton's Diary*, *op. cit.*, I, p. clxxxvi. For the Exchequer Commission in 1651, see PRO E178/6130. For those in 1657 and later, see PRO, *Lists and Indexes, XXXVII, List of Special Commissions and Returns in the Exchequer, passim*; E178/6101 relates to Middlesex. Some files are voluminous, like that for Lancs, E178/6089. The enquiry must have been initiated in April 1656. See *CSPD, 1655–6*, p. 246; *CSPD, 1657–8*, pp. 72, 110, 183, 251, 355; *CSPD, 1658–9*, p. 175. At the same date authority was also given to one Parliamentary supporter, a tanner and maltster of Worcester, who had complained of his financial losses to the Council of State, to make them up out of half of any discoveries which he made of concealed lands, goods, and monies. This seems to have been a singular concession, however, and did not inaugurate a system (*CSPD 1655–6*, p. 283).
83 Thirsk, in Hoyle, *Estates of the English Crown*, *op. cit.*, pp. 349–50. Pym was also a commissioner for Gloucestershire in 1632, directed to enquire into depopulations and conversions to pasture since 1568 in six counties from Lincolnshire to Somerset (*CSPD, 1631–3*, p. 490).
84 *CSPD, 1656–7*, p. 131. Was John Osborne perhaps the son of Sir Robert Osborne, who in 1635 was keen to discover enclosure and the conversion of arable land to pasture, and, if given a royal warrant to search for this offence, would similarly have earned profit for himself? (PRO SP16/307, no. 18.)
85 PRO E178/6084. The origins of this commission are explained in the letter from Generals Blake and Montague to the President of the Council of State. They had been riding at anchor, when some of the Deal pilots had asked them for help to save from sale their homes (built at their own cost on the beach), or at least to allow them to be the buyers. The two generals observed in support of the request that the fleet often called on these pilots for assistance (*CSPD, 1655–6*, pp. 204–05).
86 The search is best pursued first in the *Victoria County Histories*. As one possible example of an agrarian reformer, in sympathy with the Hartlib circle, at least, see *VCH, Cambs.*, VIII, pp. 44, 45. Robert Castell was a Parliamentary colonel, whose family had held East Hatley manor since *c.* 1490. Open field land survived there in 1640 but had been enclosed by 1661. It is likely that this Col. Castell was the same Col. Castle whose 'fair plantation' in Ewell Fen of onions, peas, and hemp was praised by William Dugdale (Darby, *Drainage*, p. 274).
87 Thirsk, *Rural Economy*, op. cit., pp. vii, 102. Philip Skippon was a member of the Parliamentary committee to relieve the poor in 1650 (*CJ 1648–51*, p. 374). In Chidley's case, Ian Gentles does not credit him with any idealism, (Gentles, 'The purchasers of Northamptonshire Crown lands, 1649–60', *Midland History*, III, 1976, p. 208; *idem.*, 'The sales of Crown lands during the English revolution', *Economic History Review*, 2nd Ser., XXVI, 1973, pp. 626–7). For an idealist plan for Enfield Chase, see Bucharan Sharp on Covell, below p. 268.

88 Thirsk, 'Changing attitudes', *op. cit.*, p. 535.
89 Henry, Earl of Manchester had been put on the commission to enquire into depopulations in 1635 (PRO C66/2706/3).
90 PRO C78/704/10.
91 PRO E178/5711.
92 D. A. Crowley (ed.), *VCH, Wilts*, XI, 1980, pp. 82ff., 92–3. In Enfield Chase enclosure was met at every step by continuing uproar and resistance from the commoners, but actual events could well be read as a genuine attempt by the authorities to find a fair solution. See Pam, *Enfield Chase, op. cit.*, pp. 70–72. For two less contentious enclosure agreements, both precipitated by the difficulties of farming, see the case at Marston, Oxford, where the garrison of soldiers at Oxford made farming in the open fields impossible (PRO C78/586/1(1661)), and at Bassingham, Lincs. where wet seasons forced the decision to enclose (PRO C78/637/1 (1655)). The Marston agreement is printed in G. N. Clark, 'Enclosure by agreement at Marston, near Oxford', *English Historical Review*, XLII, 1927, pp. 87–94.
93 E. P. Thompson, 'The moral economy of the English crowd in the eighteenth century', *Past and Present*, 50, 1971, pp. 79, 86–8, 95, 98, 108–11, 115.
94 S. A. Moore, *A History of the Foreshore*, 3rd edn., London, 1888, Chs. XIX–XXIII. This work was, in fact, an attempt to elucidate the current situation at the end of the nineteenth century. It seemed that every landowner had to find documentary evidence to support his individual claim against the Crown.
95 W. S. Holdsworth, *An Historical Introduction to the Land Law*, Oxford, 1927, pp. 36–7, 48, 322.
96 Thirsk, *English Peasant Farming, op. cit.*, p. 126. The more lasting effects of the eloquent defence of commoners at this time are also affirmed in James, *Social Problems, op. cit.*, p. 102.

CHAPTER EIGHT

THE EXPERIENCE OF THE GENTRY
1640 – 1660

Barry Coward

'What has been, gentlemen', said a Tory gentleman, Sir Simon Harcourt, to Buckinghamshire JPs at Aylesbury in 1704, 'may be again but God of his infinite mercy abate, soften and mollify all restless and implacable spirits . . . the turbulent libellers of 1642 were first trumpeters of sedition, and when the ferment was high enough they sounded to rebellion and engaged the country in a civil war to the effusion of much native blood . . . barbarously murdering the best of Kings even under colour of law'.[1] 'Let not 1641 come again' was a long-lived sentiment among many gentlemen after 1660, demonstrating that the English Revolution scarred the collective mentalities of generations of English gentlemen.[2] This, though, ought not to obscure the fact that at the time the impact of the English Revolution on the gentry and their responses to it were diverse. This is, of course, not surprising. Although the gentry were a fairly small, cohesive elite group (perhaps the most homogeneous social group in early modern England), there were at least 20,000 gentry on the eve of the English Revolution.[3] Such a large number of people were unlikely to have responded in exactly the same ways to the complex crises of the 1640s and 1650s. Indeed the first major feature that is apparent about the history of the English gentry after 1640 is that any gentry unity that there may have been in 1640 quickly crumbled in the months preceeding the outbreak of the Civil War in 1642. When the Civil War began the gentry community in England was split.

The main purpose of this essay is to suggest three broad themes underlying the diversity of individual gentry experiences during and after the outbreak of the Civil War. The first is the way in which in the 1640s the gentry reunited in order to try to preserve their social and political hegemony, which was being threatened (or so they thought) by events during and after the war. The Second Civil War in 1648 was essentially a revolt of the English gentry to restore social and political normality. The failure of that revolt, however, coincided with the appearance of a second theme that became increasingly apparent during the rule of the English republic. Whereas in the 1640s their fears and anxieties had driven many gentry to support a return to monarchical government, they now pushed many of them in a different direction. Reluctantly many English gentry conceded that the republic (both in the guise of the Commonwealth, 1649–53, and the Protectorate, 1653–59) was a bulwark against those they feared were working to turn the old world upside down. The English republic did not collapse in 1659 because it lacked gentry support. But its collapse heralded a third theme, which is more ambiguous than the first two. In the winter of 1659–60 many gentry turned back to the monarchy, venting their hate and anger at Dissenters and others they associated with the regimes of the 1640s and 1650s, foreshadowing the High Church-Tory views that had such a high profile in later Stuart English politics. However, not all English gentlemen, although they supported the restoration of the monarchy, were converted by the English Revolution into bigoted Tory Anglicans. Some adopted a more tolerant attitude to Protestant Dissent, suggesting that at least one of the strands of later Stuart Whiggism, as well as Toryism, can be traced to the divergent experiences of the gentry during the English Revolution.

There is little doubt that the vast majority of English gentlemen shared the widespread distrust of Charles I's government that was everywhere apparent when the Long Parliament first met on 3 November 1640. The speech of a future Royalist, the Kent MP Sir John Culpepper, encapsulates the determination of many in 1640 to get rid of the measures which had caused growing disquiet among many gentlemen since Charles's accession in 1625. 'The Grievances of the County of Kent', said Culpepper, were 'the great increase of Papists', 'the obtruding and countenancing of divers new Ceremonies in Matters of Religion', 'Military Charges', 'the [new Laudian ecclesiatical] canons', 'Ship-Money' and 'the great Customs and Compositions levied upon our Cloaths'.[4]

What is less certain than it once was, however, is whether these sentiments, which were replicated in other parliamentary speeches as well as in petitions to parliament, were purely localist responses to an innovative, centralising regime. Much that has been written recently about the English gentry leads one to question David Underdown's statement, written over twenty years ago, that 'for ... the country gentleman ... it still required an effort to think in national terms'.[5] The concept of early seventeenth-century England as a federation of insular 'county communities', on which it was based, cannot now be sustained.[6] By the early seventeenth century the integration into a national whole of the English state had proceeded further than had happened in many contemporary Continental countries.[7] Furthermore, developments like the growth of the press,[8] the increasing role of London as a means by which cultural, religious and political ideas were diffused, and the sustained experience of political debate in the parliaments of the 1620s contributed to a growing awareness among the gentry of national political issues during the early seventeenth century.[9]

Anthony Fletcher has pointed to the need for more work on 'the chronology of an emerging consciousness [by 1640] of political issues that transcended county and regional boundaries and on the nature and strength of that consciousness shire by shire'.[10] The lack of abundant source material for the 1630s makes it difficult to do this. What does emerge though, through the dark glass of inadequate sources, is a picture of gentry unity against Caroline fiscal, military and religious policies but of deep divisions about the need for further reform of the Church once the Laudian innovations of the 1630s had been abolished. The main issue that divided English gentlemen by 1640 was the question of whether the Reformation, which had begun in the mid-sixteenth century, had been completed. It is likely that a majority of English gentry believed that it had and were quite satisfied with the Church as it had developed during the reigns of Elizabeth I and James I. What set Puritans apart from these supporters of the pre-Laudian Church was not opposition to a national church or commitment to presbyterianism, but a belief that what had been so far achieved was, at best, a half Reformation; not only had there been only a partial reformation of church government and liturgy, but what was worse, was that the real reformation, the inner cleansing of men's minds – 'the reformation of manners', had made even less progress. In the opinion of these godly Puritan gentry sinfulness abounded, and until it was rooted out the nation would never benefit from the warmth of God's blessing.[11]

In the first few months of the English Revolution this division was obscured by broad opposition to the Laudian Church and a widely-shared fear of popery. In the early heady days of the Revolution, too, some English gentry were so carried away by hatred of Laudian bishops that they aligned themselves with those who demanded limitations on or even abolition of bishops. What also encouraged some gentry with moderate religious views to do this at this stage were schemes that were floated in Parliamentary committees to replace bishops with county commissions of gentlemen.[12] For many gentry, though, religious reformation was not central to their political aims in the early 1640s. What set many committed Parliamentarians apart was that for them it was. The distrust of Caroline government of zealous Puritan gentry like Robert Harley, Sir Simond D'Ewes, Sir Thomas Pelham, Lord Brooke, and Sir Nathaniel Barnardiston was maintained by a conviction that the cause of Parliament and of Protestantism could not be separated. The future existence of both depended on an ongoing religious reformation.

That this was a view not held by all gentlemen soon became apparent in the months preceding the outbreak of the Civil War, when some Puritan gentry began to back away from radical reform of the Church, illustrated by the marked contrast between the radical tone of county petitions supporting root and branch abolition of episcopacy early in 1641 and county petitions in support of Parliament a year later, which took a much more moderate line. This trend was further marked by the appearance in many counties in late 1641 – early 1642 of pro-bishop petitions, which show 'that an alternative view of the Church from the Puritan one was firmly held by substantial numbers of people in the country'.[13] Attachment to a national Church with bishops and a Book of Common Prayer was reinforced by the fear that zeal for further reformation would undermine the traditional constitution and the established social order. This was so, they believed, because further reformation would inevitably threaten the existence of one national church by unleashing religious heterodoxy and, for gentlemen like Sir Edward Dering, who early in 1642 regretted his earlier support of the root and branch cause, it was folly to abolish episcopacy without replacing it with an alternative system for maintaining discipline in the church and in society.[14] Sir Thomas Aston, the leader of the Cheshire campaign to secure episcopacy against the Puritan activist Sir William Brereton, freely admitted the need for 'the suppressing of Popery, the increase of able pastors, the removing of innovations', but he warned that those who wanted to abolish bishops intended 'to pull down 26 bishops [and] set up 9324 potential Popes'. As well as destroying church discipline, he also alleged that, for the reformers, 'freedom of their consciences and persons is not enough, but they must have their purses and estates free too … Nay they go higher, even to the denial of the right to proprieties in our estates'.[15] These fears of impending social anarchy were played on by Royalist propaganda, the best example before the Civil War being the cleverly-crafted King's Answer to the Nineteen Propositions, which alleged that soon the common people would be encouraged 'to set up for themselves, call parity and independence liberty, devour that estate which had devoured the rest, destroy all rights proprieties, all distinctions of families and merit, and by this means this splendid and excellently distinguished form of government end in a dark, equal chaos of confusion, and the long line of our many noble ancestors in a Jack Cade or Wat Tyler'.[16] What made this allegation stick was that the Parliamentary leadership was now demanding changes in the constitution, like Parliamentary appointment of the king's ministers and Parliamentary control of the armed forces, that would have greatly diminished the royal prerogative. They were also flirting with popular opinion, 'tell[ing] Stories to the People' in Dering's sneering phrase about the Parliamentary Grand Remonstrance.[17]

As a result, by the summer of 1642 a marked resurgence of traditional loyalties and ties of deference to the Crown can be seen among some gentry, who showed a willingness to fight for the king by attempting to seize local supplies of ammunition and control of the local trained bands by virtue of royal commissions of array. Nothing shows more clearly the way in which the gentry had fragmented than the clashes for control of the county trained bands in many areas of England in July and August 1642 between these Royalist commissioners and gentry claiming the authority of the Parliamentary militia ordinance.

By 1642 the pro-Parliamentary enthusiasm of many gentry had evaporated, but by no means all gentlemen who feared that events were escalating towards social and political disorder committed themselves to full-blown Royalism. The revelation of widespread neutralism among English gentry as the country slid into Civil War is one of the prime achievements of recent historical scholarship.[18] Neutralism, however, is not a subject that is without problems.[19] It would be misleading to take all neutralist statements at their face value. The Yorkshire pacification treaty of September 1642, for example, seems to be a case of pure neutralism in its intention to rid the county 'of all former unkindness and differences which have been bred by these distractions and we will hereafter be as one man to defend one another according to the law against all others'.[20] But in reality it was probably simply a temporary truce between a few committed Parliamentarians and Royalists. It is possible, however, to take too far doubts about the extent of neutralism. Many (probably a majority) of the English gentry in 1642 would probably have echoed Thomas Knyvett's heart-felt comment in his letter to his wife in May 1642, when he received a commission from Parliament by virtue of the militia ordinance and then immediately afterwards a royal declaration denouncing it: 'Oh sweet heart I am in a great straight what to do'.[21] Among the gentry in 1642 were varying kinds of non-commitment: ranging from one extreme represented by the dazed indecision of Knyvett, via the passive neutralism of those gentlemen who in 1642 contributed men and money to both sides, to, at the other extreme, the committed non-commitment of gentry in Linconshire and Staffordshire, who raised third forces to keep out rival armies, and the Cheshire gentlemen who made a local demilitarisation treaty at Bunbury in December 1642.[22]

By the outbreak of the Civil War the gentry had fragmented into minority groups of committed Parliamentarians and Royalists, but most typical of gentry opinion were those neutralist gentry who were not yet willing to commit themselves to either side. Not only was the choice an unpalatable one, since both sides were now tainted with the smear of 'absolutism' (the Royalists because of Caroline policies in the 1630s and the Parliamentarians because of the new constitutional demands that were being made), but also commitment meant civil war and gentlemen had at hand in the well-reported war in northern Europe an example of the horrors that war could bring. 'Oh let the miserable spectacle of a German devastation', said a Norfolk peace petition of January 1643, 'persuade you to decline those perilous casualties which may result from a civil war'.[23] It took no effort of the imagination to see that such 'perilous casualties' would hit not only their pockets but also their social and political dominance. 'Whensoever necessity shall enforce us to make use of the multitude', wrote a Norfolk gentleman, Sir John Potts to his nephew, Simond D'Ewes, three days before the official outbreak of the Civil War, 'I do not promise my self safety'.[24]

The prime impact of the Civil War and its aftermath on the gentry was to confirm those fears, which gradually brought most of them round to supporting a settlement with the king. As events in England slid in a radical direction after 1642 to a bloody civil war, then to army politicisation and revolt and finally to a military take-over of Parliament and the trial of the king, Charles I gained more and more support from the traditional landed elite. In many ways, of course, this conservative reaction of the gentry to radical events is not surprising. For many, their experiences of civil war and its aftermath were traumatic. For one thing, few gentry could have been insulated from the dramatic effects that the war had on the normal rhythms of social and economic life. Both sides created taxes (assessments, sequestration, forced loans and excise) that were more accurately geared to the actual wealth of individuals than any previous levies. Moreover, the cost of war to property owners also included supplying free quarter to marching armies and garrisons alike. Their rental incomes collapsed as rents fell into arrears, their tenants were conscripted and their properties plundered by soldiers. Moreover, the consequences of the war for the gentry's social and political position seemed even more severe. Everywhere they looked the existing society seemed to be under attack: from radical religious sects, who, according to Thomas Edwards' *Gangraena*, published in 1646, allowed women preachers, called for the abolition of tithes, sanctioned sexual permissiveness, and generally were subversive of the traditional social order; from the army, especially as from 1644 onwards army mutinies over wage arrears proliferated, adding to the impression of a general collapse of order; and from Parliamentary county committees that seemed to be dominated more and more by 'mean' men from outside the traditional ruling circle.

A new twist to these experiences of the gentry in the 1640s has recently been given by evidence that suggests that the gentry may have exaggerated their troubles. Recent research has justified their anguished cries in only one major respect. There is little doubt that all property owners were hit hard by the economic effects of the war;[25] the impact of the war on the gentry in other respects may have been less severe than they thought. The work of John Morrill and John Walter suggests that the scale of popular disorders in the 1640s was no greater than in pre-war England. The tendency of recent revisionist writing on radical groups like the Levellers and Diggers has been to minimise their popular support. It has also been contended that less than five per cent of the population attended religious assemblies other than in parish churches.[26] Similarly, Austin Woolrych's work on the New Model Army portrays it as being no serious threat to the traditional power of the gentry but rather that its aims before 1648 were to erect a constitution, the Heads of the Proposals, that would not have disturbed the existing social hierarchy.[27] Moreover, work on Parliamentary county committees has shown that not all were taken over by 'mean' men. There is no denying that many of the county 'bosses' who rose to prominence in the 1640s often had radical religious views and were men from outside the elites from whom local magistrates were normally drawn in pre-Civil War England. But most of them were gentlemen – if lesser gentry – and in few places did they displace a core of traditional ruling families who remained entrenched in local county administration in the 1640s.[28]

All this, though, should not minimise the fact that the gentry perception was that both threats against them and the scale of popular disorders were increasing. Why, then, did the gentry have such exaggerated fears? In the present state of knowledge it is impossible to be certain. But one possible explanation is that by 1640 the gentry were far from being the self-confident ruling elite they are sometimes said to have been. On the contrary, it is likely that they were riven with anxieties, after a long period in which there seemed to have been a sustained attack on them both from the threat of 'the many headed monster' of popular rebellion from below and from 'innovations' from the monarchy from above. Charles I's promotion of ecclesiastics to secular offices, Laudian attacks on tithes and Caroline fiscal expedients all seemed to be an overt attack on gentry interests. It is highly likely that gentry resentment in the 1640s was so deep because the wartime regimes seemed to be continuing (and indeed intensifying) a long-running threat to their power.

This is why the reactions of many gentry against armies and county committees escalated rapidly in the 1640s, from sporadic defensive actions to sustained political pressure on Parliament and, in some cases, armed uprisings by the end of the decade. Typical of gentry reaction in the early stages of the war is the revolt in Kent in 1643 against the county committee, in which the gentry petitioned against the Presbyterian Covenant, arbitrary distraint of good and taxes imposed 'contrary to the liberty of the subject'.[29] In 1643 there is also some evidence of gentry unrest against Parliamentary war taxation in Norfolk, but it did not grow in strength and coherence until 1644, when Parliamentary exactions began to bite throughout East Anglia under the energetic leadership of the Eastern Association by the Earl of Manchester and his subordinate, Oliver Cromwell. In every region that has been studied, whether under Parliamentarian or Royalist control, gentry discontent at the war became more apparent in the latter half of 1644 and the beginning of 1645. Clive Holmes has shown how in the eastern counties gentry opinion coalesced at this time in favour of a speedy settlement with the king, and that the Earl of Manchester's transformation in the months after Marston Moor (July 1644) from a dynamic win-the-war general into an ally of Political Presbyterians at Westminster, who were pressing for a speedy settlement with the king, was brought about, in part, by pressure from East Anglian gentry.[30] The conservative movement at Westminster, spearheaded by the Earl of Essex and the Political Presbyterians, also had behind it the evidence of a concerted gentry movement in Warwickshire, Staffordshire and Cheshire that focused around the earl of Denbigh, the Parliamentary commander of those associated counties, against the militant measures being adopted by Sir William Brereton. The petition to Parliament of Warwickshire gentlemen in July 1644 is typical of gentry resentment in these counties at high taxation which was 'double at the least if not treble to other neighbouring counties', 'losses suffered by free quarter, frequent plunderings almost throughout the whole county', committeemen serving as military officers, and a county committee whose members were 'men of inconsiderable fortunes, others of little or no estate and strangers in our county'.[31] In Lincolnshire Colonel Edward King's campaign against the county committee also got underway in the winter of 1644–45, as elsewhere using the local sub-committee of accounts which produced evidence of financial irregularities by the committee, which were forwarded to the central accounts committee in London to strengthen the hand of the Political Presbyterian campaign at Westminster.[32] This climaxed in 1646–47 in a sustained attempt to abolish county committees by Parliamentary ordinance, demobilise the New Model Army without satisfying its wage arrears, and reach a settlement with the king without delay. In Royalist areas, too, the gentry mobilised against the effects of the war at this time. In the first two months of 1645 Charles I had little option but to agree to the demands of gentry in Worcestershire, Shropshire, Herefordshire and Staffordshire to raise an army staffed, not by the king's officers, but by local gentry. Later in the year the scheme spread to South Wales, where a gentry-led 'Peaceable Army' was formed with the aim of restraining Royalist war measures that burst the bounds of traditional methods of government.[33] The extent of gentry involvement in the anti-war Clubman movement, which swept across many counties of southern England and Wales in 1645–46 is uncertain. A commonly-held view is that the Clubmen movement 'was a spontaneous ouburst of peasants, led by men of no social significance'. But G. J. Lynch's identification of 65 gentry among the 163 Clubmen who can be identified suggests that it might be worth testing its validity.[34]

Gentry conservatism, which had burgeoned in the mid-1640s, exploded in 1648 in the so-called 'Second Civil War'. The petitions from and rebellions in an arc of counties in southern England in the spring and summer of 1648 are aptly described by David Underdown as 'the tip of the iceberg of submerged gentry discontent'.[35] Although Brian Lyndon's recent work on the Essex rebellion has focused attention rightly on the key role played by Royalist activists in 1648, it is doubtful if any of the rebellions could have got off the ground without the active support of ex-Parliamentarian and neutralist gentry.[36] Even those MPs who had stuck by the army in putting down the counter-revolution of 1647 now deserted the army and supported the treaty negotiations which began with the king at Newport in September. By the end of 1648 the vast majority of English gentlemen were convinced that the only way of protecting themselves against arbitrary county committees, and the social revolution they feared would follow if the army were allowed to countenance religious toleration, was by a settlement with the king.

1649 was a traumatic year for the English gentry. The ruthless way in which the army established a military, regicide regime could not but fail to sustain the apprehensive and sullen mood which followed the defeats of the gentry rebellions of 1648 and the execution of the king. It is, however, more difficult to make broad generalisations about the experiences of the gentry during the next decade than it is about their history during the 1640s. The primary sources for the 1650s are less abundant and the provincial history of the republican decade has been less intensively studied.[37] Moreover, there has been a tendency to write the history of the 1650s with the restoration of the monarchy very much in mind. One major consequence has been that the extent of gentry hostility to the English republic has been exaggerated. A major argument in the following paragraphs is that by the death of Oliver Cromwell in 1658, although many gentry never gave the republican regimes enthusiastic support, they not only held aloof from Royalist plots but they eventually, albeit reluctantly, accepted and worked with those in power. In the present state of knowledge it is easier to explain why the majority of the gentry were reluctant to commit themselves fully to the republican governments of the 1650s than it is to understand why their reluctance was overcome by the later 1650s.

What makes the question of gentry allegiance to the regimes of the 1650s especially interesting is that there was much about them that served to intensify threats to gentry interests. Two aspects of the Commonwealth regime, in particular, heightened gentry fears. The first is that between 1649 and 1653 more men from outside the traditional ruling elites than in the 1640s were promoted to positions of power in local government. The Rump and Council of State may have had little alternative but to do this. Immediately after the establishment of the republic they had obviously been anxious that many gentry might withdraw from public life in horror at what had just happened. One of the first

Acts passed by the Rump on 17 February 1649 confirmed that the commissions of JPs and sheriffs were not invalidated by the king's execution.[38] These anxieties seem to have been justified, since there are many examples of the absence of JPs at quarter sessions in the first few months of the republic. On 17 March 1649, for example, only seven of the forty Devonshire JPs came to hear an address by the assize judge, John Wylde, in defence of the revolutionary events of the previous winter.[39] The new regime, therefore, had to fall back on men from outside county elites, like Robert Bennet in Cornwall and Thomas Birch in Lancashire, and to confirm in power many of the county bosses who had emerged in the 1640s. Moreover, when it became known that many gentlemen had refused to take the oath of Engagement to the new regime, the Council decided on a systematic purge of commissions of the peace, and these were undertaken in the summer of 1650. The severity of the purges varied from county to county. In one county, Glamorgan, there was 'a real transfer of power to a militant puritan clique who wanted to create a society ... radically different from the old order';[40] while Dr Roberts's study of Devon shows that the traditional ruling families remained in power.[41] But it is important that these qualifications should not obscure Anthony Fletcher's generalisation that 'the most striking feature of local politics between 1649 and 1653 was the narrowing of circles of power, as the retreat of the traditional ruling families from both administrative and political activity reached its climax'.[42]

Not only was the Commonwealth a regime that seemed to favour 'mean' men, but its reliance on the army meant the continuation of high taxation. The Rump, like the Protectorate later, attempted with some success to reduce taxation levels, but it never proved possible to bring them down to anywhere near pre-war levels, since military expenditure remained high in order to maintain a large standing army and the need to suppress rebellions in, and then garrison and govern, Ireland and Scotland. Above all, though, it was the threat of social and religious radicalism represented by the army that kept alive gentry fears about the dangers of tampering with the national church that had been raised by Laudian innovations in the 1630s and attacks on bishops in the 1640s. Despite the passage of an act abolishing the laws making attendance at the national church compulsory, few members of the Rump were in favour of allowing much liberty of religious conscience, as the punitive Blasphemy Act of 1650 illustrates. But to many gentry it must have seemed as if the political revolution, of which the Rump was the heir, would soon be followed by an even more dangerous social revolution.

The intensity of these fears of the gentry in the early years of the republic cannot be exaggerated. High prices and food shortages, the results of five successive harvest failures since 1646, raised again the spectre of rebellion by 'the many-headed monster' of the poor, and these fears seemed to be confirmed immediately after the execution of the king by reports of activities of Levellers and Diggers, as well as by the proliferation of religious sects like the Quakers and Baptists. The best and fullest illustration of the resultant gentry panic and paranoia at this time is 'the Ranter sensation', which filled the popular press in the early 1650s. In the wake of the publication of J.C. Davis's work, whether or not the Ranters existed is one of the most heated current historical question of mid seventeenth-century English history.[43] Amid the controversy, however, what is certain is that Professor Davis has clearly shown that the anti-Ranter literature of the early 1650s was 'a projection of deviance that had more to do with the reality of religious anxieties, a sense of dislocation, than with the reality of particular people and groups, their actions and beliefs'.[44] Various people had vested motives in propagating the Ranter sensation – enterprising entrepreneurs to sell newspapers and pamphlets, orthodox church ministers to underline the dangers of straying from an ordered and uniform national church, for example, – but they would not have been so hugely successful unless the fears of the propertied about imminent social revolution had not reached a state of near hysteria in the early 1650s.

The end of the Commonwealth in April 1653 was not therefore unwelcome to most gentry. But the manner in which it was ended – by the use of military force – did little to quieten gentry misgivings. The irony of Cromwell's using troops against the Long Parliament only eleven years after he had risked life and property to fight for it was not lost on contemporaries. 'if Mr. Pym were alive again', wrote a young gentlewomen, Dorothy Osborne, to her lover, William Temple, at the time, 'I wonder what he would think of these proceedings, and whether this would appear as great a breach of the Privilege of Parliament as the demanding of the 5 members'.[45] What happened next sent more chills of horror down the spines of propertied gentlemen. Austin Woolrych's brilliant reconstruction of the events of 1653 has demonstrated that Barebones Parliament, an assembly nominated largely by Cromwell and the army council, was not the body of impractical, visionary religious zealots of legend.[46] Nevertheless, that is how it came to be perceived. The sneering assessment of the Royalist Sir Edward Hyde was one shared by many of the traditional ruling elite: 'Much of the major part of them consisted of inferior persons, of no quality or name, artificers of the meanest trades, known only by their gifts in praying or preaching ... they were a pack of weak, senseless fellows, fit only to bring the name and reputation of Parliament lower than it was'.[47] Against this background even moderate reform measures in Barebones Parliament were met with alarm by a paranoid gentry fearful that any change presaged a slide towards social revolution. Therefore when a minority in Barebones Parliament introduced radical far-reaching measures – for fundamental reform of the law on Mosaic lines, for the abolition of tithes and the right of lay patronage to church livings, for example – these merely confirmed conservative fears that private property rights were in danger. Nor did the fact that in August 1653 Barebones Parliament received a proposal that 'the titles of Duke, Marquess, Earl, Lord, Knight, Esquire, and such like should be laid aside as a vain glorious thing, for God's people should be under one name, viz Christian' do anything to alter the contemporary hostile view of the assembly.[48] What made matters worse was that in the summer of 1653 Barebones Parliament undertook yet another purge of county commissions of the peace of varying severity, but enough, as David Underdown comments, 'to give the moderate gentry a severe case of fright'.[49]

The Protectorate, which was established in December 1653, was seen by many gentry as being only a minimal improvement on Barebone's Parliament. It was after all a regime heavily dependent on the army and one that was far more tolerant of religious diversity than were the majority of English gentry. The Instrument of Government which established Oliver Cromwell as Protector was drafted by army commanders, principally John Lambert, and running through it can be seen the army's distrust of parliaments. Two major incursions were made by the drafters of the Instrument into parliamentary liberties: the right given to the council to exclude elected MPs at the beginning of parliamentary sessions, and the power given to Protector and Council to legislate before Parliament met. Cromwell in 1653 accepted a constitution that infringed parliamentary liberties in ways that no monarch (with the possible exception of Charles I) had done.

Moreover, on many occasions during the Protectorate Cromwell showed a disdain for parliamentary and constitutional legality that caused constitutionally-minded gentry great misgivings. The middle years of the Protectorate provide the best example of Cromwell's 'iron-fisted' authoritarianism. It is not the purpose of this essay to explain why at this stage the dominant characteristic of Cromwell's rule was a ruthless lack of compunction in dealing with those who questioned the legality of his actions and a determination to achieve his aims regardless of constitutional and legal niceties.[50] What is important to explain is that in 1655–56 he often acted as though he believed that this was one of those occasions when (as he said in October 1655) 'the Supreme Magistrate should not be tied up to the ordinary rules'.[51] In the course of 1655–56 he imprisoned a merchant, George Cony, and his lawyers, who had the effrontery to question the legality of protectoral ordinances that levied customs dues, in a display of authoritarian power that echoed Charles I's disregard for the law in the Five Knights' Case in 1627. He also harrassed and dismissed senior judges for mounting a legal challenge to the protectoral constitution. In July 1656 Sir Peter Wentworth, a Warwickshire gentleman, was bullied by the council into withdrawing his opposition to paying taxes levied by authority of the Instrument of Government. These instances were followed shortly afterwards by the imposition of drastic press censorship. Consequently Cromwell's establishment of the rule of eleven major generals in the autumn of 1655 was merely one in a series of high-handed attempts to take England into his hoped-for New Jerusalem, if necessary by the scruff of the neck. Gentry resentment at the major-generals – 'swordsmen and decimators' – has been well-documented elsewhere.[52] Moreover, Sarah Jones's unpublished thesis on the Protectorate parliaments has brought out clearly the ways in which in all three parliaments the major cause of tension was opposition to the dominant influence of the army in political life.[53]

Ironically, the opinions of substantial landed gentry in the country were probably reflected more fully than ever before in the Protectorate parliaments, since the Instrument of Government weighted parliamentary representation in favour of counties and against boroughs, and restricted the vote to those who had £200 or more in real or personal property. Not surprisingly, therefore, Protectorate parliaments vented gentry resentment at the military, authoritarian aspects of Cromwellian rule and also their opposition to Cromwellian attempts to extend the boundaries of liberty of religious conscience. Recent work has made clear that Cromwell's commitment to religious toleration was much more limited than has sometimes been supposed.[54] This, however, is a point that would have been lost on many of the English gentry, who saw any relaxation of religious penal laws as a sure recipe for social revolution. The clearest illustration of the strength of gentry attachment to religious uniformity in the Protectorate is the treatment meted out to James Nayler, the Quaker, in the parliamentary session of 1656. The 'crime' for which Nayler was found guilty and eventually savagely punished, was that in October 1656, as part of a revivalist evangelical tour of the West Country, he had entered Bristol, riding on an ass and acclaimed by his supporters, re-enacting Christ's entry into Jerusalem. He was brought to London and charged with 'horrid blasphemy'. Those MPs who argued that Nayler was not guilty and that Parliament had in any case no right to try him under the Instrument of Government were howled down. 'Let us all stop our ears and stone him', said one MP[55] and Nayler was declared guilty by Parliament without a division and sentenced to be branded, bored through the tongue, flogged twice and then imprisoned for life. Cromwell had little sympathy for Nayler's Quaker views but he feared that gentry revulsion at Nayler (and other unorthodox individuals like Biddle) might extend to more moderate religious groups like Baptists and Independents that Cromwell was willing and anxious to tolerate. There is no doubt that he was right. As long as the Protectorate continued its religious policies and its dependence on the army the gentry would always treat the regime with the utmost suspicion.

All that, therefore, makes especially interesting the question of why the majority of the gentry did not support Royalist rebellions in the 1650s and, what is more, gradually came to give the regime their support. It is certain that both these propositions are broadly true. David Underdown's book on Royalist conspiracies in the

1650s leave no room for doubt about the very limited extent of gentry support for the Sealed Knot and other Royalist emigré groups, who devised hair-brained schemes for armed rebellion in England.[56] Moreover, studies of provincial England in the 1650s show the way in which many members of the traditional ruling classes resumed active roles in English government. The most important illustration of this is the way that during the Protectorate representatives of pre-Civil War ruling elites returned to active work as JPs in many English counties: a Pelham returning to the Sussex bench, and a Wyndham, a Luttrell and a Rogers becoming JPs in Somerset, for example. Future research on English localities in Cromwellian England may modify Underdown's account, but it is unlikely to destroy his conclusion that by the last years of the Protectorate 'the country gentry could feel that they were recovering their powers and the local independence that had traditionally been their due'.[57]

What persuaded many gentlemen to collaborate with a republican government many of them probably disliked? It is likely that it was not just cowardice or a judicious concern to protect their property and lives that caused them to give no more support to the exiled Charles Stuart than their successors were to give later Royalist pretenders, the Jacobite Stuarts, in the early eighteenth century. Like the gentlemen of Hanoverian Britain, the gentry of Cromwellian England came to realise that the existing regime suited them and their interests too well to risk all on a desperate, reckless gamble in support of a penniless Stuart adventurer. Like the Commonwealth, the Protectorate was not in many respects a revolutionary regime; nor did it conform to the stereotyped image of a military dictatorship.[58] Oliver Cromwell as protector often looked and acted like a king. Very soon after the establishment of the Protectorate the former royal palaces, St James's, Westminster, Somerset House, Greenwich House, Windsor Castle, Hampton Court and the manor house at York, were vested in Cromwell and his successors. Hampton Court was re-furnished with tapestries, paintings, statues and fountains.[59] When John Evelyn visited Whitehall in February 1656 after a long absence he found it 'very glorious and well furnished'.[60] Cromwell and his court also adopted other outward trappings of regality. Cromwell as Protector was habitually addressed as 'Your Highness' by English courtiers and foreign ambassadors and when Cromwell was re-installed as protector in 1657 the ceremony had some of the features of a royal coronation. In the following year he even created two life peers: Charles Howard was made Baron Gilsand in July and Edward Dunock Baron Burnell in August.

Furthermore, major efforts were made during the Protectorate to woo gentry support. One of Oliver Cromwell's earliest attempts to do this was by abandoning the Rump's Oath of Engagement which had required public approval of the abolition of the monarchy. The key theme of his speech at the opening of the first Protectorate parliament in September 1654 was the need for 'healing and settling'. 'Remembering transactions too particularly (at least in the heart of many of you)', he went on, 'may set the wound fresh a-bleeding'.[61] Time after time during his protectorate Cromwell tried to heal these 'wounds', interfering to protect ex-Royalists, like the Earl of Bridgewater in mid-1654, from the vengeance of the sequestration commissioners. In June that year he signed an order allowing Lady Tyringham to recover all her family's estates lost to Parliament in 1642. It is now fairly certain that many Royalists were able to recover, although at a financial cost, many of the estates they had lost by confiscation at the hands of the regimes of the 1640s and early 1650s,[62] a point given testimony by contemporary complaints from both ends of the political spectrum. The republican Edmund Ludlow was angry that Cromwell instructed assize judges on their circuits of the English provinces to show favour to Royalists, while the Royalist Sir Edward Hyde was bemused that 'Cromwell proceeds with strange dexterity towards the reconciling of all kinds of persons, and chooses out those of all parties whose abilities are most eminent. He ... has given Lord Rothes his liberty and estate, and has restored Sir John Stavell to his fortunes'.[63]

What also undoubtedly helped to reconcile some gentlemen to the Protectorate was that it became obvious to them that it was not a regime that had the bureaucratic machinery necessary to sustain a co-ordinated 'policy' of centralisation. Even during the rule of the major-generals the traditional local government machinery remained in place, staffed by local men who were able to use their local knowledge to frustrate the ambitions of even the most industrious major-general.[64] What was especially attractive to propertied gentry about republican government is that it filled the main functions expected of all early modern regimes: the maintenance of national security and of social order and stability. English foreign policy in the 1650s, though very expensive, was highly successful in meeting the first of those two aims. Equally impressive is the efficient way that local governors responded to one of the most severe economic crises of the seventeenth century: high food prices, near famine conditions and escalating poverty. Both Warwickshire and Cheshire are typical of the way in which the work concerning poor relief undertaken by JPs increased dramatically in the 1650s. In both counties grain prices were reduced, effective measures were taken to ensure that grain was not hoarded by profiteers, and greater fairness in raising taxation was achieved. At the very least, looked at from the perspective of the provinces, the government of England during the republic probably seemed no worse to the gentry than it did at other times, and, at best, it may have seemed better.[65]

Above all, though, what probably persuaded the traditional ruling families to support the republic was that, as Bulstrode Whitelocke candidly admitted in 1649, 'my obedience is only due to you, and there is no other visible authority in being but yourselves'.[66] Even more explicit was Thomas Edgar, a Suffolk JP, who told his fellow magistrates that 'those in public employment in a Commonwealth must not desert government because the way or form doth not like them. Though one kind of government be better than another, yet take that is next rather than none'.[67] Oliver Cromwell in the early 1650s was as skilful as had been Charles I's advisers a decade earlier in arguing that the existing regime was the only bulwark against a descent into anarchy. In his speech to his first Protectorate parliament in September 1654 he depicted his regime as one that had rescued the country from social revolution. 'The magistracy of the nation', he asked, 'was it not almost trampled under foot, under desire and contempt by men of Levelling principles ... for the order of men and ranks of men, did not that Levelling principles tend to the reducing all to an equality?'. He also took great pains to appear as the bastion of the traditional hierarchical social order, saying 'a nobleman, a gentleman, and a yeoman. (That is a good interest of the nation and a great one)'. Even more appealing to conservative landowning gentry was his commitment to safeguard property by claiming that it was one of 'the badges of the kingdom of Christ'.[68] Gradually it became clear that the republic was providing the stability for which the gentry yearned, and when Oliver Cromwell died in September 1658 loyal addresses flowed in from many counties to welcome the accession of his son, Richard, as the new protector.

Why, then, was Charles Stuart restored to the throne with enthusiastic gentry support within a bare twenty months of Richard Cromwell's accession? The answer is to be found in the timing of the conversion of many gentry to restoration of the monarchy – at the very end of 1659. A Royalist rising in the late summer of that year hardly got off the ground. Sir George Booth in Cheshire and south Lancashire was one of the few gentlemen to come out openly for Charles Stuart, indicating the lack of widespread gentry enthusiasm for his return even at that stage. However, during the next few months county associations and petitions began to call for the return of 'a free parliament', rallying to the support of General Monck on his march south from Scotland. 'A free parliament' meant the return of the MPs secluded by the army in 1648 and that was bound to lead to a parliamentary majority for the restoration of the monarchy. The major explanation for the suddenness of this change is that by this time Richard Cromwell's Protectorate had collapsed (in April 1659) and succeeding regimes headed by the restored Rump and the army council failed to provide effective central government. The republic collapsed because of the political bankruptcy of Oliver Cromwell's successors, not because of gentry opposition. But its collapse caused the gentry to panic, fearing as they had in the early 1650s that a social revolution would occur unless effective central government was restored without delay. This time the gentry's bogeymen were Quakers not Ranters, and this time there was substance behind their fears.

By the 1650s there were at least 50,000 Quakers, making them the most numerous of the new unorthodox religious Protestant groups to emerge during the English Revolution. Largely through the work of evangelists like James Nayler, Quaker ideas spread from the north of England throughout the country. What was horrifying to gentry opinion about this was not only the spread of unlicensed preaching, but the fact that the Quakers developed more fully than most heterodox religious groups the Protestant concept of 'the inner light' – that men and women should follow their own consciences rather than the dictates of ministers and magistrates. Many gentry feared, with some justice, that some Quakers interpreted this not only as a licence for sexual permissiveness, but also for attacks on the existing social order. Quakers refused to pay tithes or to take off their hats in the presence of those considered by others to be their social superiors, and, in great contrast to their peace-loving successors from the later seventeenth century onwards, were not against taking militant action, often violently interrupting church services. Nayler's release from prison in September 1659 wrongly gave the impression that the government was encouraging ideas like these. Barry Reay concludes that the threat seen to be posed to respectable society by the Quakers in 1659 is comparable to the 'fear of Catholics in England in the early 1640s or the Great Fear in France over a century later'. But he does present evidence that gave some substance to these fears – of Quakers (and Baptists) getting commissions in the militia, for example – making explicable the warnings of the Anglican divine, Robert South, in a sermon in Oxford in July 1659 about what would happen 'should God in his judgement suffer England to be transformed into a Münster'.[69] This kind of hysteria of 'an England turned Germany' (this time an early sixteenth-century Germany) is the context in which the gentry turned back to the Stuarts. By March 1661 nearly 5,000 Quakers had been imprisoned by Anglican magistrates, well before the Quaker Act (1662) and Conventicle Act (1664) enacted severe punishments of fines, imprisonment and transportation for those convicted of Quakerism. These were the beginnings of 'the Church in Danger' hysteria that led Anglican gentry to pass penal legislation against Protestant Dissenters from the early 1660s to the early eighteenth century. For many English gentlemen their experiences during the English Revolution ensured the continuation after 1660 of long-standing fears that their wealth and influence were in jeopardy. Therefore, like their successors exactly twenty-nine years later, they turned to a regime that could provide a guarantee of stability and a bulwark against imminent social revolution.

Was, then, the main consequence of their experiences in the English Revolution to 'reunite' the gentry behind the Church and monarchy in order to safeguard their own restoration to power in the English provinces, which is reflected in the composition of county commissions of the militia and the peace in the early

1660s? Certainly it is now much harder to detect the religious differences which had divided the gentry before the early 1640s. For many gentlemen the godly zeal which had put fire in their bellies at the outbreak of the Civil War had become less strong as the godly cause became associated with political and social radicalism, as has been seen. What makes Oliver Cromwell so unusual among propertied gentlemen is that his commitment to the cause of godly reformation intensified in the 1650s. Yet it may be that the English Revolution did not convert all gentlemen into supporters of an intolerant national church. At present most of the evidence for those who supported a 'Presbyterian' view of a comprehensive church is to be found in the parliaments of the early 1660s, among peers, like Lord Wharton and the Earl of Manchester, who had broken with the army in 1648.[70] At the provincial level the evidence of the survival of godly commitment among the gentry is patchy. In Warwickshire a petition from the leading gentry of the county to Monck at the end of January 1660 asked 'that such liberty be allowed to tender consciences as is agreeable to the revealed will of God in the holy scriptures'.[71] Philip Jenkins concludes that in Glamorgan in the early 1660s there were 'two distinct factions among the elite of county society, who were chiefly divided by attitudes to dissent. One part looked for support to Wharton and Manchester, the other to Sheldon and Ormonde ... As in neighbouring counties, some Glamorgan puritans were still tolerated by the "sober part of the gentry", who were a powerful element in county society'.[72] Elsewhere, too, gentry from families with a long tradition of godly commitment, like the Barringtons of Essex and the Hampdens of Buckinghamshire, employed nonconformist ministers as domestic chaplains.[73] Moreover, the evidence that the penal laws were not vigorously executed by some gentry magistrates in the early years after the Restoration suggests that at least among a minority of gentry their recent experiences had confirmed their attachment to the cause of godly reformation.[74] It may be that gentry Puritanism not only survived the English Revolution, but that it formed one of the bases of a later Stuart Whig tradition, which, like intolerant Anglican Toryism (reflected in the strident statement at the head of this essay), is rooted in the experiences of the gentry during the English Revolution.

Notes

1 Quoted in A. Fletcher, *Reform in the Provinces: the Government of Stuart England*, New Haven and London, 1986, p. 175.

2 J. P. Kenyon, *Revolution Principles: the Politics of Party, 1689–1720*, Cambridge, 1977, Ch. 6.

3 This is the estimate of J. Morrill, 'The Stuarts' in K. O. Morgan (ed.), *The Oxford Illustrated History of Britain*, Oxford, 1984, p. 297.

4 J. Rushworth, *Historical Collections, 1680–1722*, 10 vols., IV, p. 33. Rushworth also prints other parliamentary speeches made in November 1640. Some county petitions and other speeches are printed in J. S. Morrill, *The Revolt of the Provinces*, 2nd edn., London, 1980, pp. 148–9, 150–51, 153–55.

5 D. Underdown, *Pride's Purge: Politics in the Puritan Revolution*, Oxford, 1971, p. 24.

6 A. M. Everitt, *The Community of Kent and the Great Rebellion 1640–60*, Leicester, 1966, is the seminal work on the idea of the county community. Its main critics are C. Holmes, 'The county community in Stuart historiography', *Journal of British Studies*, XIX, 1980 and *Seventeenth-Century Lincolnshire*, Lincoln, 1980, and A. Hughes, 'Warwickshire on the eve of the Civil War: a "county community"?', *Midland History*, VII, 1981; *Politics, Society and Civil War in Warwickshire 1620–60*, Cambridge, 1987, and 'Local history and the origins of the Civil War' in R. Cust and A. Hughes (eds.), *Conflict in Early Stuart England: Studies in Religion and Politics 1603–42*, Harlow, 1989. Everitt's work, however, stimulated a flood of writings on the provincial history of mid-seventeenth-century England, many of which are cited in the following footnotes.

7 'The determinative contrast between England and the other great states of Europe [is that] in no other has there been such continuity in the exercise of effective authority over so wide an area for so long', in J. Campbell, *et al.*, *The Anglo-Saxons*, London, 1982, quoted in P. Corrigan and D. Sayer, *The Great Arch: English State Formation as Cultural Revolution*, Oxford, 1985, p. 15.

8 R. Cust, 'News and politics in early seventeenth-century England', *Past and Present*, 112, 1986.

9 A. Fletcher, 'National and local awareness in the county communities', in H. Tomlinson, (ed.), *Before the English Civil War: Essays on Early Stuart Politics and Government*, London, 1983.

10 Fletcher, 'National and local awareness', p. 164.

11 On Puritan gentry, the importance of religion and the divisive issue of 'further reformation' see J. T. Cliffe, *Puritans in Conflict: the Puritan Gentry during and after the Civil Wars*, London, 1988, J. S. Morrill, 'The religious context of the English Civil War', *Transactions of the Royal Historical Society*, 5th series, 34, 1984, and C. Russell, *The Causes of the English Civil War*, Oxford, 1990, pp. 220–6.

12 A. Fletcher, 'Concern for renewal in the Root and Branch debates of 1641' in D. Baker, (ed.), *Studies in Church History*, 14, 1977; A. Fletcher, *The Outbreak of the English Civil War*, London, 1981, pp. 104–5.

13 Fletcher, *Outbreak*, pp. 221–2, 288.

14 D. Hirst, 'The defection of Sir Edward Dering, 1640–41', *Historical Journal*, 15, 1972.

15 J. S. Morrill, *Cheshire 1630–60: County Government and Society during the English Revolution*, Oxford, 1974, pp. 49–50.

16 J.P. Kenyon (ed.), *The Stuart Constitution 1603–88*, 2nd edn., 1986, p. 20.

17 Rushworth, *Historical Collections*, IV, p. 425.

18 Morrill, *Revolt, passim*.

19 See Fletcher, *Outbreak*, Ch. 12, especially pp. 400–5, for the best discussion of these problems.

20 Fletcher, *Outbreak*, p. 391.

21 B. Schofield (ed.), *The Knyvett Letters 1620–44* (1949), quoted in Morrill, *Revolt*, p. 136.

22 Fletcher, *Outbreak*, Ch. 12; Morrill, *Cheshire*, pp. 66–9; Morrill, *Revolt*, pp. 160–1.

23 C. Holmes, *The Eastern Association in the English Civil War*, Cambridge, 1974, p. 61.

24 Cliffe, *Puritans in Conflict*, p. 28.

25 The best general accounts of this are I. Roy, 'The English Civil War and English Society' in B. Bond and I. Roy, (eds.), *War and Society*, London, 1977 and D. H. Pennington, 'The war and the English people' in J. S. Morrill (ed.), *Reactions to the English Civil War*, London, 1982. For the economic impact of the war on the gentry specifically, see C. Clay, 'Landlords and estate management in England: the Civil War and Interregnum' in J. Thirsk (ed.), *The Agrarian History of England and Wales*, V, Cambridge, 1985 and J. Broad, 'Gentry finances and the Civil War: the case of the Buckinghamshire Verneys', *Economic History Review*, 2nd series, XXXII, 1979, and Hughes, *Warwickshire*, Ch. 5.

26 J.S. Morrill and J. Walter, 'Order and disorder in the English Revolution' in A. Fletcher and J. Stevenson (eds.), *Order and Disorder in Early Modern England*, Cambridge, 1985.

27 A. H. Woolrych, *Soldiers and Statesmen: the General Council of the Army and its Debates 1647–48*, Oxford, 1987.

28 Fletcher, *Reform*, pp. 12–14; Underdown, *Pride's Purge*, pp. 34–36; Morrill, *Revolt*, p. 119.

29 Everitt, *Kent*, pp. 190–5.

30 Holmes, *Eastern Association*, p. 215.

31 Hughes, *Warwickshire*, p. 234. For Staffordshire, see D. H. Pennington and I. Roots (eds.), *The Committee at Stafford 1643–45*, Manchester, 1957, pp. lxxiv–lxxxiii, 342–44. For Cheshire, see Morrill, *Cheshire*, Ch. 4.

32 Holmes, *Lincolnshire*, pp. 185–86, 188–93; C. Holmes, 'Colonel King and Lincolnshire politics, 1642–46', *Historical Journal*, 16, 1973.

33 R. Hutton, *The Royalist War Effort, 1642–46*, London, 1982, pp. 184–89.

34 Hutton, *Royalist War Effort*, p. 159. For the Clubmen, see Morrill, *Revolt*, pp. 98–111, D. Underdown, 'The chalk and the cheese: contrasts among the English Clubmen', *Past and Present*, 85, 1979; Hutton, *Royalist War Effort*, pp. 159–65, 170–72, 180–82. The reference to G. Lynch, 'The Rising of the Clubmen in the English Civil war' (unpublished MA thesis, University of Manchester, 1973) is in Morrill, *Revolt*, p. 224, n. 42.

35 Underdown, *Pride's Purge*, p. 99. There is no full study of the Second Civil War. Underdown, *Pride's Purge*, Morrill, *Revolt*, pp. 125–31, and Everitt, *Kent*, pp. 231–70 are the best short accounts.

36 B. Lyndon, 'The Second Civil War', *History*, 71, 1986, and 'Essex and the king's cause in 1648', *Historical Journal*, 29, 1986.

37 Some of the works already cited cover the 1650s but do so much less extensively than the 1640s. Two recent county studies take the later 1640s as their starting

point: S. K. Roberts, *Recovery and Restoration in an English County: Devon Local Administration, 1646–70*, Exeter, 1985 and A. M. Coleby, *Central Government and the Localities: Hampshire 1649–89*, Cambridge, 1987.

38 C. H. Firth and R. S. Rait (eds.), *Acts and Ordinances of the Interregnum*, 2 vols., Oxford 1911, II, pp. 5–6.

39 Underdown, *Pride's Purge*, p. 299.

40 P. Jenkins, *The Making of a Ruling Class: the Glamorgan Gentry*, Cambridge, 1983, p. 110.

41 Roberts, *Devon*, pp. 30–3.

42 Fletcher, *Outbreak*, p. 15.

43 J. C. Davis, *Fear, Myth and History: the Ranters and the Historians*, Cambridge, 1986. Davis's article, 'Fear, myth and furore: reappraising the Ranters', *Past and Present*, 129, 1990, summarises the debate, as well as giving his response to it.

44 Davis, *Ranters*, p. 124.

45 G. C. Moore Smith (ed.), *The Letters of Dorothy Osborne to William Temple*, Oxford, 1928, p. 39.

46 A. H. Woolrych, *From Commonwealth to Protectorate*, Oxford, 1986.

47 W. D. Macray (ed.), *Clarendon's History of the Rebellion*, 6 vols., Oxford, 1988, V, p. 282.

48 Cliffe, *Puritans in Conflict*, p. 182.

49 Underdown, *Pride's Purge*, p. 341.

50 This question is explored in my book in the Longman Profiles in Power series: Barry Coward, *Cromwell*, Harlow, 1991.

51 Quoted in S. R. Gardiner, *History of the Commonwealth and Protectorate, 1646–49*, 4 vols., London, 1903, III, p. 260.

52 See the articles by D. W. Rannie in *English Historical Review*, X, 1895, I. Roots in J. H. Parry (ed.), *After the English Civil War* (London, 1970), and A. Fletcher in D. Baker (ed.), *Religious Motivation: Studies in Church History, Vol. 15*, (Oxford, 1978).

53 S. Jones, 'The Composition and Activity of the Protectorate Parliaments', unpublished Ph.D. thesis, University of Exeter, 1988.

54 The seminal article on this is B. Worden, 'Toleration and the Cromwellian Protectorate', in W. J. Shiels (ed.), *Persecution and Toleration: Studies in Church History*, Oxford, 1984.

55 Quoted in C. H. Firth, *The Last Years of the Protectorate 1656–58*, 2 vols., London, 1907, I, p. 21.

56 D. Underdown, *Royalist Conspiracy in England, 1649–60*, New Haven, 1960.

57 D. Underdown, 'Settlement in the counties' in G. E. Aylmer (ed.), *The Interregnum: the Quest for Settlement 1646–60*, London, 1972, p. 172. This article is the best survey of the mood of the gentry in the localities in the 1650s. The following points the way to the detailed work that needs to be done on this topic: A. Fletcher, 'Oliver Cromwell and the localities' in C. Jones, M. Newitt and S. Roberts (eds.), *Politics and People in Revolutionary England*, Oxford, 1986.

58 On the conservatism of the Rump see B. Worden, *The Rump Parliament 1649–53*, Cambridge, 1975. For the Protectorate see A. Woolrych, 'The Cromwellian Protectorate: a "military dictatorship"?', *History*, 75, 1990.

59 R. Sherwood, *The Court of Oliver Cromwell*, London, 1977.

60 E. S. de Beer (ed.), *The Diary of John Evelyn*, London, 1955, 6 vols., II, p. 166.

61 W. C. Abbott (ed.), *Writings and Speeches of Oliver Cromwell*, 4 vols., Cambridge, Mass., 1937–47, III, p. 166.

62 This is also true of landowners who had been forced to sell land as a result of the adverse effects of the Civil War noted above: J. Thirsk, 'The sale of royalist lands during the Interregnum', *Economic History Review*, 2nd ser., V, 1952–53; H. J. Habbakuk, 'Landowners and the Civil War', *ibid.*, XVIII, 1965, and 'Public finance and the sale of confiscated estates during the Interregnum', *ibid.*, XV, 1962; P. G. Holiday, 'Land sales and repurchases in Yorkshire after the Civil War, 1650–70', *Northern History*, V, 1970; B. Coward, *The Stanleys, Lords Stanley and Earls of Derby 1385–1672*, Manchester, 1983. See also Clay's article cited in note 25 above.

63 Clarendon's *History*, II, p. 323.

64 Fletcher, 'Cromwell and the localities', pp. 196–200.

65 Hughes, *Warwickshire*, pp. 277–90; Morrill, *Cheshire*, Ch. 6.

66 B. Whitelocke, *Memorials of the English Affairs*, 4 vols., 1853, II, pp. 524–7.

67 Quoted in Underdown, *Pride's Purge*, p. 262.

68 Abbott, *Writings*, III, pp. 435, 438.

69 B. Reay, *The Quakers and the English Revolution*, London, 1985, pp. 92, 100, 106.

70 D. R. Lacey, *Dissent and Parliamentary Politics 1661–89*, New Brunswick, 1969, *passim*.

71 Hughes, *Warwickshire*, p. 332.

72 Jenkins, *The Making of a Ruling Class*, p. 124.

73 Cliffe, *Puritans in Conflict*, p. 195.

74 M. R. Watts, *The Dissenters*, Oxford, 1978, Ch. 3; A. Fletcher, 'The enforcement of the Conventicle Acts 1664–79' in *Persecution and Toleration: Studies in Church History*, Oxford, 1984.

CHAPTER NINE

LANDLORD-TENANT RELATIONSHIPS
1642 – 1660

C. B. Phillips

The essential organism for landlord-tenant relationships was the manor. Historians debate whether or not the manor was introduced into England by the Normans. It was in effect abolished in 1925 so its history is some 1,000 years long. Its characteristics have changed in that span, though with seemingly infinite variation from place to place, and over time. Villeinage was replaced by cash transactions, cultivation in common by farming in severalty. Urban settlement expanded, and industry came to replace agriculture as the main source of wealth and employment. A predominantly feudal society became a predominantly capitalist one. The control of manors passed from the Crown to become the property of individuals and institutions. It is the aim of this essay to discuss the impact of the Civil War, Interregnum, and Restoration, from 1642 to 1660 on the relationship at the heart of the manor, the relationship between landlord and tenant.

However, the agrarian historian of England might be forgiven for asking whether the Civil War had any significant effect on that relationship, for secular change in population and price levels can be viewed as the major determinant of harmony or disharmony between lord and tenant. By the second half of the sixteenth century the pressure of population on land led would-be tenants to offer higher leasehold rents for land, more so in arable rather than in pastoral regions, certain that, with rising prices for agricultural commodities, their income would also go up.[1] Where manorial custom did not permit lords to increase rents, pressure to replace customary estates with leases developed, landlords tried to raise entry fines and demand their full entitlement of,

for example, boon hens, or labour dues.[2] The end of the English
Civil Wars at Worcester in 1651 roughly coincides with the clear
emergence of secular change in national population trends.[3] It is
also possible that there had been some improvement in agricultural
productivity, and/or increase in levels of output, over the late
sixteenth and seventeenth centuries. If these increases did take
place, then they may also, with stagnant population levels, have
contributed to the imbalance between the supply of agricultural
produce and the demand for food about which late seventeenth-
century commentators complained. Enclosure, and the knowledge
of new techniques, and of new forms of husbandry, at least raise
the possibility of increased output and productivity.[4] The new
economic climate which resulted shifted fundamentally the terms
upon which landlords leased and tenants rented; conflict declined
between lord and tenant over levels of rent, length of leases, and
willingness to renew. In areas where customary forms of tenure,
including rights of inheritance, dominated, the impact of population/
price levels may have been muted as some disputes over the nature
of customary estates continued into the eighteenth century.[5]
Arguably, therefore, the major differences apparent in landlord-
tenant relationships between the first quarter and the last quarter of
the seventeenth century owed little to the events of the Civil War.

II

The term landlord in this period usually refers to the lord of a
manor. Land was held of a manorial lord by frank (or freehold)
tenure, and base (or customary) tenure; all such tenants of the
manor were liable to attend the manorial court. An individual
might hold land in both ways from the same manor, and or different
manors. Customary tenants had estates or interests in their land
holding, thus a copyhold of inheritance, because it lasted for
life, was a freehold estate held by base tenure. By *circa* 1600
some ancient manorial demesne, let in the fourteenth or fifteenth
centuries had, with the passage of time, become indistinguishable
from customary land. In the seventeenth century such properties
were regarded in law as held at the will of the lord. Since seventeenth-
century demesne leases were commercial contracts between landowner and farmer, and involved the tenants in no obligation to
attend the manorial court demesne tenants are not our concern
in this essay; neither are we concerned with sub-tenancies which

may have been created by customary tenants. It is as well not to oversimplify our definitions: the spread of leaseholds as replacements for customary tenure may not have totally eliminated a concept of obligation between lord and tenant, nor a duty to attend court; in any case, there were those who were both customary and demesne tenants. Furthermore, people by custom had access to lands to which they had no title accepted in law.[6]

III

The first question is the extent of the involvement of tenants in the armies. Did tenants actually serve? Clarendon's *History of the Rebellion* is an early authority for the view that the Royalist army was a feudal host drawn from the tenants of the King's noble and gentle supporters.[7] Other contemporaries differed: Baxter noted support for the Royalist gentry from their tenants, while Chamberlayne placed 'very many of the peasantry' on the side of Parliament. Christopher Hill used the marquis of Newcastle's 'Whitecoats', made up of his tenants, to typify the Royalist army.[8] The propaganda of both sides at the start of the war was anxious to claim support from men of the economic and social status of tenants, and needs therefore to be treated with caution. The make-up of the armies of each side early in the war depended a lot on the tactics of the recruiters. Where one or other side attempted to take over the trained bands, then the resultant force would resemble the bands; where noblemen or gentry appealed for support (under either the militia ordinance or a commission of array, or even using the *posse comitatus*), then tenant levies might have resulted. It is worth noting that in the militia forces both before and after the war many who were liable attempted to avoid service by sending deputies. The concern of militia organisers was to get enough soldiers from the propertied levels of society – including tenants – to serve. In the later years of the war, say from the end of 1644, recruitment to Parliament's armies was mainly by transfer from existing forces, and for the Royalists primarily by impressment.[9] For the historian, therefore, by 1644 the question of tenant allegiance is no longer paramount, rather the issue is inverted: Clubmen riots and other risings, often associated with enclosure, witnessed the opposition of 'countrymen' (the Clubmen), including tenants and minor gentry, to both sides in the war.[10]

There is no doubt that in the summer of 1642 partisans of both sides were successful in recruiting tenants into their forces.

For the king in Lancashire the Earl of Derby held two well attended rallies in mid-July, but precisely how many who came were his tenants or those of his associates is unclear, and neither occasion seems to have produced any solid military force, despite the supposed attack on Manchester on 15 July.[11] By 16 September the Lancashire Royalists had raised a coherent force of three regiments, and these many have included tenants from the Earl of Derby's estates in south-west Lancashire, though this is not clear. The Gerard family certainly raised one regiment, while the possible presence of Welsh troops (not, apparently, from the Earl of Derby's Flintshire estates) has been used by Hutton to play down the feudal nature of this force. Malcolm has highlighted evidence that tenants were forced to participate in it, and found indications of similar strong-arm tactics by the Earl of Newcastle in north-east England.[12]

In Staffordshire, according to Hutton,[13] the Royalists recruited by beating the drum for individual volunteers, but tenants' allegiance was more obviously at work in Worcester on 12 August 1642 where there was a display of tenant loyalty to the Herbert family.[14] In Cornwall the Royalists were able to take over the county militia, and recruit additional volunteers in a climate where loyalty to landlords was important.[15] Underdown maintains that the king's troops in Somerset were mainly recruited not from manorial tenants but from the economically marginal, and that when tenants did follow their lord, they did so for only so long as he was able to offer them protection against the opposition.[16] In those parts of Lincolnshire where the Earls of Lindsey held sway, Holmes reports the royalists raising forces in 1642 by beating the drum.[17]

Early in 1643 the Earl of Derby in Lancashire was able to raise some thousands of countrymen – not necessarily his tenants – for the Royalist cause, and while Royalist gentry and their tenants figured in these forces, others participated as part of a *posse* to foil a threat of raiding by Parliamentarians. Parliament raised similar forces in those parts of Lancashire which it controlled, and on both sides such levies were ill armed and stood down after a particular skirmish. In Cumberland in May 1643 a similarly described tenant levy repulsed a Parliamentarian attack on Carlisle, but gave birth to no coherent force. In other parts of the country soldiers had deserted over the winter, and Hutton has concluded that, from the start of the 1643 campaigning season onwards, the Royalist army was recruited by impressment or by beating the drum for volunteers. While people who were manorial tenants may have been recruited in these ways (though probably not by impressment), they can hardly be said to have joined up under some feeling of tenurial obligation.[18]

In contrast, historians of strongly Parliamentarian areas, or of Parliamentarian armies, have placed little emphasis on the role of tenants. Before the war proper started, tenants of the Earl of Stamford helped him secure the magazine at Leicester against the king in June 1642, and Sir George Booth's tenants went to help Manchester resist the Earl of Derby.[19] Many of the recruits for Parliament from the counties of the eastern association were volunteers.[20] In four Suffolk villages for which detailed evidence survives, such volunteers were servants and 'poorer neighbours' of those who subscribed money. Less detailed evidence for other communities suggests that the more wealthy (that is tenants, though Holmes does not use the word) were willing to subscribe rather than serve.By mid-1643 volunteer recruits, especially for the infantry, were hard to find, and from July to August 1643 troops were being levied by impressment, and these were usually labourers or servants, but sometimes 'householders, husbandmen or men of property'. If the Parliamentary ordinance was followed those with £5 in goods or £3 in land were exempt, but the possibility that tenants were pressed is clear.[21] Bulstrode Whitelocke stated that the cavalry forces of the eastern association were recruited from 'Freeholders and freeholders' sons', but while Holmes has identified one copyholder and one husbandman amongst them, his evidence of recruits from outside the geographical area of the association has weakened Whitelocke's claim for an ideologically committed, locally raised force which would have included many tenants.[22]

Within the eastern association, recruitment in Essex in 1642 is of especial interest because of the parallels with Lancashire. In Essex the personal appearance of the Earl of Warwick was vital for recruiting Parliamentarian volunteers in 1642,[23] yet, just as in Lancashire where the Earl of Derby reflected that men had supported him for a variety of reasons, so too in Essex, support for Warwick came from economic self-interest, and because of his Puritan religious leanings. No contemporary seems to have described his supporters as his tenants, and neither have modern historians, yet in 1630 the Earl was lord of sixty-four manors in the county.[24] In contrast with Lancashire, Warwick was able in 1642 to secure the trained bands, presumably including some tenants, and bandsmen were still serving a year later, though by June 1643 many were said to have deserted.[25] It seems reasonable to conclude that great magnates in both the opposing sides could command support, but that contemporary images of those supporters differed. In Parliamentarian Essex Puritanism and personal loyalty were stressed, while in Lancashire personal loyalty was expected to come from tenants. The pamphlet, autobiographical and hagiographical source material for the early months of the war in Lancashire is difficult. Did the writers consider support from tenants a strength for the Earl of Derby, or was the emphasis on tenantry amongst his supporters understood to be a sign of weakness? That is, tenants were there because they had to be, not necessarily because they wanted to support Derby and the king? For those disappointed by the size of support for the Earl, a face-saving explanation may have been to emphasise the involuntary aspect of a feudal host; tenants who stayed away were particularly valuable to Derby's enemies. In Essex, on the other hand, the war was a godly war, and any secular obligations on tenants to support the Earl of Warwick could be seen as superfluous to religious zeal.

Much of the evidence of tenant involvement just discussed derived from contemporary pamphlets. Military records and committee papers extend our knowledge marginally but, unfortunately, little is known about the mass of the soldiers in either army. Listings of prisoners give names but their identification as individuals has usually only been possible for officers.[26] Military historians have rarely been able to find muster lists, or even casualty lists, of the common soldiers.[27] The evidence of pensions paid to disabled soldiers of both sides probably tells us little of the social status of the pensioners in the 1640s. A number of Royalist yeomen and husbandmen were sequestered and either discharged as not wealthy enough to compound, or compounded for small estates; some of these men were tenants involved in the fighting.[28] The appeal of the Staffordshire Grand Jury in 1644 for the return of men in time for the harvest implies that those missing were the lower levels of society who provided the casual labour so essential to get the crops in. There is a further implication that the tenants had been there earlier to plant the crops and tend them.[29]

Tenants did not always serve when called by their lord, and indeed, some opposed their lord. At the start of the war, twenty-four tenants of the Cheshire landowner William Davenport wrote to tell him they did not support his Royalist stance, and even sought to get him to change sides; Davenport noted that some went off to join the Parliamentarian army.[30] The Earl of Derby's tenants in West Derby and Wavertree, together with some in Bury and Pilkington would not support him at the start of the war; Derby's experience with his tenants was clearly a mixed one.[31] Sir Ralph Hopton's tenants at Evercreech in Somerset opposed him, as did those of Sir Thomas Smith.[32] I have found no examples of the tenants of a Parliamentarian landlord refusing to follow his lead in 1642 or 1643.

John Morrill's suggestion that as many as one in three males were in arms at some point in the war (Brereton Conference, Chester, 16 March 1991) implies that many tenants did in fact serve in the armies, but has to be contrasted with Manning's conclusion that '... over a great deal of the kingdom masses of them [the people] were indifferent or opposed to both sides ...'.[33] It is quite impossible to say how many tenants, or what proportion of tenants, joined the civil war armies. Equally, no enumeration can be made of those Clubmen who, although their allegiance might be claimed by one side, massed in order to keep the armies of either side away from their homes and livelihoods.

Amongst landlords more detailed figures for active involvement with one or other side are available, figures which stress the numerical importance of those gentry who avoided the war. The more important gentry, thus frequently the more wealthy families owning numbers of manors, were usually committed, and in this respect the lords of more tenants may have been involved in the war compared with those tenants whose lords took no active part. In Cumberland and Westmorland eighty-two out of 180 gentry families took no part in the first civil war, fifty-seven of these families were of the lowest gentle status in 1642, and only two were knights; in Warwickshire only half the gentry are known to have taken sides.[34] In Suffolk, a county identified with Parliament, those landlords who supported the king went to Oxford, and the active loyalty of their tenants was never put to the test.[35]

IV

How far were landlords able to control the allegiance of their tenants in the war? The army which two years earlier gathered to fight the Scots was raised by a state whose power to do so was undisputed, even if the war policy was challenged. The circumstances of 1642 were unusual, without precedent in any part of the country since the rebellion of the northern earls in 1569, when Neville and Percy had been able to call on the ancient allegiance and obligation of their followers. Was society sufficiently deferential for landlords to expect their tenants to risk their lives in a cause which the tenants themselves might not espouse? In practice, as we have just seen, some landlords expected such support, and got it; other landlords were disappointed. Even as late as 1644 a captured Royalist was told to tell his tenants not to take up arms against Parliament.[36] When a relief force threatened the siege of Chester, tenants of Royalists were allowed to reduce by half the rents paid to the sequestrators, to keep them loyal to Parliament.[37] In those parishes where homilies on obedience were frequently read to the congregations, tenants might be inclined to obey a summons from their lord. Professor Stone has argued that the power of the peerage to obtain military service had declined, and we might also apply his conclusions to the gentry. As late as 1558 the crown summoned nobles to bring their tenants to the defence of Calais, and there were later, personal, offers of military forces to Elizabeth. Nevertheless, on two occasions she had to condemn the practice of retaining. As late as the 1590s some landlords were requiring clauses about military service in time of war to appear in leases. But the shift of the militia to control by lords lieutenant as opposed to peers as individuals, the removal of the need for military service on the border with Scotland after 1603, the cessation of the custom of large bodies of tenants turning out to greet lords, and a decline in the size of noble housholds all contributed to weaken the obligation of tenants to perform military service at the call of their lords.[38] In particular, and in Charles I's reign, the increasing taxes to pay for the militia, the more frequent mustering of the individuals specifically assigned to the trained bands, and the impressment of men for army service abroad must all have served to distinguish military obligations from teneurial ones.

In this respect then, it is perhaps remarkable that landlords were as successful as they were in obtaining military support from their tenants, *qua* tenants. Professor Brian Manning has tried to explain the failure of tenants to support their lords, albeit in the context of the role of 'the people' in the Civil War, that is a much wider grouping than tenants as defined above. In Somerset he concluded that Sir Ralph Hopton, one of a party of Royalists under the Marquis of Hertford sent to recruit in the West Country, failed to get support because Hertford and his associates were regarded as outsiders, and because those gentry who supported Parliament were able to whip up a popular fear of the Royalist recruiters.[39] B.G. Blackwood showed that a number of Royalists in north Lancashire had been engaged in litigation with their tenants before the war, and that this may have cost the Crown support in Lonsdale hundred of the county. Yet he is cautious in explaining civil war allegiance by teneurial conflict, for such conflicts were widespread in the region, while some tenants of the area actually fought for the king, or provided munitions. In Cornwall, Sir Beville Grenville sued tenants who denied customs, but obtained their support in the war.[40]

Also in Lancashire, the Earl of Derby met with a mixed reaction from his tenants. Manning has emphasised opposition to the Earl from his tenants. The evidence about Derby is difficult to use, not least because one Earl died in 1642 and was succeeded by his son, so that there is some doubt as to whose teneurial policy applied. It seems likely that in 1637 relations with the tenants of the manors of Weeton and Treales were at least 'strained'. This is the only unambiguous evidence that the Earls of Derby were harsh to their tenants, on two out of the twenty or more manors they held in Lancashire. The seventh Earl was in 1655 noted as a good landlord 'until of late'. 'Of late' has usually been applied to the manors of West Derby and Wavertree, which the family only acquired in 1639, from London financiers who had bought them in settlement of Crown debts in 1628. Tenurial relations were obviously strained before Derby took over. The evidence that he was harsh to these tenants comes from a 1647 letter from the Parliamentarian Col Edward Moore, who claimed that Derby had attacked their customs, but he did not make clear whether this was before or after the tenants had fought for Parliament. In contrast to Manning and Blackwood, Hutton suggests that these tenants may have supported Derby until the

Royalists lost control of Lancashire in 1643. Indeed, it might be that these tenants' attitudes reflected their feelings towards their old landlord, the Crown, rather than their new lord, the Earl.[41] Manning points out that across the north of England, in the Fens, in Somerset and Gloucestershire, and in the forests of the central south, Crown estate policy had become much harsher to tenants in the seventeenth century, as evidenced in higher fines, attacks on custom, and the enclosure of wastes and fens; surprisingly, midland areas with a history of riot were quiescent. In the war, the defenders of fen and forest rights embroiled troops in their ongoing struggles rather than joined either of the sides.[42] Religion may also have moved tenants against their masters. Mistakenly or not, the king and the Royalists were identified with papists, who generated an irrational but widespread hostility on which some Parliamentarians played. The Royalists were also identified with Laudianism, and in Cheshire some of William Davenport's tenants who rejected his Royalism may have done so as much over a dispute about heriots, as about religion. Certainly the Cheshire MP Sir Thomas Aston resented Presbyterianism as a challenge to a landlord's authority. In Lancashire some tenants of the Earl of Derby in Bury and Pilkington opposed him for religious reasons.[43]

V

Of those who did serve in the armies, how many died as a result of their service? Wrigley and Schofield concluded that some mortality crises of the 1640s could be attributed to epidemics associated with the movement of armies, and this conclusion has recently been reinforced for the Berkshire area by Joan Dills.[44] Charles Carlton's recent work has stressed the impact of the war by comparing the 0.6 per cent of the population who died in the Second World War 1939–46 with the 3.6 per cent of the population who died in the Civil War years.[45] His figures for the 1640s include those who died of disease, and Carlton has counted 84,738 killed in the fighting, rather less than contemporary estimates of casualties which ranged from 100,000 to 300,000. Allowing that some of this mortality from disease, for both civilians and soldiers, was war induced, it is not clear to what extent deaths from these epidemics were unusually severe in comparison with deaths from other of the often highly localised epidemics, or even famines, of the period. However accurate Carlton's brave 'inspired guesses' at the level of battle casualties may prove to be, we do not know how many of them were tenants. The burials of ordinary soldiers who lingered to die of wounds after a battle were often recorded in parish registers, but those who died on the field were buried unnumbered and anonymous in mass graves. Amongst landowners casualties are better known, and on the Royalist side they were zealously recorded in the heraldic visitations of the 1660s.

In Cumberland and Westmorland three Royalist heads of family were killed, Thomas Denton of Warnell Denton, Sir Henry Fletcher of Hutton in the Forest, and Thomas Stanwix of Stanwix.[46] Their deaths would have triggered customary fines for their tenants. Of course, one cannot predict when a tenant or a lord who was killed in the war would have died of natural causes. The death of either set in train the procedures of inheritance which involved both; the death of a tenant might occasion the resumption of a holding, or its engrossment by marriage if the only heir was a female. Failure to answer at a manorial court might be crucial if the lord was ill-disposed to a tenant, and even more crucial if lives had to be inserted in copyholds or if a general fine became due. A less drastic but more common consequence of war service would be the loss to his farm of a tenant's labour and supervision, assuming that he worked at least part of the holding rather than sublet it. Manorial court records might give biographical details of customary tenants and the circumstances in which they inherited, as part of the ongoing statement of the custom of the manor, and these records need to be examined for evidence of the military service of tenants (though see below p. 238 for losses of such records in the war).

VI

The potential of civil war to devastate an economy is wide-ranging: the destruction in the 1640s of crops, occasionally of animals, the seizure of produce and stock, tools, carts and draught teams and, especially, horses, are all recorded. Even if paid for at the time or later, the loss of stock and equipment, even of seed, could be devastating to tenants with limited capital. Land itself was only rarely taken out of use and damaged by siege works, or flooded for defensive purposes. But trade in foodstuffs and industrial raw materials was disrupted and, insofar as many farmers were engaged in some form of the dual economy, industrial production also fell, with consequent loss of income; Clay has suggested that the impact of war on industry may have been greater than upon agriculture.[47] Plunder of personal goods and cash by soldiers, the costs of war taxation and quartering soldiers and horses, and the loss of income when estates were sequestrated all had their effect. But there has been no comprehensive attempt to evaluate the damage done by the war, though two schools have emerged. Professor Everitt has argued that the effects of the war may have been overstated by comparison with the epidemics, famines, and fire disasters which were common throughout the seventeenth century, and from which communities seemed to recover with remarkable rapidity; on the other hand Dr Roy has stressed the totality of wartime economic dislocation in the Severn Valley region, and drawn parallels with the economic damage caused during the Thirty Years War in Europe.[48] How did such events affect landlord-tenant relationships?

Lords commonly did not receive rents from their tenants in the Civil War period, and three explanations can be suggested: the tenants did not pay because they would not pay rent to a lord whom they opposed; or because they had insufficient income or surplus to transmit to the lord; or because the rents were diverted by sequestrators. Sometimes a complex mix of these factors was at work.

Lionel Cranfield, Earl of Middlesex, was slow to declare for either party in the war, but as early as October 1642 he was finding it difficult to collect his Gloucestershire rents, and his rights as a landlord to keep a deer forest were under attack; Cranfield's tenants appeared not to have wanted to pay, and this attack on their landlord was probably encouraged by gentry supporters of Parliament. In the 1630s Cranfield's Warwickshire rents produced £3,400 – £3,700 per annum, but in a seventeen-month period in 1643 – 44 they yielded only £2,600, a reduction of more than 50 per cent.[49] Sir John Lowther of Lowther's rental book shows no significant evidence of lost revenue from his Cumbrian estates in 1642, 1643, and for much of 1644, though it is clear that he was not receiving his Yorkshire estate revenues. There are no entries of rentals for the years beginning Martinmas 1644 and 1645, when his estates were sequestered, but in the rental for Martinmas 1647 his Cumbrian rents were again apparently fully paid, with only a few shillings stated as allowed in payment of sesses (i.e. taxes). The difference between the experience of these two men is of course that Cranfield's estates were in the war zone, whereas only Lowther's Yorkshire estates were so afflicted, until the Scots invaded Cumbria in the autumn of 1644. Then Lowther lost control of his Cumbrian estates into sequestration.[50] After he had compounded his estates were distant enough from the sieges and garrisons of Carlisle and Skipton to escape damage.

Tenants refused to pay their rents because they wanted reductions as levels of rent fell in their locality, and or because wartime pressures had reduced their income. Rent arrears in a war zone are understandable, but reports from counties such as Suffolk, or Norfolk, where the ravages of war by and large did not spread (though taxation was high), are less comprehensible. Manning and others have interpreted un-let and un-paid rent as a shift of economic advantage to tenants made possible by the war. That the tenants' perception of a choice of farms available at lower rents was both reported by, and apparently accepted by landowners, gives credibility to their threats to leave their holdings if the rent was not reduced. Of course landowners and their agents might have had motives to exaggerate their difficulties, but at least some of the evidence, such as the letters of Thomas Knyvett, appears free of such distortion. It certainly seems that by 1644 the supply of land outstripped the demand, even if it is not always clear whether such stories relate to non-residential demesne leases, or to holdings, on which tenants actually lived (for example, the case of Richard Brent of Weston and Welford in Warwickshire).[51]

How far can we attribute the inability to let holdings to the effect of Civil War? Was the impact of army service, and casualties, amongst the tenant classes so high that farms had fallen vacant? Sequestration began in 1643, but its impact varied depending on military control of an area. In Suffolk its incidence may have been severe from the beginning, and Everitt has shown that some £21,000 was raised from the county in this way.[52] Land that had been used for home farms might now be available to let, thereby reducing pressure on land, but the quantity of land involved seems unlikely to have had a major effect. In Westmorland at first sequestrators were content to let land to delinquents, and later to those who would give most; nevertheless, some estates were unlet by the sequestrators and were said to be waste. Sequestrators took leases, as they did in Cheshire, but how far this was to ensure an income rather than to favour themselves is unclear.[53]

Was the dislocation of war such that confidence had evaporated, and men would not take on farms? But if they did not farm, where did they put their money and gain their income? National price series, though of limited extent and value, suggest that as prices were steady in the years 1642 – 46 there was no shortage of foodstuffs. Was trade so disrupted as to make the sale of crops unpredictable so that land went out of production under pressure of local over-supply? On the other hand, Hughes' evidence from Warwickshire, and Roy's study of dislocation in the Severn valley, show how severe could be the disasters which befell an individual or even a region. Alternatively, given that harvests were good, were demands for rent reductions, and vacant holdings, merely the first signs of a secular turn in landlord-tenant relations which owed little if anything to the war?[54]

Sieges were an especial burden. At Carlisle the besiegers were Scots, and the mutual distrust between English and Scots exacerbated matters; there was no change when the Scots garrisoned the city after the siege, nor when they marched through Warwickshire. The Scots felt they were not getting enough supplies, while the English replied in terms of the 'wasted and needy condition of the country', and urged the Scots to think of the locals 'as brethren not slaves'. The Royalist garrison took corn and cattle. The area covered on the ground by the siege at Carlisle was large enough to allow the garrison to graze its own herd of cattle; there were siege works a mile to the west and north, and four miles to the south of the city.[55] The close works on the ground at Chester were some five square kilometres, but the area affected by the siege covered much of the west of the county, from Puddington in the Wirral east to Beeston Castle, and as far south as Nantwich and then round towards North Wales via Farndon to Hawarden. There were two subsidiary sieges at Beeston and Hawarden castles. The main siege works were of course much closer to Chester. The massive siege works of Newark, of which much still survives, were at a radius of about two miles from the town, and involved some eight villages, with other villages up to four miles away being fortified. Some of the individual siege works even now occupy the area of a whole field. In addition to the demands for forced labour on military works, the potential for agrarian dislocation in these localities was clearly enormous.[56]

War brought new forms of taxation, extended the size of the

tax-paying groups in society, and by military might ensured high levels of payment. At Nether Whitley in Cheshire by the end of 1644 £372 had been raised on the community in taxes; for 1642 to 1645 Lymm paid £1,164, and fifty-one horses were taken as well. Robert Whittingham of Over lost twelve cows and three heifers plus a calf, valued at £40, at a time when the median number of cows on a Cheshire farmer's estate was sixteen or seventeen.[57] From 1646 onwards, at least in Warwickshire, some attempt was made to check the accuracy of claims about expenditure and taxation through parish accounts prepared for the Parliamentarian Sub-committee of Accounts. Such was the impact of war on Warwickshire that communities found themselves paying taxes and giving quarter to both sides. The abandonment of holdings, already referred to, made tax collecting harder, and in Staffordshire and Worcestershire in the summer of 1644 it was alleged that there were fewer people working the land who could be taxed.[58]

Plunder was often another form of taxation, though the looting and burning of great houses (as opposed to military sleighting) has been seen as evidence of popular hatred. When court rolls and other documents were plundered or burnt, the loss of evidence opened the way for tendentious argument in later law suits between lord and tenant, for example between the Curwens of Rottington (Cumberland) and their tenants in 1662. But, in the current state of research, too few attacks on records are known to warrant a conclusion that attempts to destroy manorial records were widespread.[59]

An early reaction to all these forms of economic disruption from tenants was to attempt to pass the cost of quarter and taxation on to their landlords by reducing rents to cover these charges, and they were possibly encouraged to do this by the wording of Parliamentary ordinances.[60] There was a direct pressure on landlord-tenant relationships when tenants found themselves sued by their lords for arrears of rent when the alleged arrears were, it was argued, sums deducted for quarter and taxation.[61] Sir John Lowther of Lowther seems to have been unforgiving about his Yorkshire losses, and was still listing them as arrears in 1672.[62] It seems clear that assessed taxes by both sides, the impact of quarter, and the cost of the excise, together added up to significantly higher levels of taxation. But the evidence of tenants' incomes against which to assess the impact of these taxes is lacking, while the fact that taxes were paid suggests they could be afforded.

VII

It could be argued that sequestration had little impact on landlord and tenant, for it was the *force-majeure* of the state that diverted the tenants' rents from the lord. But it was not unknown for lords to sue tenants for rents which they had paid sequestrators.[63] On the other hand, there was room for ingenuity: the possibility that the sequestrators leased land to a lord's own tenants is raised in the career of Richard Pindreth. He was sub-sequestrator (14 August 1645) and collector for sequestrations (17 December 1645) in south Westmorland, and in 1645 and 1646 he was lessee, with others, of Curwen's wood, Holme Park, part of Clawthropp demesne, and the tithe barns of Burton, Farleton, Gaitbeck, Holme, and Preston; his rent obligations on these leases totalled well over £200 per annum. Most of these properties belonged to the Preston family, of whom he was a customary tenant, which leaves open the possibility that by taking the leases he was acting in their interests. (Note the Prestons were in minority and Parliament had appointed a guardian. The income to the sequestrators was assigned to Trustees to pay off John Pym's debts.)[64] Sequestrators leased estates back to the delinquent (later forbidden), who could then continue to collect their rents in the established way. The longer sequestration went on, the greater likelihood of the delinquent securing a nominee leaseholder.[65] Sequestration impinged directly on the landlord-tenant relationship when the sequestrators tried to act as lords, hold courts, admit tenants and receive entry fines. It is clear that the sequestrators held a number of manorial courts in Cambridge, probably in Buckinghamshire,[66] and certainly in Westmorland. Here in the north-west between June 1650 and December 1651 they held courts for ten manors, including the manor of Thornthwaite, which was to be sold by the Treason Trustees. For particular entry fines they charged six- or eight-fold multiples of the old rents, a precedent which as we shall see, was to embarrass the Royalist owner when he regained his lands. The tenants, except those of Thornthwaite, refused to pay fines to the sequestrators, though whether out of loyalty to their lords, or because of disagreement over the level of the fines is not clear. The Goldsmiths Hall Committee in London ordered the county commissioners to evict the tenants, according to the custom of the manor![67] The traditional relationship between lord and tenant was certainly put aside in these cases.

VIII

Many Royalist landlords paid their composition fine and recovered their sequestered estates, but the lands of a number were confiscated and sold by the state; Crown and church estates were also put on the market. Royalists recovered their estates, but often had to mortgage them to secure the loans which repurchased them. Thus Gilbert Crouch, who acted as agent for the recusant-delinquent Howards of Corby, bought Sir Francis Howard's life estate in the manor of Thornthwaite from the Treason Trustees, and jointly funded a £30,000 mortgage for them in 1657, became Lord of Thornthwaite manor in Westmorland in 1657. The tenants of Thornthwaite (above, p. 239) had accepted low entry fines from the Westmorland sequestration commissioners in 1651, and in 1657 sued in Chancery to attempt to prevent the levying of fines at a multiple of twenty times the ancient rent. The lordship was clearly confused: it was Sir Francis Howard who was levying the fines, but Gilbert Crouch who held the manor as security. Customary tenure in Cumbria had been a source of prolonged litigation for over a century, for the Thornthwaite tenants the Civil War added a complication which could be exploited at law.[68]

What was sold by the state in the 1650s varied from a fee simple interest to a life estate, and the custom of few, if any, manors obliged tenants to pay an entry fine to a new lord by purchase. The first act of sale allowed tenants a pre-emption to purchase, but this was not repeated in the second and third acts. Detailed studies suggest that a few tenants were to be found amongst the purchasers in either private or state initiated transactions. On estates in the south-east, only eight yeomen or artisans, who might have been tenants, bought confiscated land directly from the Treason Trustees, but by 1660 forty-one such people were in possession of confiscated lands.[69] Part of the Earl of Cleveland's manor of Toddington went to two tenants, one of whom was his bailiff who bought another estate as well; a third tenant was also involved.[70] Major-General Skippon was given confiscated land in Buckinghamshire, and after taking fines for new leases as the old ones fell in, began to dismember the estate by selling in small plots. His customers included nine existing tenants. Dr Thirsk postulated that Skippon may have co-operated with a Leveller initiative to sell land to those who lived on it. Certainly the Leveller Samuel Chidley re-sold the Crown manor of Greensnorton in Northamptonshire to tenants.[71]

In a parallel move Peter Legay, an Independent, sold lands once owned by the Earl of Derby in Bury and Pilkington which he had purchased from the Treason Trustees, to co-religionist tenants who had been opposed to the Stanleys in the Civil War.[72] The Stanleys encouraged some of their tenants there to buy from the Trustees, and then the Earl released them the property hoping thereby to establish a claim. These moves backfired on the Earl at the Restoration when the tenants refused to give up their holdings, and were supported by the House of Lords. But other Stanley tenants were more willing to support the Earl, and in February 1651–52 seventeen Macclesfield tenants assigned their rights of pre-emptive purchase to the Earl, provided he did not alienate the land, and provided he kept to the old customs. This arrangement collapsed when Derby could not raise the money.[73] In all, through direct purchases, the use of agents, and in re-sales, some 130 Stanley tenants (not all yeomen or husbandmen) bought properties. Those in the Puritan parts of Lancashire held on to it.[74] Elsewhere in Lancashire the tenants of the Townleys of Towneley tried to buy their holdings in opposition to their lord; only five succeeded. Tenants of two other gentry families were also successful. It is perhaps again significant that the Townleys lived in the Parliamentarian/Puritan part of Lancashire. Blackwood concluded that purchases by yeomen in Lancashire were of little overall significance in terms of acreage, but that the Stanley family may have lost influence in south-east Lancashire because of the sale of land.[75] In Yorkshire three estates were sold privately to tenants.[76]

Those ancient tenants of Crown or church land who had purchased it were favourably regarded at the Restoration, and many got leases. Other purchasers were held to have been compensated for the outlay on land by the profits they had made in the Interregnum. There is nothing to indicate that land sales to tenants brought about any sort of revolution in the 1650s and 1660s, though the independence of some Derby ex-tenants is a significant regional qualification to this conclusion.[77]

IX

In the aftermath of the war compounding landlords, Parliamentarians with damaged estates, and those with money to raise for the purchase of confiscated estates, all needed to maximise their estate income, and the question arises as to what impact such imperatives had on their tenants. After the war lands were fully let, for complaints about lack of tenants disappear, and the rentals of some estates, though they did not increase, began to approach their prewar levels.[78] In the Home Counties some Royalist lords attempted to pay off their debts and fines through increasing the productivity of their estates by enclosing land. The Verneys began to think about enclosure in 1648, and enclosures began in 1653. These were able to proceed relatively smoothly because leases granted over the previous forty years had included a clause to permit enclosure, assigning new holdings to tenants.[79] Here there is a parallel with Professor Everitt's argument over the comparative effects of Civil War mortality, and crisis mortality at other times in the seventeenth century: the only thing that links these Verney enclosures to the Civil War is that the debts they would help to pay off now included their losses incurred during the war.

Other landlords attempted to put up entry fines, and fines were levied on some leasehold lands in Essex, which had not previously been fined. Land hitherto let at rack rents could be set on beneficial leases, which would generate ready cash in fines. Such policies presuppose that there were tenants capable of paying the fines, and paying them quickly because instalments would not meet the lords' cash needs. Leases on these conditions, with lower rents over the term, could have worked to the tenants' advantage provided the price of produce increased; in practice, national price indices suggest that over the 1650s this happened only for meat and wool, but not for grains.[80] On four of five Royalist estates in Lancashire, with varied tenurial customs, Blackwood concluded that, on average, fines were higher between 1646 and 1688 than those levied before the war; other Royalists also levied high fines after the war.[81]

In Cumberland and Westmorland in the 1650s, where entry fines were arbitrary, lords were demanding high fines. Arguments over whether fines were or were not arbitrary, and what was a reasonable fine, had been widespread in the two counties for more than a century before the Civil War. Latterly, landlords had tried to abolish customary tenure and replace it with leasehold, with a few successes and some notable failures, as when the Crown lost its case over the barony of Kendal. It is against that background that the claims of the 1650s have to be seen. Henry Tolson of Bridekirk (a Parliamentarian) and Alan Bellingham of Levens (Parliamentarian until 1648, then Royalist), John Aglionby (Royalist) and Anthony Duckett (Royalist and indebted) were all attempting to levy fines twenty times the ancient customary rent. Aglionby's tenants admitted that this level of fine was not unknown, while Bellingham's claimed that a multiple of six had been used by his father. As Bellingham pointed out, his father could afford to be a kindly lord. He died in 1642 and had not been weighed down by composition fines, irksome inherited obligations to pay bequests, and by the legal expenses involved in fighting off a challenge to his title. The balance of the evidence is that the fines demanded were high, but not improperly so, and the nature of the suits quite in keeping with longstanding disputes over tenure.[82] But it was possible to plead to Cromwell for aid against 'those Delinquents which are our landlords [who] break all our customs and rob us of all ancient and just privilege' because so many landlords in Cumbria had been Royalists. On the manor of Kentmere the tenants' resistance to higher fines sparked a new opportunist tactic from their hard-pressed lord (Parliamentarian, then Royalist in 1648) who put in suit penal bonds given him by tenants when he paid a composition to soldiers to recover the tenants' goods seized by General Munro's Scottish troops in 1648.[83]

The Royalist John Stanley of Dalegarth was accused by his tenants in 1648 of trying to destroy custom on his manor, presumably to replace it with leasehold tenure, or to exact a lump sum payment from the tenants to confirm the customs.[84] The only Royalists to sell confirmations did so years after the war. The recusant Royalist Henry Curwen of Camerton did this on three manors between 1659 and 1665; on the manor of Greysouthen he was paid £365 10s. 0d. Curwen's debts centred not only on the war, but also on a 1657 family settlement.[85] The delinquent George Denton of Cardew, close to Carlisle and damaged during the siege, was long indebted after the war, but not until 1676 did he enfranchise his tenants on the manor of Parton.[86] These payments were substantial, and although the re-statement of customs was useful for the tenants, they had in the recent past been overturned by landlords. It is tempting, with the date 1676, to point to long-term effects of the war for at least some tenants, just as Habakkuk has shown how late into the seventeenth century the financial effects of the war were still being experienced by landlords. But in fact re-statements of customs were drawn up and paid for in the sixteenth century, the making of arbitrary fines into fines certain was advocated in the judgement on the Crown's case with its barony of Kendal tenants in 1625, and there had been a number of such agreements thereafter. One was made in 1662 by a Dissenting squire, and Parliamentarian, George Fletcher of Tallentire, in return for the payment of sixty-three times the ancient rent.[87] In other words, the re-statements of customs by Curwen and Denton can be seen as just further episodes in the long struggle over tenant right in Cumberland and Westmorland which went on into the eighteenth century,[88] and as having little to do with the Civil War.

One type of lawsuit which probably does owe something to the Civil War for it is unusual outside the early 1650s, is the attempt by lords to enforce suit of mill: four cases were brought by compounding Royalists, including the Anthony Ducket mentioned above, and Thomas Dykes of Wardhall, who was also in financial difficulty. Ducket's suit was, according to the defendants, attempting to re-establish suit of mill after an eighteen-year lapse to a now derelict mill.[89]

There is thus evidence from places as far apart as Essex and Cumberland of attempts by landlords to raise their return from their tenants in the painful aftermath of the war, in circumstances which seem to relate directly to the war. Other forms of conflict between lord and tenant, because they fall into place in more long-term wrangles between lord and tenant, appear to coincide with the war rather than result from it. By and large, these wrangles took place with an established body of landlords. The conclusion of Dr Thirsk (the south-east), supported by Habakkuk (Home Counties), Holiday (Yorkshire), Blackwood (Lancashire), and Phillips (Cumberland and Westmorland), that the purchases of the 1650s combined with the Restoration land settlement, put Crown, church, and the Royalists (very largely), back as owners of their own land, turned aside arguments of an older generation of historians that a new type of more commercially-orientated, and less paternalistic, landlord emerged from the Civil War.[90] Recent scholarship has shown that such a group can only have existed, for at most, a few years in the 1650s, or on those Royalist estates which were sold privately. Even purchasers by private treaty do not stand out as significantly different from the purchasers of land who characterised England's normally fluid society and land market. Land sales did not, therefore, expose the tenant body to a more commercial, more exploitative type of landlord.

It remains true of course that landlords shook off the Crown's rights of wardship and became more absolute owners of their estates in consequence. On the other hand, tenants did not benefit. Customary tenants with estates of inheritance continued, presumably, to be subject to some form of wardship of heirs in minority. It is also true that balance of taxation was shifted down the social scale by the war, as the war-time excise bit across a wide social swathe and continued to do so after the Restoration, and as the hearth tax, which helped to replace Crown revenue lost with wardship, was levied on many tenants from 1662.

X

Two caveats to begin my conclusion: first, the circumstances of individual landlords and individual tenants differed at the start of the war, and were accentuated by it, not only because one man survived when another was killed, but because the economic damage caused by the war, while widespread, was at the same time localised. Its impact on individual communities is the subject of another chapter in this volume. Second, one strand of this essay has argued that, in comparison with famine, plague, and the effect of bad weather on the harvest, the mortality and plunder of the Civil War was neither a new nor an exceptional experience. But, it witnessed violence, formal battles, and occasional savagery, on a scale not seen in England for over seventy years.

It is clear that landlords did call on their tenants' obligation to fight with them, and that tenants responded. But it seems equally clear that the vast majority of tenants were not welded into an effective force to serve where required over a period of time. In this respect, they differ only in degree from the trained bands. Both sides quickly depended on volunteers or pressed men. 1643 saw massive dilution of the tenant element in the soldiery. No Parliamentarian tenants are known to have refused to serve their lord, but some tenants of Royalists did. The Earl of Warwick's role in person in Essex makes it likely that at least some of his tenants there joined up, but they are portrayed as men of religious principle rather than a feudal mass. The renewal of war in 1648 was altogether different from 1642, and tenant allegiance seems unimportant.

Tenants forced down rents in the years of the fighting simply by paying at reduced levels. Such reductions were easier to make where rents were 'improved', rather than where 'old', evidently anachronistic customary rents obtained. Genuine hardship linked to death, war damage, plunder, and dislocation of demand for produce, received some understanding from lords and their stewards, who also accepted, if less willingly, abatements to offset taxation. Refusal to pay rent to a lord on the other side was rare, especially after sequestration began. How far cheap leases of sequestered land encouraged the withholding of rent is unclear. Rents recovered at the end of the war, but did not continue on the rising trend apparent before the war. Hughes has suggested that by withholding rent, and by pressing for arrears, tenants and lords reduced the bonds of social obligation between them, and postulated that in another major political crisis landlord-tenant co-operation would weaken. But the limits to any change in relationships are suggested by the turn out of the tenants of the Booths and others in 1688 in Cheshire to support the Protestant cause, and by deferential voting in English eighteenth-century elections, before rising rents and increased demand for land gave lords a coercive power of eviction. Throughout the period long established struggles on fen and in forests between enclosers and commoners continued, with only the ability of one or other party to attract support from the military linking these long-term changes to the Civil War. On cultivated land, enclosure to increase income was a policy well known before the war.

Raising fines, or cash sums on cofirmation of customs, to pay off war expenditure seems an obvious expedient for lords, and the tenants' pleas to the state about oppression by delinquents an equally obvious defence. The litigation that resulted fits easily into a longer term pattern of friction between lord and tenant. Small numbers of tenants bought themselves out of such friction in the 1650s, but only a minority were able to keep their land after 1660, though those whose purchases were then resumed were either given favourable leases or seem already to have paid off their expenditure with the profits of farming. In the 1650s some new purchasers did exploit estates for short-term cash returns, but the idea that a new body of grasping commercial landlords bought their way into landowning society has been disproved. The effects of the Civil War and its aftermath on landlord-tenant relationships were dramatic, and, depending on one's place in society, disturbing or exciting in the short term; in the long term the secular change in population, the gradual extension of enclosure, and the evolution of tenure did more to shape the landscape and its inhabitants.

Notes

1 E. Kerridge, 'The movement of rent 1540–1640', *Economic History Review*, 2nd ser., VI, p. 28; *Agrarian History of England and Wales. IV: 1500–1600*, ed. Joan Thirsk, Cambridge, 1967, p. 688.

2 R. Hoyle, 'Lords, tenants, and tenant right in the sixteenth century: four studies', *Northern History*, XX, 1984; E. Kerridge, *Agrarian Problems in the Sixteenth Century and After*, London, 1969, Ch. 3; C. B. Phillips, 'The gentry in Cumberland and Westmorland 1600–1665', unpublished Ph.D. thesis, University of Lancaster, 1973, pp. 127–39.

3 As projected by E. A. Wrigley and R. S. Schofield, *The Population History of England 1541–1871*, London, 1981.

4 J. V. Beckett, *The Agricultural Revolution*, Oxford, 1990, pp. 6, 7, 10.

5 C. G. A. Clay, 'Landlords and estate management in England', in *The Agrarian History of England and Wales. V: 1640–1750, pt. 2*, ed. Joan Thirsk, Cambridge, 1985, pp. 198–229; Phillips, thesis, p. 134.

6 Kerridge, *Agrarian Problems*, Ch. 2, especially p. 61; cf. D. Veall, *The Popular Movement for Law Reform 1640–1660*, London, 1970, pp. 51–4. And see also A. W. B. Simpson, *An Introduction to the History of English Land Law*, Oxford, 1961, and B. G. Blackwood, 'The Lancashire cavaliers and their tenants', *Transactions of the Historic Society of Lancashire and Cheshire*, [hereafter *THSLC*], CXVII, 1965.

7 R. Hutton, *The Royalist War Effort 1642–1646*, London, 1982, p. 22.

8 C. Hill, *The Century of Revolution*, London, 1961, pp. 122–4.

9 Hutton, *Royalist War Effort*, pp. 92–3; M. Kishlansky, *The Rise of the New Model Army*, Cambridge, 1979, e.g. pp. 44–5.

10 G. J. Lynch, 'The Risings of the Clubmen in the English Civil War', unpublished MA thesis, University of Manchester, 1973.

11 A. J. Fletcher, *The Outbreak of the English Civil War*, London, 1981, p. 361; R. Hutton, 'The failure of the Lancashire cavaliers', *THSLC*, CXXIX, 1980, pp. 50–1.

12 Hutton, *THSLC*, CXXIX, p. 52; B. Coward, *The Stanleys, Lords Stanley and Earls of Derby, 1385–1672*, Chetham Society, 3rd ser., XXX, 1983, p. 108; J. L. Malcolm, *Caesar's Due: Loyalty and King Charles 1642–1646*, London, 1983, pp. 62–3, 82.

13 Hutton, *Royalist War Effort*, pp. 22–3.

14 Fletcher, *Outbreak*, p. 359.

15 M. Coate, *Cornwall in the Great Civil War*, Oxford, 1933, pp. 34–8; Malcolm, *Caesar's Due*, pp. 75–9.

16 D. Underdown, *Somerset in the Civil War and Interregnum*, Newton Abbot, 1973, p. 85.

17 C. Holmes, *Seventeenth-Century Lincolnshire*, Lincoln, 1980, p. 158.

18 Hutton, *Royalist War Effort*, pp. 92–3. I. Tullie, *The Siege of Carlisle*, ed. S. Jefferson, Carlisle, 1840, reprinted Whitehaven, 1988, p. 1.

19 Fletcher, *Outbreak*, pp. 351, 359.

20 C. Holmes, *The Eastern Association in the English Civil War*, Cambridge, 1974, pp. 88, 94, 96, 162, 164, 165.

21 Holmes, *Eastern Association*, pp. 76, 77, 167.

22 Holmes, *Eastern Association*, pp. 171–3.

23 Holmes, *Eastern Association*, pp. 26, 28, 36–40.

24 W. Hunt, *The Puritan Moment*, Cambridge, Mass., 1983, p. 15; GEC, *Complete Peerage*.

25 Holmes, *Eastern Association*, pp. 35, 77.

26 R. N. Dore (ed.), *The Letter Books of Sir William Brereton*, 2 vols., Record Society of Lancashire and Cheshire, CXXIII, CXXVIII, 1984, 1991, II, pp. 70–8.

27 C. H. Firth and G. Davies, *The Regimental History of Cromwell's Army*, London, 1940; P. Young, *Marston Moor*, Kineton, 1970, pp. 271–4; Holmes, *Eastern Association*, p. 279, n. 1.

28 For example, see *Yorkshire Royalist Composition Papers*, ed. J. W. Clay, Yorkshire Archaeological Society Record Series, XV, 1893, p. 78, XVIII, 1895, p. 205; Royal Commission on Historical Monuments [RCHM], *Newark on Trent, the Civil War Siegeworks*, London, 1964, p. 91; *Calendar of the Committee for Compounding* [hereafter *CCC*], ed. M. A. E. Green, London, 1889–1892, p. 124; Public Record Office, London, State Papers Domestic, SP. 23/213/43; SP. 23/58A/457.

29 M. James, *Social Problems and Policy during the Puritan Revolution 1640–1660*, London, 1930, p. 63.

30 J. S. Morrill, *Cheshire 1630–1660*, London, 1974, pp. 78–9; B. S. Manning, *The English People and the English Revolution*, London, paperback edn., 1978, pp. 205–5.

31 Coward, *The Stanleys*, p. 175.

32 Underdown, *Somerset in the Civil War*, p. 39.

33 Manning, *English People*, p. 247.

34 C. B. Phillips, 'The royalist north: the Cumberland and Westmorland gentry, 1642–1660', *Northern History*, XIV, 1978, p. 175; A. Hughes, *Politics, Society and Civil War in Warwickshire, 1620–1660*, Cambridge, 1987, p. 162.

35 A. M. Everitt, *Suffolk and the Great Rebellion 1640–1660*, Suffolk Record Society, III, 1960, p. 17. See also B. G. Blackwood, *The Lancashire Gentry and the Great Rebellion*, Chetham Society, 3rd ser., XXV, 1978, pp. 10, 37, 56, 58, where 53% were committed in both wars; J. T. Cliffe, *The Yorkshire Gentry from the Reformation to the Civil War*, London, 1969, p. 336, where some two-thirds were committed.

36 Underdown, *Somerset*, p. 44.

37 Morrill, *Cheshire*, p. 115.

38 L. Stone, *The Crisis of the Aristocracy, 1560–1641*, London, 1965, pp. 202, 207, 212, 215.

39 Manning, *English People*, pp. 230–4.

40 Blackwood, *THSLC*, CXVII, pp. 24–31; Coate, *Cornwall*, p. 9.

41 Blackwood, *THSLC*, CXVII, p. 23, n. 17; Coward, *The Stanleys*, pp. 204–8; *A discourse of the Warr in Lancashire*, ed. W. Beamont, Chetham Society, old ser., LXII, 1864, p. 77; *Victoria History of the County of Lancashire* [hereafter VCH Lancs.], ed. W. Farrer and J. Brownbill, III, 1907, p. 21; Manning, *English People*, p. 205; Hutton, *THSLC*, CXXIX, p. 52.

42 Manning, *English People*, esp. pp. 202–15; J. S. Morrill and J. D. Walter, 'Order and disorder in the English revolution', in A. Fletcher and J. Stevenson (eds.), *Order and Disorder in Early Modern England*, Cambridge, 1985, pp. 139–40; B. Sharp, *In Contempt of all Authority*, Berkeley, 1980, pp. 224–35, 237; C. Holmes, 'Drainers and Fenmen', in Fletcher and Stevenson, *Order and Disorder*.

43 Aston is quoted in Morrill, *Cheshire*, p. 50; Coward, *The Stanleys*, p. 75.

44 Wrigley and Schofield, *Population History*, p. 681; J. A. Dills, 'Mortality and civil war in Berkshire', *Southern History*, XI, 1989, p. 51.

45 C. Carlton, 'The impact of the fighting', in J. S. Morrill (ed.), *The Impact of the English Civil War*, London, 1991, p. 20.

46 *Pedigrees Recorded at the Heralds' Visitations of the Counties of Cumberland and Westmorland*, ed. J. Foster, London, [1891], pp. 38, 49, 128.

47 C. G. A. Clay, *Economic Expansion and Social Change: England 1500–1700*, I, London, 1984, p. 48.

48 A. M. Everitt, *The Local Community and the Great Rebellion*, London, 1969, pp. 24–6; I. Roy, 'England turned Germany? The aftermath of the civil war in its European context', *Transactions of the Royal Historical Society,* [TRHS] 5th ser., 28, 1978.

49 M. O. Prestwich, *Cranfield. Politics and Profit under the early Stuarts*, Oxford, 1966, pp. 568–70; Manning, *English People*, pp. 213, 215; Hughes, *Warwickshire*, p. 265.

50 *Lowther Family Estate Books, 1617–1675*, ed. C. B. Phillips, Surtees Society, CXCI, 1979, pp. 61, 77–84; Cumbria Record Office, Carlisle, D/Lons/Lons, A1/4, ff. 120–124.

51 Manning, *English People*, p. 214; *The Knyvett Letters 1620–1641*, ed. B. Schofield, London, 1949, pp. 134, 137; Prestwich, *Cranfield*, pp. 575–77.

52 Everitt, *Suffolk*, p. 13.

53 PRO, SP.23/171/171sqq; PRO, Commonwealth Exchequer Papers, SP.28/216, account book of Richard Pindreth; *CCC*, pp. 176, 585, 588; Morrill, *Cheshire*, pp. 113–17.

54 Hughes, *Warwickshire*, pp. 256–64; Roy, *TRHS*, 5th ser., XXVIII.

55 *CSPD, 1644–45*, p. 543; *CCC*, pp. 232, 1694; Hughes, *Warwickshire*, p. 256; Tullie, *Siege of Carlisle*, pp. 7, 30.

56 Tullie, *Siege of Carlisle*, pp. 10–11; Dore, *Letterbooks*, I, pp. 9–10; II, p. xxvii; RCHM, *Newark, passim*, esp. p. 27; Hughes, *Warwickshire*, p. 255.

57 Morrill, *Cheshire*, pp. 108, 109; David Hey, 'The North Midlands', in Thirsk, *The Agrarian History of England and Wales*. V. pt. 1, pp. 152–153.

58 Hughes, *Warwickshire*, pp. 231, 256, 264.

59 Manning, *English People*, pp. 189–197; PRO. Chancery Proceedings before 1714, Bridges Division, C.5/419/159; Morrill and Walter, *Order and Disorder*, p. 144.

60 Prestwich, *Cranfield*, pp. 568, 570.

61 Hughes, *Warwickshire*, p. 264.

62 Phillips, *Lowther Books*, p. 148.

63 Hughes, *Warwickshire*, pp. 268–9.

64 *CCC*, pp. 1898–1904; VCH, *Lancs.*, VIII, p. 312; PRO, SP. 28/216, account book of Richard Pindreth.
65 Phillips, *Northern History*, XIV, p. 179.
66 *CCC*, pp. 208, 241.
67 *CCC*, pp. 585, 588.
68 PRO, C.5/31/69.
69 Joan Thirsk, 'The sales of royalist land during the Interregnum', *Economic History Review*, 2nd ser., V, 1952, pp. 206, 207.
70 Thirsk, *Economic History Review*, 2nd ser., V, p. 197.
71 *Ibid.*, p. 202.
72 *Ibid.*, pp. 201–2; Coward, *The Stanleys*, pp. 175, 185.
73 Coward, *The Stanleys*, p. 72.
74 Blackwood, *Lancashire Gentry*, pp. 131–6.
75 *Ibid.*, pp. 117, 130, 136, 154.
76 P. G. Holiday, 'Land sales and repurchases in Yorkshire after the civil wars, 1650–1670', *Northern History*, V, 1970, p. 76.
77 Joan Thirsk, 'The Restoration land settlement', *Journal of Modern History*, XXVI, 1954; Blackwood, *Lancashire Gentry*, p. 136.
78 J. Broad, 'Gentry finances and the civil war: the case of the Buckinghamshire Verneys', *Economic History Review*, 2nd ser., XXXII, 1979, p. 192; Hughes, *Warwickshire*, p. 267; Clay, *The Agrarian History of England and Wales*, V, pt. 2, p. 146.
79 H. J. Habakkuk, 'Landowners and the civil war', *Economic History Review*, 2nd ser., XVIII, 1965, p. 138; J. Broad, 'The Verneys as enclosing landlords, 1600–1800', in J. Chartres and D. Hey (eds.), *English Rural Society, 1500–1800*, Cambridge, 1990, pp. 31, 33, 34.
80 Habakkuk, *Economic History Review*, 2nd ser., XVIII, p. 138; Clay, *Economic Expansion*, p. 49.
81 Blackwood, *Lancashire Gentry*, pp. 14, 145–7.
82 PRO, C.5/13/144; C.5/31/10; C.5/380/116; C.5/41/49.
83 Petition from tenants of Thomas Dykes of Wardhall, quoted in James, *Social Policy*, p. 89; PRO, C.5/397/58.
84 PRO, Chancery Proceedings, Series II, C.3/434/54.
85 PRO, C.5/31/62; PRO, Chancery, enrolled decrees, C.78/597 no. 13; C.78/601.
86 Cumbria County Record Office, Carlisle, Lonsdale MSS, D/Lons/Lons, Brough box 1, bdle 1.
87 PRO, C.78/597, n. 5.
88 Phillips, thesis, pp. 134.
89 PRO, C.5/397/38; PRO, Exchequer, depositions by commission, E.134/1654/Mich.25; PRO, C.5/378/125. For Dykes see also James, *Social Policy*, p. 89; PRO, C.5/603/132.
90 E.g. James, *Social Policy*, pp. 85–7.

CHAPTER TEN

RURAL DISCONTENTS AND THE ENGLISH REVOLUTION

Buchanan Sharp

Over the last three decades our knowledge of the social, economic, and religious history of English rural communities in the seventeenth century has been extended and deepened by an impressive array of studies of individual communities and particular economic and geographical regions. From such studies three related themes have emerged, which bear directly on questions of popular political allegiance and activities during the revolution. The themes are the rise of a godly middling sort, the implementation of a reformation of manners or a reform of popular culture, and the cultural distinction between wood pasture and arable fielden districts. An exploration of these themes and the extent of their usefulness in explaining the rural population's experience of the Revolution is the aim of this chapter.[1]

In his earlier work on Somerset during the revolution David Underdown relied on the distinction between the politically active godly minority and the inactive, deferential majority to explain patterns of popular allegiance in the county. The godly minority came from the middling sort: 'The traders and craftsmen of the small towns, the husbandmen or small farmers, the freeholders and wealthy yeomen of the countryside'.[2] This middling sort in Taunton, Wellington, and Bridgwater and in the cloth-making area of north-east Somerset provided the popular backing for Parliament. In such places, marked by a considerable degree of independence from gentry control, the middling sort exercised community leadership. Elsewhere in the county, especially in the west and the south-east, the people – the poorer sort of journeymen, small holders, labourers, and servants – deferred to their social betters or, perhaps more accurately, to a different sort of betters, the gentry instead of the middling sort. These areas, 'with their more traditional social structure, more exclusively agrarian economy, and fewer wealthy yeomen to challenge the gentry, tended naturally to royalism'.[3]

In his emphasis on the support of the godly middling sort for Parliament and on the natural inclination of the poorer sort to follow their betters, Underdown drew on a historiographical tradition that stretches back to the mid-seventeenth century.[4] A more modern version is to be found in the work of Lawrence Stone: 'the small merchants, tradesmen, shopkeepers, artisans and apprentices tended to be Puritan in sympathy and Parliamentarian in allegiance, with a view to breaking the ramparts of privilege which protected the entrenched oligarchy'. At the same time the poorer sort were politically inert: 'the labouring poor, both rural and urban, played no part in the Revolution except as cannon fodder for both sides'.[5]

Somewhat similar views are to be found in the work of Brian Manning, although here the middling sort has an even more important role to play. While in Stone's work the middling sort followed the lead of the Parliamentary gentry, in Manning's they had an autonomous role as a class conscious revolutionary vanguard who provided the ideological fervour to push the relatively moderate gentry leadership of the Parliamentary opposition to adopt a more radical stance in politics and religion, thereby producing armed conflict with the king and his supporters.[6] Manning's views of the poorer sort, however, coincide with Underdown's and Stone's; they are dismissed as a constituent part of *The People and the English Revolution*: 'The poor – servants, journeymen, labourers and paupers – tended to be passive instruments or victims of the conflict of their superiors, but they are not the subject of this book'.[7]

More recently, Underdown has woven the rise of the godly middling sort together with the concept of a reformation of manners and the cultural distinction between wood pasture and arable fielden areas to explain different patterns of popular allegiance in the revolution. Underdown's concept of a reformation of manners appears to owe a great deal to the work of Keith Wrightson, who has argued that a cultural division occurred at the parochial or village level during the seventeenth century. On the one side was the local elite, composed of minor gentlemen, yeomen, substantial husbandmen, prosperous craftsmen and small traders, a middling sort who were, largely, Puritan in religion. On the other side was the poorer sort of alehouse-haunting marginal smallholders, journeymen, labourers, and servants, who lacked religious zeal. In the communities that Wrightson studied, the godly middling sort, who held parochial, village, and hundredal offices, pursued a campaign for the reform of traditional festive culture through the imposition of new standards of sobriety, sexual propriety, and orderliness of their poorer neighbours.[8]

The distinction between wood pasture and arable fielden settlements was first elaborated by Joan Thirsk and further developed by Alan Everitt.[9] According to them wood pasture settlements, often in and around royal forests, were characterised by scattered hamlets and townships, large parishes, loose or non-existent manorial organisation, weak or absent gentry landlord control over the community, and a dominant, broad-based middling sort of reasonably prosperous yeomen and substantial husbandmen with enclosed land holdings and access to relatively abundant common pasture and waste. In the absence of strong social controls such settlements experienced in-migration of poor people who squatted on the commons. In some wood pasture areas the availability of a relatively abundant supply of cheap labour helped to stimulate the development of industries such as cloth-making, mining, and iron-making. Manufacturing, in turn, attracted yet more poor migrants seeking work. Fielden areas were, on the contrary, characterised by strong gentry-landlord control, reinforced by the Anglican parson, over nucleated village communities of manorialised husbandmen tilling the soil in traditional open fields. Such fielden communities generally lacked abundant commons and that, plus supervision by the landlord or his agent, prevented in-migration of the landless poor in search of work.

In Underdown's hands the three themes come together to create a coherent picture of the revolution as a conflict between two cultures. One was the individualistic culture of the industrious, sober Puritan middling sort situated in the economically progressive, market-oriented wood pasture manufacturing districts, where control over the poorer sort was exercised through an imposed reform of popular festive culture. The other was the traditional festive culture which bound together, in an organic whole, the Anglican gentry and their deferential social inferiors, situated in the economically more backward, subsistence-oriented arable fielden districts.

There is, however, considerable distance in Underdown's work between large, universal claims for the significance of the cultural divide and what his evidence actually demonstrates. In some of his earlier work he claimed that 'popular support for Puritanism before 1640, and for Parliament during the war, is likely to have been stronger in the fen, forest, and pasture regions than in the more traditionalist arable districts'.[10] But, elsewhere, he notes that any neat division between Parliamentary wood pasture and Royalist arable fielden districts is an oversimplification.[10]

Sometimes Underdown presents the dichotomy between the two types of areas in the starkest terms, as if they were the equivalents of bourgeois and feudal cultures. The implication is that the dichotomy existed throughout the whole kingdom and that the revolution was a conflict between two clearly defined cultures.[12] As a result, one now finds other historians invoking cultural distinctions between the two kinds of communities to explain patterns of allegiance in various parts of England.[13] Yet on Underdown's own admission the clearly defined and contrasting cultures represent only ideal types, useful, one supposes, for pointing out distinctions but difficult to discover in any specific historical setting.[14] In fact, his actual conclusions on the division between the two cultures are substantially limited to three western counties: Dorset, Somerset, and Wiltshire. Moreover, in Underdown's latest work, the cultural region of the Puritan middling sort is confined to the wood pasture textile regions of north-east Somerset and north-west Wiltshire, which were pro-Parliament in political allegiance.

There were, according to Underdown, three general kinds of rural settlement in the western counties. One was the gentry-landlord dominated nucleated village where the inhabitants were engaged in traditional open field agriculture. Another was the scattered settlement in wood pasture areas where yeomen and husbandmen actively enclosed land and other members of the middling sort were engaged in textile production. In Underdown's scheme the culture of each kind of settlement was shaped by the extent of market influence or development. The traditional arable community, organised for co-operative subsistence production, was least affected by the market while the wood pasture manufacturing community was most affected.[15]

Between the two extremes lay the third kind of community, which Underdown calls the intermediate, a wood pasture settlement only partially influenced by the market. Here middling sort yeomen and husbandmen were enclosing land and otherwise engaged in profitable agriculture but there was less industry and, in some instances, the influence of the gentry remained significant. Market forces had not yet completely shattered the cohesive cultural values of the intermediate communities and replaced them with the individualism characteristic of the industrial areas.[16] In terms of political allegiance the traditional community was Royalist, the wood pasture industrial was Parliamentarian, and the intermediate was neutralist tending to royalism.

Such a typology is not only overly schematic but the idea that arable fielden areas were less affected by the market than wood pasture flies in the face of modern scholarship on English agriculture, which has demonstrated the capacity of the arable sector to produce more bread grains to feed a rising population in this period. Underdown appears to believe that the best measures of market development are rural industrialism and small-scale enclosure at the hands of middling sort yeomen and substantial husbandmen located in wood pasture regions. But it is in the production and marketing of grain – still the main commodity produced by the traditional fielden regions – that the impact of market influences in rural settings can be most clearly observed.[17]

It is difficult to see the distinction that Underdown attempts to draw between the market-oriented wood pasture district of north-east Somerset and north-west Wiltshire and the intermediate districts in south-east Somerset and north Dorset. Bruton, in south-east Somerset within the traditional bounds of Selwood forest, and the region of Gillingham forest in north Dorset were reputed to be strongholds of Royalist and neutralist sentiment in the revolution.[18] Bruton was a market centre connected to a dispersed rural cloth industry, typical of wood pasture industrial regions. Around Gillingham, in the course of the first half of the seventeenth century, market-oriented yeomen and husbandmen, no different from the middling sort to be found in similar districts elsewhere in the country, engaged in small-scale enclosures of manorial commons in the interest of improved agriculture.[19] During the same period, Gillingham also experienced a substantial growth in the population of poor cottagers living on the commons. Part of the area's attraction for migrants was the existence of woollen and linen textile manufacturing. Given the evidence of quite considerable employment in textiles in the areas around Bruton and Gillingham, it is hard to see why Underdown categorises them as intermediate districts rather than wood pasture industrial ones, except that they did not follow the expected pattern of pro-Parliament allegiance.[20]

A similar problem is to be found in Underdown's treatment of south-west Wiltshire, the area around the towns of Westbury, Warminster, and Mere. Based on an examination of the pensions paid to Royalist soldiers or their widows after the Restoration, Underdown argues that Royalist recruitment efforts had minimal results in north-west Wiltshire, where the godly middling sort gave their full support to Parliament, while they enjoyed great success in the south-west of the county where, in the depressed market towns of Warminster, Westbury, and Mere, the impoverished poorer sort were Royalist, if for no other reason than necessity, which compelled them to accept the king's shilling. The distinction that Underdown makes between the two areas is related to the extent of market development. North-west Wiltshire was a wood pasture industrial area while south-west Wiltshire was literally an intermediate zone, which straddled the dividing line between the wood pasture and the arable fielden districts of the county.[21]

There is, in fact, no obvious distinction between the textile towns of north-west Wiltshire – Calne, Chippenham, and Trowbridge – whose inhabitants were Parliamentarians and the decaying market towns of south-west Wiltshire – Westbury, Warminster, and Mere – whose inhabitants were Royalists. As Underdown himself notes, Westbury and Warminster were important centres of the cloth industry.[22] Both market towns were well within the traditional bounds of Selwood forest and, like the textile towns to the north, they were surrounded by extensive wood pasture hinterlands dotted with the cottages of weavers and other workers employed by urban clothiers.[23] Mere, further to the south, was also in a clothing area, perhaps one not as important as that around Westbury and Warminster, and bordered on Gillingham forest in Dorset.

In the end, no significant differences in occupational structure or settlement pattern can be found between north-west and south-west Wiltshire that would satisfactorily explain the split in popular allegiance. The entire region can be classified as wood pasture. Moreover, given the depressed nature of the Wiltshire textile industry during the 1640s, the argument that necessity compelled the inhabitants of the decaying market towns to join the Royalist army could also be applied to the recruits for the Parliamentary army drawn from the northern textile area.[24]

What of cultural differences between the various wood pasture areas? If it was certain, as Underdown claims, that a godly middling sort waged a campaign for the reformation of the manners of the disorderly poor in the textile district of north Somerset and Wiltshire, one might be able to argue that cultural differences, embodied in godly zeal, distinguished the northern wood pasture area from similar districts in south-west Wiltshire and elsewhere in the west. Unfortunately, the concept of a reformation of manners or a reform of popular culture, as currently used by some historians, is a far from unproblematic measure of Puritan religious sympathies or middling sort cultural sensibilities.

Aside from the problem of defining Puritanism, it is difficult to be certain when faced with evidence of the kind of regulations usually associated with the Puritan reformation of manners – control of alehouses, enforcement of the poor law and vagrancy statute, campaigns against illegitimacy, and the suppression of festivities – whether one has come across a genuine example of that reformation or simply responsible magistrates carrying out duties laid on them by the Crown to enforce regulatory statutes designed to maintain good order and relieve distress.

No doubt Puritanism, which until the rise of Laudianism appears to be quite similar to the mainstream Calvinism of the Church of England, gave an added moral edge to magisterial enforcement of social regulation and thereby produced a real reformation of manners, as at Terling in Essex, or energised into action individual godly magistrates like Sir Thomas Barrington in Essex.[25] But, in many instances, it is difficult to distinguish the activities of Puritans from those of other magistrates. Patrick Collinson has argued persuasively that Puritan magistrates were part of the established hierarchy and, at least in the reign of James I, acted vigorously to sustain order and enforce regulations and instructions that emanated from the Crown and its agents. Even when such an apparently Puritan reform as the attempted suppression of Somerset Churchales in 1633 is examined more closely it becomes clear that the attempt was motivated not by godly zeal but by a complex of local political considerations, including a desire to maintain order.[26]

There is no doubt that Underdown is right when he argues that the Puritan reformation of manners needs to be seen as a response to the economic situation of the period from the late sixteenth century through the first half of the seventeenth.[27] But it was only one dimension of a larger societal and governmental response to pressing problems of poverty and economic dislocation, which those in positions of authority perceived as having the potential to disrupt the social order. For example, in Keevil, a parish in the north-west Wiltshire textile area, compelling economic necessity rather than Puritan religiosity explains stricter 'attitudes to bastardy and bridal pregnancy', during the early seventeenth century.[28]

It is currently fashionable to play down the novelty of Charles I's Book of Orders of 1631.[29] Nonetheless, as applied in the 1630s, with an emphasis on arresting vagrants, setting the poor on work, binding out the children of the poor as apprentices, the suppression of alehouses, and the punishment of those who blasphemed or failed to attend church, the Book of Orders constituted, if not a blueprint for a reformation of manners, then a programme for stricter maintenance of order and a rational response to social and economic problems.[30] Virtually all magistrates, whether Puritan or not, could agree with the Book's aims. In Essex, Puritan magistrates were among the most vigorous enforcers of the Book of Orders. This 'suggests that there was no fundamental conflict between the social welfare objectives proclaimed by the Crown and the aspirations of the godly. The paternalism embodied in the Book of Orders cannot plausibly be listed among the causes of the Civil War in Essex'.[31] In the course of the decade, reports from local magistrates, recording their efforts to comply with the Book of Orders, became routine and uninformative, indicating less than enthusiastic compliance.[32] Nonetheless, the Crown's commitment to enforcement, which lasted for nine years, compares favourably with reforms attempted locally by the Puritan middling sort or nationally, for little more than a year, by the Major Generals during the Protectorate.

As presented in Underdown's work the poorer sort in the north

Somerset and Wiltshire wood pasture districts offered virtually no resistance to what he calls a Puritan reformation of manners. Many of the reformers were, in another guise, presumably clothiers who employed labour or, at least, controlled the sale and distribution of the raw materials on which journeymen worked. Journeymen clothworkers were, undoubtedly, participants in the festive culture of the alehouse and targets of the reformers. In a location of a depressed industry, where in 1647 there were protests over the scarcity and high price of grain, one would expect other evidence of social tension as discontent with rising food prices, declining wages, and unemployment fused with resistance to the cultural reforms imposed by the godly who were also masters.[33] Perhaps, in some cases, small masters, the so-called yeoman clothiers, were close enough in status in journeymen that social and cultural tensions were at a minimum. But this was not generally the case: the northern Wiltshire and Somerset textile area, which produced largely for international markets, was noted for the concentration of control in wealthy and substantial clothiers and for the impoverished state of the workers.[34]

It may be that the effects of the long-term depression in the western broadcloth industry during the 1630s and 1640s sapped the will of clothworkers in north Somerset and Wiltshire to resist the imposed reformation of manners. Possibly the iron hand of Puritan discipline successfully clamped down on the disorderly poorer sort. Whatever the nature of the reform that the Puritan godly managed to impose on the populace of the area during the first half of the seventeenth century, it was a temporary phenomenon. In the late seventeenth and early eighteenth centuries, the rural clothworkers of the area were regularly characterised as a drunken and improvident lot.[35]

Some of Underdown's other assertions about the culture of the individualistic wood pasture textile area of north Somerset and Wiltshire are equally problematic, such as the claim that Skimmington Riding was virtually unique to the area: 'in the early seventeenth century this form of ritual was a localized one centred in Somerset and north Wiltshire'.[36] The only significant, politically charged Skimmingtons of the seventeenth century occurred elsewhere, in other western wood pasture areas and involved protests against disafforestation and enclosure. The first anti-enclosure riots at Gillingham forest in 1626 were led by a man dressed as a woman, who adopted the alias Lady Skimmington. In Braydon forest, east of the textile area of north-west Wiltshire, three Lady Skimmingtons led the riots of 1631. The most famous Lady Skimmington of all was John Williams, leader of the protests against enclosure in the forest of Dean in 1631 and 1632; the Dean protests of 1631, in particular, followed the ritual pattern of a Skimmington Riding.[37]

Given Underdown's emphasis on the individualistic and independent nature of the inhabitants of wood pasture industrial areas, compared with the dependent and deferential nature of the populace elsewhere, it is surprising that there were no major protests against the disafforestation and enclosure of Chippenham and Melksham forests in the early 1620s and Frome Selwood forest in the late 1620s. These forests were at the geographical heart of the textile area of north Somerset and Wiltshire and home to large numbers of cottagers employed in the cloth industry. While there were rumours in 1631 that Lady Skimmington would visit Chippenham and Melksham, it is unclear whether she did.[38] Perhaps this relative lack of protest should be taken as another indication of the energy-sapping effects of the long-term depression in the cloth industry.

The forests where popular resistance to enclosure was most intense and lasted longest were Gillingham and Dean. In terms of their settlement pattern, occupational structure, and level of market influence both are classifiable as wood pasture industrial areas but the political allegiance of their inhabitants did not follow a simple pro-Parliament pattern. Moreover, the poorer sort in both forests demonstrated a degree of political autonomy and activism, which raises doubts about assertions regarding their deference and lack of capacity for independent action. No evidence has ever been offered to contradict my earlier conclusion that the protesters were largely cottagers – artisans, marginal husbandmen and labourers. Some may have been from the lower end of the middling sort but many were drawn from the poorer sort. The reason for their resistance is not far to seek. Among forest inhabitants the labouring poor were the most dependent on free access to unstinted common and other resources to help meet their subsistence needs; that access was directly threatened by enclosure and disafforestation.[39]

Not only did the population of Gillingham forest strenuously resist the loss of their customary rights in the forest through the period from 1626 to 1632, but during the revolution they maintained a campaign of resistance from 1642 to at least 1648 against the leading beneficiary of the enclosure, Thomas Bruce, Earl of Elgin, a supporter of Parliament, whose local allies included William Whitaker, a friend of John Pym and a member of the Long Parliament for Shaftesbury. Given Elgin's political connections the protesters, who destroyed the enclosures at Gillingham during the revolution and prevented the Earl from receiving his rents from the forest land, could be considered Royalist sympathisers. But it would be more accurate to describe them as defenders of customary rights and opponents of enclosure who knew their enemy and used every available means to oppose him. Their Royalism can, at best, be called functional, something they could use to urge on Royalist troops to destroy the Gillingham enclosures of a pro-Parliament peer. The relative insignificance of conventional political allegiance in this conflict is nicely illustrated in the case of Sir Edward Nicholas, Charles I's former secretary of state in exile to avoid impeachment by the king's opponents, whose lands enclosed out of Gillingham forest were also a target of the rent strike.[40]

If Underdown's notion of the intermediate wood pasture district offered real insights into the determinants of popular allegiance then the inhabitants of Gillingham should have deferentially followed the leading local landowner, the Earl of Elgin, into Parliamentary allegiance (with a minority following Secretary Nicholas in his Royalism). Instead the people of Gillingham clung to a stubborn neutrality, which continues, erroneously, to be equated with Royalism. A similar situation was to be found, nearby, at Bruton in Somerset. Here the most prominent local landowner was the Royalist Sir Charles Berkeley. But instead of meekly following his political lead, the local inhabitants during the period 1642 and 1652 regularly destroyed Berkeley's enclosures of former Selwood forest land at Kilmington Heath and Bernard's Combe.[41]

Another striking example of the independent political stance of forest-dwellers is to be found in the forest of Dean where, in a struggle for control of the forest's iron ore and the wood supply available for smelting, small producers resisted the intrusion of relatively large-scale capital intensive enterprises. From around

1612 through the late 1630s large-scale market forces in Dean were represented by the farmers of the royal ironworks, a changing group of courtiers, financiers, and ironmasters, who leased monopoly rights to produce iron from the ore and wood fuel within the 20,000 acres of Crown demesne in the forest. Their opponents were the 'free miners', who claimed the customary right to mine iron ore in the royal demesne along with other extensive rights of common in the forest. The struggle over resources was intensified as the growing demand for wood to fuel the royal ironworks required the enclosure of increasingly larger areas within the forest to protect coppices against the depredation of commoners' grazing animals. The climax came when Charles I granted monopoly rights over the ore in Mailescott woods, a particularly rich deposit, to Sir Edward Villiers, along with the right to enclose the land and exclude the free miners from digging there. Riots against the enclosure of Mailescott began in 1631 and for much of the rest of the decade the forest was in an unsettled state.[42]

In the late 1630s Charles I, driven by financial necessity and plagued by continuing problems of order in the forest, decided to disafforest Dean and sell it off. Thereafter, the representative of large-scale capitalism in the forest was its purchaser, Sir John Winter, a local ironmaster who aimed to enjoy the benefit of the monopoly position held by the farmers of the royal ironworks. Unfortunately for Winter the holder of that position inevitably became the object of the local inhabitants' hostility, deepened, perhaps, by Winter's Catholicism. Superficially, at least, Winter's religion and subsequent Royalism resulted in the inhabitants of Dean allying themselves with Parliament in the revolution. But, like the Royalism of Gillingham's inhabitants, the Parliamentarianism of Dean's was largely functional. Once the enemy, in the person of Winter, was defeated and lost possession of the forest, popular suspicions became increasingly focused on the new Parliamentary administration of the forest, established in 1645, which was trying to revive production at the old royal ironworks. Faced with the Protectorate's attempt to enclose a sizeable portion of the forest in 1657 Dean's inhabitants became openly hostile; by 1659 they were reputed to be negotiating with Royalist agents to support the return of Charles II. The shift to functional Royalism did not alter matters much. In 1668 Charles II reafforested Dean, but this left untouched enclosures that predated Winter's disafforestation of 1640-41. Predictably, in 1671 riotous miners again destroyed the enclosures at Mailescott woods, the very enclosures which had been the occasion for Lady Skimmington's first protests in 1631.[43]

The inability of the presumed cultural distinction between wood pasture and arable fielden areas to account for popular allegiance in the revolution calls for the re-conceptualisation of the problem. There is no doubt that the development of the market was important, but the key to understanding it is to be found in the idea that, while there were economic winners and losers in the mid-seventeenth century, they are not identifiable with Parliamentarians and Royalists.[44] Behind social and economic change lay dire conditions. Just as a specifically Puritan reformation of manners was only one aspect of a larger societal and governmental response to those conditions, so too the market-oriented activities of the middling sort were only one part of a more broadly based set of economic responses. Underdown has offered a largely neo-Whig or neo-Marxist view of the revolution; it was a conflict between progressive forces, identified with the market-oriented and individualist middling sort, and the traditionalist, identified with the subsistence-oriented and hierarchical Crown and gentry.[45] In fact the necessity of the times forced the Crown and its friends as well as the middling sort to maximise income; a main road to maximisation for every landholder, whether king or middling sort, was through sponsoring or engaging in enclosure and other improvements.

Agricultural improvement, as conceived by modern historians, means largely enclosure of common fields or of common waste and pasture undertaken by both gentry landlords and yeomen and substantial husbandmen in order to introduce up and down husbandry that, with the implementation of new crop rotations, artificial grasses, marling, and other new techniques, resulted in increased grain yields as well as more nutritious animal feed. The overall result was a growth in the volume of agricultural production for the market. Among the seventeenth-century advocates of improvement no one better represents the outlook of the middling sort of yeomen and husbandmen than Walter Blith.

Blith's father was a yeoman or substantial husbandman who held land around the forest of Arden in Warwickshire. Blith, himself, was an active supporter of Parliament in the revolution and held various minor posts under the Commonwealth. He is best remembered for his agricultural treatise published in two editions as *The English Improver* (1649) and *The English Improver Improved* (1653). In it he advocated improved husbandry, which involved the enclosure of common pasture, including forest land, and bringing it into a system of up and down husbandry.[46] Blith's proposals were rooted in actual agricultural practice in the forest of Arden where, in the first half of the seventeenth century, middling sort yeomen and husbandmen were active enclosers and improvers.[47]

Not only did Blith embody the economic aspirations of the middling sort but he was also connected to Samuel Hartlib and his group of social reformers that flourished in the 1650s. Hartlib and his friends, along with other social commentators around mid-century, regarded agricultural improvement as the means to solve social problems. They viewed undeveloped land as an untapped resource, which if enclosed and improved would feed the hungry and employ the poor.[48] Beyond such practical effects, social reformers believed that enclosure and agricultural improvement would lead to improvement in the manners of forest inhabitants. Forests were seen as wild, untamed places akin to primordial chaos, inhabited by the dissolute, disorderly, drunken, and irreligious poor. Enclosure would be the means to civilise these wild places, turn them to improved arable and pasture, and create opportunities to remake their inhabitants into sober, hard-working yeomen, husbandmen, and small holders. In the 1650s reformers hoped that the state would implement such grand schemes through the disafforestation of royal forests, which had been confiscated by the Protectorate along with all other Crown lands.[49] While Blith did not necessarily share all the grander visions of reformers like Hartlib, he regarded the prosperity of yeomen and husbandmen as important for England's social and economic progress.

Such schemes for agricultural improvement and social or cultural reform, which emanated from the opponents of the Crown in the revolution and which were designed to enhance the economic and social position of the middling sort of yeomen and husbandmen, resembled proposals for the enclosure and improvement of forests and other waste places entertained by the Stuart monarchy. Beginning in the first decade of the seventeenth century, surveys of royal forests routinely advocated enclosure and improvement as the way to increase income and to suppress the destructive activities of the poor, who despoiled woods and overcharged commons with beasts. While the disafforestations of the seventeenth century were clearly driven by the Crown's fiscal necessity, some official statements justifying the policy, especially those made by James I, were tinged with the rhetoric of moral reform. Moreover, the effect of disafforestation on agricultural practice and land use was very much in line with the later proposals of the Hartlib circle and other reformers. On the extinction of common rights at disafforestation all landholders, who could prove right of comon, received compensatory allotments of land. The rest of the forest land, to which the Crown claimed title and which was first granted in a single parcel to a group of courtiers, monopolists, or other concessionaires, was then divided into smaller enclosed parcels and made available for lease by local yeomen and husbandmen. There is evidence for a number of western forests, including Gillingham, Neroche, Selwood, Chippenham, and Melksham that disafforestation was closely connected to the spread of improved husbandry and that middling sort of yeomen and husbandmen were among the beneficiaries of the process.[50]

During the seventeenth century there thus existed a constellation of overlapping interests which pushed for the enclosure of waste ground and the advancement of agricultural improvement. One was the Crown and its associated allies among the nobility and gentry and monopoly financial interests. Another included middling sort of yeomen and husbandmen with an eye to the main chance. A third constituted the advocates of moral and social reform like Hartlib and his friends. These and other market-oriented interest groups could be considered winners, in that they responded positively to market forces and began to whittle away at customary rights. Furthermore, the way in which the winners responded, especially big landowners like the Crown, made them the agents of yet further economic and social change. If we are to seek then for the kind of transformative process that the phrase reformation of manners implies, and for evidence of popular resistance, we need look no further than disafforestation and enclosure of waste during the period from the late 1620s through the late 1650s, no matter the political situation or the regime in power.

In thinking about the apparently odd conjunction of interests among what are assumed to be the Royalist elite and the Parliamentary middling sort we can go back to Keith Wrightson's idea of the reformation of manners as a cultural distancing in which the middling sort moved away from their poorer neighbours and drew closer in outlook to the elite. The implication of this idea for conclusions about patterns of middling sort allegiance in the revolution is unclear. One could infer, however, that the process made the middling sort more like the enterprising gentry in their market-oriented activities and more willing to rely on, or defer to, their political leadership. '

So far we have been talking about the winners, what of the losers? They were the poor commoners or, in the specific case of Dean, the miners whose customary subsistence rights and way of life were threatened by enclosure, improvement of the waste, and the general spread of market values. For the poorer sort it did not matter whether improvement was directed by the Crown and associated projectors, by Royalists or Parliamentarians, or by the Protectorate and its Hartlib-like sympathisers with the middling sort, the outcome was always the same. No doubt improvement was necessary to increase the food supply to feed a growing population, but it did not do much immediately to improve the condition of the growing population of poor. The self-sufficiency of the labouring poor, sustained by free access to common, was often replaced, as result of enclosure, with the need to resort to charity in bad times.[51]

At the same time the social and cultural, as well as the economic, distance between the middling sort and the poorer sort became greater by the middle of the seventeenth century and was reflected in the changing language used by contemporaries to describe the social structure.[52] While the middling sort yeomen and substantial husbandmen continued to prosper, the numbers of smallholders, poor artisans, labourers and undifferentiated poor had increased. From the hearth tax returns of the early 1660s for five parishes in the Arden forest region Victor Skipp has determined that among the householders there were 85 middling sort (17.9% of the total), 170 (35.8%) smaller husbandmen, poorer artisans, and labourers, and 189 (39.8%) excused from payment because of poverty. Skipp estimates that the total population of the five parishes in 1660 was 3,400 and that the landless poor comprised 29 per cent or 1,000 of that total. The most striking figure of all is that while the population of the Arden parishes in the period 1570 to 1660 rose from 2,200 to 3,400, a 35 per cent increase, the number of landless poor rose from

100 to 1,000, a ten-fold increase.[53] The social differentiation indicated by these figures was certainly not unique to the forest of Arden. Another well-documented example, also drawn from the hearth tax records, is Brigstock village in Rockingham forest.[54]

While riot was one form of resistance to improvement and the reform of manners, others may have included the embracing of radical social and religious ideas as can be seen at Enfield Chase, Middlesex, a few miles north of London, an area whose history was a virtual microcosm of wood pasture areas in the seventeenth century. Enfield Chase comprised 7,900 acres of royal demesne surrounded by a number of densely populated townships whose inhabitants were engaged predominantly in agricultural pursuits, although there were some attempts in the first three decades of the seventeenth century to establish cloth-making as employment for the poor.[55] In the late sixteenth and early seventeenth centuries improving yeomen and substantial husbandmen in the surrounding townships engaged in small-scale enclosure to increase grain production.[56] The population of poor labourers and cottagers in and around the chase grew markedly, drawn there by the subsistence opportunities offered by its woods and pastures. In the 1664 hearth tax returns 36 per cent of the households in Enfield parish, 34 per cent in Edmonton, and 46 per cent in Tottenham were exempt from paying the tax because of poverty.[57]

Like virtually every other forest or chase in the country, Enfield had a reputation as a disorderly place. In reports from local officials or from the agents of the Cecil family, the most prominent local landowners, the people of the chase were regularly condemned as stealers of wood and killers of the king's deer; as in other wooded areas deer poaching was especially common during the revolution.[58] In 1589 and 1603 the inhabitants of the town of Enfield rioted to preserve their rights to common of pasture and to firewood in the chase from any limitations imposed by the Crown or its agents.[59]

The inhabitants of Enfield, like other forest-dwellers, showed a stubborn streak of political independence. The chase was one of the Crown properties first designated in 1656 to be sold to cover arrears of soldiers' pay, but the process of enclosure did not begin until late 1658 when the chase was surveyed. An area totalling 3,189 acres was set out to compensate the commoners of the neighbouring parishes, while the Protectorate took title to the other 4,537 acres. One-third of the government's share was soon divided into smaller holdings and some of it sold to former soldiers who enclosed the land and began to grow grain. The result, predictably, was disorder, which appears to have run from May to early July, 1659. On 1 June local inhabitants threw down the enclosures and drove cattle onto the growing corn. Then on 10 July soldiers were sent to restore order and bloodshed followed, resulting in the death of three people of Enfield and one soldier. Whatever the original political allegiance of the Enfield populace, one report of their protests in 1659 has them declaring for the king in exile.[60]

While this, almost stereotypical, history of a wood pasture area was unfolding other, perhaps more intriguing, developments were underway. By 1650 a Digger colony, about which virtually nothing is known, had appeared.[61] In 1659 William Covell, an inhabitant of Enfield, a former Cromwellian officer, and a sectarian preacher of radical antinomian views, proposed to use Enfield to try out his ideas for the social transformation of England. While his plan may have owed something to the influence of the Diggers, it reads more like an extreme radical version of some of the improvement schemes proposed by Hartlib and his circle. Covell advocated, among other things, the abolition of money, the establishment of small scale co-operative communities, and the cultivation of waste land by the poor as the solution to endemic poverty. He proposed that, of 1,500 acres set aside on the division of the chase to compensate the commoners from the town of Enfield, 1,000 acres should be enclosed and devoted to improved agriculture while on the other 500 acres almshouses for the impotent poor and a manufactory employing the idle poor were to be established.[62]

It hardly needs saying that Covell's proposal never got off the ground. But the problems of poverty at Enfield Chase continued. Late in 1660 the inhabitants of the town of Enfield, no doubt respectable middling sort ratepayers, petitioned the restored Charles II concerning the large numbers of poor who destroyed the woods in the chase and had become a heavy charge on parish poor rates. The solution they proposed was a Bill in Parliament authorising the enclosure of the common fields in the parish, thereby leading to the improvement of their lands. To solve the problems of poverty the petitioners proposed levying a rate on each acre of enclosed ground and using the money to raise a stock to employ some of the able-bodied poor and to pay for the transportation of the rest to Ireland or any English Plantation abroad.[63] In making this proposal the respectable inhabitants of Enfield were not only attempting to impose order on the disorderly poor but participating in the ongoing cultural separation between the middling sort and the poorer sort typical of the time.

Notes

1 Earlier versions of some of the ideas in this chapter were first tried out in an unpublished paper, 'Popular discontents and the English Revolution', delivered at the Pacific Coast Conference on British Studies, on 23 March 1984.

2 D. Underdown, *Somerset in the Civil War and Interregnum*, Newton Abbot, 1973, p. 16.

3 Underdown, *Somerset*, p. 117.

4 See the historiographical discussion in D. Underdown, *Revel, Riot and Rebellion: Popular Culture and Politics in England 1603–1660*, Oxford, 1985, pp. 1–4.

5 L. Stone, *The Causes of the English Revolution*, London, 1973, p. 145.

6 B. Manning, *The English People and the English Revolution 1640–49*, London, 1976. For assessments of Manning's argument see J. S. Morrill, 'Provincial squires and 'middling sorts' in the Great Rebellion', *Historical Journal*, 20, 1977, pp. 229–36 and B. Sharp, 'The place of the people in the English Revolution', *Theory and Society*, 13, 1984, pp. 93–110.

7 Manning, *People*, p. v.

8 K. Wrightson and D. Levine, *Poverty and Piety in an English Village: Terling, 1525–1700*, New York, 1979, pp. 116–86; K. Wrightson, 'Two concepts of order: justices, constables and jurymen in seventeenth century England', in J. Brewer and J. Styles (eds.), *An Ungovernable People*, London, 1980, pp. 21–46.

9 J. Thirsk, 'Industries in the countryside', in F. J. Fisher (ed.), *Essays in the Economic and Social History of Tudor and Stuart England*, Cambridge, 1961, pp. 70–88; J. Thirsk, 'Seventeenth-century agriculture and social change', and A. Everitt, 'Nonconformity in country parishes', in J. Thirsk (ed.), *Land, Church, and People*, Reading, 1970, pp. 148–77 and pp. 178–99.

10 D. Underdown, 'Community and class: theories of local politics in the English Revolution', in B. C. Malament (ed.), *After the Reformation*, Manchester, 1980, p. 160.

11 Underdown, *Revel*, pp. 5–8.

12 Underdown, *Revel*, pp. 18–20, pp. 40–2. See also J. Morrill, 'The Ecology of Allegiance in the English Revolution', *Journal of British Studies*, XXVI, 1987, pp. 451–2.

13 For example in A. Hughes, *Politics, Society and Civil War in Warwickshire, 1620–1660*, Cambridge, 1987, pp. 4–6.

14 D. Underdown, 'A reply to John Morrill', *Journal of British Studies*, XXVI, 1987, p. 469.

15 Underdown, *Revel*, p. 12 and pp. 17–20.

16 Underdown, *Revel*, pp. 4 – 8.
17 Agricultural changes in the period are comprehensively surveyed in J. Thirsk (ed.), *The Agrarian History of England and Wales. IV: 1500 – 1640*, Cambridge, 1967 and E. Kerridge, *The Agricultural Revolution*, London, 1968. See also J. S. Morrill and J. D. Walter, 'Order and disorder in the English Revolution', in A. J. Fletcher and J. Stevenson (eds.), *Order and Disorder in Early Modern England*, pp. 137 – 66, where a central argument is that market development was most notable in fielden areas.
18 Underdown, *Revel*, pp. 95 – 9, pp. 103 – 5, pp. 197 – 8, and pp. 204 – 5.
19 Underdown, *Revel*, pp. 204 – 5; B. Sharp, *In Contempt of All Authority: Rural Artisans and Riot in the West of England, 1586 – 1660*, Berkeley, Calif., 1980, p. 140; V. Skipp, *Crisis and Development: An Ecological Case Study of the Forest of Arden 1570 – 1674*, Cambridge, 1978, pp. 42 – 54.
20 Sharp, *In Contempt*, pp. 159 – 60, p. 167.
21 Underdown, *Revel*, pp. 193 – 5.
22 Underdown, *Revel*, p. 195; G. D. Ramsay, *The Wiltshire Woollen Industry in the Sixteenth and Seventeenth Centuries*, Oxford, 1943, contains repeated references to the significance of Westbury and Warminster as centres of the broadcloth industry.
23 See the map of Selwood forest in *Victoria County History of Wiltshire*, IV, London, 1959, p. 449.
24 Ramsay, *Wiltshire Woollen Industry*, pp. 112 – 13.
25 Wrightson and Levine, *Poverty and Piety*, pp. 110 – 85; W. Hunt, *The Puritan Moment: The Coming of Revolution to an English County*, Cambridge, Mass., 1983, pp. 248 – 50.
26 P. Collinson, *The Religion of Protestants*, Oxford, 1982, pp. 141 – 88; T. G. Barnes, 'County politics and a puritan *cause célèbre*: Somerset churchales', *Transactions of the Royal Historical Society* [TRHS], 5th ser., 9, 1959, pp. 103 – 22. Another example of godly magistrates effectively upholding the established order is to be found in Salisbury, see P. Slack, 'Poverty and politics in Salisbury 1597 – 1666', in P. Clark and P. Slack (eds.), *Crisis and Order in English Towns 1500 – 1700*, London, 1972, pp. 164 – 203.
27 Underdown, *Revel*, pp. 17 – 40; see also Wrightson and Levine, *Poverty and Piety*, pp. 1 – 18.
28 M. Ingram, 'Religion, communities and moral discipline in late sixteenth and early seventeenth century England', in K. von Greyerz (ed.), *Religion and Society in Early Modern Europe 1500 – 1800*, London, 1984, p. 190. See also Morrill, 'Ecology of Allegiance', pp. 460 – 1.
29 B. W. Quintrell, 'The making of Charles I's book of orders', *English Historical Review*, 95, 1980, pp. 553 – 72; P. Slack, 'Book of orders: the making of English social policy, 1577 – 1631', *TRHS*, 5th. ser., 30, 1980, pp. 1 – 22.
30 T. G. Barnes, *Somerset 1625 – 1640: A County's Government during the Personal Rule*, Cambridge, Mass., 1961, pp. 172 – 202; Slack, 'Book of Orders', pp. 16 – 18; K. Sharpe, 'The Personal Rule of Charles I', in H. Tomlinson (ed.), *Before the English Civil War*, London, 1983, pp. 60 – 3.
31 Hunt, *Puritan Moment*, p. 250.
32 This is based on reading all of the surviving reports in the State Papers Domestic. Current scholarship on the rule of the Major Generals has undermined the traditional view that it was a near perfect example of the Puritan reformation of manners, coherently conceived and consistently enforced,

and has, unintentionally, highlighted the achievements of Charles I's personal rule in comparison, see A. Fletcher, 'Oliver Cromwell and the localities: the problem of consent', in C. Jones *et al.* (eds.), *Politics and People in Revolutionary England*, Oxford, 1986, pp. 187–204.

33 J. Walter, 'The geography of food riots 1585–1649', in A. Charlesworth (ed.), *An Atlas of Rural Protest in Britain 1548–1900*, London, 1983, pp. 77–9.

34 Ramsay, *Wiltshire Woollen Industry*, pp. 65–100.

35 J. de L. Mann, 'Clothiers and weavers in Wiltshire during the eighteenth century', in L. S. Pressnell (ed.), *Studies in the Industrial Revolution*, London, 1960, pp. 72–6. See also the stunning contemporary descriptions of life on Warminster common in the eighteenth century contained in J. J. Daniell, *The History of Warminster*, Warminster, n.d., pp. 87–92.

36 Underdown, *Revel*, p. 102. Oddly in the next chapter, beginning at p. 107, Underdown discusses the Skimmington-led forest riots as examples of the culture of wood pasture areas generally, as if he had never made the quoted statement and without reference to his own category of intermediate wood pasture settlements.

37 Sharp, *In Contempt*, pp. 82–96.

38 Sharp, *In Contempt*, p. 93.

39 Sharp, *In Contempt*, pp. 126–74. The precise point of the criticism in Morrill and Walter, 'Order and Disorder', p. 153 n. 79, escapes me; they certainly offer no evidence to challenge my conclusions.

40 Sharp, *In Contempt*, pp. 224–45. These points are worth remaking because Underdown in his discussion of the riots at Gillingham and elsewhere in *Revel*, pp. 107–12, leaves the impression that resentment at disafforestation created a willingness in the inhabitants of forests to follow the Crown's opponents in the revolution. Nowhere, either in this section or later on pp. 160–2, does he mention Elgin's political connections with the Parliamentary opposition, thereby creating the impression that the inhabitants of Gillingham were vaguely pro-Parliament.

41 Sharp, *In Contempt*, p. 244. Underdown's various attempts to explain the situation at Bruton and the role of the Berkeleys as the socially dominant figures in an intermediate wood pasture community can be followed in *Somerset*, p. 116, 'The Chalk and the Cheese: Contrasts among English Clubmen', *Past and Present*, 85, 1979, p. 46, and *Revel*, p. 215.

42 Sharp, *In Contempt*, pp. 94–6 and pp. 190–216.

43 Sharp, *In Contempt*, pp. 217–19 and pp. 252–4. For the riot of 1671, see PRO PC 2/63, fo. 67, Privy Council to JPs near the Forest of Dean, 30 November, 1671; K.B.9/927/230, information against Dean rioters, Hilary, 1671/72.

44 This idea derives from my reading of Morrill and Walter, 'Crisis and Order' where on p. 152 they talk of beneficiaries and victims of economic change; my preference is to call them winners and losers.

45 In this regard Underdown is no different from Manning and Stone, except that while Underdown, like Manning, regards progressive forces as embodied in the rising middling sort, Stone finds them in the rising gentry.

46 The best introduction to Blith and his work is J. Thirsk, 'Plough and pen: agricultural writers in the seventeenth century', in T. H. Aston *et al.* (eds.), *Social Relations and Ideas*, Cambridge, 1983, pp. 307–314.

47 Skipp, *Crisis and Development*, pp. 42–54.

48 C. Webster, *The Great Instauration*, London, 1975, pp. 465–83.
49 B. Sharp, 'Common rights, charities and the disorderly poor', in G. Eley and W. Hunt (eds.), *Reviving the English Revolution*, London, 1988, pp. 113–18. There is an interesting, and so far unexplored, problem in whether the pamphlet discussion of forests reflected actual conditions or simply drew on certain long-standing literary conventions. A related problem concerns contemporary depictions of the 'natives' of Ireland and North America. In the meantime see K. Thomas, *Man and the Natural World*, London, 1983, pp. 41–50 and pp. 192–7.
50 Sharp, 'Common rights', pp. 118–20; Kerridge, *Agricultural Revolution*, pp. 215–16; G. V. Harrison, 'The southwest: Dorset, Somerset, Devon, and Cornwall', in J. Thirsk (ed.), *The Agrarian History of England and Wales. V: 1640–1750: Regional Farming Systems*, Cambridge, 1984, pp. 358–9.
51 Sharp, 'Common Rights', pp. 128–34.
52 K. Wrightson, 'The social order of early modern England: three approaches', L. Bonfield *et al.* (eds.), *The World We Have Gained*, Oxford, 1986, pp. 177–202.
53 Skipp, *Crisis and Development*, pp. 78–89.
54 P. A. J. Pettit, *The Royal Forests of Northamptonshire: A Study in their Economy, 1558–1714*, Northants Record Society, XXIII, 1968, pp. 181–2.
55 D. O. Pam, *The Rude Multitude: Enfield and the Civil War*, Edmonton Hundred Historical Society, Occasional Paper, 33, 1977, pp. 4–7 and p. 11; *Historical Manuscripts Commission: Calendar of Salisbury MSS*, XXII, London, 1971, pp. 80–1.
56 D. O. Pam, *The Fight for Common Rights in Enfield and Edmonton, 1400–1600*, Edmonton Hundred Historical Society, Occasional Paper 27, 1974, pp. 8–10.
57 Pam, *Rude Multitude*, p. 7 and p. 13.
58 *Salisbury MSS*, XV, pp. 83–4; XVII, p. 116; XXII, p. 5, p. 139 and pp. 411–15; Pam, *Rude Multitude*, p. 10.
59 British Library, Lansdowne MSS 59/30 and 31, petition of inhabitants of Enfield to Lord Burghley, August, 1589 and the names of women of Enfield indicted for riot and sent to Newgate, August, 1589; PRO SP 14/1/25, Vincent Skinner to Robert Cecil, April 15, 1603.
60 Pam, *Rude Multitude*, pp. 11–12.
61 Pam, *Rude Multitude*, p. 10.
62 William Covell, *A Declaration unto the Parliament. Council of State and Army … with the Method of a Commonwealth*, London, 1659; Pam, *Rude Multitude*, pp. 12–13; J. M. Patrick, 'William Covell and the troubles at Enfield in 1659', *University of Toronto Quarterly*, 14, 1944, pp. 45–57.
63 PRO SP 29/22/153, petition of the tenants and inhabitants of Enfield to the king [Nov. 1660?].

INDEX